ELEMENTARY EDUCATION FOR THE POOREST AND OTHER DEPRIVED GROUPS

Elementary Education for the Poorest and Other Deprived Groups

THE REAL CHALLENGE OF UNIVERSALIZATION

JYOTSNA JHA and DHIR JHINGRAN

MANOHAR
2005

First published 2005

ISBN 81-7304-631-X (Hb.)
ISBN 81-7304-643-3 (Pb.)

Published by

Ajay Kumar Jain for
Manohar Publishers & Distributors
4753/23 Ansari Road, Daryaganj
New Delhi 110 002

Typeset at

Digigrafics
New Delhi 110 049

Printed at

Lordson Publishers Pvt Ltd
Delhi 110 007

Distributed in South Asia by

FOUNDATION BOOKS

4381/4, Ansari Road
Daryaganj, New Delhi 110 002
and its branches at Mumbai, Hyderabad,
Bangalore, Chennai, Kolkata

Contents

Tables and Charts

TABLES

CHARTS

Preface

Another book on elementary education! Yes, we are aware that several reports and books have been written on the issue of universalizing elementary education in India during the past five to six years. We were aware of the existence of these books and reports even when we set out to undertake this study. Still, we felt that there existed a need to go deeper into a number of issues, issues that have been neglected or even considered non-issues in the 'changed' Indian context by many of those working or writing on education. Before discussing what these issues are, and how we think we have added value to their understanding, we would like to highlight certain specific developments and debates that dominated, and continue to dominate, the elementary education scenario, and provide the perspective for our endeavour.

The 1990s witnessed a renewed interest in the issue of the universalization of elementary education both in terms of policy and programming, and research and academic debate. The government came up with mega schemes such as the District Primary Education Programme in the mid-1990s followed by the countrywide programme, Sarva Shiksha Abhiyan in 2000, as the main vehicles for achieving universalization. The debates on elementary education centred on several main themes. The need for larger financial allocations for the expansion of provisioning in order to make universal elementary education a reality continues to be a major issue. An increasing number of states with significant gaps in access and provisioning have been adopting alternative models of opening a large number of schools which are not 'formal' in terms of basic infrastructure. Most states with adverse teacher–pupil ratios are also resorting to the hiring of contractual teachers on lower remuneration in formal schools, leading to heated debates on whether such initiatives signify a greater commitment to universalization through a faster pace of expansion or whether it merely implies cheaper solutions for poorer people. The topic of dysfunctional schools in general has been discussed widely, and so has the issue of the effectiveness of regular teacher versus para teacher. On the whole, inadequate budgetary resources and the poor quality of teaching were regarded as the two key constraints in achieving universal participation.

While working in the sector as researchers or administrators, we followed the debates and felt that though all arguments were valid in some manner or the other, they did not address the issue of non-participation of children in schooling in its entirety. We came across issues and experiences of children not going to school that told a different story and deserved a deeper understanding. It was, and is obvious, that universal elementary education demands a significant increase in financial allocation, but it was also evident that finances alone would not ensure regular attendance of children coming from families which face uncertainty and instability due to a variety of reasons. While a lot has been said about the poor quality of teaching and learning in government schools, the dimensions of equity and exclusion within classroom processes did not seem to find any place in this debate, making the discussion on quality somewhat unidimensional. The belief and assumption that all parents are deeply interested in educating their children, and do not send their children to schools only due to the poor quality of teaching, failed to explain why young children carry water on their heads for miles or help their parents at brick kiln sites or ... the list is endless.

Available indicators and experiences show that the poor and the deprived form the overwhelming majority of out-of-school and irregular children, but ongoing debates did not help us fully understand the different dimensions of the problem. Therefore, we felt the need for an exercise that helps to understand the interplay of different processes, including the life situations of children, school functioning, classroom processes and parental aspirations, and their implications for children's regular attendance and schooling in different contexts. The reality is more complex than the simplistic generalizations that were being made. We considered it essential to understand these dimensions if the universalization of elementary education is to be achieved in India.

The study covers a wide range of contexts and varying circumstances through intensive fieldwork in both rural and urban areas. In rural areas, fieldwork was conducted in eleven districts across the ten states of Assam, Bihar, Jharkhand, Orissa, Uttar Pradesh, Madhya Pradesh, Maharashtra, Gujarat, Andhra Pradesh and Karnataka. The five urban centres covered in the study included a metropolitan city, Delhi, an industrial town Kanpur, and three smaller towns—Malda in West Bengal, Warangal in Andhra Pradesh, and Parbhani in Maharashtra. Within each context we tried to understand all critical dimensions that impact participation, including school, household, community, area and their inter linkages through a variety of methods. The analysis attempts to deconstruct the various dimensions to understand their relationship with schooling participation without losing sight of other dimensions.

The design had implications for financial resources as well as the research team. The tools for fieldwork in rural areas had to be translated into six different languages—Hindi, Assamese, Marathi, Gujarati, Telugu and Kannada—and those in urban areas into four languages—Hindi, Bengali, Marathi and Telugu. A senior researcher was identified for each state and urban centre in a manner that together they formed an interdisciplinary team of social scientists, social activists and practitioners with substantial work experience in education. The initial set of tools was shared with this team for deliberations, followed by a joint field training in one of the rural districts. The varied backgrounds and experiences of the team contributed towards revising the tools, making them more robust in the process. A team of field researchers were selected and trained in each state. The training focused on orientation to the study and the use of tools in particular contexts. Some of the tools were prepared to enable reflective exercises among the field teams so that their own observations and reflections would also find a place in the overall understanding. The same set of tools were later adapted for urban slums after familiarity visits and trialing, and a similar process of selection and training was followed for field researchers. Between the two of us, we visited each and every district and urban centre while the fieldwork was being conducted so that our analyses and interpretations were not devoid of first-hand understanding and we were able to comprehend the interplay of processes in a proper perspective. It also helped us to integrate the insights of the field teams in the final analysis.

We present our work with the hope that it will prove useful for a wide range of people, including analysts, researchers, activists, policy makers, and practitioners. We have deliberately tried to paint a picture of life situations of children facing poverty at home, deprivation in society, and exclusion or indifference in school rather than depending on sophisticated statistical analyses to establish relationships and associations. In order to be sure about these relationships, we did regression analyses but have refrained from presenting those in the book because we did not want to limit our study to a particular type of reader. We hope we have been successful in our endeavour of communicating what we saw and understood.

During the post-research phase, one of us, Dhir Jhingran, worked as Mission Director of Sarva Shiksha Abhiyan in Assam and saw this as an opportunity to put some of the emerging understanding into practice. However, it was not easy and he shares his experiences in a note attached as Appendix IV.

We are grateful to senior researchers without whose contributions the study could not have been completed. They coordinated the fieldwork and led the research teams in selected districts and urban centres. They include Mr Julian Boyle, Development Network (Shravasti, now part of Bahraich, Uttar Pradesh), Dr Harishwar Dayal, St. Xavier's College, Ranchi (Araria, Bihar and Palamu, Jharkhand), Dr Javed Akhtar, University of Allahabad (Sidhi, Madhya Pradesh), Prof. S.N. Ratha, Director, Council for Analytical Tribal Studies, Koraput (Nuapara and Koraput, Orissa), Mr Uddalak Dutta, independent researcher, Guwahati (Dhubri, Assam), Mr Jasvir Singh, independent researcher, Bangalore (Chamrajnagar, Karnataka), Dr Shailesh Shukla, independent researcher, Ahmedabad (Dangs, Gujarat), Prof. Shiva Reddy, Osmania University, Hyderabad (West Godavari and Warangal,

Andhra Pradesh), Mr Vivek Kulkarni, Jnana Probodhini, Pune (Pune and Parbhani, Maharashtra), Ms Vandana Mahajan, Alarippu, Delhi (Delhi), and Ms Shukti Pal, Unmesh (Kanpur). We are also grateful to all our field investigators for collecting the information sincerely and diligently. We would like to specifically mention Alka Singh (Sidhi, Madhya Pradesh), Sadananda (Chanrajnagar, Karnataka), Amarendra Srivastava (Shravasti, Uttar Pradesh) and B.K.N. Singh (Araria, Bihar and Palamu, Jharkhand) for their inputs into processing the information and preliminary analysis.

Gurdeep Singh Sappal and Manju Katoch tirelessly processed volumes of quantitative information and patiently met our virtually endless demands. They deserve our special thanks. Deepa Jain helped us in analysis of data for urban areas. Rubina Jasani, Rubina Mohan, Sudakshina Mallick, Prem Bahukhandi and Amitha provided research assistance for varying periods during the life of the project.

We extend our sincere thanks to our Advisory Group which includes Prof. Shyam Menon, Prof. Shubhashis Gangopadhyay, Dr Geetha Nambissan, and Yogendra Ji. Their advice, ideas and support at various stages of the work was extremely helpful. We thank Dr Geetha Nambissan, Prof. Shyam Menon and Vinoba Gautam for reading parts of this report and giving us useful feedback. We express our gratitude to Prof. Tapas Majumdar for discussing various arguments in this study. Our sincere thanks are also due to Dr Ashley Tellis for editing the original manuscript.

We are grateful to the Centre for Policy Research (CPR), New Delhi, for granting us affiliation and providing institutional support. We were based at the CPR for the better part of our study and received full cooperation on all fronts. The Janshala team deserves special thanks for their readiness to provide all kinds of support at all stages of the study. We also thank the district administration, DPEP functionaries and the staff of various government departments for their cooperation during fieldwork in all areas covered in the study. Rajiva Sinha, the then State Project Director, and Roma Bannerjee of DPEP, West Bengal deserve special mention for supporting the fieldwork in Malda. A study of this kind draws heavily on the support of a large number of individuals and institutions. Thanks are due to all, though it is not possible for us to name each one of them. We are grateful to the thousands of parents, children, teachers, and villagers who shared information and insights with us, and cooperated in many other ways.

Financial support for this study came from three agencies—CARE India, the European Commission's Education Programme Office, and the Royal Netherlands Embassy in New Delhi. We are grateful to Geeta Menon, Mervi Karikorpi, and Nandini Prasad from these agencies for their appreciation and support of this study. The photographs on the cover are courtesy CARE India.

We would like to thank our families for being understanding and supportive. Jyotsna extends her appreciation to her family and friends for going beyond the call of duty and acknowledges that it would have been difficult to complete the project without their active help and participation. Dhir Jhingran would like to express his thanks to the Ministry of Human Resource Development, Government of India, for granting him study leave to undertake this study in an independent capacity.

We need hardly add that we alone are responsible for the errors and omissions that remain in the book.

New Delhi
March 2005

JYOTSNA JHA
DHIR JHINGRAN

Abbreviations

AP	:	Andhra Pradesh
APL	:	Above Poverty Line
AS	:	Alternative Schooling
BPL	:	Below Poverty Line
BSP	:	Bahujan Samaj Party
CABE	:	Central Advisory Board on Education
CPI-M	:	Communist Party of India-Marxist
CWC	:	Concerned for Working Children
DIET	:	District Institute of Education and Training
DPEP	:	District Primary Education Programme
ECCE	:	Early Childhood and Care Programme
ECE	:	Early Childhood Education
EGS	:	Education Guarantee Scheme
FIR	:	Female Illiteracy Rate
GOI	:	Government of India
HYV	:	High Yielding Variety
ICDS	:	Integrated Child Development Scheme
IMR	:	Infant Mortality Rate
LBPL	:	Lower (segment of) Below Poverty Line
LCM	:	Lower Caste Muslims
MFP	:	Minor Forest Produce
MHRD	:	Ministry of Human Resource Development
MP	:	Madhya Pradesh
NAR	:	Net Attendance Rates
NCAER	:	National Council of Applied Economic Research
NCERT	:	National Council of Educational Research and Training
NCLP	:	National Child Labour Project
NFE	:	Non-Formal Education
NFHS	:	National Family Health Survey
NGO	:	Non-Government Organization
NPE	:	National Policy of Education
NSSO	:	National Sample Survey Organization
OB	:	Operation Blackboard
OBC	:	Other Backward Castes
PDS	:	Public Distribution System
PHC	:	Primary Health Centre
POA	:	Programme of Action
PTA	:	Parent Teacher Association
PTR	:	Pupil Teacher Ratio
SC	:	Scheduled Caste
SSA	:	Sarva Shiksha Abhiyan

ST	:	Scheduled Tribe
UBPL	:	Upper (segment of) Below Poverty Line
UCH	:	Upper Caste Hindu
UCM	:	Upper Caste Muslim
UEE	:	Universal Elementary Education
UP	:	Uttar Pradesh
VEC	:	Village Education Committee

1. Introduction

The Issue

The need to extend eight years of basic education to all children in India is almost universally accepted. Nevertheless, in view of the fact that millions of children in the country are still, in the fourth year of the twenty-first century, not attending school, and that this does not appear to be any great cause of concern, makes it imperative to re-assert the rationale behind investing in and strategizing for universal elementary education. The role of education in expanding choices, enabling greater participation at individual levels, and facilitating change and development at social levels are well delineated in the literature of development economics.[1] Apart from being of intrinsic value to a person, education also facilitates wider individual and social processes, leading to the all-round betterment of the society. Research and experiences have clearly established that education leads to broad economic as well as social benefits in the shape of higher productivity, lower child and infant mortality rates, and better health. Education also leads to the empowerment of girls/women and other disadvantaged groups having widespread redistributive effects. Education, therefore, is a basic right in a modern democracy committed to equity and social justice.

The authors of the Indian Constitution were definitely aware of the empowering and instrumental role of education, which impelled them to make a commitment to achieve universal elementary education on a priority basis. Article 45 of the Directive Principles of the Constitution states that 'the State shall endeavour to provide within a period of ten years from the commencement of this Constitution, for free and compulsory education for all children until they complete the age of fourteen years.' The recent move to amend Article 45 and make the provision of free and compulsory education a fundamental right only affirms this old commitment.

The fact that not only has this goal not been achieved even after 57 years of Independence, but also that the numbers that have to be brought into the fold of schooling remain dauntingly large, reflects the lack of priority assigned to this issue and points to the enormity of the task that lies ahead. According to the NSSO (1998), only 66 per cent of the total children in the age group of 6-10 years (both inclusive) and 43 per cent of those in the 11-13 years age group (both inclusive) were attending school at the primary and upper-primary levels respectively.[2] However, many children in the higher age group of 11-13 years attend the primary level and a few children in the 6-10 years age group attend higher classes. As such, the attendance ratio of

Table 1.1: Schooling Participation Patterns (India) in the 1990s

NSSO (1995-6)									
Class/age group	Rural			Urban			Total		
	Male	Female	Total	Male	Female	Total	Male	Female	Total
Net Attendance Ratio									
I-V	68	56	63	80	77	78	71	61	66
VI-VIII	44	32	39	60	57	58	48	38	43
Age-specific Attendance Ratio									
6-10	71	58	65	84	82	83	73	63	69
11-13	75	57	67	87	83	85	78	64	72
NFHS (1998-99)									
Age group	Rural			Urban			Total		
	Male	Female	Total	Male	Female	Total	Male	Female	Total
School Attendance Ratio									
6-10	83.2	75.1	79.3	91.7	89.1	90.4	85.2	78.3	81.9
11-14	78.5	61.6	73.9	85.1	82.8	84.0	80.2	67.0	73.9
6-14	81.4	69.7	75.7	88.7	86.3	87.6	83.1	73.7	78.6

SOURCES: National Sample Survey Organization, Government of India, 1998.
National Family Health Survey–2, International Institute for Population Sciences, 2000.

children in the 6-10 years age group went up to 69 per cent and that of children in the 11-13 years age group to 72 per cent. The NFHS-II presents a somewhat better picture with 74 per cent girls and 83 per cent boys in the age group of 6-13 years attending schools in 1998-9. Taking the population projections and estimates of age-specific enrolments into account, the Tapas Majumdar Committee Report (1999) estimated the size of out-of-school children in 2001 to be about 60-70 million.[3] By any account, this is a huge number and getting them to school not a mean task.

At this juncture, it is important to raise two other important questions—what does the universalization of education at any stage mean and can universal enrolment alone be taken as the definite indicator of universalization? Schooling, especially at the elementary stage, requires regular attendance at school, and enrolment indicators do not always reveal the actual situation regarding attendance. Although the NSSO survey has taken this problem into account by asking whether the child is attending school instead of asking if she or he is enrolled in school, this may still be an overestimate due to the inclusion of highly irregular and occasionally attending children. In typical rural Indian situations, characterized by seasonality, ill-health, and the involvement of children in some economic work, on the one hand, and irregularly functioning schools and teacher absenteeism, on the other, long and frequent absences from school are not uncommon, at least in certain parts of the country. Therefore, it is likely that the real size of out-of-school children is larger than estimated by most studies.

It is not only the size of out-of-school children which poses a challenge for policy makers and the civil society. Recent trends in enrolment also make it clear that it is more difficult to get children who remain outside the school system now, even at the beginning of the new century, to school, as compared to those who were brought into the fold of schools in the past one or two decades. This is obvious from the stagnation or decline in overall enrolments seen in many districts during the second half of the 1990s (Agarwal, 2001). What is disconcerting is the fact that this trend is seen not only in districts where the age-specific population ratio is on the decline but that it also includes many districts from states yet far from that plateau.

Although stagnation in enrolment ratios is an almost universal phenomenon, it is generally experienced after attaining a high rate of enrolment. Once any nation, state or district reaches the net enrolment level of higher than 90 per cent, it is not uncommon to witness a slowing down in the rate of increase of this ratio. Kerala is finding it difficult to increase its current level of enrolments in the range of 90-94 per cent at primary and upper-primary levels. However, what is really disturbing is the fact that many states or districts in educationally backward states appear to have reached, or are going through, a period of stagnation in school participation rates at a much lower stage. For instance, nine districts in Assam, a state with an overall Net Attendance Rate (NAR) of only 72 per cent (NSSO, 1998) in 1995-6, registered a decline of about 9 to 11 per cent during the second half of the 1990s. About three-fourths of the 57 districts that registered a decline in enrolments (out of the 125 districts analysed) during 1999-2000 to 2000-1, belonged to states with NARs between 58 and 85 per cent (Agarwal, 2001).

The fact that this is the situation in districts that have been implementing the DPEP, a central government-sponsored programme investing substantially in several aspects of primary education including infrastructure, teacher training, institutional strengthening, etc., for the last five to seven years, makes the issue more serious. This, coupled with the fact that a substantial proportion of the so-called 'enrolled' and 'attending' children do not attend school regularly, necessitates a deeper understanding of the issue of non-participation if the goal of the universalization of elementary education is to be realized.

Poverty, Deprivation and School Participation

The available evidence, based on analyses of large sample survey-based statistics, clearly reveals that the majority of in-school children come from economically better off, and the majority of out-of-school children from the poorer sections of society. The analysis of enrolment patterns for different income groups in NFHS-I data showed that only half of the children in the bottom 40 per cent households were estimated to be studying in schools as against more than 94 per cent in the top 20 per cent in 1992-3 (Table 1.2). The analysis, based on NSSO data for 1995-6, also revealed similar disparities between the poorest 20 per cent and the richest 20 per cent in rural India (Table 1.3). *The India Human Development Report* (NCAER, 1999) based on a large, countrywide sample survey, in 1994, confirmed these trends by showing that children in poor families are less likely to be enrolled in school than children in better-off families. In the 15 states surveyed by the NCAER, the ever-enrolment rates in the lowest annual income households are on an average 25 percentage points lower than the rates for the highest income households. The discontinuation rates for the poorest children were almost two times higher than those for children in the highest income households. Also, the disadvantage of being poor operates much more severely at the higher age group. The discontinuation rates for children in the 11-14 years age group are much higher in low-income households compared to those in high-income households (Table 1.4).

Table 1.2: Proportion of 6 to 14-year-olds Currently in School

Economic Group	Proportion of 6 to 14-year-olds currently in school (per cent)
Bottom 40 per cent	50.0
Middle 40 per cent	76.7
Top 20 per cent	94.2

SOURCE: Filmer & Pritchett, 1998. Calculated from NFHS-I data, 1992-3.

Table 1.3: Average Primary School Enrolments in Rural India

Quintile (Based on expenditure estimates)	Average Net Enrolment Rate (per cent) Boys	Girls	Total
Poorest	42.6	31.6	37.2
2nd	53.4	43.1	48.6
3rd	60.5	50.3	55.8
4th	66.1	58.6	62.6
Highest	69.9	65.2	67.7

SOURCE: Lanjouw & Ravallion, 1998, Based on NSS, 1993-4.

Table 1.4: Age-specific Ever-enrolment and Discontinuation Rates

Population groups (household annual income group)	Ever-enrolment Rates (per cent)			Discontinuation Rates (per cent)		
	6-9 years	11-14 years	6-14 years	6-9 years	11-14 years	6-14 years
Up to Rs. 20,000	63.4	69.5	65.3	2.9	15.8	7.2
Above Rs. 86,000	87.4	93.1	89.3	1.0	7.1	3.2

SOURCE: *India Human Development Report*, NCAER, 1999.

Table 1.5: Proportion of 15 to 19-year-olds who have completed Grade 8

Economic Group (Households in)	Proportion of 15 to 19-year-olds who have completed grade 8 (per cent)		
	Male	Female	Gender Gap
Bottom 40 per cent	31.3	9.5	21.8
Top 20 per cent	85.2	79.6	5.6

SOURCE: Filmer & Pritchett, 1998. Calculated from NFHS data, 1992-3.

A gender gap, which exists in the form of differences in enrolment and completion ratios in all groups, is also higher for the bottom economic groups. The proportion of 15 to 19 year-olds having completed grade 8 is not only abysmally low for females in the bottom 40 per cent households, but the differences between men and women are also much wider (Table 1.5).

A significant fact is that states or regions with a larger concentration of poor people are usually also those with the largest concentration of out-of-school children. This includes the whole or parts of Bihar, Orissa, Assam, West Bengal, Madhya Pradesh and Uttar Pradesh. What is more telling is that the enrolment disparity among different economic groups is also sharper in some of these states. The disparity in enrolment rates between the top and bottom economic groups declines with a reduction in the number and proportion of the poor, and with an overall improvement in enrolment ratios. While Kerala, Tamil Nadu and Maharashtra show little difference in enrolment rates across different income groups, in states like Bihar, Madhya Pradesh, Rajasthan and Uttar Pradesh, enrolment rates are considerably lower in the last two income categories. The enrolment rates for the household income category of an annual income less than Rs. 20,000 are very low for states like Bihar, Rajasthan, Madhya Pradesh, Uttar Pradesh and West Bengal [Table 1.6 (a)].

The positive and strong correlation between poverty and school participation rates for children makes it clear that the issue of non-participation needs to be understood in the specific context of low income or expenditure households. The incidence of poverty is high in India, and though different estimates for the number of poor persons living in India vary depending upon the base used and the method applied, nearly 300 to 350 million persons are estimated to be living below the poverty line (BPL).[4] The higher incidence of non-participation among poor families, large in number, makes it almost essential to base policy formulations for universalization on an improved and deeper understanding of poor families and the processes that impact on schooling related decisions in such families.

It is important to assert that income or expenditure poverty is only one aspect of deprivation. It is well recognized now that there are many dimensions to deprivation, and a complete understanding calls for an alternative approach. The emergence of the concept of human development

Table 1.6 (a): Ever-enrolment Rates (per cent) for States

State	Ever-enrolment Rates (per cent) for Household Income Groups (Rs. per year)			
	Up to 20,000	20,001-40,000	40,001-62,000	Above 62,000
Haryana	69.2	78.5	86.2	86.4
Himachal Pradesh	90.6	96.0	94.7	90.1
Punjab	83.3	85.8	88.9	96.4
Bihar	49.8	66.5	70.9	83.6
Uttar Pradesh	54.7	67.7	75.5	85.3
Madhya Pradesh	54.6	67.7	73.2	79.4
Orissa	65.2	81.6	83.9	90.7
Rajasthan	53.9	61.9	75.4	79.2
North-eastern Region	78.3	80.1	90.1	84.5
West Bengal	59.9	77.1	80.0	92.5
Gujarat	74.0	89.1	82.8	91.5
Maharashtra	82.8	84.8	90.9	76.5
Andhra Pradesh	77.4	77.9	88.5	98.8
Karnataka	75.9	79.7	82.0	81.1
Kerala	98.6	98.7	97.9	98.9
Tamil Nadu	86.0	89.0	93.4	94.7
All India	65.3	75.1	80.9	86.9

SOURCE: *India Human Development Report*, NCAER, 1999.

encompassing various aspects of well-being, including access to health and education opportunities and capabilities of coping with crises and changes, has firmly established that poverty cannot be understood by looking at income and expenditure alone.[5] Food insecurity, illnesses, lack of choices and opportunities, forced livelihood options, vulnerability to crises and lack of access to basic services such as safe drinking water, school or health facilities are some other aspects of deprivation. Although some of these are correlates of income or expenditure poverty, this may not always be true. Many ill-provided-for urban neighbourhood slums in India provide classic examples of a low state of well-being despite the level of income or expenditure not being so low. If income poverty puts one set of constraints, other aspects of deprivation put another set of constraints and when they operate in combination, which they do more often than not, they not only reinforce each other but also create new restrictions on the choices or opportunities available.[6]

Social deprivation, arising out of the ascribed status of caste, tribe or religion, is another form of deprivation, especially in highly stratified rural areas. Social exclusion and discrimination faced by certain social groups are known to adversely affect the economic status as well as participation of children in the schooling processes. Caste in Indian society interacts with the education of children from poor families at two levels, one because of the correspondence with poverty and the other due to exclusion from a number of social processes, including education. Social as well as physical distance

Table 1.6 (b): Ever-enrolment Rates (per cent) for Social Groups

Social Groups	STs and SCs	Hindus	Muslims	Other Minorities
	61.8	72.0	61.6	83.5

SOURCE: *India Human Development Report*, NCAER, 1999.

between castes has been sharpest for ex-untouchables or the Scheduled Castes. The majority of the tribal population has also remained outside the fold of formal education because of their physical isolation. The statistics clearly reveal that the level of participation is lower among these groups as compared to others [Table 1.6 (b)].

It seems apparent that deprivation of any kind is generally linked negatively with school participation of children. However, in order to understand the linkages between poverty and deprivation, on the one hand, and school participation, on the other, it is important to understand the process through which any particular form of deprivation operates on the decision-making processes in families, as decisions regarding schooling at the elementary stage are taken by parents. Different forms of deprivation, however, do not necessarily work in isolation; they also act in varying combinations and affect the decision-making processes at the level of family or household. A number of recent research studies[7] have established that the household, village and school together impact on decisions regarding the schooling of children in rural areas. But here also, the process and the manner in which these factors act and impact upon each other leading to a particular decision have received less attention.[8] Therefore, we felt strongly that there was a need for a deeper understanding of this interplay in the specific context of poor and deprived households. Although a number of points highlighted and the conclusions arrived at in this study may appear to be known, if not through research then because of hunches and insights, the significance lies in a systematic enquiry and analyses, and also in necessary reiterations and confirmations of the known.

THE OBJECTIVES

The broad objectives of the present study as emanating from the above discussion are as below:

- To understand the challenges involved in making the universalization of elementary education a reality.
- To understand the ways and manner in which poverty and other forms of deprivation affect school participation decisions in a variety of contexts.
- To discern and understand the factors and processes which have an enabling impact from those that have a depressing impact on decisions about the schooling of children in poor households.[9]

- To analyse the current policy and programme frameworks in the sub-sector with the perspective developed through the above understandings.

Conceptual Framework and Assumptions

This section outlines some of the important concepts that have provided the framework for the choice of approach, methodology, tools and modes of analyses. These have been derived from the available theoretical and empirical knowledge base.

Two Domains of Decision-Making in Education[10]

There are two domains of decision-making in education, which, in simplified form, can be named the individual and institutional domains. The individual refers to children or students and their parents who decide to spend their time and other resources, and institutional refers to the state which will decide to invest in provisioning and other related aspects. Both have to act *in tandem* for education to be facilitated. But the two sets of decision makers, the state and individual families, have different sets of objectives, time horizons, and purposes that guide their decisions. The state takes a macro-perspective and considerations of education whereas families go by micro-level perspectives and uncertainties. The state also has a longer time horizon as compared to an individual family. Nevertheless, since it is essential to match the two to reach wider, long-term macro-goals, it is critical for macro-policies to be guided by an understanding of the decision-making process at the individual level and, if required, make efforts to influence these in the desired direction.

Individual and Collective Choices

In a socially and economically stratified society like India, decision making at the individual level is closely linked with collective or group behaviour. Individual preferences and collective or social norms may or may not move in the same direction. Complex socio-cultural-economic phenomena and issues such as caste, alienation, world-view, attitudes towards gender, livelihood choices, etc., interact with each other and at times create dilemmas in the making of choices. For instance, individual parents might express the desire to educate their daughters but may not be actually sending their daughters to school because there exists a norm in the community against sending girls to school. On the other hand, a few parents might not be convinced of any benefits of education *per se* but could still be sending their children to school because everybody else in the group or area does so. Therefore, it is important to make the distinction and understand phenomena in the light of the complexities that exist on the ground (Chart 1.1).

Chart 1.1: Subjects and Dimensions of Enquiry

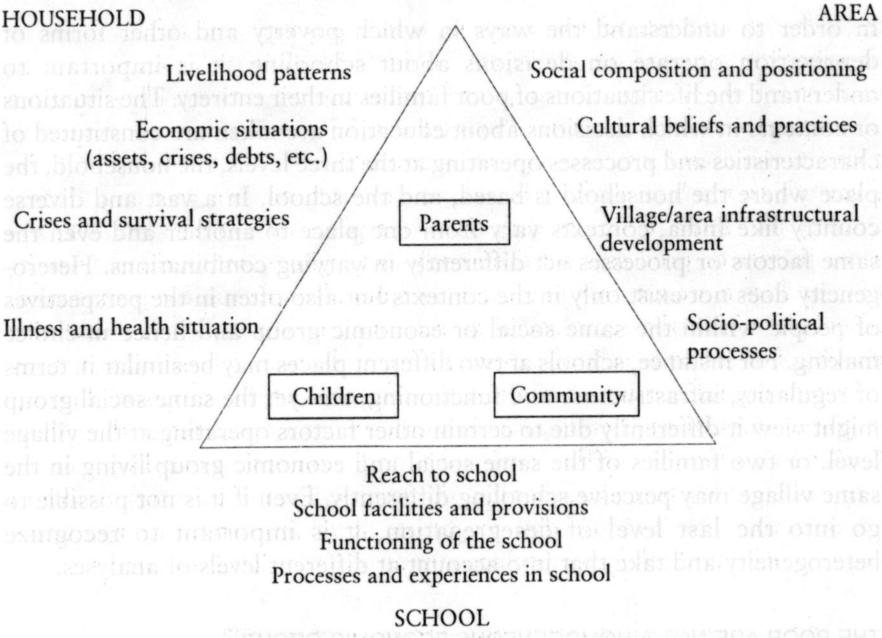

DESIRE AND DEMAND FOR EDUCATION AND A COMMITMENT TO EDUCATION

It is essential to make a difference between a desire for and the demand for education. Demand is a stage where the desire is backed by willingness to pay or make efforts and adjustments to transform it into a reality. The existing literature on education often does not make a distinction between the two and takes one for the other.[11] The distinction is necessary in order to identify the processes that can help in changing the state of indifference or desire into a state of demand. If elementary education is a basic right, which it indeed is, it is important that the state facilitates processes that enable demand among those who remain outside the schooling fold. The distinction is also necessary to understand that there are many layers when it comes to the demand for education and it would be simplistic to assume it is either this way or that.

We have used the term Commitment to Education, admittedly some-what inaccurately and obviously, for want of a more appropriate term, to denote a stage where children's education becomes a priority, leading to a demonstrated decision or revealed demand for education. It is, however, different from parental motivation and depends upon a number of factors, including ones external to parents and households. This, in some way, is a parameter or boundary defining parental resolve, or the lack of it, to educating their children, given the multiple contexts in which they live. Commitment to education itself, as subsequent analyses will show, remains varied among poor families and changes with alterations in certain factors and processes.

HETEROGENEITY OF CONTEXTS AND SITUATIONS

In order to understand the ways in which poverty and other forms of deprivation operate on decisions about schooling, it is important to understand the life situations of poor families in their entirety. The situations or contexts in which decisions about education are taken are constituted of characteristics and processes operating at the three levels, the household, the place where the household is based, and the school. In a vast and diverse country like India, contexts vary from one place to another and even the same factors or processes act differently in varying combinations. Heterogeneity does not exist only in the contexts but also often in the perspectives of people within the same social or economic group and hence in choice making. For instance, schools at two different places may be similar in terms of regularity, infrastructure and functioning, and yet the same social group might view it differently due to certain other factors operating at the village level, or two families of the same social and economic group living in the same village may perceive schooling differently. Even if it is not possible to go into the last level of desegregation, it is important to recognize heterogeneity and take that into account at different levels of analyses.

THE POOR ARE NOT A HOMOGENEOUS ECONOMIC GROUP[12]

The poor are usually identified by their position beneath the Poverty Line. However, within the poor, there are generally many layers, characterized by varying levels of deprivation. Similarly, there may not be much difference among those living just below or above the Poverty Line, even if they are positioned in the two opposite categories. Within the poor, some families are more marginalized than the others. As mentioned earlier, some aspects of deprivation may be operating at the level of the non-poor as well. For instance, gender-related discrimination is known to operate in all social and economic groups. Still, it is likely to operate differently for the poor and the non-poor and also within different layers of poor households. Extending the need for recognizing heterogeneity, it becomes essential to differentiate between at least the two layers of those who are designated poor. We have tried to identify the lower segment of Below the Poverty Line (BPL) families and understand the differences in their situations as well as their outlook towards schooling. The analyses of various indicators have taken this distinction into account.

THE APPROACH AND THE METHODOLOGY

The study is primarily based on detailed fieldwork conducted in both rural and urban areas during the first half of the year 2001. The three important players in the decision-making process at the micro-level—parents, children and community—were our main subjects of enquiry. There are three main dimensions to the enquiry—characteristics and processes within households, within the village or the neighbourhood area, and within the school. Within these three dimensions, a number of aspects were examined, some in greater detail than others. The interplay of these aspects and dimensions was analysed with thorough qualitative as well as quantitative modes. The focus is on the use of quantitative information to present the larger picture and on the use of qualitative information to understand processes. The dimensions of area or external context and household are closely associated and, hence at the level of analysis they have been viewed together wherever considered more appropriate. Efforts have been made to understand the life situations of children belonging to poor families and to try and explain schooling decisions.

Identification of Areas and Coverage

For identification of villages in rural areas at the first level, eleven districts were chosen on the basis of a composite index developed for all the districts in the country. The index was developed on the basis of the percentage of BPL population, Infant Mortality Rate (IMR) and Female Illiteracy Rate (FIR).[13] Nine out of eleven districts were identified from among the 100 highest-ranking (high BPL, IMR and FIR) districts, taking one from each bigger state that figured. The exceptions were Bihar and Orissa from where two districts each were identified as these two states had 20 and 14 districts respectively in the list of 100. Bihar was subsequently divided and one identified district, Palamu, fell into the new state of Jharkhand. Ten districts from Arunachal Pradesh and a few more from other north-eastern states figured in the list of top 100 districts, but none except Dhubri in Assam could be included for detailed fieldwork due to logistical bottlenecks. However, an exploratory case study was conducted in Arunachal Pradesh and has been used in the analysis. The rationale for selecting districts from different states was in order to understand the variety of situations. In addition to these nine, two more districts were identified from among those 'low' on the list—one from Andhra Pradesh and one from Maharashtra. The rationale was to widen the variety of situations and also see the picture in the areas where the incidence of poverty or deprivation is lower.

Two blocks were identified in each district, except for Dangs (which is a single block district), West Godavari and Pune where only one block each was identified. It was ensured that the two blocks were also different from each other in terms of development. Two villages were identified within each selected block based on the perusal of data and consultation to ensure that they represented at least one particular feature of the district in terms of (1) poverty/backwardness, (2) social composition, and (3) certain natural features (forest dependence, flood or drought proneness). The size of the identified villages varied between 40 to 200 households, with at least 20 BPL families with children at school-going ages. The necessary condition in the

Table1.7: List of Selected Districts for Fieldwork in Rural Areas

State	District	Per cent Population Below Poverty Line (1997-8)	Infant Mortality Rate (1991)	Female Illiteracy Rate (1991)	Female Illiteracy Rate (2001)	Largest Social Group in the Population	Important Additional Features
Assam	Dhubri	80.26	131	85.99	57.36	Muslims & OBCs	Large riverine areas present
Bihar	Araria	75.17	116	83.85	53.50	Muslims & SCs	Flood prone, remote
Jharkhand	Palamu	84.60	128	86.91	69.50	SCs & STs	Naxalite groups active
Orissa	Nuapara	78.31	–	87.22	73.99	SCs and STs	Drought prone, single crop
Orissa	Koraput	56.48	136	82.6	75.19	STs & SCs	Forest areas, many languages
Madhya Pradesh (MP)	Sidhi	56.91	155	89.27	63.57	STs & SCs	Large forest areas, feudal
Uttar Pradesh (UP)	Shravasti*	75.03	143	71.25	81.25	SCs & Muslims	Remote, parts flood prone
Gujarat	Dangs	80.27	100	64.69	51.01	STs	Forest, single crop area
Karnataka	Chamraj-nagar	72.00	75	80	56.98	SCs & STs	Forest, strong Dalit movement
Andhra Pradesh (AP)	West Godavari	35.00	68	53.02	30.55	SCs & OBCs	Irrigated multiple crop
Maharashtra	Pune	19.54	58	40.23	27.68	Marathas and SCs	Economically well developed

NOTE: * The three figures are for Bahraich, the district from which Shravasti was carved out recently.

SOURCES: Census of India (1991, 2001), Below Poverty Line Survey (Department of Panchayat and Rural Development, GOI (not published), District and Village Reports (Fieldwork)

identification of the village was the presence of a primary school within it, or at a radius of 1.5 km.

The choice of five urban centres was also guided by the need to include a variety of situations. One mega city, one industrial city, and three smaller cities in three different states were identified on the basis of consultation and interaction with a number of persons active in working with the urban poor. Since the majority of the neighbourhood slums remain unrecognized, it is

Table 1.8: List of Selected Cities for Fieldwork in Urban Areas

State	City	Population* (Total–2001)	Female Illiteracy Rate (2001)	Specific Feature
Delhi	Delhi	12,819,761	35.2	Mega city, national capital, growing at a fast rate
Uttar Pradesh	Kanpur	2,772,212	28.8	Metropolitan, old industrial city, known for cotton, wool, leather
Andhra Pradesh	Warangal	620,791	36.5	Many engineering colleges, small industries
Maharashtra	Parbhani	485,103	43.0	Trade-oriented city with close ties to neighbouring rural areas
West Bengal	Malda	240,915	34.6	Flood prone, important railway junction

NOTE: * These are population figures for the district's urban areas. This, at times, could be a little higher than the population of the city *per se*. Female illiteracy rates are also the rates for the district's urban female population.

SOURCE: Census of India 2001, City Appraisals.

not easy to get statistics for these. In each identified city, a number of slums were visited and interactions held with the local population and activists before identifying the final ones for fieldwork. In all, 37 villages and 15 neighbourhood slums were covered by the detailed fieldwork. The focus was on understanding the identified villages and slums, which provided a variety of situations in their entirety, rather than looking only at education in isolation in a larger number of areas.

Identification of Households

Detailed household surveys were conducted for about 25 families in each village. This included 20 BPL and 5 APL families. BPL households were identified through the list collected from the panchayat or block office. Households with no child at school-going ages (6-13 years) were excluded and a fresh list prepared. Twenty families were then identified randomly from this revised list and substituted by the next family on the list whenever the need arose. The approach remained similar for urban areas except for the fact that the identification of households was not done on the basis of the BPL list. Households were selected on a random basis from the list obtained through the municipality office. Wherever the list was not available, a fresh list was prepared with the help of people and then households identified on a random basis. The following tables provide an indication of the coverage of the surveys in rural and urban areas.

It is apparent that the work covered diverse parts of the country and a spectrum of social groups and sub-groups speaking different languages and following a variety of socio-cultural practices. This helped in understanding and assessing the life situations and schooling decisions among the poor in

Table 1.9: Number of Households, Children and Schools Covered in the Survey

Coverage	Rural	Urban	Total
Total Number of Families	913	164	1,077
Total Number of Children	1,842	348	2,190
Total Number of Schools	42	45	87

NOTES: 1. Percentage distribution of the households by economic group (Rural)

Above Poverty Line (APL)	:	16.6
Below Poverty Line (BPL)	:	83.4
Upper Below Poverty Line (UBPL)	:	51.5
Lower Below Poverty Line (LBPL)	:	31.9

2. Percentage distribution of the households by social group (Rural)

Upper Caste Hindu (UCH)	:	9.0
Other Backward Castes (OBC)	:	19.1
Scheduled Caste (SC)	:	28.5
Scheduled Tribe (ST)	:	30.3
Muslims	:	12.2
Others	:	0.9

diverse circumstances and differing sites. The broad commonalities and finer diversities seen across these groups helped in affirming conclusions and discerning implications valid for disadvantaged groups in a wider sense. However, there are specific groups of children who suffer educational disadvantages for specific reasons. These include children with disabilities, children of sex workers or child sex workers, children on the streets, child labour in industries, children in jails, etc. These have not been covered directly by fieldwork in this study.

Research Methods and Tools

A mix of qualitative and quantitative methods was used for conducting fieldwork in rural as well as urban areas. A team of four to eight members stayed in the villages for 8 to 12 days to complete the fieldwork. The tools and guidelines used in rural areas were as below:

Village Appraisal: This covered general information about a number of aspects of the village and village life, including population profile, land type, quality and distribution, cropping patterns, ownership of other assets, general level of infrastructure and services available, livelihood patterns and trends, wage payments and debt practices, caste and social dynamics, children's life, work and education, etc. This was to facilitate an initial familiarization and understanding at a later stage.

Poverty Perception Exercise: This was conducted to facilitate the differentiation between two segments of BPL households and also to identify indicators used to define different levels of poverty.

Focus Group Discussion (FGD): FGDs were conducted with five different groups in each village—Poor Men, Poor Women, Extremely Poor Families, Out-of-school Children, and Village Education Committee (VEC) members. Poor men and women were drawn from the same social group in most cases.

Household Survey: The survey included interviews with the household head or spouse as well as interviews with children. At least one boy and one girl were interviewed from whichever category (school-going, drop-out, never-enrolled) of child was present in the family.

Case Study: At least two families were identified from among BPL families for detailed case studies to be conducted over the entire period of the team's stay in the village. This was to provide a complete and unbroken picture of processes in the family.

School Survey: All schools (primary and upper-primary) located in the selected villages were surveyed through an interview with the headmaster, a study of the records, and detailed observations of schools, teachers, and classes.

Interview with Teacher: At least one teacher was interviewed in depth from all the schools surveyed.

Interview with Educational/General Administrators: This was to get their perspective and assess their sensitivity towards the problems of the area.

Teams' Discussion Notes (Village Analytical Reports): This was an analytical report prepared by the field team for each village against some of the identified issues and research questions.

The tools were prepared initially after undertaking a few familiarization visits to some of the districts. These were then shared and discussed with the larger team of key persons from the states in a workshop mode organized in one of the study districts. The tools were field-tested there followed by another round of discussions. These were then modified, based on feedback from discussions as well as from field testing. The same set of tools/guidelines was modified to adapt to suit situations in urban, low-income neighbourhood areas. We also visited several slums in one mega city and one small city before adapting the tools for the urban fieldwork. The fieldwork in all identified villages and urban slums was conducted between February and September 2001. Therefore, all data presented in the report pertain to this period.

THE STRUCTURE OF THE REPORT

The report comprises ten chapters in all. The first chapter outlines the issues, objectives, conceptual framework, coverage, methodology and approach. Chapter 2 discusses the three sites—area, household and school—as life situations in which families live and operate. The focus is on presenting a picture of the contexts in which children live and the kinds of lives they lead. This contextualizes explanations and understandings of school participation patterns in the following chapter. The discussions of area and household focus on the different aspects of life situations, including access to basic needs such as water and health, connectivity to towns, work availability, livelihood choices and their implications, wages, seasonality, indebtedness, illnesses, education among adults, ownership of assets, crises faced, children's roles and responsibilities, etc. The idea is to provide a background to the villages and families studied and to present a picture of the prevailing conditions in different places. The issue of caste, tribe or religion has not been highlighted at great length here; these have been discussed separately later. This is followed by an analysis of sample schools for their provisions, mainly physical infrastructure, teachers and functioning. School functioning has been assessed and analysed taking two perspectives into account, observations by the research team and perceptions of the parents/community.

Chapter 3 first discusses school participation patterns as emerging from the field survey across various parameters of economic groups, social groups, regions, gender, age groups, etc. This is followed by an analysis of the reasons for non-participation and linkages between school participation patterns and the families' life situations discussed in the previous chapter. The chapter also presents a first-level analysis of the families' decision-making process about the schooling of children in the face of poverty and the multiple facets of deprivation.

Chapters 4 to 8 present the second level of analysis for different social groups and for girls. Groups such as Dalits, STs, Muslims, and girls remain socially and educationally deprived, and hence need special attention in terms of understanding. While the earlier chapters present an aggregate and, at times, fragmented picture, these five chapters present a disaggregated, more holistic picture. The focus here is on understanding the interplay of external environment, school, and the internal environment of households *vis-à-vis* schooling participation decisions.

The chapters on different social groups analyse aspects of intra-group differences across villages and intra-village differences between the chosen group and others in school participation. The aspects of typical life situations of these groups, including living in separate clusters, access to basic requirements, livelihood choices, traditional occupations, etc., have also been looked into. The issues of social exclusion, culture, self-image, identity and their linkages with people's aspirations for their children have been analysed. The focus is on looking at these groups in varying contexts of economic opportunities (work availability, production relations, etc.), development conditions (access to roads, hospitals, transport systems, etc.), socio-cultural-political processes (practices, beliefs, organizations, etc.) and school functioning (facilities and processes). The chapter on girls looks at them within each social group and tries to outline the common constraints they face, often accentuated by the caste, tribe or religious group to which they belong.

The next chapter (Chapter IX: Nowhere to Belong: Schooling in Urban Low-income Neighbourhoods) discusses the issue of the poverty, deprivation, and schooling of the urban poor. It adopts a similar approach, first analysing the profiles of slums, families, and schools followed by an analysis of schooling status, reasons for non-participation, and linkages between different aspects of deprivation and decision-making in the schooling of children. Social positioning and gender have also been examined. The features that distinguish urban from rural scenarios have been highlighted.

The concluding chapter first presents the course of household decision making in the shape of a simple chart highlighting the role of different factors and processes. Deriving from all the previous chapters, this chapter discusses the issues in their entirety. It then goes on to examine and analyse the policies, programmes, and interventions from the specific perspective of the emerging issues. The chapter also analyses some NGO initiatives in the same light. The last section highlights the implications for policy and action emanating from the analyses so far, keeping in mind the elusive goal of the universalization of elementary education in India.

NOTES

1. Refer to Drèze and Sen (1995; 2002) for detailed arguments on the role of education and health in enabling personal and social change.
2. The Primary level refers to Classes I to V and the Upper Primary level to Classes VI to VIII.
3. Annual government statistics based on school sources usually do not provide age-specific enrolment ratios. Moreover, the gross ratios provided by the Education Department are often at variance with the statistics provided by household surveys. The extent of variance between government and household survey-based data can be seen from the following table:

Comparison of statistics from two sources for the year 1995-6

Indicators	Source	Classes I-V			Classes VI-VIII		
		Male	Female	Total	Male	Female	Total
Gross enrolment ratio	Deptt. of Education	115	93	104	80	55	67
Gross attendance ratio	NSSO	92	77	85	74	56	65

SOURCE: National Sample Survey Organisation, Government of India, October 1998.

Two large sample-based surveys by the National Sample Survey Organisation (NSSO) and the National Family Health Survey (NFHS) are almost universally relied upon for age-specific enrolment ratios and for estimating out-of-school children by researchers in this area.

4. Below Poverty Line is defined on the basis of the minimum normative food basket and the prescribed calorie consumption norm. See Dubey and Gangopadhyay (1998) for a detailed discussion on the practices being followed in India to estimate the number of poor.
5. See Sen (1986), Chambers (1992) and Rahman and Hussain (1995) for a detailed discussion of the definitions of well-being, deprivation and poverty.
6. We have used the terms 'poor' and 'deprived' interchangeably.
7. See Vaidyanathan and Nair (2001) for detailed studies done in different Indian states on the issue of school participation and the varying factors that operate at the grass-roots level. These studies mainly rely on multivariate statistical analysis for explaining the role of multiple factors on enrolment rates.
8. Vaidyanathan and Nair (2001) themselves have pointed out that these studies focus more on quantitative measurement and analysis, and mention the need for further studies 'for a deeper understanding of educational disparities and their dynamics' (p. 31).
9. It is important to point out that this study does not look at curriculum content, how it is being taught in school, and how children are evaluated. There is no denying that these aspects are of critical importance in view of equity. However, we have deliberately avoided them in order to maintain our focus.
10. The two-domain framework, as well as individual versus collective choice, are based primarily on Majumdar (1983). These have been modified and reinterpreted to build the argument for the contemporary context.
11. For instance, the PROBE Report (1999) takes a positive response to a question not even linked directly to the respondent's son: 'Is it important for a boy to be educated?' as evidence of strong parental interest in their children's schooling.
12. See Sen (1995) and Chambers (1992) for a discussion of distinctions within the category of the poor.
13. A survey conducted by the Department of Rural Development, Government of India in 1997-8 has been used for the percentage of BPL population. The Census of India, 1991, has been used for IMR and Female Illiteracy Rate (FIR). The NSSO data do not provide information below the level of region. The size and composition of NSS regions vary widely, and sometimes one region includes districts quite dissimilar in terms of infrastructural and human development indicators. For instance, the ten poorest regions on the basis of 1993-4 Head Count Ratio included 2 to 18 districts. A further level of disaggregating was considered desirable, and hence the Department of Rural Development data available for the district level was used. However, it was not correct to rely upon a single indicator, and hence IMR and FIR were included as well. IMR is considered a good indicator to depict access to health facilities, backwardness of the area, and uncertainties in families. Similarly, the FIR was included for its direct linkages with poverty, the condition of women, and socio-cultural backwardness. The profiles of the districts were also matched with the Centre for Monitoring the Indian Economy's district profiles.

2. The Multivalent Contexts of Poverty and Deprivation

Poverty and Deprivation in Indian Villages

Poverty and deprivation are essentially linked with the characteristics and processes in an area where any group lives. In other words, factors such as assetlessness, occupation, income, etc., in a particular family are also influenced by the factors and practices prevalent in the village. The specific features of this study's villages with a significant bearing on the extent of poverty and the nature of deprivation are discussed in this section. The discussion in the next section further elaborates the issues and highlights the linkages between them. These villages represent varying situations found commonly in different parts of the country. However, it must be remembered that the villages selected for this study are not necessarily the poorest in the country or even in the selected district.

ACCESSIBILITY AND CONNECTIVITY

The accessibility and connectivity of a place play important roles in opening up opportunities. They facilitate the movement of people, goods and information. The wide network of roads in Kerala has allowed children to attend schools, especially at upper primary and secondary levels, even if they live at a good distance. However, a large number of villages remain badly connected and only a few states in the southern and western parts of the country have succeeded in developing a good network of roads and transport systems. While about 54 per cent of the study villages were located within a kilometre of metalled roads, only 13.5 per cent had good and reliable public transport systems in operation (Table 2.1). The transport facilities were reported to be either bad or very bad, which in many cases meant no public transport facilities at all, in more than half of the villages. The distance from towns is also important, especially from the point of view of seasonal work opportunities. More than three-fourths of the villages were located at a distance of 9 km or more.

This state of village accessibility exists in spite of the fact that block and village selection processes by us were biased in favour of slightly more developed villages, due to the mandatory need to have a primary school within the village. In other words, these villages do not represent the remotest and worst of villages in terms of connectivity and accessibility. Despite an emphasis on selecting villages at varying stages of development within each

Table 2.1: Accessibility and Connectivity of the Study Villages

	Distribution of villages			
Distance from Metalled Road	Less than 1 km	1-3 km	4-5 km	More than 5 km
	20 (54.1)	*7 (18.9)*	*5 (13.5)*	*5 (13.5)*
Distance from the Nearest Town	Up to 3 km	4-8 km	9-14 km	More than 14 km
	3 (8.1)	*15 (40.5)*	*12 (32.4)*	*17 (46.0)*
Public Transport Facilities	Good *5 (13.5)*	Average *12 (32.4)*	Bad *4 (10.8)*	Very Bad *16 (43.3)*

NOTE: Figures in parentheses reveal the percentage distribution of villages.
SOURCE: Village Appraisal Reports.

district, in every state, the relatively better position observed in southern and western states reveals that the general situation is better in these states. The majority of villages with no or very bad public transport services were in Bihar, Orissa, Uttar Pradesh (UP) and Madhya Pradesh (MP) and most villages with better transport facilities, despite being located at large distances from towns, belonged to districts in Andhra Pradesh, Maharashtra, Gujarat and Karnataka.

AVAILABILITY OF BASIC SERVICES AND FACILITIES

One of the important facets of deprivation arises out of access, or the lack of it, to certain basic facilities and services. The situation in rural areas is far from satisfactory in this respect. Nearly 67 per cent villages had no electricity. *Anganwadi* facilities were available within the village in only 13, and upper-primary schools in only 8, out of 37 villages (Table 2.2). The upper primary schools were only within villages that were better connected through roads. Access to safe drinking water is a far cry in most villages. Hand-pumps or tube-wells are the main sources of drinking water, but the location and availability per family is extremely limited. The sight of long queues of women and children, generally girls, with vessels standing near hand-pumps is one of the most common sights in rural India. At times, it takes hours to collect enough water for the daily needs of one family. Moreover, the distribution of hand-pumps in terms of location is also highly unequal in many places with the majority, or all, being placed in the *tola* or *purba* inhabited by more influential households.

Access to basic health facilities is worse as more than half of the villages have no Primary Health Centre (PHC) or hospital at a distance of less than 6 kilometres. Distance from a PHC or hospital becomes a real issue in villages located away from roads and with no proper transport facilities. Moreover, the functioning of PHCs in terms of availability of doctors or

Table 2.2: Availability of Selected Basic Services and Facilities

	Distribution of Villages			
Drinking Water Facilities	Good *7 (18.9)*	Average *19 (51.4)*	Bad *7 (18.9)*	Very Bad *4 (10.8)*
Distance from Primary Health Centre (PHC) / Hospital	Up to 2 km *7 (18.9)*	3-5 km *10 (27.0)*	6-10 km *15 (40.5)*	More than 10 km *5 (13.5)*
Electricity	Yes *16 (43.3)*		No *21 (56.7)*	
Upper Primary School within Village	Yes *8 (21.6)*		No *29 (78.4)*	
Anganwadi within Village	Yes *13 (35.1)*		No *24 (64.9)*	

NOTE: Figures in parentheses reveal the percentage distribution of villages.
SOURCE: Village Appraisal Reports.

medicines is such that in most areas, people prefer not to rely upon them. The use of public facilities is more common in some villages of Chamrajnagar district in Karnataka, despite greater distance, due to good transport facilities and functional hospitals. The lack of basic services, coupled with poor accessibility and connectivity, causes a lot of hardships in specific circumstances. The villages in Araria and Shravasti districts witness a number of deaths due to delays in providing medical help. The use of private doctors, many of them quacks, is common in almost all villages, especially in the eastern and central parts of the country. Only 27 per cent of those who suffered major illnesses ever, and 23 per cent of those reported to have suffered minor illnesses during the previous four months, made use of public health facilities, while the rest had either not taken any medical help or had gone to private sources. The poor make less frequent use of public services, which is obvious from the fact that while 39 per cent of APL families went to hospitals/PHCs, only 21 per cent of BPL households did so for treatment of major illnesses (Table 2.3). Later discussions reveal that this has severe implications for the economic position, levels of indebtedness, and vulnerability in poor families.

NATURE OF AGRICULTURE AND AGRICULTURAL PRACTICES

In rural contexts, where the economy still remains primarily agrarian and labour markets are imperfect and highly segmented, poverty is essentially linked with the nature of agriculture. This determines the nature of livelihood options to a large extent, which in turn guide a number of decisions at the household level. The quality of land, irrigation practices, cropping patterns, land distribution patterns, wage payment systems and rates, everything

Table 2.3: Accessing Medical Help: Common Practices in Rural Areas

	Source of medical support: Percentage distribution of those who reported illness					
	Not gone to anyone for medical support	Local private doctor	Private doctor in nearby town	Quack	Primary health centre/ hospital	Any other
Major Illness*						
APL	7.7	7.7	38.0	–	38.3	7.7
BPL	49.6	4.3	16.0	6.1	20.9	3.5
Total	45.3	4.7	18.0	5.5	22.7	3.9
Minor Illness**						
APL	12.3	11.8	23.6	19.3	36.6	0.5
BPL	17.8	5.5	9.5	27.9	33.6	4.3
Total	17.0	6.8	11.6	26.5	34.4	3.7

NOTES: * Ever suffered.
** During last four months.
SOURCE: Household Survey.

matters in determining the extent and incidence of poverty in an area. Land distribution is unequal, with concentration in the hands of a few landlords in most places, including Pune (Maharashtra), Chamrajnagar (Karnataka) and West Godavari (Andhra Pradesh), except in the tribal areas of Palamu (Jharkhand), Koraput and Nuapara (Orissa), Sidhi (Madhya Pradesh) and Dangs (Gujarat) where the distribution is somewhat more equitable. The ownership of small landholdings is not always the best position for most respondents, as later discussions will reveal. Small and marginal farmers basically practise subsistence farming. They use primitive farming techniques, especially in tribal areas, with little use of fertilizers or HYV seeds. Agriculture is almost entirely rain-dependent and yields are low. Furthermore, the nature of agriculture has undergone a change in areas where irrigation facilities are available and heavy investments made by large farmers in growing cash crops. The villages in Pune (Maharashtra), Chamrajnagar (Karnataka) and West Godavari (Andhra Pradesh) districts provide such examples. The wage work availability is much higher in these villages.

The wage rates for agricultural work within villages or neighbouring areas are abysmally low at about Rs. 25-35 per day in all districts except, once again, in Pune (Maharashtra), Chamrajnagar (Karnataka) and West Godavari (Andhra Pradesh). The prevalent wage rates in these districts are about twice those in other parts of the country. The wage payment systems are complex as the rates as well as modes of payments vary for different agricultural operations. Wages are paid as a particular portion of produce harvested or bundles made at the time of harvesting in most places (Box 2.1).

BOX 2.1: WAGE RATES AND PAYMENT SYSTEMS

- Wage rates for agricultural work in the districts of Araria, Palamu, Sidhi and Shravasti are abysmally low—around Rs. 25-35 per day. In peak agricultural season, the wages could go up to Rs. 40. The payment is lower if food is provided by the landowner. It is also common to pay in kind or in a combination of cash and kind. The following table provides an example of the difference in wages for different agricultural operations in Mudballa village, Araria, Bihar:

Nature of work	Time	Wages
Sundry tasks	8 a.m. to 12 p.m.	Rs. 15 : 750 gm. rice
Preparing the field	8 a.m. to 4 p.m.	Rs. 25 : 250 gm. rice
Sowing/transplanting	8 a.m. to 4 p.m.	Rs. 15 + 750 gm. rice
Weeding, etc.	8 a.m. to 4 p.m.	Rs. 15 + 750 gm. rice
Harvesting paddy	8 a.m. to 4 p.m.	1/8th share in grain prepared
Harvesting wheat	Own convenience	1/8th share in grain prepared

- Wage rates for children are much lower. Young children get about half the wages of adults, while older children get almost as much as adults.
- Wage rates are lower in Sidhi district and Doriya village of Bihar for working as attached labour with high caste landowners. The entire family is generally involved in responding to the demand for odd jobs mostly on no or very low wages.
- Wage rates are significantly higher in Pune, Chamrajnagar and West Godavari districts. The average wage rate for agricultural work for men is about Rs. 70, which is nearly double the rate prevalent elsewhere. One of the reasons is the cultivation of labour-intensive commercial crops and also higher crop intensity.
- Wage rates for women are lower but not notably different from those of men, except in the districts of Pune, Chamrajnagar and West Godavari, where they get almost half of what men get. However, the areas with high differentials in wage rates for men and women are also areas with a higher wage work availability and women get work around the year. Otherwise, women are generally employed for particular agricultural operations only.
- Non-agricultural unskilled labour wage rates are slightly higher than rates for agricultural work. Wages for unskilled work like loading, rickshaw-pulling, etc., in neighbouring small towns are Rs. 10-25 more than those in the village. The following table provides an example of the rates prevalent for non-agricultural casual work in Mudballa village, Araria, Bihar:

Nature of work	Time	Wages
Mason (construction work)	8 a.m. to 4 p.m.	Rs. 15-80
Loading	8 a.m. to 4 p.m.	Rs. 30
Carpenter/wood work	8 a.m. to 4 p.m.	Rs. 50
Kuccha construction	8 a.m. to 4 p.m.	Rs. 30

- Work in brick kilns or sugar cane harvesting is usually done in pairs/groups. Several members of a family work together and get paid a family wage. The average earning per adult varies between Rs. 50 to 75 per day.
- Wage rates are higher for agricultural work at places of migration such as Punjab and Haryana (Rs. 70 to 100 + food) and also for non-agricultural work in cities like Delhi, Gwalior, and Nainital.

In certain villages of Araria (Bihar) and Sidhi (MP), traditional feudal relations between landlords and labourers still prevail. The highly inequitable land distribution, with a small number of upper caste families owing a major portion of the land in the village is characteristic of Naudhiya, Kursa and Jogini villages in Sidhi district in MP, Doriya village in Araria in Bihar, as well as Gavaravaram village in Andhra Pradesh. However, while in AP this has resulted in a high demand for agricultural wage workers and an upward movement of wages, in MP and Bihar it has contributed to furthering the traditional patron–client relationship, including the incidence of attached labour, known as *harwahi* in Sidhi. This involves one or more members of the SC/ST families, often including children, working for the landlord's household, often on wages lower than those prevalent in the area and for longer than the usual wage hours. Advances to attached labourers, in cash or kind (of small amounts) from landlords are usually without interest, in contrast to the high interest rates prevalent in the village. With greater opportunities for work outside the village, the dependent relationship as well as the exploitative element is on the decline in most places.

In Honnahalli village in Chamrajnagar district (Karnataka), there is incidence of work as attached labour (often with reduced wages), almost invariably associated with a borrowing from a landlord which results in the commitment of wage work for about a year. In most places, the borrowing of money or grains takes place during the difficult season of low work availability. However, in Chamrajnagar, this practice does not have any caste basis; the landlords are Tamil migrants with huge landholdings acquired over a period of time. All these villages are characterized by seasonal food shortages which makes security of work, even on unfavourable terms, crucial. However, despite the sense of security, the desire to get out of this situation is strong everywhere and evidence of breaking away from this practice can be seen.

THE AVAILABILITY OF WAGE WORK

Based on land distribution and wage work availability, the 37 villages could be grouped in the four categories shown in Chart 2.1. Areas of high wage work availability have a higher cropping intensity due to the availability of irrigation facilities. The district-wise distribution of women reporting wage work as the primary occupation clearly indicates a high incidence of women's wage work in areas where wage work availability is high. These are the only villages where poor families are not usually required to adopt multiple strategies for survival and, therefore, the livelihood situation is more stable. It is obvious that there is a convergence of better transport and communication facilities, better provisioning of health, education and other basic services, generally better governance and high investment in agriculture leading to higher wage work availability. Wage work availability within

Chart 2.1: Classification of Villages According to Land Distribution and Work Availability

District (State)	Inequitable land distribution & low wage work availability	Better land distribution & low wage work availability	Inequitable land distribution & high wage work availability	Better land distribution & high wage work availability
Dhubri (Assam)	Jhakuapara, Tiapara	–	Ramrai Kutti	–
Araria (Bihar)	Mudballa, Khabaspur, Rahatmina, Doriya	–	–	–
Palamu (Jharkhand)	Ayodhya Kolhua	Khurakhurd, Lanka, Ukamand	–	–
Sidhi (MP)	Naudhiya	Barambaba, Kursa, Jogini	–	–
Chamrajnagar (Karnataka)	Chandukatte Mole	Maddur Colony	–	Doddathapur, Honnahalli
Pune (Maharashtra)	Malegaon	–	Karandi	–
Nuapada (Orissa)	–	Kermeli, Ratapalli, Cheri Chaun, Bhardua Munda	–	–
Koraput (Orissa)	–	Mohul Bhatta, Padheiguda	–	Mulasar
Shravasti (UP)	–	Balanagar Kodri, Sultana, Kathkuiyan Kalan, Masaha Kalan	–	–
Dangs (Gujarat)	–	Mahal, Wakarya	–	–
West Godavari (AP)	–	–	Gavaravaram, Bayyanagudem	–

the village significantly determines the need for adopting other means for survival. One of the common means adopted for survival is seasonal migration in search of work. The rate of migration is higher from villages where wage work availability is lower. In contrast, villages with high wage work availability witness some in-migration during peak agricultural seasons. Migration as a livelihood strategy has been discussed at greater length in the next section.

SEASONALITY

Poverty is not static, and the number of poor as well as the intensity of deprivation changes from year to year depending upon a good or bad harvest, and, from time to time, within a year due to seasonality as well as other sudden crises. The seasonal nature of agriculture in India and other agrarian economies quite significantly influences life patterns in rural areas. This generally means high work availability for some parts of the year and lean periods for the rest. For the poor, low work availability is linked with periodic food crises and changes in consumption patterns for poor families, reported in different measures in all the study villages. Another dimension of seasonality observed in the villages, especially in Bihar and Orissa, is the outbreak of diseases such as malaria and cholera almost every year during the rainy season. Water logging and lack of proper drainage leads to the eruption of these diseases and causes hardships accentuated by the fact that many such areas get cut-off during this period. This is also a period of food crisis coupled with hard work for paddy-growing areas, especially for women engaged in transplantation.

PROXIMITY TO FORESTS

Some villages are located in interior, remote locations in the districts of Koraput and Nuapada (Orissa), Palamu (Jharkhand), Dangs (Gujarat) and some parts of Sidhi (MP) district. Most of these are ST-majority villages. The forest generally offers avenues for additional earnings in the shape of various kinds of leaves and seeds, including *tendu* and *mahua*, and also certain foodstuffs used during periods of seasonal food shortages. However, such areas now face a crisis owing to the denudation of the forest cover. In a few tribal villages in Orissa and Jharkhand, the traditional right to and practice of utilizing minor forest produce has been severely curtailed since the forest area has been, or is proposed to be, converted into a sanctuary.

SOCIAL COMPOSITION, RELATIONS, AND PROCESSES

Villages reflect varying social compositions in terms of social groups and their inter-relationships. Some villages are mixed while others are dominated by one or two social groups in terms of population proportions. STs covered more than 60 per cent population in about one-third of, and were present in more than half, the villages. ST-dominated villages were located in Koraput and Nuapara (Orissa), Palamu (Jharkhand), Sidhi (MP), Shravasti (UP) and Chamrajnagar (Karnataka). Dalits were present in 20 (covering all study districts except Dangs) of the 37 villages, comprising more than half in 7, and between one-fourth and half in 4 of them. In almost all villages with Dalit inhabitants, the population also included either Upper Caste Hindu (UCH) or Other Backward Caste (OBC) groups, or both, in varying proportions. This is not always true for ST-dominated villages. The proportion of UCH families is generally small in most places. There are many villages with both SC and ST populations, generally true for Orissa and MP villages. A few villages in Dhubri (Assam) and Chamrajnagar (Karnataka) were entirely inhabited by a single OBC caste group, a phenomenon not seen for any other social group. A few villages in Araria (Bihar), Dhubri (Assam) and Shravasti (UP) have a significant Muslim population.

These varying compositions along with other factors significantly influence social processes and determine the life situations of poor families. Social distances and inequalities lead to various forms of deprivation and add to hardships caused by economic disparities. The study villages provided many examples and confirmed the existence of definite trends in these matters, implying that these are not isolated incidents but the usual factors that operate most of the time. However, these are deliberately not discussed here as they have been looked into at greater length in subsequent chapters.

HIGHER INCIDENCE OF DEEP POVERTY AND POWERLESSNESS

The Poverty Perception exercise undertaken with people in every village clearly indicated layers within BPL households and also identified the indicators used by people to distinguish 'very poor' from 'poor'. Almost 40 per cent of the total poor were categorized by people as being in the lower segment of BPL families. The incidence of deep poverty is much higher in certain areas; more than 40 per cent of the BPL families were put in this category in Araria (Bihar), Palamu (Jharkhand) and Shravasti (UP) as against only around 20 per cent in Pune (Maharashtra) and West Godavari (AP). This confirms that numbers alone are not enough to depict the nature of poverty, and that the intensity is also crucial.

Therefore, a higher incidence of deep poverty in any village is linked, to some extent, to other features such as poor connectivity, lack of access to basic services, subsistence agriculture and low wage structures, seasonality, social distances, exploitation, etc. These, when present in combination or even in isolation, reflect and add to the powerlessness of poor people. Powerlessness is a common state for the poor which determines their relations with the state and other 'powerful' groups in society. The poor do not appear to really question their position; they appear to accept their condition somewhat fatalistically; a feeling of hopelessness is paramount. This was evident in varying degrees among poor families in all villages, the situation being worse in areas where the incidence of deep poverty was higher.

POVERTY AND DEPRIVATION AT THE LEVEL OF THE HOUSEHOLD

LOWER AND UPPER SEGMENTS AMONG THE POOR

In order to discuss and understand poverty and deprivation at the household level, it is important to refer to indicators used to distinguish the two segments within poor families. This would also help in arriving at the parameters that define or determine the level of poverty or deprivation in a family. The indicators used by people at different places to distinguish between 'not poor', 'poor' and 'very poor' were surprisingly similar to each other. Although there were small variations, they largely followed the same pattern. The indicators used by people are a mixed bag; some of these could be seen as leading to poverty, some as a fallout of poverty, and some as simply reflecting the state of poverty. These indicators are:

1. Landlessness or small/poor quality landholdings.
2. High dependence on wage work; migration in search of work; dependence on Common Property Resources (CPR).
3. Absence or inadequacy of livestock holdings.
4. Chronic or occasional food shortages, accentuated during lean agricultural seasons; poor nutrition levels.
5. Lack of creditworthiness for large borrowings; borrowing food during lean seasons.
6. Long-term illness or physical weakness of an earning member of the household or frequent occurrence of illnesses.
7. Engagement of children in work.
8. Illiteracy in the family.

Deriving from the above analysis, the context of deprivation in poor households is discussed under the four major aspects of (i) livelihood strategies, (ii) food insecurity, (iii) illness, other crises and indebtedness, and (iv) literacy and education.

LIVELIHOOD STRATEGIES

Landownership

The ownership of assets, especially land, draught and milch animals largely determines the livelihood strategies of most poor people in rural areas with a very limited diversification of occupations, which holds largely true for the majority of this study's villages. Land distribution patterns clearly show that non poor families own more land than the poor, and within the poor, the lower segment owns much less than the upper segment BPL households. Landlessness is very high among the poor, especially among the lower segment. Nearly 58 per cent of very poor families were landless and another 23 per cent possessed land up to 1 acre only. Less than 1 per cent of the lower segment and 3.4 per cent of the upper segment of poor families as against 43 per cent non-poor families own more than 5 acres of land. The mean landholding owned by non-poor families is about five times higher than that for the upper BPL households and ten times higher than that for the lower BPL households. The social group to which a household belongs is important in determining the size of landholding owned even within poor families. The size of the mean landholding owned is the smallest for Dalits followed by OBCs, Muslims, the STs, and the UCH. The difference between UCH and the rest of the households is especially significant (Table 2.4).

Landownership patterns for poor families across different districts show notable variations yet indicate a definite design. One important feature is that despite variation, the mean size of landholding owned by poor households remains small, the highest being 2.14 acres at Sidhi (MP). Landlessness is usually high in districts where the study villages have a higher proportion of Dalit or OBC population. This includes West Godavari (AP), Araria (Bihar), Pune (Maharashtra), Dhubri (Assam), Chamrajnagar (Karnataka) and Koraput (Orissa). The size of the mean landholding owned is also smallest in these districts.

It is important to note that the extent of landlessness or ownership of only marginal landholdings is quite high among poor households in the two economically developed districts of West Godavari and Pune. Although the extent of landlessness is not so high in Shravasti (UP), which has a significant Dalit population, the average landholdings are very small. This is reflected in a large share of households owning less than 1 acre of land each. The extent of landlessness is less in districts where the study villages had a higher proportion of tribal families. This includes Palamu (Jharkhand), Nuapara (Orissa), Sidhi (MP) and Dangs (Gujarat) (Table 2.5). There are, however, two points of significance here: one, that there are important differences within districts, and two, that the differences exist even within one broad social group whether Dalit, ST, OBC or Muslim. These differences and their implications have been looked at later on in greater detail.

Table 2.4: Landownership Patterns across Economic and Social Groups

Economic Groups	Landownership Distribution (per cent) (in acres)					Mean landholding
	Landless	0.1-1	1.1-2.5	2.5-5	More than 5	
APL	10.6	8.6	13.9	23.8	43.0	6.59
UBPL	39.2	18.6	20.6	18.2	3.4	1.44
LBPL	57.9	22.8	14.1	4.5	0.7	0.64
All poor (BPL)	46.4	20.2	18.1	12.9	2.4	
Total (913)	40.4	18.3	17.4	14.8	9.1	2.04
Social group-wise distribution within BPL families	Landless	0.1-1	1.1-2.5	2.5-5	More than 5	Mean landholding
UCH	37.0	14.8	8.6	11.1	28.4	4.4
OBC	41.9	15.1	18.0	18.6	6.4	1.86
SC	49.6	19.9	15.2	10.5	4.7	1.25
ST	29.0	18.5	24.6	18.8	9.1	2.19
UC Muslim	49.1	23.6	10.9	10.9	5.5	1.27
LC Muslim	41.8	23.6	9.1	10.9	14.5	2.99

SOURCE: Household Survey.

Table 2.5: Landownership Patterns among BPL Households across Districts

District (state)	Mean landholding (in acre)	Per cent BPL households landless	Per cent BPL households owning up to 1 acre
Dhubri (Assam)	0.53	60.8	82.3
Araria (Bihar)	0.24	79.8	90.5
Palamu (Jharkhand)	1.48	32.9	54.4
Nuapara (Orissa)	1.66	35.8	42.7
Koraput (Orissa)	0.78	54.5	75.7
Sidhi (MP)	2.14	35.5	51.3
Shravasti (UP)	1.36	13.8	62.6
Dangs (Gujarat)	2.06	12.2	36.6
Chamrajnagar (Karnataka)	1.27	54.2	62.6
West Godavari (AP)	0.01	97.4	100.0
Pune (Maharashtra)	0.41	62.5	92.5
All India	1.11	40.4	58.7

SOURCE: Household Survey.

Ownership of small and uneconomic holdings does not make much difference in the economic or occupational status. The productivity of such land is low, it is largely unirrigated, and little investment is made in the use of fertilizers, HYV seeds, etc. Such marginal farmers are not able to survive only on the basis of agricultural produce and hence one or more members of the households are engaged in wage work of some kind to supplement the meagre income from farming.

Livestock Ownership

Despite the fact that only a small proportion of families depend entirely on cattle rearing, livestock holds a very important place in the lives of poor people in most parts of rural India. This is mainly because cattle are very crucial to farming and also in getting land on a sharecropping basis. Ownership of a couple of bullocks sometimes also fetches higher wages. But, most importantly, this provides security, often the only security available to poor families in times of crises. It is common for poor households to sell their goat or pig to earn cash at the time of any crisis such as illness, marriage or death. It also serves as an important source of earning 'big' cash at one go to be spent on clothes, etc. during festivals. These are the reasons why about 97 per cent of household heads considered owning livestock very important. This included those who do not own any cattle.

Nearly one-third (31.4 per cent) of the total families interacted with did not own any livestock. The ownership of livestock is closely linked with ownership of land. Fifty four per cent of landless households do not own any livestock and 70 per cent of them own only small animals, but no large or milch animal. More than one-third of the households owning up to 1 acre of land do not own any livestock (Table 2.6). The situation of households with

Table 2.6: Livestock Ownership Patterns across Landholding Groups

Landholding groups	Distribution of households according to livestock ownership (per cent)		
	Big animal*	Small animal**	No livestock
Landless	30.0	15.9	54.1
0.1 to 1 acre	62.7	13.3	24.1
1.1 to 2.5 acre	71.7	9.4	18.9
2.5 to 5 acre	81.3	9.0	9.7
More than 5	91.6	4.8	3.6
All	56.4	12.3	31.4

NOTES: *includes cow, buffalo, bullock, etc.
**includes mainly goat and pig.
Those owning both big and small animals are included as owning big animals. Therefore, the two groups are mutually exclusive.

SOURCE: Household Survey.

no land or livestock remains quite vulnerable as they do not get any land for sharecropping and do not even have any security to fall back on in times of financial crisis.

Primary and Secondary Occupations

The most significant feature of the livelihood scenario for poor families in rural areas is that most families have a mix of different occupations—cultivation/sharecropping, wage work within the village, wage work outside the village, forest produce collection, and cattle rearing—adopted in varying combinations by different family members at different points of time. However, wage work is the dominant occupation of poor families. Half of BPL household heads reported wage work as their primary occupation. Dependence on wage work is even higher for the lower segment of BPL families (Table 2.7). A substantial proportion (47 per cent) of families dependent on wage work as the primary occupation were involved mainly in the non-agriculture sector, reflective of a change that has taken place in the last one or two decades. This has close links with the phenomenon of seasonal migration and going to neighbouring towns for work. These occurrences were quite common in many villages. This issue is discussed later in this chapter.

Cultivation is the other major primary occupation for rural households, both among the poor and the non-poor, the proportion obviously being higher for the former. However, there is a major difference between a non-poor or a poor family being cultivator because of the basic difference between the size of the landholding and the investments made in that landholding. The average period for which their own grain production (including shares from sharecropping) for the previous year would have sustained a family is about two months for very poor families as against nearly six months for the upper segment of BPL families and about two and a half

Table 2.7: Primary Occupations of Household Heads

(in percentage)

Economic Groups	Cultivation	Agri. labour	Non-agri. labour	Non-agri. skilled	Salaried & self-employed	Others
APL	61.6	3.3	3.3	3.3	21.2	7.3
UBPL	45.9	23.9	13.9	5.1	6.2	5.0
LBPL	24.0	35.3	19.3	5.4	7.5	8.5
All poor (BPL)	37.4	28.3	16.0	5.2	6.7	6.4
Total	40.4	24.4	14.3	4.9	9.2	6.8
Social Groupwise Distribution within BPL Families	**Cultivation**	**Agri. labour**	**Non-agri. labour**	**Non-agri. skilled**	**Salaried & self-employed**	**Others**
UCH	49.4	31.3	2.4	–	10.8	6.1
OBC	33.6	31.2	9.1	9.1	9.1	7.9
SC	31.6	28.6	19.3	5.0	8.9	6.6
ST	54.9	16.0	15.6	2.2	5.8	5.5
UC Muslim	26.9	26.9	17.3	17.3	11.5	0.1
LC Muslim	43.6	16.4	10.9	–	16.3	12.8

SOURCE: Household Survey.

years for APL families.[1] Poor families need to supplement their income from farming by working for wages. More than 60 per cent of poor families reporting their primary occupation as cultivation cited wage labour (agricultural, non-agricultural, domestic work, or cattle grazing for others) as their secondary occupation.

Sharecropping is very common in most areas. Usually small and marginal farmers who also possess livestock (buffalo/bullock) lease-in land for sharecropping from bigger landowners. Different systems of sharing of costs and harvested produce are prevalent across the country. While sharecropping enhances the availability of grains for the household, the economic condition remains poor in the majority of cases. They often need to borrow money to invest in cultivation, and the returns depend on the rains and other factors leading to a good or bad harvest in a particular year. During droughts, the returns may be very low. In some areas, like Sidhi (MP), the terms of sharecropping are adverse and the sharecropper is barely able to break even. Nevertheless, being a cultivator and not a daily wage earner is considered more respectful in most areas.

A district-wise analysis (not shown in table form) of the primary and secondary occupations of household heads indicates that the highest proportion of households is dependent entirely on wage labour in West Godavari district followed by Palamu, Araria and Chamrajnagar. The incidence of wage work as a secondary occupation in the districts of Shravasti and Sidhi indicates that marginal and small farmers work as casual wage earners as well. In West Godavari district, wage work is locally available and is largely agricultural. In Araria district, agricultural wage work includes work within the village as well as wage work recorded for migrants going to Punjab and Haryana on a regular basis. There is also incidence of migration for non-agricultural wage work to distant destinations. In Palamu district, however, wage work is mostly of the non-agricultural kind, including work in brick kilns, manual labour work in nearby towns, and limited migration to distant destinations. Poor land quality and entirely rain-dependent agriculture, coupled with the absence of large landholdings, result in low availability of agricultural wage work in the villages of Palamu. The implication of being a wage worker on one's economic condition as well as on other aspects of life, however, varies from one area to the other depending on the nature of seasonality, work availability, wage rates, and nature of employment.

Female Work Participation

Quite expectedly, housework emerges as the most dominant primary occupation of adult (15+) women in rural areas. In fact, housework figures for about 90 per cent either as primary or secondary occupation. Housework includes daily chores at home, child care, and collection of water and fuelwood for self-consumption. This is generally not easy in places where it includes the tough task of carrying water or fuelwood over long distances, generally the responsibility of women in poor families, in places with poor basic facilities. The situation is tougher on women who are also engaged in some wage-earning activities. Nearly 18 per cent of women in poor households are primarily wage workers and about 10 per cent more are either engaged in cultivation or some other earning activity such as making baskets at home. Nearly 30 per cent of adult women in poor households reported wage labour as their secondary occupation. This indicates a large proportion of them being engaged in seasonal labour during specific agricultural operations such as transplanting. The involvement of women from APL families in paid labour outside the home is minimal (Table 2.8). Both parents reported being engaged in earning activities in about one-fourth of the total households, most of these belonging to poor families.

Women's participation in wage work is the highest in the villages of Chamrajnagar. This means that a high proportion of the poor in the total population coupled with a high demand for labour leads to a high participation of women in wage work. Usually, women work as agricultural labour in their own/nearby villages in specific agricultural operations. No significant differences across social groups exist for primary occupations of adult women except that the participation of ST women in work outside the home is higher than it is for women of other social groups, followed by SC and OBC women.

Table 2.8: Primary and Secondary Occupations of Adult Women*
(Economic Groups)

(in percentage)

Primary Occupation	Cultivation	Agri. labour	Non-agri. labour	Self-employed	House work
APL	9.1	1.0	0.3	3.6	73.9
BPL	7.3	15.9	2.1	2.5	67.5
Secondary Occupation	**Cultivation**	**Agri. labour**	**Non-agri. labour**	**Self-employed**	**House work**
APL	24.2	5.5	0.3	2.2	13.2
BPL	19.6	22.0	7.8	2.3	20.7

NOTE: * This includes all females in the age group of 15+.
The total does not add up to 100 as (i) other occupations reported in small numbers have not been included, (ii) everybody did not have a secondary occupation.

Dependence on Forests

In villages located near forest areas, poor households are able to utilize forest produce like *mahua* and *tendu* leaves, fuelwood, fruits, etc., to gain additional earnings. The forest offers certain foodstuffs used during periods of seasonal food shortage. During the *mahua* season and *tendu* leaf-collection season, the entire family, including children, is involved in this activity. In some of these villages, cutting and selling of fuelwood is a major source of livelihood or additional income. In several villages of Nuapara and Koraput (Orissa) and Palamu (Jharkhand), forest-linked economic activity was reported as a primary or secondary occupation for a significant number of adults.

Migration

Seasonal migration for a few months to near and faraway places is an important survival strategy for the poor during lean months. Roughly one-fourth of poor households reported migration[2] of the household head or spouse or both at least once during the last one year. If migration of other family members, especially boys in their teens, is taken into account, the incidence would be much higher. The phenomenon is apparently on the increase and is now often used as a regular source to supplement income. However, in most cases, it is simply a coping mechanism without which it would be difficult to sustain oneself during lean months. At most, in some cases it leads to expenditure on conspicuous consumption during the period immediately after the period of migration. In very few cases, it has also led to investment in assets such as the purchase of land and cattle.

The pattern of migration varies in terms of who migrates and to which place, for what kind of work, and for how long. Single male migration (the male head of the household migrating alone and not with his wife or/and children) is common in some villages of Dhubri (Assam), Araria (Bihar),

Chart 2.2: Migration Patterns in the Study Districts

District	Type of Migration	Extent	Nature of Work	Place to which Migrated	Duration	Remarks
Dhubri (Assam)	Single male	70 per cent of total migration	Sawing, construction	Far off, within state	Throughout the year	
	Whole family	30 per cent of total migration	Brick kiln	Far off, within and outside state	Six months [October-April]	
Araria (Bihar)	Single male	Almost entirely	Agriculture, construction, factory	Punjab, Haryana, Delhi, MP, UP	Throughout the year or 6-8 months	Children between 13-15 years get initiated
Palamu (Jharkhand)	Men and women [some with children]	70 per cent of total migration	Agricultural work	Aurangabad (Bihar)	20-40 days three times a year	High participation of women in migration
	Whole family	30 per cent of total migration	Stone breaking, brick kiln	Bihar, UP, Haryana	Between 2-6 months	
Dangs (Gujarat)	2-3 persons of a family or whole family	About 30 per cent of the migration is whole family migration	Sugar cane harvesting, some families also go to grape orchards	Bardoli and other places in Gujarat and Nasik	Mostly 6 months [September-April], so go for 3 months [December-April]	Two adults work in a pair; children also contribute
Nuapara (Orissa)	Whole family migration	Individual male migration limited	Brick kiln	Andhra Pradesh, Madhya Pradesh	Six months [November-June]	
Shravasti (UP)	Single male migration	10-15 per cent	Brick kiln, construction, rickshaw pulling, and labour	Ludhiana, Mumbai, Rajkot, etc.	August-October & January-March	Limited family migration (caste group)
Chamraj-nagar (Karnataka)	Essentially single male migration, women and children for 3-4 months	15-20 per cent	Plantation - agricultural farm work	Kerala	Throughout the year, single male; entire families away between January-April	Also limited single male migration in lean season the district

Shravasti (UP), and Chamrajnagar (Karnataka), whereas family migration is common in Nuapara (Orissa), Dangs (Gujarat), and some parts of Palamu (Jharkhand) and Dhubri (Assam). In Dangs (Gujarat), and some parts of Palamu (Jharkhand), it is also common for a few members of a family, and not the entire family, to migrate. Single male migrants generally work as rickshaw pullers or daily wage earners in factories and agriculture, whereas those who migrate with part or entire families generally work on piecemeal rates at brick kilns, stone quarries, orchards, sugarcane cutting, paddy or wheat harvesting, etc. The duration of migration varies depending on the nature of work and the state of requirement in the village (Chart 2.2). Migration generally takes place in groups when several families or individuals migrate together. Even when it is not group migration, the role of information flowing from those who migrated earlier is crucial, and that is why people from one village are seen to be migrating to the same places and for similar kinds of work.

FOOD INSECURITY

The issue of acute food shortage faced by poor people in drought-affected areas in Orissa, Rajasthan, Maharashtra and Madhya Pradesh in the midst of gigantic 'surplus' food stocks rotting in godowns has been an area of debate and discussion in many national dailies and magazines during the last two years (2000-1). What is important to point out in this respect is that food insecurity is not faced by the poor only during drought or drought-like situations. In many places, periodic food crises are an annual phenomenon; the intensity of the crisis and the length of the period increases during years of bad or no crop. Despite the fact that the year preceding our fieldwork had been a relatively good crop year, about three-fourths of poor families reported facing a food crisis for several months, and described this as an annual occurrence. Nearly one-third of these families usually face a food crisis for more than four months in a year, and the rest go through this for about two-three months.

A food crisis has a distinct seasonal character related to a lean agricultural season when availability of work is low and whatever little stock of grains, if any, the families had are finished. Typically, these are the months between the sowing and harvesting of the *kharif* crop, the worst months being July, August and September. In some places in Sidhi (MP) and Shravasti (UP) districts, the pre-harvest season for the *rabi* crop, i.e. the months of January and February, have also been recorded as leading to food shortages. All poor families face food crises in the villages of Dangs district in Gujarat, a rain-fed, mono-crop area with no alternative employment available within or close to the villages (Table 2.9).

The extent and intensity of the food crisis is not a direct result of landlessness or low 'own grain production'. While the extent of the

Table 2.9: Period for which Households Faced Crisis during a Year (per cent of Households)

Districts	Percentage of households facing food crisis for the period of				
	No crisis	0-2 months	3-4 months	5-6 months	7-12 months
Dhubri	51.9	27.8	12.7	6.3	1.3
Araria	26.2	19.0	38.1	13.1	3.6
Palamu	43.0	21.5	31.6	2.5	1.3
Nuapara	21.3	47.2	22.0	6.7	2.2
Koraput	37.9	39.4	15.2	7.6	–
Sidhi	–	6.6	15.8	50.0	27.6
Shravasti	12.5	8.8	35.0	33.8	10.0
Dangs	2.4	7.3	9.8	39.0	41.5
Chamrajnagar	27.7	15.7	47.0	9.6	–
W. Godavari	25.6	23.1	41.0	10.3	–
Pune	62.5	27.5	2.5	–	7.5
Total	27.8	22.6	26.1	16.1	7.4

SOURCE: Household Survey.

landlessness is the highest in West Godavari (AP), the availability of wage work almost around the year contributes to food security. Similarly, in the irrigated villages of Koraput (Orissa), Pune (Maharashtra) and Chamrajnagar (Karnataka) districts, the extent of food shortage is significantly lower. The coping strategies adopted by the poor include a shift to the consumption of coarse grains such as maize, barley or *ragi*, usually cheaper than rice or wheat, and a shift from three meals to two or from two to one a day. The meal generally consists of only one cereal for many poor families even during non-crisis periods, but during this period it becomes true for a larger number of families. In areas close to forests, the dependence on fruits, herbs and leaves collected from forests increases. Seasonal food crises in the family means reduced food intake for everybody in the family, including children.

Food crisis refers to a failure to maintain the food consumption levels of the 'normal' or 'non-crisis' period. This does not refer to adequate food intake from a nutritional point of view; consumption levels of nutritional inputs are quite low even during non-crisis periods. Although it was not possible to go into the finer aspects of nutritional intakes and levels, some of the common questions asked about consumption of *dal* and vegetables, commonly taken inputs for protein, suggested very low levels of use among poor families. Seventy per cent of BPL families reported taking *dal* only rarely or occasionally. Only 18 per cent of poor families have *dal* on a daily basis. Consumption of vegetables is also not common; more than half of BPL households eat vegetables only rarely or occasionally. By contrast, about 88 per cent of APL families take *dal* as well as vegetables either daily or quite frequently (Table 2.10).

Food shortage is one of the worst crises faced by families, making them

Table 2.10: Consumption Patterns of *Dal* and Vegetables

	Percentage distribution of households based on consumption patterns			
	Consumption of *dal*		Consumption of vegetables	
	APL	BPL	APL	BPL
Rarely	4.0	25.7	8.0	20.0
Occasionally	7.9	35.3	5.3	29.8
Frequently	35.1	21.6	24.7	29.0
Daily	53.0	17.5	62.0	20.5

SOURCE: Household Survey.

vulnerable and their lives quite insecure. This is one of the major reasons leading people to look for various opportunities to earn, including migration. Tackling this crisis is of paramount importance to people and determines their life decisions quite significantly. The fear of an imminent food crisis is also responsible for continued practices of attached labour at certain places. Food crises also force families to borrow at high rates of interest, and borrowing for food has been identified by people as an indicator of being very poor.

ILLNESS, OTHER CRISES, AND INDEBTEDNESS

Periodic food crises are something poor families can anticipate, and be prepared for, in whatever measure possible. However, there are several other crises, both anticipated and unanticipated,[3] which affect their lives quite significantly. While some of these are general in nature affecting everybody in the village or area such as drought or crop failure and flood, others are more personal in nature such as illness or death. About 30 per cent of BPL families reported a financial crisis due to some external occurrence at least once during the period of two years immediately preceding the fieldwork. Drought (or a drought-like situation) or crop failure was the most common reason (63 per cent) followed by flood (29 per cent). A drought-like situation was reported in villages in Palamu (Jharkhand), Nuapara (Orissa) and Sidhi (MP) districts, while a restriction on growing tobacco due to a glut-like situation in the global market leading to a lowering of the demand for labour was reported in West Godavari (AP). Palamu and Nuapara (carved out of the erstwhile Kalahandi district) have been infamous for being drought-prone, leading to the worst forms of food insecurity and starvation deaths.[4] Flood appeared as a common cause leading to crises at Araria (Bihar), Shravasti (UP) and Dhubri (Assam).

Illness of a family member is the most common reason leading to a financial crisis and causing a lot of insecurity. Nearly 40 per cent of BPL families reported having faced some financial crisis during the period of last two years and about 69 per cent of these was on account of illness, another

11 per cent on account of the death of a family member. The marriage of a son or daughter, an otherwise happy event for the family, is also one of the major reasons leading to financial crises (the remaining 20 per cent) among poor families and more often than not long-term indebtedness as well. Borrowing is the most common coping mechanism for personal as well as general crises and, in most cases, it is borrowing from local moneylenders at exorbitant rates of interest. Eating less, increased dependence on forest and migration are some other common coping mechanisms during times of general crisis.

A large proportion (63 per cent) of poor households reported being currently in debt. More than three-fourth of these households have borrowed from informal sources such as moneylenders, landlords, shopkeepers and friends. Borrowing from friends and relatives is preferred as it generally means lower rates of interest. However, this is generally available only for short terms. Although borrowing is not so uncommon in APL families either

Table 2.11: Indebtedness among the Poor in Rural Areas

District	Extent of indebtedness from informal sources (per cent)	Mean rate of interest from money-lenders*	Most dominant purpose for borrowing	Second most dominant purpose for borrowing	Prevalence of committed wage work against borrowing
Dhubri	63.3	59.33	Illness (55.6 per cent)	Marriage (11.1 per cent)	Yes
Araria	84.5	100.4	Illness (34.4 per cent)	Marriage (21.9 per cent)	Yes
Palamu	35.4	75.0	Illness (43.8 per cent)	Food (31.3 per cent)	No
Nuapara	7.8	78.0	Illness (50.0 per cent)	Agriculture (50.0 per cent)	Yes
Koraput	5.6	46.7	Agriculture (100 per cent)	–	No
Sidhi	59.2	62.2	Food (36.4 per cent)	Illness (27.3 per cent)	Yes
Shravasti	47.5	80.7	Marriage (31.8 per cent)	Food (22.7 per cent)	Yes
Dangs	17.0	48.0	Food (28.5 per cent)	Agriculture (22.9 per cent)	No
Chamrajnagar	100.0	75.5	Pilgrimage (32.4 per cent)	Illness (22.5 per cent)	Yes
W. Godavari	76.9	58.2	Food (40.0 per cent)	Illness (20.0 per cent)	No
Pune	25.0	60.0	Illness (25.0 per cent)	Marriage (25 per cent)	No
All India	40.4	76.8	Illness (27.9 per cent)	Food (17.2 per cent)	

NOTE: * The rate of interest is annual in per cent terms.

(about 59 per cent), there are stark differences in the purposes of borrowing. They borrow more to invest in agriculture and house-building rather than due to illness or a shortage of food. The poor have less access to institutional sources of borrowing (banks and government schemes) as compared to the non-poor. While about 50 per cent of the total APL households have borrowed from banks or government schemes, only about 22 per cent of poor households had taken loans from these sources.

Nearly one third of the borrowing from informal sources among the poor is due to illness. The general health condition, especially of women and children, in rural areas, remains precarious due to the lack of access to safe drinking water and nutritious food and hard work. Successive pregnancies often add to this and make women weak. Absence or dysfunctionality of basic public health services force them to go to private sources which invariably means arranging money by borrowing. If the person falling sick happens to be an earning member, borrowing also becomes essential in many cases to sustain the rest of the family. Illness, thus, severely adds to the state of vulnerability in poor families.

The average annual rate of interest for borrowing from landlords was as high as 50 per cent and from moneylenders an unbelievable 77 per cent, these being higher than average at many places. Apart from marriages and deaths, a good number of poor families reported having borrowed to go on pilgrimages. The borrowing of grains is common not only for consumption during lean seasons but also for sowing, to be paid back after harvesting. Often, the amount of grains to be returned is double that borrowed. Borrowing against committed labour is also a common practice in many areas. Many such practices do not get reflected in quantified presentations.

LITERACY AND EDUCATION

The presence of educated or at least literate members in the family makes a difference in terms of exposure and attitude, which gets reflected in many ways. Literate members are better informed and deal better with others including government functionaries. The absence of basic literacy makes people more vulnerable. However, the situation is dismal on this account. The extent of illiteracy among adults is very high for both men and women. 84 per cent women and 62 per cent men are illiterate in poor households, the proportion being higher for the lower segment of BPL families. Only about 11 per cent women and 25 per cent men among poor households have completed the primary level of schooling or above. The situation is much better for APL families, especially for men, as more than 60 per cent of them have completed at least primary school education.

Wide regional variations exist in terms of literacy among adults. More than 60 per cent of the men in Koraput (Orissa), Chamrajnagar (Karnataka), Shravasti (UP) and West Godavari (Andhra Pradesh) are illiterate, whereas

Table 2.12: Literacy and Schooling among Adults (14 years and above)

(in percentage)

Economic groups	Illiterate	Literate	Primary completed	Upper-primary completed	Class X completed	Graduate and above
Female						
APL	60.6	8.4	14.1	8.1	6.7	2.0
BPL	83.9	5.5	6.7	2.6	1.0	.4
UBPL	82.7	5.4	7.5	3.4	1.2	.6
LBPL	87.4	5.8	5.2	1.0	.5	0.0
Male						
APL	23.8	14.6	15.5	14.9	21.1	10.1
BPL	61.9	13.9	11.0	7.6	3.9	1.7
UBPL	59.4	14.2	11.1	8.3	5.0	1.9
LBPL	66.5	13.3	10.9	6.1	1.9	1.3
District						
Female						
Dhubri	60.2	12.2	16.3	5.7	4.8	–
Araria	85.0	6.2	8.1	–	.6	–
Palamu	88.0	5.6	3.2	1.6	1.6	–
Nuapara	79.8	11.8	6.3	1.4	.7	–
Koraput	94.7	1.0	2.1	–	–	2.1
Sidhi	84.4	3.5	5.7	3.5	1.4	1.4
Shravasti	92.3	1.8	3.5	.6	1.8	–
Dangs	69.1	11.6	10.2	7.6	1.5	–
Chamrajnagar	71.8	3.4	8.6	10.9	5.2	–
W. Godavari	71.0	5.8	10.1	4.3	4.3	4.3
Pune	50.6	8.2	25.9	9.4	2.3	3.5
Male						
Dhubri	28.87	26.05	19.01	11.26	10.56	3.52
Araria	46.62	13.50	12.67	6.13	13.50	7.7
Palamu	49.30	11.80	15.3	10.41	9.73	3.5
Nuapara	49.6	21.0	8.4	11.8	7.7	.7
Koraput	82.0	9.0	4.5	–	1.1	3.4
Sidhi	59.8	12.1	9.5	8.3	3.8	6.4
Shravasti	63.4	10.3	10.3	7.7	5.7	2.0
Dangs	36.2	24.5	14.5	15.9	7.2	1.4
Chamrajnagar	63.7	4.3	11.3	11.3	6.3	3.1
W. Godavari	60.3	10.3	8.7	7.7	10.3	2.5
Pune	30.7	16.0	22.7	13.3	13.3	4.0

SOURCE: Household Survey.

this share is less than 40 per cent in Dangs (Gujarat) and Pune (Maharashtra). The proportion is much higher for women in comparison to men everywhere, the disparity in terms of per cent points being smallest at Chamrajnagar (Karnataka). This situation is despite the fact that this literacy has been taken for all those in the age group of 14 years and above and the incidence of illiteracy will be higher if those between 14 and 18 years are not included. This becomes clear when one takes the status of parental literacy levels into account. Both parents were illiterate in the case of more than 70 per cent of BPL households. In about 18 per cent of the families, the fathers were literate while the mothers were illiterate. Only in about 6 per cent of the poor families were both parents literate, and in the remaining 5 per cent, the mothers were literate while the fathers illiterate. This means the mothers are literate in only about 11 per cent of poor households.

Poor households in most places live in conditions where they have very little control over their own lives in terms of choice of occupation, leading to a characteristic uncertainty about life and future. The lack of basic services and institutional support, either due to sheer absence or dysfunctionality, or simply because the poor cannot negotiate, makes them vulnerable to small crises and open to exploitation in various forms. They, therefore, tend to be engaged with immediate concerns of survival most of the time and find it difficult to have a long-term perspective. On the whole, the life-situation for poor families in rural areas is largely characterized by:

- Uncertainty and instability
- Vulnerability to small crises—lack of institutional support
- Heavy dependence on debt from informal sources at exorbitant interest rates
- A very short-term view of life and engagement with immediate concerns
- Daily life full of drudgery, especially for women
- Lack of education, exposure and wider world-view.

This is not to say that there are no differences across all poor families in the villages or regions. There are villages where life is at least relatively more secure and there are families within very deprived areas experiencing change due to one or more factors. The various circumstances and the processes crucial in bringing change will be discussed at a more disaggregated level in different chapters.

Children's Lives and Roles in the Family's Survival

General poverty, coupled with uncertainty and instability of life situations, significantly influence children's lives. They are part of everything that happens in the family and often play a crucial, albeit at times invisible and unaccounted for, role in coping with crises. Unlike non-poor families, where children are rarely engaged in any kind of work, except, of course, girls in household chores, children in poor families are generally engaged in a variety of activities—paid and unpaid, full-time and part-time, seasonal and round the year, within the home and outside. Engagement in some work for their own household is more common than working for wages. Engagements for their own families include cattle grazing, own farm activities, household chores, and sibling care. Often, though they are not directly employed for

Chart 2.3: Broad Patterns for Children's Work

Younger boys (6-9 years)	Younger girls (6-9 years)	Older Boys (9-13 years)	Older girls (9-13 years)
Cattle grazing Employed by another family as grazers Forest produce collection	Sibling care & household work Cattle grazing Employed as domestic workers Forest produce collection	Seasonal work for own farming Agricultural wage work Forest produce collection Wage work, including independent work at place of migration of family Work as member of team at brick kiln, sugarcane harvesting Independent wage employment in towns	Seasonal work for own farming Agricultural wage work, often with mother Forest produce collection Work as member of team at brick kiln, sugarcane harvesting

wages, they contribute towards family labour. The pattern seen for children's work across the study villages are broadly categorized in Chart 2.3.

Children's engagement in work can be best understood in the light of the situations observed for poor families and the context of the villages that they live in. Cattle grazing, for instance, is important because cattle are crucial for small and marginal farmers and they cannot afford to hire a grazer for the purpose. Culture also plays a role as sending one child for this purpose is customary among certain groups such as Gonds (STs) in Barambaba village in Sidhi (MP) district. However, this culture itself could have come to be established over course of time because of the importance of cattle in maintaining livelihood. Similarly, the economics of farming on small uneconomic holdings is such that most families perform all the agricultural operations themselves; it is not possible to hire outside paid labour. Moreover, most labour-intensive agricultural operations are such that they need to be completed within a short period of time and this means a high demand for labour for a limited period. Since most marginal and a few small farmers also double up as wage labourers, they prefer to finish their own work fast so that they can also earn outside. As such, it becomes almost inevitable to engage all hands available in the family for sowing or harvesting. In fact, during harvest seasons, it is also not uncommon to engage children for help in paid work as wages are linked to the quantity cut and bundles made.

The nature of the seasonal collection of forest produce is also not very different. The season for *mahua* or *tendu* does not last long and to make the most of it, it is common for the entire family to be engaged in the act for the whole day. Household chores and sibling care are other common engagements for children, especially girls. Tough daily life and engagement of women in various kinds of jobs brings the need to have somebody else to support in domestic chores and sibling care. More than 90 per cent of BPL households are nuclear where there is no elder person to take care of children. Invariably, it is the girl, if there is a girl in the family, who gets this responsibility. Ill-health of women coupled with successive pregnancies adds to this requirement (see Box 2.2).

BOX 2.2: CHILD LABOUR IN INDIA

There are very widely varying perceptions of the magnitude of the child labour problem in India. As per the 1991 census, children whose main activity was economic, and could be called working children, number about 12.7 million, i.e. about 5.2 per cent of the total child population in the 6-14 years age group. Another 10.5 million were marginal workers. Thus 23.2 million children were engaged in some paid economic activity. The definitions as well as estimates for working children vary from each other ranging between 17 to 44 million children. The estimates go up if children engaged in sibling care/household chores are included.

Child work is a very varied phenomenon and cannot be seen as a homogeneous category. One classification that is often made, based on provisions of labour legislation, is:

1. Children working in notified hazardous occupations in the organized sector. They number between 5-10 per cent of the total number of working children.
2. Children working in other non-hazardous occupations in the organised or unorganized sectors.
3. Children working in agriculture or as domestic servants for landlords and farmers.
4. Children working in their own homes and on their own farms.

The Child Labour Regulation and Prohibition Act, 1986 permits the employment of children in non-hazardous occupations for 4-6 hours a day provided the employer provides 2 hours of non-formal education every day at the worksite. The Act does not cover children working in agriculture and allied activities and also in hazardous or non-hazardous work within the household. The unorganized and informal sector, both in urban and rural areas, not covered by this legislation, accounts for almost 85 per cent of the total child labour. Work in hotels, *dhabas*, shops and establishments is not covered under this Act. Children working in such establishments usually work 10-12 hours everyday. In a survey of out-of-school children in Guwahati city, almost 35 per cent of them were found working in tea shops, restaurants and shops. There has been virtually no country-wide assessment of children working in roadside *dhabas* and restaurants. Most such establishments do not get covered during house-to-house surveys conducted in rural and semi-urban areas. Seventy-six per cent of male child workers and 81 per cent of female child workers are in the agricultural sector. In agriculture, the percentage of child workers working for wages is on the increase while those engaged in own farm work on the decline. Almost 85 per cent of the children working for wages work in rural areas.

In agriculture and allied activities, as well as cottage industries like coir, *papad*-making, gem-polishing, *beedi*-making, carpet-weaving, embroidery, etc., children get paid much less than adults. Also, girls get even lower wages than boys and are employed in jobs requiring the lowest skills. Children are employed despite large-scale adult unemployment or underemployment. The major part of NGO effort and international concern is directed to the problem of child labour in the manufacturing sector, while wage-earning child labourers in agriculture outnumber those in the manufacturing sector 6:1.

According to an estimate, there are 4 lakh child labourers in Delhi city alone. Out of these, about half are in non-manufacturing sectors—roughly one lakh are domestic workers, about 30,000 work in *dhabas* and tea shades, 40,000 in construction and allied work, and 20,000 in scooter/car repairing. As per the 1991 census, the states of Andhra Pradesh, Madhya Pradesh, Maharashtra, Uttar Pradesh, West Bengal and Bihar have the highest absolute number of child workers. A small proportion of working children are "bonded" to the employers to work in servitude usually to return a debt. Agriculture employs far more bonded labourers than all industries and services put together.

Children who migrate with their families often work with their parents. This is common for households engaged in family-based labour, i.e. labour is hired on the basis of the family as a unit. The examples are sugar cane harvesting in Gujarat and Maharashtra; brick-kiln work in Andhra Pradesh, Uttar Pradesh, West Bengal, Assam and other states; building and road construction work throughout the country.

The proportion of children from poor households engaged in such activities is high even if one separates occasional engagements and those regular but not involving long hours. More than half of the children in the age group of 6-13 years (both inclusive) are engaged in these activities for long hours and for a substantial number of days in a year. Household chores and/or sibling care and cattle grazing are year-long activities, while engagement in own work is generally seasonal. There is a good amount of overlap and almost all children who figure in 'own work' are also engaged in one or the other activities. Girls outnumber boys in these activities, whether household chores, sibling care and own farm or forest work. The mean hours of work in all these activities is high for both boys and girls.

CHILDREN WORKING FOR WAGES

About 13.2 per cent of BPL children work for wages. The incidence is high in two kinds of places, one where land distribution is highly unequal and big landlords hire children to work as full-time graziers or domestic workers and, two, where the incidence of migration is high, influencing older children also to migrate. Boys in the age group of 11-13 years move out of the village to work in urban areas in shops, hotels, etc., especially from areas where adult, long-term migration is common. This percentage is an underestimate because of exclusion of certain categories which the families did not view and report as wage labour. For instance, a good number of children migrate with their families, and often contribute to family labour but do not get reported because they were not employed directly. Children's engagement in earning activities is also common among social groups traditionally engaged in some caste-linked occupation; one such group was Kaparias in Sultana village at Shravasti (UP) district. Almost all families in this group migrate to distant places for about eight months every year and are engaged in a

Table 2.13: Engagement of Children in Economic Activities and their Mean Hours of Work

Kind of Work	Per cent of Total (BPL) children engaged in this work			Mean Hours of work	
	Boys	Girls	Total	Boys	Girls
Wage work	20.2	5.9	13.2	8.58	7.84
Own Work	8.5	14.2	11.1	5.80	6.14
Cattle grazing	12.3	8.6	10.6	7.64	7.56
Household chores/ sibling care	6.1	47.8	25.5	5.1	5.8

NOTES: 1. Own work includes cultivation, forest collection for earning purposes, home-based skilled work for earning purposes, etc. Only those children have been included who reported working for more than 20 days in a year.

2. Cattle grazing refers to own cattle grazing. Cattle grazing for others comes under wage work. Only those children have been included for whom it is almost a year-round activity.

3. Only those children have been included who are engaged in household chores/ sibling care for more than three hours. A substantial number are engaged for three hours or less who have not been included. By deleting all those who are engaged in household work for three hours or less (who form another 12.5 per cent of total children), it is ensured that there is no over-estimation.

4. No APL child, boy or girl, was reported to be engaged in own cattle grazing or wage work. Very few (less than 10) children from APL families were reported to be engaged in own work. Almost all from APL families engaged in household chores/sibling care worked for three hours or less.

5. This includes both school-going and out-of-school children.

6. It is common for children, especially girls, engaged in household chores to also get involved in seasonal farm and forest work. Boys mainly engaged in cattle grazing also get involved in own farm and forest work. At times, children engaged in full-time work also work on their own farms during sowing or harvesting seasons, or during *mahua* or *tendu* leaves collection season. Thus, there are overlaps and the proportion of total children engaged in work is less than the total of all these.

SOURCE: Household Survey.

number of activities including begging. This kind of engagement is also often not included as involvement in paid labour.

The incidence of working for wages is much higher among the lower segment of BPL families as compared to the upper segment. Nearly 17.5 per cent of very poor families reported working for wages as against 10.5 per cent in the upper segment of BPL families. The average annual earning of children in paid work, though not very high, contributes significantly to their family's total earnings simply because earnings are so limited. The decision to send a child for paid labour is often linked with some crisis or the other. It is common to start sending a child for wage work when families are in debt and are required to pay heavy interest rates. However, once the practice starts, it generally continues even if the family gets out of that particular crisis. This is very significant as it points to children's vulnerability

Chart 2.4: Incidence of Children Working for Wages

High	Moderate	Low
Naupara (Orissa)	Dhubri (Assam)	Palamu (Jharkhand)
Araria (Bihar)	Sidhi (MP)	Shravasti (UP)
Dangs (Gujarat)	West Godavari (AP)	Chamrajnagar (Karnataka)
Koraput (Orissa)		Pune (Maharashtra)

Table 2.14: Average Annual Earnings of Children Working for Wages

(*in Rs.*)

Age	Average Annual Earnings	
	Boys	Girls
6-10 years	1,393	1,095
11-13 years	2,585	1,989

NOTE: (i) The earnings have been recorded on the basis of an estimated contribution where income accrues jointly to a group of family members, including those who work together, for example in sugarcane harvesting, etc.

(ii) The value of food / clothes included as a part of the wages has not been added. This is a common practice for children working as grazers or domestic servants on a full-time basis with other households.

to their circumstances. The perusal of a large number of case studies of families with children in wage work showed that the situation generally improves after children join the work force and start contributing. But that does not lead to the withdrawal of children from work because this is likely to push them back to the earlier situation. The workload is generally quite heavy and majority of children expressed their discomfort and a desire to get out of their present situations. However, they do not appear to have any say in this regard. It is obvious that poverty and related circumstances in the households impact on children's lives and choices made about them quite significantly. Involvement in long hours of work at an early age definitely clashes with a childhood that every child deserves.

SCHOOLS: ANOTHER DIMENSION OF POVERTY AND DEPRIVATION

School[5] is the third dimension in addition to village and household constituting the context for children's education-related decisions. The functionality of school is important in determining whether the school present in an area is really 'available' to people, people in this case consisting of children from poor and deprived families. The issues of the regular functioning of schools, attitudes of teachers towards children from poorer and so-called lower-caste groups and the reliability of the school as an institution in delivering the goods came up almost everywhere, with very few exceptions. At many places, people also expressed indifference towards the issue of school functioning in view of the 'futility of educating children up to only primary level' as it was perceived to be leading to no benefits given the lack of access to and affordability of educating children up to a higher stage which could be meaningful. It was clear that the voicelessness and powerlessness of poor people also affects the relationship between poor parents and schools.

In general, schools in Pune (Maharashtra), West Godavari (AP), Chamrajnagar (Karanataka) and Dangs (Gujarat) are functioning better than the ones in the northern and eastern parts of the country. The functioning of the school seems to follow a pattern similar to the working of other government delivery systems like the Public Distribution System (PDS), Primary Health Centres and Rural Development schemes. Subsequent chapters present a disaggregated picture of school functioning in varying situations and contexts, this section presents an aggregate analysis of school functionality. This aggregate analysis pertains to primary schools only as the number of upper primary schools is too few for any meaningful aggregation. The functionality of school is discussed here under three broad aspects of school provisioning and functioning, aspects important in determining the disposition of parents:

1. Basic pre-requisites of a 'functioning school'
2. Inputs into teaching learning and classroom processes.
3. School Supervision, Academic Support and Incentives.

In addition, certain efficiency indicators are also discussed.

BASIC PRE-REQUISITES FOR SCHOOL FUNCTIONING

Basic Physical Infrastructure

Physical infrastructure including the classrooms, blackboards and a few other basic facilities determines the learning space and environment to some extent and, hence, is important. However, the condition of this physical infrastructure in rural areas as observed in study villages was far from satisfactory everywhere. Only 6.7 per cent of the primary schools and 12.5 per cent of the upper primary schools have a fully *pucca* building. About 73 per cent have partially *pucca* building and rest have either a *kuchcha* structure, a dilapidated one or no building at all. Although the maintenance of a building did not appear to be a major issue, especially in districts where the DPEP has been in operation, many primary schools did not have basic drinking water or toilet facilities. What is, however, more telling is the fact that only 53 per cent of the observed classrooms have blackboards in good condition. About 30 per cent of the classrooms did not have any blackboards.

Physical infrastructure, however, needs to be seen in totality and understood in relation to enrolment. We tried to make an overall assessment of the adequacy of the school's infrastructure based on the condition of the building, available floor space and the enrolment of the school and rate them in four categories. Only for 4 per cent of the schools, the infrastructure could be considered average to good, these schools were located mainly in MP, Karnataka, Gujarat and Maharashtra. School infrastructure was rated as inadequate in case of 38 per cent schools and the remaining 22 per cent was considered to be very inadequate.

Number of Teachers

An adequate number of teachers is critical for creating the desired learning environment and ensuring the required attention that every child deserves. More than one-fifth (21 per cent) schools had only one teacher in position; these included three Alternative Schools (AS) and Education Guarantee Schools (EGS) in Sidhi, Madhya Pradesh. Another 50 per cent schools had only 2 teachers posted at the school. Seventy-one per cent of all surveyed schools, therefore, had two or less teachers and only 29 per cent had more than two teachers in position. This means the existence of multi-grade teaching situations in majority of the schools. About 28 per cent have a Pupil-Teacher Ratio (PTR) of between 60 and 100, 23 per cent schools between 40 and 60 and 35 per cent schools 40 or less.

Table 2.15: Distribution of schools across Certain Indicators

	Proportion of Schools in Each Category (per cent)			
Type of Building	*Pucca*	*Partially Pucca*	*Kuchcha*	*Dilapidated*
Primary (37 schools)	5.4	73.0	10.8	10.8
Upper Primary (8 schools)	12.5	75.0	12.5	–
Total	6.7	73.3	11.1	8.8
Adequacy of Infrastructural Facilities**	Good	Average	Inadequate	Very inadequate
Primary (37 schools)	8.1	24.3	43.2	24.3
Upper Primary (8 schools)	12.5	62.5	12.5	12.5
Total	8.8	31.1	37.8	22.2
Student-Classroom Ratio	*Up to 30*	*31-50*	*51-70*	*More than 70*
(Primary)	20.0	27.5	15.0	37.5
Pupil-Teacher Ratio	*Up to 40*	*41-60*	*61-100*	*More than 100*
(Primary)	35	23	28	14
Attendance as proportion of enrolment***	*5-20 per cent*	*20-40 per cent*	*40-60 per cent*	*60-70 per cent*
(primary and upper primary)	10.0	33.3	20.0	37.7
People's perception of school functioning (primary and upper primary)	*Good* 40.0	*Average* 25.0	*Bad* 20.0	*Very Bad* 15.0

NOTES: * Includes no building.
** Based on the research team's observations.
*** On the day of the visit.

SOURCE: School Survey and Focus Group Discussions

Regular Opening of Schools for Prescribed Hours

The regularity of the schools in terms of opening daily for the prescribed hours has been assessed on the basis of people's perception as gathered through FGDs. In several villages of Dhubri (Assam), Araria (Bihar), Sidhi (MP) and Shravasti (UP), people complained that the school functioned irregularly; there were many holidays or the teachers were involved in many meetings or other responsibilities which resulted in the frequent closure of the school (Chart 2.5).

Chart 2.5: Regularity of School: Peoples' Perception

Regular	Irregular (Very and Somewhat)
45 per cent Dangs (Gujarat) Chamrajnagar (Karnataka) West Godavari (AP), Pune (Maharashtra) and *some* tribal areas of Palamu (Jharkhand), Koraput and Nuapara (Orissa)	55 per cent Dhubri (Assam), Araria (Bihar), Sidhi (MP), Shravasti (UP) and *some* areas of Palamu (Jharkhand), Koraput and Nuapada (Orissa)

Teachers' Attendance

In almost all the villages, people commented on the irregularity of individual teachers. Particular teachers were known to be coming only occasionally and in some cases there appeared to be an understanding—one teacher remains absent for few days, then the other remains absent for the next few. Or one teacher comes late in the morning, while the other comes on time, but leaves early. This way the school opens and functions regularly for the prescribed hours. However, the teaching time is reduced and there is no way this can be assessed. In Dhubri (Assam), Araria (Bihar), Shravasti (UP) and Sidhi (MP), people questioned the quality of teaching in view of the irregular attendance of teachers and their lack of interest in teaching. It is important to add that even if a teacher is present in the school, she or he need not necessarily be teaching or be engaged in some school-related activity. Field observations show that while in 27 per cent cases, teachers were not present in the school, in 21 per cent cases, they were present but were neither teaching nor doing any

Table 2.16: What were the Teachers Doing?*

Teacher's Activity Observed	Per cent distribution
Not present in school	27
Teaching in a class	38
Checking students' work/other teaching-related work	14
Present in school/ class but not teaching	21

NOTE: * Three observations were collected for each teacher in position in the surveyed schools.
SOURCE: School Survey.

teaching-related work. This means that in only slightly more than half the cases, teachers were either found to be teaching or doing some related work, mostly checking students' notebooks (Table 2.16).

INPUTS INTO TEACHING: LEARNING AND CLASSROOM PROCESSES

Teacher Qualification and Training

Teaching is a professional job and requires that teachers have minimum education and training. Sixty-five per cent teachers had the basic qualification of Class XII or more, the remaining 35 per cent were Class X Pass or less. The teachers with lesser qualifications were all older, recruited long ago. Ninety-four per cent of teachers had received pre-service or equivalent teacher training, only 6 per cent had not received this training. It may be mentioned that although a minimum level of education and competence is essential, it was apparent that teachers' educational qualifications and their pre-service training are not discriminating factors in teacher performance. The aspects of teacher motivation and empathy with children were found to be more crucial for the marginalized areas/groups covered in this study. Teacher performance is here referred to as a sum total of regularity in attendance, interest in teaching, relationship with children in classroom, attitude towards disadvantaged children and teaching methodology and seen through the school/classroom observations and people's perceptions.

Multi-grade Teaching Situations

The inadequate number of teachers positioned, and their frequent absence even when they are adequate in number, result in one teacher handling several classes at a time. Almost in one-fourth of the classes observed, teachers were handling four to five classes together and in another 16 per cent of cases, teachers were handling three classes together. This was most common in Araria (Bihar), Sidhi (MP) and Shravasti (UP) districts. The situation of one teacher-one class was present only in Pune (Maharashtra) and West Godavari (AP), and in some parts, mainly the primary sections of upper primary schools, in Chamrajnagar (Karnataka). The observations clearly showed that most teachers who had to teach more than one class at the same time were just managing to keep the children disciplined or engaged in some routine, repetitive tasks and there was hardly any learning taking place (Box 2.3). This was also perceived by people to be one of the most serious factors hindering the 'quality' of the school.

Availability of Textbooks

In the absence of a library and any other learning aid as such, the textbook is the only learning aid. Most children had textbooks in about 75 per cent of the classrooms observed. However, many of them did not have all the textbooks. Fewer children had exercise books for all subjects as required.

BOX 2.3: AVERAGE CLASSROOM SCENE IN A SCHOOL WITH TWO TEACHERS

- Children writing letters in alphabetical order on a slate and showing this to teachers (some very young children look lost) and the teacher sitting on a chair, disinterested.
- Some children writing, some looking at textbooks, and some idling/playing (not by design, but because the teacher is disinterested).
- Some questions written on the blackboard, a few children writing, others not bothered and nobody to monitor them.
- Children doing something on their own (reading from book), teacher scolding/beating those around him but not teaching.

Inside the Classroom[6]

Children doing some repetitive work (either written or verbal) was the most common observation in the classrooms. As such, it is not surprising that children were observed to be keenly interested in the classroom only in 18 per cent of cases. They were completely passive in 37 per cent cases and only somewhat interested in the remaining 45 per cent of cases. The teacher-child relationship could be described as friendly in 11 per cent cases and somewhat friendly in another 20 per cent cases. Children were reported to be afraid of teachers in 37 per cent cases and in another 32 per cent cases, only a few children were getting attention from teachers.

Corporal punishment was very common in almost all schools. It may be added that household survey and FGDs showed that parents also consider this important for 'maintaining discipline' and making children learn. Parents objected only if the teacher beat the children 'savagely' or discriminated in the punishment against children of a particular caste. Children were much less appreciative of beatings by teachers. This was the most common factor identified by children in distinguishing between good and bad teachers (Box 2.4).

BOX 2.4: CORPORAL PUNISHMENT

In Balanagar Kodri village in Shravasti district (UP), there are two teachers at the local primary school, one head teacher, one assistant. The assistant teacher beats the children regularly and is particularly harsh towards Dalit children. The head teacher generally does not beat the children. The attendance in the school improves on days when the head teacher is present. The children first see whether the head teacher has come, and on many occasions decide not to come to school if he hasn't. However, the head teacher is not very regular but the assistant teacher is regular!

In some schools in Koraput district (Orissa), the teachers were seen to be having difficulty in understanding the children's language. The teachers were thus unable to initiate such children gradually to the regional language. These were mainly non-tribal teachers posted in tribal areas. Actually, in several parts of the country, the home language of children is quite different/distant from the medium of instruction and textbooks and training programmes do not address this issue.

It is often difficult to ascertain teachers' attitudes towards children from poor and lower-caste families over a short period of observation. However, obvious instances were recorded and there were many of these. Certain obvious observations such as the serving of the midday meal separately to Dalit children in Koraput district (Orissa) did not require any special skill. Neglect of poorer, ill-clad children was commonly observed in several schools across almost all districts. While subtle discrimination based on caste was reported from many other places, obvious discrimination on the basis of caste by teachers in terms of attention and interaction was reported in Sidhi (MP). The school here appears to be reflecting the caste-based feudal set-up of the larger society. These aspects are discussed later on in detail.

SCHOOL SUPERVISION, ACADEMIC SUPPORT AND INCENTIVES

School supervision and support are, or at least should be, crucial for the monitoring and facilitation of school functioning. However, in reality, school supervision in rural areas is infrequent and perfunctory. Inspecting personnel had not visited the surveyed schools for 6 to 28 months prior to the fieldwork survey in Shravasti (UP), Dhubri (Assam), Palamu (Jharkhand), Araria (Bihar) and some schools of Sidhi (MP). As in some other aspects, the position is somewhat better in Pune (Maharashtra), West Godavari (AP) and parts of Chamrajnagar (Karanataka). The inspecting personnel at block and sub-block levels are of the opinion that they have too many administrative responsibilities and the number of schools in their jurisdiction is too large, making regular supervision impossible. Nevertheless, most block-level education administrators are aware of the problems of school performance in these disadvantaged areas. However, most also (especially in the eastern and central states) thought that nothing could be done to improve the situation at the administrative level. They rather took the lack of awareness and poverty of parents to be a 'given', which cannot be changed and saw no role for school or the schooling system in changing the situation (Box 2.5).

Supervision is not oriented to school improvement issues. It is more important for inspectors to complete the required number of school visits, what they actually do on those visits does not really matter. They are not oriented to discuss and provide support on issues of school improvement. However, the system of having Cluster Resource Coordinators, as separate from school inspectors, oriented towards the task of providing academic support has helped in providing some academic support in districts where the DPEP is operation. No evidence of active interest from any parent or community body was found, with a few exceptions. This was true even for

> **BOX 2.5: PASSING THE BUCK**
>
> Discussions with the teachers and education administrators at different levels reveal that they love to pass the responsibility to 'others'. For teachers, it is 'too many non-teaching tasks, unnecessary meetings called by superiors, no recognition of any good work, no support and supervision from above, very difficult and remote areas making commuting difficult', which does not make them work. For supervisors and inspectors, it is 'teachers' apathy, absenteeism, insensitivity towards poor and lower caste children, lack of competence, and their inability to monitor due to too many responsibilities', which lead to the failure to attract and retain children from poor families in schools. They are, of course, united in thinking and often concluding that 'poor parents are not interested in sending their children to school. These children also do not have adequate capacities to learn and hence the school cannot do much to ensure their schooling.' The lack of the system's accountability towards people or even the need to develop any such accountability, the lack of any orientation among functionaries to issues of equity and the existence of corrupt practices which help both teachers and administrators in maintaining their vested interests, did not find any mention, barring very few exceptions.

those states where an institutional role has been given to either the panchayat or a parents' body, for example in Madhya Pradesh, Andhra Pradesh and Karnataka.

Village Education Committees or School Management Committees have been formed in almost all schools, but only very few take any interest. In 62 per cent schools, they play no role at all, they normally do not even come for school meetings. The headmaster who happens to be the member-secretary, sends the register and gets the required signatures to complete the quorum required to show the conduct of the 'meeting'. The level of interest varies in schools where they are not so indifferent—in some cases, some members come to meetings whenever called but mostly keep quiet; in some others, they come, voice their opinions but do not take any responsibility; and in a very few, they take the initiative, make suggestions, take responsibilities and work in collaboration with schools for school improvement and increased participation.

The functioning of the VEC, however, depends to a great extent on the initiative of teachers. Although the composition of the VEC ensures that there is representation from disadavantaged social groups and women, they have rarely been involved in the formation of VECs and made aware of the accountability of schools to people. The responses from teachers suggest that they expect VEC members to be very respectful to them and consider the VEC 'problematic' if they raise a number of questions. In their opinion, a 'good' VEC is one which unquestioningly supports the teachers' suggestions and makes contribution in terms of land or labour.

Several incentive schemes are in operation in almost all states, mainly with an objective to motivate parents and compensate for at least some part of the private costs of sending a child to school. The most common incentive schemes other than the midday meal are attendance scholarships, free textbooks and free uniforms. Parents in most places stressed the importance of incentives in ensuring the regular attendance of children. This was also obvious from the fact that they raised the issue of the management of incentives and delays whenever the issue of school functionality was raised in FGDs. The provision for free textbooks was considered the most important by the majority of parents, including those belonging to the lower segment of BPL families. BPL families, unlike APL households, attached a lot of importance to the midday meal as well. APL families considered scholarships more important than the mid day meal (Table 2.17).

The coverage of incentives is, however, extremely limited (Table 2.18). Specific incentive schemes such as the Attendance scholarship or Free uniform are in operation for children belonging to SC or ST families, but they do not really cover all children coming from these groups. Very few children belonging to these groups actually receive these. The criteria for selecting these children remain unclear and most head teachers apply their own criteria. It was reported that there is mismanagement, delay and corruption in the delivery of these incentives. The schools in Araria (Bihar), Palamu (Jharkhand) and Sidhi (MP) had the greatest delays. Delays in some cases defeat the whole purpose. For instance, the whole logic of the attendance scholarship is to provide a monetary incentive at the end of the day or month to motivate parents to send their children regularly to school.

Table 2.17: Preference for Particular Incentives

Economic Group	Rating of the particular incentive as the 'Most Critical' (per cent)*			
	Free Textbooks	Midday Meal	Cash Scholarship	Free Uniform
APL	51.3	14.3	31.3	10.4
UBPL	43.1	34.2	14.7	11.0
LBPL	37.6	34.3	16.8	14.5
ALL	43.2	30.8	18.4	11.9

NOTE: *Many parents rated more than one incentive as the 'most critical' and gave the same rating. That is the reason why these cannot be added for any group to arrive at 100.

SOURCE: Household Survey.

Table 2.18: Common Incentives and their Coverage

S. No.	Incentive Schemes	Coverage of Children (per cent of total enrolment)*
1.	Attendance Scholarship	8.0
2.	Free Textbooks	50.0
3.	Free Uniform (ever received)	16.0
4.	Exercise Books	7.7

NOTE: *This denotes that this percentage of children have received the particular incentive at least once during the previous two years unless otherwise specified, for example in case of uniforms, it depicts the percentage of enrolled children who have ever received uniforms.

SOURCE: School Survey.

When this comes as a lump sum several months after the actual period for which it is meant, it loses its meaning and relevance. The provision for free textbooks exists for all children from SC and ST communities and all girls in districts where the DPEP is operational. However, schools do not receive these books in time and, often, the number is not adequate for all eligible children (Box 2.6).

BOX 2.6: A FEW NUGGETS FROM SCHOOL VISITS

- A teacher often sends his son to teach in place of himself (Dhubri, Assam).
- A *maktab* functions inside the government primary school. The maulvi teaches on the veranda of the school building (Araria, Bihar).
- A private school is started by upper caste villagers within a defunct government primary school (Araria, Bihar).
- The school (EGS) functions for 1-2 hours whenever the high caste, politically connected Guruji decides to come (Sidhi, MP).
- The teacher beats lower caste children more savagely (Shravasti, UP).
- The teacher distributes textbooks meant for one class among all children; after some time, he distributes textbooks meant for the other class, and so on. This device is to avoid the tearing of all the books in the first few months of the session (Koraput, Orissa).
- The names of several children reported to be 'enrolled and attending' by parents could not be found in the school register in three villages (Dhubri, Assam; Araria, Bihar; and Nuapara, Orissa).

The provision of midday meals (actually only foodgrains, except in Orissa, among all the study states) has helped enhance enrolment. Parents insist on enrolling even under-age children to get the foodgrains. The nationwide norm requiring 80 per cent attendance in a particular month to be eligible for food grains is not followed anywhere. Despite low attendance rates, teachers have to distribute grains to all parents of enrolled children because of the fear of pressure from parents. In Sidhi (MP), some teachers reduce the amount of food grains in proportion to the actual attendance. Clearly, the midday meal has not been able to ensure the regular attendance of children. Delays and corruption were reported for this as well. Several parents at different places complained about receiving much less than the norm. In Bihar and Assam, the scheme was non-functional for a long time and has only recently been resumed.

EFFICIENCY AND EFFECTIVENESS OF SCHOOLS

We wanted to use three simple indicators to look at the efficiency and effectiveness of schools, (i) attendance rates (attendance on the day of visits as against enrolment), (ii) retention rate (Class IV or V enrolment of 2000/2001 as a proportion of class I enrolment 4 or 5 years back) and (iii) the research teams' perception of children's learning.[7] However, we could not do any aggregate analysis for retention or completion rates as the record for the last five years' enrolment were not available in a number of schools. However, the completion rate was low for most schools for which records were available.

Attendance rates were low in most parts of the country, except in Pune (Maharashtra), West Godavari (AP) and parts of Chamrajnagar (Karnataka) and Nuapara (Orissa). Only 38 per cent of the schools had an attendance of 60 per cent or more on the day of the visit. About 43 per cent of the schools have attendance rates of less than 40 per cent. Inflated enrolment figures, especially for Class I, contributed to some extent to these low rates. The end-of the year examination figures for those who appear is a more realistic assessment of 'real' enrolment, but even that was not available from all the schools. On the issue of learning, most state research teams reported that children in Class III or IV could not read or write properly or carry out simple multiplication/division exercises.

The above discussion makes it clear that the school functioning in the context of poor children leaves much to be desired and in many cases adds another dimension to their deprivation. However, this is not true everywhere. There are places where school functioning is somewhat satisfactory. How the functionality of school interacts with other factors related to area and household and act upon school-participation decisions has been discussed in detail at several places in different contexts. The next chapter discusses school participation patterns followed by reasons for non-participation and traces the linkages between poverty, deprivation and school-participation.

NOTES

1. This is based on an analysis of the total production of foodgrains during the previous year and the daily requirements of a family, taking into account the differences in the consumption patterns of different food grains.
2. Only if the person/s has/have stayed outside their village for at least one month, has it been termed migration. Daily commuting to town or going away even for a few days together for work has not been categorized as migration.
3. The terms anticipated and unanticipated crises are borrowed from Rahman (1995).
4. These areas are single-crop, rain-dependent areas with heavy dependence on forests, and the reasons for frequent droughts range from faulty policies to natural topography. A discussion of these aspects has been avoided as this would have really meant going outside the purview of this study.
5. All full-time educational institutions have been taken as schools, including Alternative Schools (AS) or Education Guarantee Schools (EGS). However, if an institution is running for less than four hours, it is not taken as a school.
6. Classroom observations are based on simple tools that could be handled by field workers efficiently.
7. We did not conduct any achievement test for children in our fieldwork.

3. Reality Bites: Schooling the Rural Poor

Schooling Participation Patterns: Lows within Lows

The picture of the schooling status of children in rural areas is far from encouraging. Less than two-thirds (64.4 per cent) of children in the age group of 6-13 years[1] are currently enrolled in schools; more than one-third, 35.6 per cent of the total children, therefore, are out-of-school. It is also noteworthy that contrary to popular belief, it is not drop-outs who largely constitute out-of-school children. The number of never-enrolled children is much higher than drop-outs; they comprise about 55 per cent of out-of-school children. If children going to unrecognized madrasas[2] are included, never-enrolled students constitute 62.2 per cent of the total out-of-school children. Madrasa-going children form 2.6 per cent of the total, 7.3 per cent of the out-of-school, and 13.3 per cent of never-enrolled children (Table 3.1).

The most striking feature of participation patterns in rural areas is the various forms of disparity that exist within an overall low level of participation. There are disparities across economic, social, regional, gender and age groups but it does not stop here. There are disparities within disparities, e.g. between social groups within the very poor or between the poor and the very poor within a social group and so on. Hence, there are lows and lows within a general low level of school participation.

DISPARITIES ACROSS ECONOMIC GROUPS AND DISTRICTS

Enrolment rates are lower for families from lower economic levels. Only 61 per cent of the total children among BPL families are enrolled as against more than 81 per cent families in APL families. The disparities are sharp even among BPL families, and nearly half (47 per cent) of the children in the lower segment of BPL families are not enrolled in schools. The share of never-enrolled also increases for poorer families; it is as high as 30.5 per cent in the lower segment of BPL families (Table 3.1). A high concentration of out-of-school children among poor families (comprising a high number of never-enrolled) has significant implications for policy planning.

The disparities in school participation patterns between poor and non-poor families are not uniform for all regions. Except for the three districts of Dhubri (Assam), Dangs (Gujarat) and Chamrajnagar (Karnataka), the difference in enrolment rates is higher than the difference of 20.2 per cent points for the rest of the districts. However, the difference is sharpest for

Table 3.1: Enrolment Status—Economic Groups (per cent)

	Enrolled	Drop-out	Never enrolled	Madrasa	Total
APL	81.2	5.2	8.1	5.5	100 (308)
BPL	61.0	15.1	21.9	2.0	100 (1493)
UBPL	66.0	14.1	18.3	1.6	100 (929)
LBPL	52.8	16.7	27.8	2.7	100 (564)
Total	64.5 (1163)	13.4 (243)	19.5 (352)	2.6 (47)	100 (1805)

NOTES: APL = Above Poverty Line, BPL = Below Poverty Line, UBPL = Upper strata of BPL, LBPL = Lower strata of BPL.
Figures in parentheses show the number of children in that category.
SOURCE: Household Survey.

Table 3.2: Enrolment Status—Economic Groups in Districts (per cent)

District	Economic group	Enrolment Status (per cent)			
		Enrolled	Drop-out	Never enrolled	Madrasa
Dhubri (Assam)	APL	89.2	10.8	00	00
	BPL	75.7	16.7	2.8	4.9
Araria (Bihar)	APL	42.2	2.2	20.0	35.6
	BPL	48.9	5.3	34.7	11.1
Palamu (Jharkhand)	APL	83.3	00	16.7	00
	BPL	59.7	9.7	30.5	00
Nuapara (Orissa)	APL	84.2	15.8	00	00
	BPL	62.3	19.1	18.5	00
Koraput (Orissa)	APL	100	00	00	00
	BPL	53.1	20.4	26.5	00
Sidhi (Madhya Pradesh)	APL	92.0	4.0	4.0	00
	BPL	69.4	13.5	17.1	00
Shravasti (Uttar Pradesh)	APL	82.5	00	15.0	2.5
	BPL	38.9	7.6	52.2	1.3
Dangs (Gujarat)	APL	79.2	12.5	8.3	00
	BPL	71.9	22.5	5.6	00
Chamrajnagar (Karnataka)	APL	91.3	4.3	4.3	00
	BPL	72.2	20.5	7.3	00
West Godavari (Andhra Pradesh)	APL	94.1	5.9	00	00
	BPL	64.0	17.3	18.7	00
Pune (Maharashtra)	APL	93.8	6.3	00	00
	BPL	61.9	31.7	6.3	00

NOTE: APL = Above Poverty Line, BPL = Below Poverty Line.
SOURCE: Household Survey.

Koraput in Orissa and Shravasti in Uttar Pradesh. Only about 53 per cent children from poor families are enrolled as against all children (100 per cent) in non-poor families in Koraput. In Shravasti, only about 39 per cent children from poor families are enrolled as against 82.5 per cent children from non-poor families. The difference is also very high for the two economically advanced districts of West Godavari (Andhra Pradesh) and Pune (Maharashtra) (Table 3.2). Although the absolute number of poor families and their share in the total population is much smaller in these districts, participation patterns for children from poor families present a somewhat similar picture as elsewhere.

Araria in Bihar presents an exception as the enrolment percentages are low for both poor and non-poor families. However, this needs cautious interpretation as the district has a sizeable Muslim population and a good number of children from both poor and non-poor families go to madrasas. Regional variation exists not only in the levels of disparities but also in the enrolment percentages themselves. About 70 per cent or more children from poor families are enrolled in Dhubri (Assam), Sidhi (MP), Dangs (Gujarat) and Chamrajnagar (Karnataka) whereas this share is lower than 50 per cent in Araria (Bihar) and Shravasti (UP) (Table 3.3).

THE ISSUE OF REGULARITY

A critical issue, raised earlier as well, is whether enrolment alone can be taken as an indicator of effective participation, especially when it concerns children from deprived and vulnerable families. Effective participation in schooling demands regular attendance for learning to be more real and permanent. If children, especially those who do not have educated parents and a supportive environment at home, do not attend school regularly, their enrolment does not have much significance as it may not lead to any effective learning. Irregular children may also have a higher potential of becoming drop-outs in the foreseeable future. As such, it is important to distinguish between regular and irregular children among those enrolled.

Only about 65 per cent of the total enrolled children regularly attend[3]

Table 3.3: Enrolment Status—Districts (per cent)

District	Enrolment Status			
	Enrolled	Drop-out	Never enrolled	Maqtabs
Dhubri (Assam)	78.5	15.5	2.2	3.9
Araria (Bihar)	47.7	4.7	31.9	15.7
Palamu (Jharkhand)	63.6	8.2	28.3	00
Nuapara (Orissa)	64.6	18.8	16.6	00
Koraput (Orissa)	55.8	19.2	26.5	00
Sidhi (Madhya Pradesh)	74.1	11.5	14.4	00
Shravasti (Uttar Pradesh)	47.7	6.1	44.7	1.5
Dangs (Gujarat)	73.5	20.4	6.2	00
Chamrajnagar (Karnataka)	74.7	18.4	6.9	00
West Godavari (Andhra Pradesh)	69.6	15.2	15.2	00
Pune (Maharashtra)	68.4	26.6	5.1	00
Total	64.5	13.4	19.5	2.6

SOURCE: Household Survey.

school, taking all the districts together. More than 7 per cent of enrolled children attend school only occasionally and can hardly be categorized as school going. They go to school once in a while, mostly just to collect their share of food grains distributed under the midday meal scheme or to collect some other such incentive like a scholarship or a textbook. For all practical purposes, these occasionally going children do not attend school and should be treated as drop-outs. The remaining 28 per cent of enrolled children attend school irregularly, i.e. for about half the working days. Irregularity is also higher among children from poor families; only 62 per cent of enrolled children from BPL families are regular as against 76 per cent children in non-poor families. The share of occasional children is also higher at 8 per cent of those enrolled from BPL families as against 4 per cent for APL families. Irregular attendance is much higher for the lower segment of BPL families. Eleven per cent of enrolled children attend school only occasionally and another 35.6 per cent are irregular. This is remarkably worse than the patterns observed for the upper segment of BPL families. Low enrolment coupled with high irregularity presents a dismal picture of school participation for children in the lowest economic strata.

Regularity among enrolled students is relatively high in the southern and south-western parts of the country. No instance of irregularity comes from Pune district, not even among poor families. This indicates that though there is a gap in enrolment among children in poor and non-poor families in this district, there is none in terms of regularity. Once enrolled, all children, including those from poor families, attend school regularly. More than 90 per cent of enrolled children go to school regularly in Chamrajnagar, 84.1 per cent in West Godavari, and 82.7 per cent in Dangs. The case of occasionally attending children is almost non-existent or minimal in these districts. The greater availability of wage work, the high level of wages, and the better functioning of schools—these factors possibly contribute to this phenomenon. The districts in the eastern and north-eastern parts of the country with high levels of irregularity among enrolled children present a contrast to the picture seen for the southern and western parts. Irregularity is the highest in Dhubri district where only about one-third of enrolled children attend school regularly. The share of those occasionally attending school is also the highest here, with 29.3 per cent of enrolled children falling into this category. Irregularity is high in all the remaining districts (the share of regularly attending children varying between 44 per cent in Shravasti to 65 per cent in Palamu) except in Nuapara (Orissa) where only about 11 per cent of enrolled children do not attend school regularly (Table 3.4).

The picture of participation patterns changes in many places if the issue of regularity is taken into account. The share of regularly attending children among the total children is much smaller than the share of enrolled children, and that of drop-outs increases if occasionally attending children are treated as virtual drop-outs, which is what they are. This is especially true for high

Table 3.4: Patterns of Regularity* among the Enrolled

National		Distribution of enrolled children on the basis of regularity in attending school (per cent)		
		Regular	Irregular	Occasional
APL		75.8	19.7	4.5
BPL		62.0	30.0	8.0
UBPL		66.2	27.3	6.5
LBPL		53.4	35.6	11.0
Total		64.9	27.9	7.3
District	Economic Group	Regular	Irregular	Occasional
Dhubri (Assam)	APL	30.4	52.2	17.4
	BPL	33.3	34.4	32.3
Araria (Bihar)	APL	73.7	15.8	10.5
	BPL	45.5	46.6	8.0
Palamu (Jharkhand)	APL	90.0	10.0	00
	BPL	58.9	40.0	1.1
Nuapada (Orissa)	APL	100.0	00	00
	BPL	87.6	10.3	2.1
Koraput (Orissa)	APL	71.4	28.6	00
	BPL	50.0	37.9	12.1
Sidhi (Madhya Pradesh)	APL	66.7	26.2	7.1
	BPL	43.4	45.9	10.7
Shravasti (Uttar Pradesh)	APL	53.3	43.3	3.3
	BPL	39.3	50.8	9.8
Dangs (Gujarat)	APL	94.1	5.9	00
	BPL	79.7	17.2	3.1
Chamrajnagar (Karnataka)	APL	100.0	00	00
	BPL	89.5	9.5	1.0
West Godavari (Andhra Pradesh)	APL	100.0	00	00
	BPL	78.7	21.3	00
Pune (Maharashtra)	APL	100.0	00	00
	BPL	100.0	00	00

NOTES: *Regular: Attending school for more than 15 days per month on an average (assuming that the school opens for about 22-23 days).
Irregular: Attending school for about 10-15 days per month on an average.
Occasional: Attending school only occasionally, for example to collect the dry ration being distributed, etc. (less than 5 days a month).
SOURCE: Household Survey.

enrolment districts such as Dhubri and Sidhi where there is a large divergence between enrolment and regularity patterns. The situation becomes worse even for those districts where low enrolments are combined with high irregularity, e.g. Shravasti, Araria and Koraput. The share of regularly attending children among the total children is as low as between 20 to 30 per cent for Shravasti, Araria, Dhubri and Koraput and between 35 to 42 per cent in Sidhi and Palamu. However, the proportion of never-enrolled children still remains higher compared to drop-outs at several places.

Table 3.5: Participation Patterns taking Regularity into Account (per cent)

District	Enrolled		Drop-out	Never Enrolled	*Maqtabs*
	Regular	Irregular			
APL	61.68	15.90	8.76	8.71	5.51
UBPL	43.70	17.97	18.40	18.30	1.60
LBPL	28.19	18.79	22.55	28.36	00
Total	41.79	17.96	18.10	19.50	2.60
Districts					
Dhubri	25.41	29.83	38.70	2.20	3.90
Araria	24.25	19.57	8.52	31.91	15.74
Palamu	41.30	21.73	8.74	28.36	00
Naupada	58.01	5.52	19.90	16.60	00
Koraput	29.16	20.83	25.03	25.00	00
Sidhi	36.62	30.40	18.51	14.40	00
Shravasti	20.81	23.35	9.64	44.67	00
Dangs	61.06	10.61	22.16	6.20	00
Chamrajnagar	67.97	5.61	19.66	6.74	00
W. Godavari	58.69	10.89	15.21	15.21	00
Pune	68.35	00	26.60	5.06	00

NOTES: (i) The figures under the columns enrolled and regular show the percentage of children attending school regularly from the total number of children in the 6-13 age group.

(ii) The figures under the column enrolled and irregular show the percentage of children attending school irregularly from the total number of children in the 6-13 age group.

(iii) Children going to school only occasionally have been added to the number of drop-outs and then the percentage of drop-outs in the total age group of children worked out to arrive at a more real estimate of drop-out percentages.

(iv) The proportions of never-enrolled and madrasa going children remain the same.

It is important to point out that notable inter-village differences exist both in enrolment and regularity in all the districts. The differences are huge in some, while not so sharp in others. Enrolment patterns in the villages are not very different from the district average in Dhubri, Sidhi, Koraput, Dangs, Chamrajnagar, West Godavari and Pune districts, whereas there are large variations in Araria, Palamu and Nuapara. The variations are, however, less marked in Shravasti district. Inter-village variations are more common for irregularity, and the shares of regularly attending children between villages vary sharply in all the districts, except for Pune. This is true even for districts that present a better picture of overall enrolment and regularity rates. For instance, only 53 per cent children attend school regularly in the village Mahal[4] of Dangs district, as against 69 per cent in Wakarya village. The same is true for West Godavari where only 46 per cent children attend school regularly in Gavaravaram as against 70.2 per cent in Bayyanagudem. It is, therefore, evident that situations change drastically even within a district or a block, although some regional practices and norms may be influencing local contexts significantly.

DISPARITIES ACROSS SOCIAL GROUPS

Disparities in the participation patterns of children exist quite distinctly not only at the level of region and economic group, but also among social groups. Social groups such as Dalits[5] (Scheduled Castes), Scheduled Tribes, and Muslims fare much worse than other groups. The share of enrolled among all children is only 50.78 per cent for Muslims, 59.8 per cent for Scheduled Tribes, 67.3 per cent for Dalits, and 70.5 per cent for Other Backward Castes, as against 83.2 per cent for upper caste Hindus. Irregularity is also the lowest for upper caste Hindus as compared to all other groups. The share of drop-outs is the highest for STs and that of never-enrolled among Muslims and Dalits. About 41 per cent of Muslim children have never been enrolled in a school. Although caste is essentially linked with Hindu society, the notion exists among, and serves as a base for social stratification for, non-Hindu groups as well in the Indian subcontinent.[6] There is a marked difference in school participation patterns between upper caste and lower caste Muslims;[7] 70 per cent of children in the upper caste group are enrolled in schools and only 9 per cent are enrolled in madrasas as against the lower caste group where 25 per cent go to madrasas and only 36 per cent are enrolled in schools. However, irregularity is higher for upper caste as compared to lower caste Muslims (Table 3.6).

Inter-social group differences in participation rates exist within poor as well as non-poor groups. It can be clearly seen that the percentage of enrolled children is higher for the higher economic strata and the lowest for the lowest economic level within each social group. This is true for the so-called lower castes as well as upper castes. However, participation rates remain the highest for upper castes as compared to all other social groups within every economic group. Also important is the fact that inter-group differences nar-

Table 3.6: Patterns of Enrolment and Attendance—Social Groups (per cent)

Social Groups	Enrolled	Enrolled			Drop-out	Never enrolled	*Maqtab*	Regular among Total*
		Regular	Irregular	Occasional				
UCH	83.2	90.75	8.40	0.85	11.2	5.6	–	75.52
OBC	70.5	64.52	27.77	7.7	13.9	15.7	–	45.48
SC	67.3	61.86	32.08	6.06	9.7	22.8	0.2	41.63
ST	59.8	71.30	24.60	4.10	19.4	20.8	–	42.64
UCM	70.0	27.27	38.96	33.77	10.9	10.0	9.1	19.09
LCM	36.1	34.61	51.92	13.47	6.3	32.6	25.0	12.50
Muslim	50.78	30.7	43.8	14.3	8.26	22.8	18.1	15.59
Total	64.5	64.9	27.9	7.3	13.4	19.5	2.6	42.0

NOTES: * Number of children attending school regularly as a proportion of the total number of children in the age group.
UCH: Upper Caste Hindu; OBC: Other Backward Caste; SC: Scheduled Caste; ST: Scheduled Tribe; UCM: Upper Caste Muslim; LCM: Lower Caste Muslim.

Table 3.7: Patterns of Enrolment and Attendance—Social and Economic Groups

Social Groups	APL		UBPL		LBPL		Total	
	per cent enrolled	per cent regularly attending among enrolled	per cent enrolled	per cent regularly attending among enrolled	per cent enrolled	per cent regularly attending among enrolled	per cent enrolled	per cent regularly attending among enrolled
UCH	94.7	86.0	77.9	92.3	66.7	100.0	83.2	90.75
OBC	87.2	68.3	66.1	64.2	63.6	60.	70.5	64.52
SC	91.5	80.0	72.3	65.8	54.4	48.1	67.3	61.86
ST	82.5	89.1	61.8	70.7	48.6	62.5	59.8	71.30
Muslim	49.1	40.0	55.7	28.7	46.2	27.0	50.8	30.23
Total	80.9	75.6	66.3	27.1	52.6	53.6	64.5	42.00

row down in the upper segment and variations are much larger for poorer groups. This obviously means that belonging to a 'lower' caste/group means a greater disadvantage for those in the lower economic groups (Table 3.7).

This indicates two significant aspects. First, belonging to a particular caste remains important and has some bearing on the school participation of children, irrespective of economic status. Two, that a change in economic status helps in narrowing down disparities experienced on account of an ascribed caste status. However, these two conjectures need further analysis, especially in view of the fact that there are wide regional variations and the position of the same caste group is not the same everywhere. The share of enrolled children varies from one district to the other for the same social/caste group. The inter-group positioning also changes from one place to the other, reflecting the fact that differences exist even within these broad groups and need to be seen in the context in which they are living. These aspects are examined in detail in the chapters on Dalits, tribals, Muslims, and Others.

It is important to mention that although participation rates for Muslims are always lower than for other social groups, different economic groups within Muslims do not reveal as sharp and unidirectional differences. The percentage of enrolled children is not very different for different economic groups and not necessarily lower for lower levels. This needs to be seen also in the light of the fact that an alternative in the form of religious education is available and has a bearing on choices made by families regarding schooling. This aspect is dealt with elsewhere in the report at greater length.

GENDER DISPARITY

Another form of disparity, perhaps the sharpest and the most common, is based on gender differentiation. Girls are at a disadvantage simply because of their gender. Within each economic, regional or social group, girls are behind boys in terms of school participation. Only 59 per cent of girls are enrolled as against 69 per cent of boys. The difference lies in a greater proportion of girls remaining never-enrolled (25.1 per cent) as compared to boys (14.7 per cent) (Table 3.8). The highest boy-girl differential in terms of enrolment exists in Palamu in Jharkhand, followed by Sidhi in MP and Shravasti district in UP. This differential is higher than the national average for all the districts except for Dhubri and Nuapara. A greater proportion of girls are enrolled in comparison to boys in Chamrajnagar, West Godavari and Pune. Sidhi and Shravasti present a poor picture for girls as large differentials exist even in terms of regularity. Girls are, however, either as, or more, regular than boys in Dhubri, Araria, Nuapada, Koraput and Pune. In West Godavari, where the proportion of girls is higher in enrolment, the proportion of boys is much higher in regular school attendance. These facts indicate that though gender differentials exist almost everywhere, the extent of differences as well as their nature varies from one place to the other.

The proportion of out-of-school girls increases in poorer groups and only 46 per cent girls in the poorest section are enrolled in schools. However,

Table 3.8: Patterns of Enrolment and Attendance (%) across Districts—Boys and Girls

District	Sex	Enrolled	% Within Enrolled			Drop-out	Never enrolled	Madrasa	Regular among Total
			Regular	Irregular	Occasional				
Dhubri	Boys	82.1	28.20	41.03	30.77	14.73	00	3.15	23.2
	Girls	74.4	39.2	31.4	29.4	16.3	4.7	4.7	29.1
Araria	Boys	52.4	48.6	42.7	9.3	4.2	28.7	14.7	25.2
	Girls	40.2	51.3	40.5	8.2	5.4	37	17.4	20.7
Palamu	Boys	74.3	65.3	34.7	00	7.6	18.1	00	48.6
	Girls	49.4	64.1	33.3	2.6	8.8	47.8	00	31.6
Naupara	Boys	69.2	90.4	6.4	3.2	23.1	7.7	00	62.6
	Girls	60.0	88.8	11.2	00	14.4	25.6	00	53.3
Koraput	Boys	61.9	51.3	38.5	10.2	22.2	15.9	00	31.7
	Girls	44.4	57.1	32.14	10.50	15.8	35.1	00	25.4
Sidhi	Boys	82.5	56.63	39.82	3.55	11.7	5.8	00	46.7
	Girls	63.2	37.32	42.28	19.40	11.3	25.5	00	23.6
Shravasti	Boys	57.1	55.36	39.28	5.35	6.1	33.7	3.1	31.6
	Girls	38.4	28.95	60.53	10.52	6.06	55.55	00	11.1
Dangs	Boys	79.1	86.79	11.33	1.88	16.4	4.5	00	68.7
	Girls	65.2	76.66	20.0	3.33	26.1	8.7	00	50.0
Chamraj-nagar	Boys	72.7	94.64	5.36	00	18.2	9.1	00	68.8
	Girls	75.2	89.47	9.21	1.32	19.8	5.0	00	67.3
West Godavari	Boys	64.2	94.12	5.88	00	15.1	20.8	00	60.4
	Girls	76.9	73.33	26.67	00	15.4	7.7	00	56.4
Pune	Boys	61.1	100	00	00	33.3	5.6	00	61.1
	Girls	74.4	100	00	00	20.9	4.7	00	74.4
Total	Boys	69.1	65.8	27.9	6.3	13.4	14.7	2.8	45.5
	Girls	59.1	64.1	27.3	8.7	13.5	25.05	2.40	37.8

SOURCE: Household Survey

Table 3.9: Patterns of Enrolment and Attendance (per cent)
(Economic Groups and Gender)

Economic Group	Sex	Enrolled	% Within enrolled			Drop-out	Never enrolled	*Maqtab*	Regular among total
			Regular	Irregular	Occasional				
APL	Boys	85.7	79.9	14.6	5.6	4.2	4.8	5.4	68.4
	Girls	75.7	69.8	27.4	2.8	6.4	12.1	5.7	52.9
UBPL	Boys	70.4	65.0	28.8	6.2	14.5	13.5	1.6	45.7
	Girls	61.2	67.8	25.3	7.0	13.7	23.5	1.5	41.5
LBPL	Boys	58.2	56.0	37.0	7.1	16.8	21.8	3.2	32.6
	Girls	46.0	48.2	34.2	17.5	16.5	35.5	2.0	22.2
Total	Boys	69.1	65.8	27.9	6.3	13.4	14.7	2.8	45.5
	Girls	59.1	64.1	27.3	8.7	13.5	25.05	2.40	37.8

SOURCE: Household Survey.

it is also important to note that though a higher proportion of girls is enrolled in non-poor families in comparison to poor families, the extent of the difference between boys and girls does not undergo much change. The same is true for different strata within the poor, where the enrolment rate for girls is higher for the upper segment, but the differences between boys and girls are roughly the same. The disparities are not so sharp for regularity patterns. However, the gender gap is high for non-poor and extremely poor groups, the gap being wider for the latter (Table 3.9).

Although it is obvious that the girls are relatively deprived and discriminated against even in non-poor families, the situation for school participation is worst for the poorest section. A very high proportion of enrolled girls from the poorest families attend school only occasionally and hence can be termed virtual drop-outs. Low enrolment with high irregularity, many of them being on roll only nominally, means abysmally low participation for girls from this section.

DISPARITY ACROSS AGE GROUPS

The age group of children is another dimension that is important in understanding participation patterns. The share of enrolled children is the highest for the 9-11 year age group in comparison with the lower (6-8 years) or higher (11-13 years) age groups. The proportion of drop-outs is understandably higher for the higher age groups, this being very high for 11-13 year-olds. It appears that though some drop outs occur at an early age, the rate really intensifies after the age of 10-11 (Table 3.10). Class-wise drop-out patterns confirm this. The majority of drop-outs had left school at the primary level (Table 3.11).

The proportion of never-enrolled is high for 6-8 and 11-13-year-olds. The smaller share of never enrolled among children in the 9-11 years age group could be taken as reflecting an actual increase in enrolment during the

Table 3.10: Patterns of Enrolment and Attendance (per cent)—
Age Group (Boys and Girls)

Age	Sex	Enrolled	Regular within enrolled	Irregular within enrolled	Occasional within enrolled	Drop-Out	Never Enrolled	*Maqtab*
6 to 8 years	Boys	72.3	58.2	31.1	10.9	5.1	18.4	4.3
	Girls	67.3	61.9	26.5	11.6	4.8	24.7	3.3
	Total	69.9	60.5	29.3	10.2	4.9	21.4	3.8
9 to 11 years	Boys	75.9	70.4	24.6	5.0	11.9	10.2	2.0
	Girls	64.7	62.9	29.0	8.1	11.5	22.7	1.0
	Total	70.8	67.7	26.6	5.6	11.7	15.9	1.5
12 to 13 years	Boys	54.0	66.4	27.0	6.5	28.9	15.5	1.7
	Girls	37.7	65.2	24.6	10.1	30.4	29.0	2.9
	Total	46.4	69.2	27.0	3.8	29.6	21.7	2.2

SOURCE: Household Survey.

Table 3.11: Class of Drop-outs

Sex	Class (Grade) in which children dropped out (per cent)							
	1	2	3	4	5	6	7	8
Boys	20.3	24.2	14.1	10.2	12.5	12.5	4.7	1.6
Girls	24.3	20.7	13.5	15.3	13.5	9.9	2.7	00
Total	22.2	22.6	13.8	12.5	13.0	11.3	3.8	0.8

SOURCE: Household Survey.

late 1990s as compared to the first half of the 1990s. Around the mid-1990s, some of the major initiatives, including the midday meal, were initiated which had a positive impact on enrolment. The high share of never-enrolled in the 6-8 years age group could be due to the common practice of late entry into schools in rural areas. Irregularity as well as the share of occasionally attending is also quite high for this age group. It appears that a fair percentage of enrolments for the younger group are actually only on the register; these children do not go to school regularly. The midday meal and other campaigns/drives initiated during the period could have a role in increasing the enrolment for younger age groups.

Regularity improves among higher age group children reflecting the fact that those who continue for a longer period tend to become more regular. The share of occasionally attending children falls in the higher age groups. However, this is not entirely true for girls. Though the proportion of enrollment for girls is lower than that for boys for all age groups, the magnitude of the gap is higher for the 12-13 years age group. Unlike boys, among whom the proportion of occasionally attending becomes less with

Table 3.12: Percentage of Enrolled Children at Primary and Upper Primary Levels*

District/State	Male		Female		Total	
	Primary Level (Classes I to V)	Upper Primary Level (Classes VI to VIII)	Primary Level (Classes I to V)	Upper Primary Level (Classes VI to VIII)	Primary Level (Classes I to V)	Upper Primary Level (Classes VI to VIII)
Dhubri (Assam)	87.4	12.6	89.1	10.9	87.4	12.6
Araria (Bihar)	95.5	4.5	96.9	3.14	95.9	4.1
Palamu (Jharkhand)	79.5	20.5	92.3	7.7	83.8	16.2
Nuapara (Orissa)	95.2	4.8	94.7	5.3	95.0	5.0
Koraput (Orissa)	100.0	0.0	100.0	0.0	100.0	0.0
Sidhi (MP)	84.5	15.5	85.0	15.0	84.5	15.5
Shravasti (UP)	90.9	9.1	100.0	0.0	94.4	15.6
Dangs (Gujarat)	75.5	24.5	90.0	10.0	80.7	19.3
Chamrajnagar (Kar)	84.2	15.8	84.4	15.6	84.2	15.8
W. Godavari (AP)	78.8	21.2	83.3	16.7	81.0	19.0
Pune (Maharashtra)	55.0	45.0	75.0	25.0	66.6	33.3
Total	85.7	14.3	88.9	11.1	87.0	13.0

NOTE: * The primary level consists of only four classes and the upper primary is only up to class VII in some states. However, this table has taken classes I-V for primary and classes VI–VIII for the upper primary, irrespective of the prevalent practice in particular states.

SOURCE: Household Survey.

age and is the lowest for 12-13 year-olds, this is higher for 12-13 year-old girls as compared to 9-11 year-olds. The widely prevalent practice of early marriage and engagement in household responsibilities as well as sibling care could be some of the reasons for this.

The lower rates of participation for higher age groups obviously means that the participation is much less for the upper primary level as compared to the primary level. Only 13 per cent of the total enrolled children are in the upper primary classes. The situation is worse for girls with only 11 per cent of them enrolled at the upper primary level, the share being 14.3 per cent for boys. Pune is the only district where one-third of the total enrolled children are at the upper-primary level. The situation is the worst in Araria, Palamu, Nuapada and Koraput. The low share of upper primary enrolment also makes it apparent that many children in the age-group 12-13 years are still enrolled at the primary level (Table 3.12).

TYPE OF SCHOOLS

The government continues to be the main provider, about 93 per cent of enrolled children are enrolled in government schools, the share being higher (95 per cent) for girls. A miniscule per cent attend private aided schools, the reason being the very limited availability of such schools in rural areas in

Table 3.13: Type of School in which Children are Enrolled (Economic Groups)

Sex	Group	Type of School in which children are enrolled [in per cent]			
		Government	Private Aided	Ashram School	Private Unaided
Boys	APL	75.7	0.7	2.2	21.3
	UBPL	87.9	2.8	3.7	5.6
	LPBL	96.5	00	1.2	2.3
	Total	87.6	1.6	2.7	8.1
Girls	APL	81.6	1.0	2.0	15.3
	UBPL	95.2	00	3.6	1.2
	EPBL	94.9	1.0	1.0	3.0
	Total	92.2	0.4	2.7	4.7
Grand Total		89.5	1.1	2.7	6.7

SOURCE: Household Survey.

Table 3.14: Type of School in which Children are Enrolled (Districts)

District	Sex	Type of School in which Children are Enrolled [per cent]			
		Government	Private Aided	Ashram School	Private Unaided
Dhubri	Boys	96.6	3.4	00	00
	Girls	100.0	00	00	00
Araria	Boys	76.7	00	00	23.3
	Girls	71.4	00	00	28.6
Palamu	Boys	93.6	2.6	00	3.8
	Girls	86.8	5.3	00	7.9
Nuapada	Boys	100.0	00	00	00
	Girls	100.0	00	00	00
Koraput	Boys	91.2	00	2.9	5.9
	Girls	100.0	00	00	00
Sidhi	Boys	86.2	00	00	13.8
	Girls	92.2	00	3.1	4.7
Shravasti	Boys	92.6	00	00	7.4
	Girls	100.0	00	00	00
Dangs	Boys	78.4	9.8	11.8	00
	Girls	86.7	00	13.3	00
Chamraj-nagar	Boys	80.0	1.8	18.2	00
	Girls	90.7	00	9.3	00
West Godavari	Boys	79.4	00	00	20.6
	Girls	86.7	00	00	13.3
Pune	Boys	86.4	00	00	13.6
	Girls	96.9	00	00	3.1
Total	Boys	87.6	1.6	2.7	8.1
	Girls	92.0	0.4	2.9	4.7

SOURCE: Household Survey.

these districts. About 8 per cent the boys and 5 per cent of the girls attend private unaided schools, the incidence being much higher for APL households. About 21 per cent boys and 15 per cent girls from the APL households attend private unaided schools (Table 3.13). The practice of sending children to private schools is limited to six out of eleven districts. These are Araria (Bihar), West Godavari (AP), Pune (Maharashtra), Sidhi (MP), Palamu (Jharkhand) and Shravasti (UP). The proportion of girls is lower than that for boys in all the districts, except Araria and Palamu. The likely explanations are the specific conditions in the villages. There are many Christian missionary schools running in Palamu providing free education and some incentives to girls and that has motivated parents to send their daughters. In Araria, many upper caste parents prefer to send their daughters to nearby private schools for reasons of security (Table 3.14).

PRE-SCHOOL ENROLMENT

In this context, it becomes relevant to see the patterns for younger children in the age group of 3-5 years. Pre-school facilities are available, if at all, through the *Anganwadi/Balwadi*[8] in rural areas. Table 3.15 shows that only one fifth of this age-group's children are enrolled in *Anganwadis*, about 15 per cent are enrolled in schools and the rest remain unenrolled. Since the initiation of the midday meal scheme, it is not uncommon to enroll even younger children in schools. Enrolment in school at a young age appears to be more common for Shravasti and Palamu (not shown in the table). Enrolment in an *Anganwadi* depends on its availability and functioning and almost the entire enrolment has been reported from districts in the western and southern parts of the country, except Orissa.

PATTERNS OF ENROLMENT ACROSS HOUSEHOLDS

There are many families from which all children do not attend school. It is common to find families with enrolled as well as unenrolled children. Table 3.16 shows that no child is enrolled in one-fourth of the total families and all children are enrolled only in 52.5 per cent families. The remaining 22 per cent families have both enrolled and unenrolled children. The proportion of

Table 3.15: Enrolment Patterns for Children in the 3-5 years Age Group (per cent)

	Enrolled in primary school	Not going	Never enrolled	Anganwadi	Madrasa
Boys	14.7	4.5	61.5	17.3	1.9
Girls	15.0	4.1	55.8	23.1	2.0
Total	14.9	4.3	58.7	20.1	2.0

SOURCE: Household Survey.

Table 3.16: Patterns of Enrolment across Households

District	Distribution of families on the basis of enrolment status of children (%)		
	Families with all children in school at least	Families where one child is in school	Families with no child in school
Dhubri	61.6	29.3	9.1
Araria	41.1	20.2	38.4
Palamu	53.8	19.8	26.4
Nuapada	52.6	20.6	26.8
Koraput	45.8	16.7	37.5
Sidhi	52.1	41.7	6.3
Shravasti	41.6	16.8	41.6
Dangs	56.9	15.7	27.5
Chamrajnagar	62.5	18.8	18.8
W. Godavari	58.0	22.0	20.0
Pune	58.0	10.0	32.0
Total	52.5	21.9	25.6

SOURCE: Household Survey.

households with all children in school is the lowest for Araria (Bihar), Shravasti (UP) and Koraput (Orissa). However, it is crucial to note that the proportion of households with all children in school is not very high even in Pune (Maharashtra), West Godavari (AP) and Chamrajnagar (Karnataka) indicating the practice of sending some children and keeping some at home in these places as well.

It is obvious from the above discussion that there are many layers of disparity operating at the societal level reflected in school participation patterns as well. Although issues related with caste, community and gender have linkages with schooling in all economic classes, the impact on poor families is generally much sharper, making children in this group much more vulnerable to circumstances as far as decisions regarding their schooling is concerned. Regional variations in schooling status, even among the poor, reinforce the need to understand the factors that could explain this. A discussion of the reasons for remaining-out-of school further elaborates this aspect.

REASONS FOR BEING OUT OF SCHOOL

PARENTS' PERCEPTIONS

It is not easy to understand the reasons which keep a particular child or a group of children out of school. The most commonly applied method for understanding the reasons for children remaining out of school is to ask parents and add micro-responses to create a macro-picture. This has its limitations as this provides a linear view as perceived by parents at the time of the interview. This does not help understand the interplay of a number of factors within and outside the family. However, despite limitations, it does provide important pointers towards the issue and definitely presents the perceptions of the most crucial link in the decision-making process with regard to the schooling of children. A preponderance of family-related reasons is noticeable in both discontinuation and non-enrolment, for both boys and girls. The need to engage in income-generating activities is the largest single reason for both discontinuation and non-enrolment among boys and the need for support in household chores or sibling care is the single largest reason in case of girls. School-related reasons, especially the distance at which the school is, are prominent for the non-enrolment of both boys and girls and for discontinuation among girls.

Children seldom remain out-of-school for only one reason. Discontinuation does take place at times due to a sudden change in family circumstances or a serious illness. Otherwise, generally, a combination of factors operates in keeping the child away from school. This is clear from the fact that the parents cited more than one reason for the majority of out-of-school children. This is true for both drop-out and never-enrolled children. A perusal of first as well as second reasons provided by parents (not shown in tables) establishes that economic factors are crucial for poor families, especially the poorer amongst the poor. The need to earn appears to be one of the reasons of discontinuation for about 42 per cent of children and high

Table 3.17: Reasons for Child's Dropping Out of School: Parents' Perceptions (per cent)

Reasons	Boys			Girls		
	UBPL	LBPL	Total	UBPL	LBPL	Total
Child related	*40.3*	*16.3*	*30.3*	*8.1*	*12.9*	*11.4*
1. Child remained ill most of the time	11.5	2.3	8.1	2.0	3.2	3.4
2. Child not interested	28.8	14.0	22.2	6.1	9.7	8.0
Family related / economic	*36.5*	*69.8*	*51.6*	*57.1*	*61.3*	*56.2*
3. Migrated and discontinued	–	2.3	1.0	–	16.1	5.7
4. Sibling care/household chores	1.9	16.3	9.1	28.6	16.2	24.1
5. Cattle grazing/own farm work	11.5	–	7.1	6.1	9.7	6.9
6. Wage/income-generating activities	21.2	37.2	27.3	10.2	16.1	11.5
7. Costs of textbooks/dress, etc.	1.9	14.0	7.1	12.2	3.2	8.0
School related	*7.7*	*7.0*	*7.1*	*14.2*	*9.7*	*13.7*
8. School remained closed	–	2.3	1.0	2.0	6.5	3.4
9. Was not learning anything	5.8	4.7	5.1	2.0	–	2.3
10. School was very far	–	–	–	8.2	3.2	6.9
11. Teacher was abusive	1.9	–	1.0	2.0	–	1.1
Other	*13.5*	*7.0*	*10.1*	*18.3*	*16.1*	*17.2*
12. No advantage/use of education		–	–	6.1	–	3.4
13. Any other	13.5	7.0	10.1	12.2	16.1	13.8

NOTE: The figures in italics show the addition of those reasons that are clubbed under one head. The addition of italics as well as non italics should be the same.

SOURCE: Household Survey.

Table 3.18: Reasons for Child's Remaining Never-enrolled: Parents' Perceptions (per cent)

Reasons	Boys			Girls		
	UBPL	LBPL	Total	UBPL	LBPL	Total
Child related	*18.0*	*13.3*	*16.1*	*14.4*	*10.5*	*13.8*
1. Child remained ill most of the time	4.9	1.3	2.6	3.1	1.2	2.4
2. Child not interested	13.1	12.0	13.5	11.3	9.3	11.4
Family related/economic	*50.8*	*58.7*	*48.7*	*54.7*	*64.1*	*54.2*
3. Migrated and discontinued	–	–	–	–	1.2	0.5
4. Sibling care/household chores	1.6	12.0	6.4	20.7	29.1	23.8
5. Cattle grazing/own farm work	11.5	8.0	9.0	8.2	3.5	5.7
6. Wage/income-generating activities	21.3	20.0	17.9	5.2	7.0	5.2
7. Costs of textbooks/dress, etc.	16.4	18.7	15.4	20.6	23.3	19.0
School related	*14.8*	*8.0*	*10.2*	*14.5*	*8.2*	*11.5*
8. School remained closed	–	–	–	–	1.2	0.5
9. Was not learning anything	3.3	–	1.9	5.2	–	2.4
10. School was very far	11.5	6.7	7.7	9.3	7.0	8.6
11. Teacher was abusive	–	1.3	0.6	–	–	–
Other	*16.4*	*20.0*	*25.0*	*16.5*	*17.5*	*20.5*
12. No advantage/use of education	–	2.7	3.2	2.1	1.2	3.8
13. Going to madrasa	1.6	4.0	3.2	3.1	2.3	2.4
14. Any other	14.8	13.3	18.6	11.3	14.0	14.3

NOTE: The figures in italics show the addition of those reasons that are clubbed under one head. The addition of italics as well as non-italics should be the same.

SOURCE: Household Survey.

schooling expenses for 23 per cent of boys in the poorest families. School-related reasons also cause drop-outs from school for 18 per cent of boys and 22 per cent of girls, and the child's disinterest for one-third of the boys and one-fourth of the girls. Again, the picture is similar for never-enrolled children. Wage-earning is one of the reasons for 27.5 per cent of all never-enrolled boys and 33.3 per cent of boys from the poorest families. Similarly, the share of those required for household chores is very high (27 per cent) for never-enrolled girls, especially those from the poorest families (38.4 per cent).

CHILDREN'S PERCEPTIONS VERSUS PARENTS' PERCEPTIONS

In the context of understanding the reasons for remaining out-of-school, it may be meaningful to see children's own perceptions, and also how far they match parents' perceptions. The analysis of children's responses suggests that though they cite largely similar kinds of reasons for remaining out of school, there are significant divergences in some cases. A child's disinterest, a difficult category to analyse, is one such example, where the perceptions of parents and children seem to differ significantly. In this context, it may be added that the majority (56 per cent) of never-enrolled children said that they wanted to go to school but could not attend due to some family-related factor or the other.

The difference between parents' and children's responses also lends weight to the fact that there is more than one reason for depending upon how an individual views the situation and links it with the child's out-of-school status, one cites one or the other reason. It is also difficult to trace some of the reasons to their roots, for example, a child's disinterest could have been due to several reasons, including the teacher's behaviour, lack of any support at home or the need to earn. The reasons cited are at times discrete and the interplay between one reason and the other does not get

Table 3.19: Reasons for being Out-of-school: Parents' and Childrens' Perceptions

Reasons	Parents	Boys	Parents	Girls
I. DROP-OUT				
Child related	*30.3*	*18.8*	*11.4*	*16.5*
Child's own illness	8.1	10.0	3.4	5.1
Child's disinterest	22.2	8.8	8.0	11.4
Family related	*51.6*	*50.1*	*56.2*	*62.1*
Migration	1.0	2.5	5.7	2.5
Household and sibling care	9.1	10.0	24.1	31.7
Farm work and cattle grazing	7.1	16.3	6.9	10.1
Wage work	27.3	17.5	11.5	12.7
High cost of schooling	7.1	3.8	8.0	5.1
School related	*2.0*	*10.1*	*11.4*	*7.6*
School remained closed	1.0	1.3	3.4	0
School was far	0	0	6.9	7.6
Teacher was abusive	1.0	8.8	1.1	0
II. NEVER ENROLMENT				
Child related	*16.1*	*22.3*	*13.8*	*14.6*
Own illness	2.6	0.03	2.4	1.5
Child not interested	13.5	22.3	11.4	13.1
Family related	*48.7*	*42.5*	*53.7*	*54.6*
Household and sibling care	6.4	3.2	23.8	34.6
Farm work and cattle grazing	9.0	11.7	5.7	7.7
Wage work	17.9	19.1	5.2	4.6
High cost of schooling	15.4	8.5	19.0	7.7
School related	*7.7*	*5.3*	*9.1*	*10.0*
School was far	7.7	5.3	8.6	9.2
School remained closed	0	0	0.5	0.8

NOTE: These do not add up to 100 as all the reasons have not been included here.
SOURCE: Household Survey.

explained. The analysis is also limited in indicating intra-family considerations leading to differences in decisions regarding the schooling of different children. Nevertheless, an analysis of the reasons clearly establishes the dominance of economic factors in keeping children from poor families away from schools. The next section deals with the issue of deprivation and its linkages with schooling. This aspect has been examined both from a macro-perspective of seeing the broad linkages between household characteristics and school participation patterns and a micro-perspective of individual families in an attempt to understand the logic of these linkages.

DEPRIVATION IN THE FAMILY AND SCHOOL PARTICIPATION

DIRECT COSTS OF SCHOOLING

The economic reasons cited by parents and children refer to both direct and indirect costs involved in sending a child to school. Parents need to spend substantial amounts on schooling even if the school does not charge any tuition fee *per se*. Per student annual expenditure is estimated to be about Rs.170.50 for a government primary school, an amount that does not appear large itself (Table 3.20). However, poor families located in rural areas and surviving in cash-starved situations, perceive this amount as large enough to make them think twice. The requirement for a particular expenditure, say for textbooks or notebooks, at a particular time, makes it more difficult as they might not be having any cash then. This explains why free textbooks is the most preferred incentive (discussed in the previous chapter).

Table 3.20: Per Student Private Expenditure on Schooling (Annual in Rs.)

Particulars	Primary Govt.	Primary Pvt.	Upper Primary Govt.	Upper Primary Pvt.
Tuition Fee	7.90	196.39	13.89	143.75
Other Fee	9.41	52.65	16.85	49.75
Uniform*	70.35	165.11	125.00	250.00
Textbooks	26.11	129.41	89.07	100.00
Notebooks & other stationery	56.70	90.69	118.24	75.00
Total**	170.50	634.27	363.07	618.50

NOTES: * This has been taken into account only if a particular dress (not necessarily a school uniform) has been stitched especially for the purpose of sending the child to school. Many poor families reported that they would not have spent on this if the child was not going to school. However, the child cannot be sent to school without any clothes or in tattered clothes, hence this expenditure.

** This does not include other expenditure such as daily pocket expenses of 50 paise to one rupee which was found common at several places and fee for private tuition, found only among APL and a few UBPL families and that too only in a few villages.

SOURCE: Household Survey.

At the upper-primary level, the average per student expenditure at government schools is more than twice that of the primary level. This is obviously seen as unaffordable by many poor parents. The per student expenditure for private schools is about four times higher at the primary level. This explains why generally only APL families send their children to private schools. There is not much difference in private expenditure between the primary and upper primary levels in private schools.

CONSTRAINTS OF LIFE SITUATIONS AND SCHOOL PARTICIPATION

Discussions in the last chapter have amply shown that for the majority of poor families in different parts of rural India, poverty is absolute and daily life a constant struggle to survive and cope. This inevitably has a bearing on the schooling of children. This is obvious from the fact that only about 40 per cent of households in the lower segment of BPL families have all children in school as against 73 per cent in APL families and 53 per cent in the upper segment of BPL families (Table 3.21). The proportion of households with no child in school is as high as 38 per cent in the lower

Table 3.21: Engagement of Children from BPL Households in Work

Kind of Work	% of out-of-school children engaged in this work			% of in-school children engaged in this work			% of children engaged in this work		
	Boys	Girls	Total	Boys	Girls	Total	Boys	Girls	Total
Wage work	57.8	11.7	33.8	0.4	00	0.2	20.2	5.9	13.2
Own work	10.3	25.7	18.2	7.5	6.9	7.5	8.5	14.2	11.1
Cattle grazing	29.8	18.9	24.1	5.7	2.8	4.5	12.3	8.6	10.6
Household chores/ Sibling care	7.1	64.2	36.3	4.4	34.6	18.8	6.1	47.8	25.5

NOTES: 1. Only those children have been included in own work who reported working for more than 20 days in a year. Most of them are usually engaged for about 30 to 60 days.

2. Cattle grazing refers to one's own cattle grazing. Cattle grazing for others comes under wage work. Only those children have been included for whom it is almost a year-round activity.

3. Only those children have been included who are engaged in household chores/ sibling care for more than three hours. By deleting all those who are engaged in household work for three hours or less (who form another 12.5 per cent of total children), it is ensured that there is no overestimation.

4. It is common for children, especially girls, engaged in household chores to also become involved in seasonal farm and forest work. Boys engaged in cattle grazing also get involved in own farm and forest work. At times, children engaged in full-time paid labour also work on their own farm, or collect *mahua* or *tendu* leaves during particular seasons. Thus, there are overlaps and that is why the total of all these is more than 100. Hence, the proportion of total children engaged in work is less than the total of all these.

SOURCE: Household Survey.

segment of BPL families as against 11 per cent in APL and 23 per cent in upper segment BPL families. Borrowing for food and illness denote severity of deprivation and the schooling status in these families is worse than those who have either no debt or are in debt for some other reason (Table 3.22).

We have seen that children's involvement in economic activities is also one of the common strategies adopted. These children include both in-school and out-of-school children in substantial numbers. As mentioned earlier, out of the four types of activities in which children are mainly engaged, own work is essentially seasonal in nature. Barring a small proportion of children who work for a greater number of days, children's involvement in farming-related work varies from 20 to 60 days a year. However, children are not usually engaged in only one type of activity. The child who normally takes his or her cattle for grazing also works in the field during the sowing or harvesting seasons, or goes to forest to collect *mahua* seeds and so on. There are some overlaps even between those engaged in

Table 3.22: Households' Attributes and Children's Schooling Participation Patterns

Households' Attributes	Distribution of households as per children's schooling participation patterns (per cent)		
	All children in school	At least one child in school	No child in school
Social Group			
Upper Caste Hindu (UCH)	74.1	7.4	18.5
Other Backward Caste (OBC)	57.1	25.9	17.1
Scheduled Caste (SC)	57.8	19.9	22.3
Scheduled Tribe (ST)	45.1	20.9	34.1
Upper Caste Muslim (UCM)	49.1	36.4	14.5
Lower Caste Muslim (LCM)	23.6	29.1	47.3
Economic Group			
LBPL	40.5	21.8	37.7
UBPL	53.2	24.1	22.6
BPL	48.3	23.2	28.4
APL	73.3	16.0	10.7
Landownership			
More than 2.0 acres	59.6	26.5	13.9
1.1 to 2.0 acres	54.5	15.9	29.7
0.1 to 1.0 acres	50.6	20.7	28.7
Landless	48.1	22.0	29.9
Primary Occupation of Household Head			
Salaried	77.8	14.8	7.4
Skilled + Self-employed	58.0	22.0	20.0
Cultivation	54.2	24.1	21.7
Non-agriculture wage work	46.7	21.3	32.0
Agriculture wage work	48.2	18.9	32.9

No earning occupation	45.9	29.7	24.3
Parents in Wage Work			
No wage work	54.8	23.3	21.9
Only father in wage work	56.4	14.5	29.1
Both parents in wage work	43.8	22.4	33.8
Mother's Wage Work (no. of days)			
Up to 50 days	39.5	32.6	27.9
50-100 days	66.1	14.3	19.6
More than 100 days	42.2	26.1	31.7
Debt (reasons)			
No Debt	52.4	21.5	26.1
Debt due to other Reasons	59.3	19.5	21.1
Debt due to Illness	49.3	25.4	25.4
Debt for Food	39.5	30.2	30.2
Migration			
No Migration	55.1	22.6	22.3
Single Migration	50.0	19.2	30.8
Migration with Spouse/Children	25.0	19.6	55.4
Parental Literacy			
Both Literate	80.5	5.7	13.8
Father Illiterate, Mother Literate	74.4	14.0	11.6
Father Literate, Mother Illiterate	61.4	21.7	16.8
Both Parents Illiterate	44.2	25.0	30.8
Total	52.5	21.9	25.6

SOURCE: Household Survey.

cattle grazing and household chores. In all, about 90 per cent of out-of-school children and 25 per cent of in-school children are engaged in some kind of work. The proportion of girls is higher than boys in both (in-school and out-of-school) groups. While almost all girls not in school are engaged in some activity, this proportion is about 85 per cent for boys. Among in-school children, only about 10 per cent boys as against 30 per cent girls are engaged in work.

Seasonality and School Participation

In-school children's engagement in seasonal work, whether farm or forest related, affects attendance in school quite severely. It is common for school attendance to dwindle during the harvest and sowing seasons, especially the former. The same holds true for schools located in areas close to forests during the *mahua* or *tendu* seasons. School attendance is also adversely affected during the rainy season in certain areas due to water-logging, flood and outbreak of diseases (Box 3.1). Since this is also the period of the severest food shortages in most areas, it becomes difficult for children to attend school. In most areas, teachers identified these periods as recording the lowest attendance levels (Table 3.23).

Table 3.23: Seasonality and School Attendance: Teachers' Experiences

District	Village	Period of Lean Attendance	Reason/s for Lean Attendance	School Attendance (%) during this period	Period of Lean Attendance	Reason/s for Lean Attendance	School Attendance (%) during this period
Dhubri	Jhakuapara	Jan.-Feb.	Paddy transplantation	50 %	Mar.-Apr.	*Mahua* collection	10-15 %
	Tiapara	May-June	Transplantation & brick kiln	25-30 %	–	–	–
	Ramraikutti	Feb.	Paddy transplantation	30 %	–	–	–
Araria	Khabaspur	Jul.-Aug.	Raining	20 %	Mar.-Apr.	Wheat harvesting	35 %
	Rahatmina	Jun.-Jul.	Raining	40 %	–	–	–
	Mudballa	Mar.-Apr.	Wheat harvesting	25 %	Jun.-Jul.	Paddy sowing	25 %
	Doriya	Mar.-Apr.	Wheat harvesting	20-30 %	Jul.-Aug.	Paddy sowing	20-30 %
Palamu	Ayodhya Kolhua	Mar.-Apr.	*Mahua*/wheat harvesting	10-12 %	Jul.-Aug.	Sowing/migration	15-20 %
	Ukamand	Mar.-Apr.	*Mahua* collection	25 %	Jul.-Aug.	Paddy sowing	20 %
	Khurakhurd	Jul.-Aug.	Agricultural work	15-20 %	Mar.-Apr.	*Mahua* collection	10-15 %
	Lanka	March	*Mahua* collection	30 %	Jul.-Aug.	Paddy sowing	35 %
Nuapara	Khaligaon	Jun.-Jul.	Transplantation	30 %	Nov.-Dec.	Harvesting	30 %
	Karmeli	Jul.-Aug.	Agricultural work	40 %	–	–	–
	Cheri Chuan	Jun.-Jul.	Transplantation	8-10 %	Nov.-Dec.	Harvesting	8-10 %
Koraput	Pahadiguda	Mar.-Apr.	Local festival	0 %	–	–	–
	Mohul Bhatta	Jul.-Aug.	Raining	30 %	Nov.-Dec.	Harvesting	30 %
	Mulasar	Jul.-Aug.	Raining	5 %	Nov.-Dec.	Harvesting	5 %
	Bharua Munda	Oct.-March	Migration—brick kilns	50 %	–	–	–
Sidhi	Barambaba	Mar.-Apr.	Monsoon harvesting	50 %	September	Raining	45-50 %
	Jogini	Jul.-Aug.	Paddy sowing	50 %	July	Raining	50-60 %
	Kursa	Apr.-May	*Mahua* collection, rains	35-40 %	Sept.-Oct.	Paddy harvesting	50 %
	Nauriya	Jul.-Aug	Raining	50 %	Dec.-Jan.	Winter—very cold	55 %

Shravasti	Kathkuiyan Kalan	Mar.-Apr.	Wheat harvesting	30 %	–	–	–
	Kathkuiyan Kalan	Nov.	Cultivation	50 %	Mar.-Apr.	Wheat harvesting	60 %
	Balanagar Kodri	Jul.-Aug.	Raining	40 %	January	Very cold	50 %
	Mashakalan	Mar.-Apr.	Harvesting	20-30 %	–	–	–
Dangs	Wakaria	Oct.-May	Migration (sugarcane)	28-29 %	–	–	–
	Mahal	Oct.-Jan	Migration	60 %	Jun.-Jul.	Agriculture	35 %
Chamraj-nagar	Doddathapur	Jun.-Aug.	Paddy sowing	90-100 %	–	–	–
	Chandukatte Mole	Jun.-Nov.	Raining	80 %	March	Festivals	50 %
	Moddur Colony	Sept.-Oct.	Harvesting	25-35 %	Dec.-Jan.	Winter	20-30 %
West Godavari	Bayyanagudem	Feb.-Mar.	Rabi harvesting	60-70 %	–	–	–
	Gavaravaram	Jul.-Aug.	Kharif sowing	50-60 %	Nov.-Dec.	Rabi sowing	50-60 %
Pune	Karandi	Jun.-Jul.	Raining	62 %	September	Harvesting	62 %
	Malegaon	November	After Diwali	25-35 %	March	Festival	20-35 %

BOX 3.1: CHILDREN WITH DISABILITIES

The last decade of the twentieth century has recognized that children with disabilities and special needs constitute a significant group, needing attention. Based on the type of disability, the group can be categorized into: orthopaedically handicapped, hearing impaired, visually impaired, speech impaired, locomoter impaired, mentally retarded, epileptic, and children with multiple disabilities. Across disabilities, it is generally found that orthopaedically disabled children are better identified than children with other disabilities. For over a century, the prevalent model of offering education to children with special needs has been the special school. At that time, it was believed that children with special needs could not be educated alongside others. Therefore, special schools were offered as the only option. Even today, about 2,500 special schools operate in the country. The limitation of the special school is that only a small number of children, drawn largely from urban communities, have access to education and it did not help these children to be mainstreamed into the community after completing their education.

India is still in the process of refining the procedures by which children with special needs can be identified. The first effort was made with the policy of 1986 and POA, 1992, which estimated that there were 12.59 million children in the school-going age with disabilities for whom provision had to be made. Different surveys have given widely divergent estimates of the disabled population in the country. According to NSSO (1991), about two and a half million children suffered from one or the other disability.

Projected population of children with disabilities (5-14 years)

(*in million*)

Category	Rural	Urban	Total
Visual	0.080	0.014	0.094
Hearing	0.219	0.053	0.272
Locomotor	0.393	0.122	0.515
Speech	1.525	0.478	2.003
Any physical disability	1.898	0.578	2.476

Malnourishment, unhealthy living conditions, maladjustment and a host of other difficulties, together with ignorance, lead to disability in children. Once a disability develops, the stigma of being 'disabled' is labelled by the society. Cultural attitudes play a major role in aggravating the problem as parents go to quacks, *ojhas* and gurus and a large amount of money is spent in the process. Illiterate parents are unaware of what could be done for their children, and the idea of sending them to school sounds quite far-fetched, except for those with orthopaedic disabilities. Currently, less than 1 per cent of the disabled children have access to education, although the Persons with Disabilities Act, 1995, promises free access to education for every child between 3-18 years of age.

The period beginning from 1981 has witnessed a number of decisions, Acts and resolutions in this regard. In 1974, the centrally-sponsored scheme for Integrated Education of Disabled Children (IEDC) was launched by the Department of Social Welfare, later transferred to the Department of Education. Today, several special schemes are in operation and a number of general education programmes, including the DPEP, are giving a special thrust to the issue. Voluntary organizations have played a major role in serving the cause of children and persons with disabilities. Over the years, the number of such NGOs has grown and their approach has witnessed an increased strength of commitment, professional soundness, and a favourable attitude towards inclusive education. There are more than 2,456 voluntary organizations working in the area of disability.

Despite a number of efforts and the presence of many agencies, there still remains a lot to be done. Parental awareness, societal sensitivities, and the inclusiveness of schooling systems need to be built in a manner which will help these children to become integrated in to the mainstream. There is also a strong need to identify children with mild and moderate disabilities as they often tend to be neglected.

Parental Occupation, Assets and School Participation

Parental occupation or the family's livelihood options are closely linked with children's schooling participation patterns. Engagement in seasonal agricultural operations for children is common among marginal and small cultivators. However, their engagement in own work is not always limited to seasonal agricultural operations or forest produce collection. There are many other skill-based tasks, usually caste-based, traditional occupations, where it is common to engage children. These include basket making, pottery and begging. In many such cases, including those of small cultivators, children's engagement in work does not only affect attendance adversely, but it also contributes to keeping some children away from school altogether.

The ownership of livestock is an important factor in providing security and some stability in the lives of the poor in rural areas. However, as discussed earlier, it also necessitates having someone to take the cattle for grazing. Due to depleting common property resources in most places, fodder is not easily available everywhere, and in many villages children walk for miles to take cattle for grazing. It, therefore, becomes a day-long activity, making it difficult for children to attend school. In areas close to forests, these children generally collect dry leaves and firewood at the same time. For children taking cattle for grazing almost daily and who are also enrolled in school, this means being irregular in their attendance. Though the majority of children involved in this work are boys, girls also form a good proportion (38.2 per cent). Both younger and older children are engaged in cattle grazing, though it is more prevalent among 9+ children. There is not much difference in the workload for children of different age groups engaged in this activity (Box 3.2).

Women's participation in work forces somebody else to support them in domestic chores and sibling care. The majority of poor families are nuclear (87 per cent), where there is no older person to take care of children. Invariably, it is the girl, if there is a girl in the family, who gets this responsibility. The need of a girl to lend support at home also arises because of a mother's illness or simply due to an increase in the size of the family and, therefore, the workload. Whatever the reason, the involvement of the girl in household chores severely affects participation for both in-school and out-

BOX 3.2: 'WE ARE POOR, WE HAVE NO OPTION'

Bhola Singh, the 13-year-old son of Lakshman Singh, works in a hotel at Daltonganj, the district headquarters of Palamu district in Jharkhand, for a monthly payment of 600 rupees. He started working when he was 10. His younger brother, Jeetu Singh (11), also started working in another hotel for a monthly payment of 450 rupees last year. They have never been to school. The youngest brother, Chathu Singh (7), too, does not go to school. Whenever his mother is busy, he takes the only goat that the family owns for grazing. He also helps his mother in taking care of the younger sister, Geeta, who is only 3 years old. Whenever he is not busy in cattle grazing or child care, he plays and roams around the village with his friends.

Bhola and Jeetu do not have any friends in the town. They say, 'there is no time to make friends; we work from early morning to late evening.' Both brothers have a number of friends in the village and whenever they are here for some festival or the other, they love to spend time with them. They hate their work 'because it is very hard and the employer keeps shouting all the time'. 'I keep remembering my village, parents and friends and long to come back', says Jeetu.

Lakshman Singh, a *khiarwar* tribal (ST), owns one acre of land which he cultivates himself with the help of his wife, Bharouliya. But he is not a full-time cultivator. He has many occupations. He works as a wage labourer in construction and does other non-agricultural work in neighbouring villages and towns. He migrates to Aurangabad district in Bihar twice a year during the paddy sowing and harvesting seasons to work as an agricultural wage labourer. Bharouliya also works as an agricultural wage labourer in the village. Unlike most other women in the village, she does not migrate with her husband because she has small children to look after. She does not keep too well either. Wage work is the main source of livelihood. The produce from the land is grossly insufficient for the family. Apart from the fact that the quality of land is not good, crops are frequently destroyed by elephants and other wild animals living in the nearby forest. This is a common problem in this village situated close to the Betla reserve forest. Lakshman Singh feels it is necessary to send children to work so that there is sufficient food to eat in the family and also to maintain some flow of cash necessary for arranging basic necessities like clothing, etc. In Aurangabad, he gets wages in kind and the availability of non-agricultural wage work is infrequent and unreliable, which is why there is no source of earning any regular cash. I sent Bhola for work when my wife fell ill and we badly needed cash for her medication, says Lakshman. He borrowed money at that time from the local moneylender at a high rate of interest which he has been able to clear because of his children's earnings. He says he did not ever send his children to school 'because I was not able to afford the high expenses'. But he adds, 'My children were not interested in the future and, in any case, they have to do wage work when they grow up, so why educate them?' Bhola differs in his response, saying, 'I want to go to school and study but we are poor; we have no option but to help our parents in running the household. Whenever I come to the village, I never feel like going back to town, but I have no choice.'

of-school girls, and if boys are engaged, then boys as well. In the case of in-school children, it does not only mean irregularity, but also the inability to do any follow-up studying at home.

Household chores, as discussed in the previous chapter, are tough and time consuming in rural areas, and sibling care is a continuous and demanding task. Moreover, most children also become involved in other tasks such as collecting firewood, agricultural operations, helping others in cattle rearing, and other similar activities. Even if they are not engaged during all hours of the day, the timings are such that it is difficult to take out a chunk of four to five continuous hours for school everyday. Needless to say, the girls' engagement in household chores and related work is also guided by the belief in 'feminine' socialization and aspirations for their future, an aspect that will be dealt with in detail at a later stage.

We have seen earlier that the majority of parents in rural areas are engaged in wage work, often a combination of several types of labour. The schooling status of children in families where either one or both parents go for wage work is much worse than those where parents have some other occupation. The situation is particularly bad for families where both parents work for wages; about 34 per cent of such families have no child in school and another 22.4 per cent have at least one child out of school. The mother's participation in wage work for a very limited number of days appears to be linked with deep poverty and low levels of school participation for children. However, participation improves with an increase in the number of days up to some point, say about 100 days a year. It appears to improve the family's financial condition and brings stability, leading to a positive impact on school participation of children. However, with a further increase in the number of days in the mother's participation in work, the schooling participation of children goes down, perhaps because of the need for children to lend support at home and lack of monitoring (Table 3.22).

Migration and School Participation

As discussed earlier, seasonal migration for short or long periods to other areas for agricultural or non-agricultural wages is a common strategy to cope during lean seasons or to add to the family's income. Single migration is more common as compared to family migration. The impact of single migration, almost entirely male migration, does not appear to be uniform in all families and at all places. In some cases, it means greater exposure leading to a positive attitude towards education, translating itself into the enrolment of children in school. Additional income also brings greater

Table 3.24: Family Migration: Children's Engagements at the Place of Migration

Children's Engagement at the Place of Migration	Proportion of Children (per cent)
Cooking, cleaning and other household chores	15.0
Sibling care	12.3
Accompanying parents to work	17.8
Help in earning activities	24.6
Studying	00
Any other	30.3

SOURCE: School Survey.

stability and aspirations for the future, leading to an enhanced interest in the schooling of children. However, parental migration does not usually lead to this positive change everywhere. The migration of the father also means additional responsibility for the children. They are expected to help their mothers in taking care of all big and small requirements at home and outside. Also, it means greater freedom, and children, especially boys, are completely on their own in such situations. In such circumstances, even if the child is enrolled, it is not uncommon for him to drop out or be irregular due to the lack of monitoring. The exact impact of migration also depends on a number of other aspects, including the kind and duration of migration, and the social and economic positioning of the family. These aspects are examined in the chapters on social groups.

Family migration, though less common than single male migration, is widely practised in certain areas. Children's migration with parents is mainly on account of two reasons—there is nobody to look after them in the village or they are needed at the place of migration for work or to take care of younger siblings. Whatever the reason, when children migrate with parents, it becomes difficult for them to continue with their education. The need for survival is paramount in such cases and education becomes secondary. None of the children migrating with families reported going to school at the place of migration. Around forty three per cent of these children are engaged in earning activities either directly or indirectly and another 27.5 per cent are engaged in household chores/sibling care. A good proportion of these children do not do anything specific (Table 3.24). Table 3.22 shows that the proportion of households with no child in school is higher (30.8 per cent) among those with single migration as compared to those where no migration takes place (22.3 per cent). However, the situation is the worst among families where children are also migrating; only one-fourth of the families have all children in school, with 55.4 per cent of them with no child in school.

Wage Work and School Participation

Barring a few exceptions, all children engaged directly in paid work are out of school. There is a basic difference in being engaged in other economic activities and being engaged in wage work, even if there is no significant difference in mean hours of work. Wage work is the least flexible. All other work allows for some flexibility and possibility of adjustment in the hours if there is a need or desire to do so, but this is not the case with wage work. The majority of child wage workers in rural areas are either annual/seasonal contract labourers with local landlords or working outside their village. In either case, it is not possible to be even enrolled in school as children are engaged in many other activities.

As discussed earlier, all families with children in wage work may not be in distress, even if many of them initially sent their children due to some crisis. Nevertheless, for children, once they start working for wages, life becomes tough, and though they like the fact that they are earning, they do not like their daily life situation *per se*. This is in contrast to those who are mainly engaged in cattle grazing. This is perhaps because they get time to play and roam around with their peers whereas children in full-time wage work do not have any space for peer interaction and any other form of entertainment. Many wage-earning children who had been to school earlier now miss school even if they did not particularly like going to school then.

WHAT IS DIFFERENT FOR THOSE WHO ARE GOING TO SCHOOL?

A fair proportion of children attend school even from families which are in similar deprived situations. Many of them attend school because they have somebody else, a sister to take care of household chores or a brother to work for wages, behind them. But there are many families which also send all their children to school. In order to understand non-participation, it is important to understand participation as well. In many cases, where all the children are going to school, it is simply a matter of not having had to face any crisis as such. The experience of non-participation points to children's vulnerability to any small change in the home situation, whether it is the arrival of more children, the need for money for someone's treatment or wedding, or just to add to the family's income so that there is a sufficient amount to eat for everybody in the family. These circumstances could suddenly lead to the withdrawal of the child from school. However, there are families which make adjustments in the face of these changes and continue sending their children; these families can be taken as having made a considered decision in favour of education. It is important to understand what leads these families to make this choice.

Literacy and Education in the Family

One important influence appears to be that of education in the family. The literacy and schooling levels of parents, especially mothers, are positively linked with the schooling participation of children. Around 80 per cent of households with both parents literate have all children in school as against only 44.2 per cent where both parents are illiterate. School participation rates are much better for families where only the mother is literate in comparison to those where only the father is literate. The proportion of families where no child is at school is lowest in families where mothers are literate (Table 3.22). Parental education helps in seeing the intrinsic value of education more clearly.

Parental Aspirations for Children

Parental aspirations are notably different for children in school as opposed to those who are not. The basic difference is that of a desire and hope for change in the child's life and status as compared to their own. An over-

Table 3.25: Parental Aspirations for Children (In-school and out-of-school)

Parental aspirations for child's future (per cent)	Boys	Girls
In-school children		
To find a government job	73.0	31.0
To be able to get out of present life situation	13.4	19.8
To be able to take care of one's own self	2.9	8.5
To get married to an educated person	0.4	22.7
To take good care of the family	3.7	8.0
Any other	6.9	9.9
Out-of-school children		
Gets married and goes to her 'real' home	–	73.1
Earns for and sustains the family	64.1	6.9
Leads the life similar to mother/father	24.9	9.1
Any other	11.0	10.9

SOURCE: Household Survey.

Table 3.26: Parental Interest and Regularity in School Attendance (in-school children)

Parental interest* in child's schooling	Regularity in School Attendance (per cent)					
	Boys			Girls		
	Regularly attending	Irregularly attending	Occasionally going	Regularly attending	Irregularly attending	Occasionally going
Not interested	48.8	36.6	14.6	45.4	43.6	10.9
Somewhat interested	66.4	27.0	6.5	67.0	24.9	6.1
Interested	70.6	24.6	4.7	75.3	20.7	4.0

NOTE: *This is based on an index made on the basis of parental visits to school, pestering their children to go to school, children discussing school events at home, and parents' resolve to the child to the next level.

whelming majority of parents expect their sons to get a government job and lead a more secure life. In the case of girls, too, the desire for change is visible, though not necessarily through a job. On the other hand, a clear sense of hopelessness and a belief that nothing is going to change their children's lives as they, too, will continue to be poor and will earn by working for wages seem quite prevalent among those not sending their children to school (Table 3.25). It is important to understand that hope itself comes from a long-term view of life, and life situations for many poor families are too difficult and pressing to allow for any long-term thinking. Life is lived on a day-to-day basis, making survival itself very precarious. Continued education, which demands a long-term commitment, does not enter into the range of possibilities in this kind of situation.

Parental Interest in Schooling and Regularity

Parental interest is important to ensure that children who are enrolled attend school regularly. In situations where there are pressures from several sides, children can go to school regularly only if parents take an active interest. The linkage between parental interest and children's regularity in school attendance can be seen clearly from Table 3.26. This shows that the level of regularity is significantly higher for families with a high level of interest and vice versa. This is especially true for girls' attendance (Box 3.3).

BOX 3.3: HIGH ASPIRATIONS AND A STRONG COMMITMENT

Mahadevamma (24) got married to Mahadevshetty (31) at the young age of 11 and came to his house at the age of 12. Early marriage is common in the Uppara (OBC) community. They are required to get the daughter married off either before or immediately after puberty. Mahadevamma and Mahadevshetty have three sons, Shankara (9), Shivmalla (7), and Parashiva (2). She was pregnant with her fourth child. Mahadevamma had been doing wage work in agriculture since she was 7. She continued working at her husband's place till three years ago. She stopped when she was expecting her third child, Parashiva. This has resulted in a financial crisis; their daily earnings are the only source for their daily survival. They have no land or cattle and in the absence of one person's wages, it became difficult to sustain themselves. This despite the fact that their needs are minimal. They cook only once a day in the evening and eat the leftovers in the morning. This led to frequent borrowings at a high interest rate of 10 per cent per month. Despite spending about 10 rupees out of the daily earnings of 50 rupees on the repayment of debt, the total debt now amounts to 10,000 rupees.

Both Shankara and Shivmalla are enrolled and go to school regularly. Shankara is in Class III and Shivmalla in Class I. The couple is interested in getting their sons educated at least up to Class X. They feel that it would 'equip them to face city life better'. Although they do not have any definite aspirations, they hope that 'education will ensure at least a secured income in private occupation if the government job does not come through'. They believe that 'at least one of the three sons would be able to get out of this daily wage work life which itself would be an achievement'. They are not very hopeful of their sons getting government jobs. 'They would be very lucky if they get one', they say.

Both Mahadevamma and Mahadevshetty believe that the incentive schemes of the government are very important for poor children's participation in schooling. 'If the government had not provided us with free uniforms, textbooks and rice, it would have been difficult to send our children to school,' says Mahadevshetty. He adds that other benefits should also be extended to all poor families, including OBCs, rather than confining them only to SCs and STs. But the couple appears to be determined to continue with their sons' education even in adverse circumstances. The three sons are aware of the parents' hardships and want to fulfil their desires. 'I will study up to Class X and then take up some job in the city. I will not leave going to school whatever happens,' says Shankara and adds, 'I know my parents want the same.' They are also careful in keeping their sons away from unhealthy influences like alcoholism, common among adolescents in the village. Their interest in schooling is also visible from the fact that they regularly visit the school to enquire about their sons' progress. Though illiterate, they are aware that it is important to be regular at school. The school opens regularly and teachers take an interest in calling children from home. The couple praise the teachers for their efforts in convincing parents about the importance of children's education.

Employment Linkages and Perceived Benefits of Schooling

Parental interest and aspirations are linked with the issue of the perceived value of education. The lack of any hope that education will bring about a change in their family's status, low aspirations for children, and low level of interest in schooling, all reflect the low perception of the value of education. Interactions and discussions with poor families brought out clearly that though they perceive education to be something valuable per se, they do not see much value in it for themselves. A distant value is attached to education, parents are ambiguous about it, even if not for any other reason than the simple fact that all those who hold power in any manner also happen to be educated. But they also see that even those who are powerful are educated, all those who are educated are not necessarily powerful. Given their own situation of despair and hopelessness, they fail to relate education with any foreseeable tangible benefits or relevance in their own lives (Box 3.4).

BOX 3.4: PREPARING FOR THEIR ADULTHOOD

Both Bhaiyalal and his wife Sanaua work for about twelve to fourteen hours everyday in order to ensure sufficient earnings for their family of six. Bhaiyalal gets up at about 5:00 a.m., collects water for the day, gobbles last night's leftovers and leaves home in search of work. It is not easy to get work in this village, Barambaba, where the majority of the families are Gond (ST), with very small pieces of land. And when work is available during the season, one needs to compromise on wages because there are too many people looking for work. Though Bhaiyalal did receive two acres of redistributed land from the government, it is as good as having no land. It is hilly land on slopes, very difficult to cultivate. In such circumstances, cutting firewood from the nearby forest and selling it in Sidhi town is their permanent source of livelihood. It is Sanaua's responsibility to go to Sidhi everyday to sell firewood. She gets up at about 3:00 a.m. to make bundles of firewood. At about 5:00 a.m., like other Gond women from the village, she is also ready with her bundle. She covers the distance of about 20 km. on foot everyday in about three hours. It does not take her more than half an hour to sell her bundle and by 10:00 a.m., she is ready to leave for her village.

Sushila (11), the oldest of Sanaua's four children, generally stays behind to do household chores in her absence. Sushila's forenoons are packed with work. Her day starts early, at about 4:00 a.m. She does all the cleaning work in the morning besides taking care of the two cows that the family owns. The most difficult task, however, is to collect water for her house located on a hilltop. It takes her more than two hours to collect sufficient water for the entire day's needs. While doing all these chores, she also needs to take care of the younger siblings, Ranno Bai (7) and Hiran Singh (1). However, most of the time, there is nothing at home to cook and Sanaua gets something from Sidhi after selling firewood. Everybody waits for her eagerly at home so that they can get something to eat. Sanaua earns about 25 rupees from the sale of firewood from which she gives 5 to the forest guard and 5 at the check-post as bribe. Fifteen rupees are not sufficient for the family's two meals, and after finishing her household chores Sanaua leaves in search of work. Sushila accompanies her almost everyday. Her life is not very different from other Gond girls in the village.

> Jaibhan (8), the second of their four children, leaves home at about 7:00 a.m. after eating last night's leftovers. He takes two cows for grazing, and does not really like this work. He is often seen roaming around school, and Sanaua gets very angry if she gets to know this. Though none of the children were ever enrolled by their parents, Jaibhan had started going to school on his own. The teacher had written his name in the register. The school has Gond teachers who take a lot of interest in the enrolment and attendance of Gond children. However, Jaibhan's name was removed from the register after his mother gave him the responsibility of taking the cattle for grazing. 'My mother does not want to send me to school but I want to study,' asserts Jaibhan. 'Yes, I don't send my children to school. Who would take care of the cattle and how will we eat if children also don't work?' counters Sanaua. Then slowly, she adds, 'They are my kids. I want them to be educated, but what can I do? Two of us alone can't take up all the responsibilities. Whatever we do, their life is going to be like ours. They had better be prepared for this.'

The most tangible benefit visible to poor people is in the form of employment linkages. The awareness that employment is associated with a particular level of education—at least matriculation—is very high. There is also a 'realization' that it is difficult to provide education up to that level and hence it does not serve any purpose to educate children up to Class V or VIII. Unemployment among the educated youth serves as a disincentive and is often cited as evidence of education having no use for the very poor. In view of the 'unattainability' of a higher level of education, many poor families often take a very limited view of education. It is generally seen as the acquisition of certain literacy and numerical skills. Families which can link education with larger benefits, and not necessarily with direct employability, reflect greater commitment to sending their children to school regularly.

SCHOOL, EXTERNAL ENVIRONMENT, AND SCHOOL PARTICIPATION

The decision to send children to school on a regular basis is a difficult one for poor families in rural areas and, therefore, the perception of the value of education plays an important role in determining their decision. Perceptions of education are not entirely disassociated from poor people's state of instability and vulnerability. However, it is not the status of the household alone, either in terms of its life situation, literacy, or anything else, that shapes its perception. School, as well as external, say village, environments, play important roles in building this perception and commitment towards education and schooling or the lack of it.

SCHOOL AND SCHOOLING PARTICIPATION

School provisioning and functioning have several dimensions such as physical infrastructure including space per child available, indicators such as pupil-teacher ratio, attendance-enrolment ratio, Class V to Class I ratio, etc., and people's perception of the school's functioning, and on the basis of these, they can be slotted into different categories. However, it is not necessary that these different aspects always match; often, in fact, they do not. Many schools with good infrastructure have a very high PTR or vice versa, or a school with low PTR may have an adverse classroom—student ratio and so on. In a few villages, it was seen that the so-called indicator of good provisioning and high efficiency, like a low PTR, is low because of a very low enrolment level. People's perceptions, which is the poor people's perceptions (and which may not always match with those of the non-poor in the same village), in most cases was linked more to teachers' behaviour, sincerity and empathetic understanding of children's circumstances rather than provisioning. The management of incentives in terms of their timely and fair distribution also makes a difference in people's perceptions. Appendix table (Table A.2) shows the rating of each school covered in the survey on the basis of three different kinds of indicators (school efficiency based on an index of several indicators, student—classroom ratio, and people's perceptions), and, except in three cases, the three ratings for the same school vary from each other everywhere.

It became clear that the impact of school functioning on school participation patterns of children in terms of enrolment and regularity needs to be understood more in the context of the entire environment and positioning of the poor. It is difficult to establish linkages between school participation patterns and school functioning without taking into account the larger contexts of the household and the external environment. There are cases where the school is perceived to be functioning well and yet participation levels are low, while in other cases participation is high despite the functioning being perceived as not good. There are also cases of improvement in school functioning due to a change of teacher, leading to an increase in participation levels. The issue is discussed in the context of villages and the social positioning of different social groups in detail at a later stage.

EXTERNAL ENVIRONMENT AND SCHOOL PARTICIPATION

The role of the external environment becomes very crucial in determining / influencing people's perspectives on life and views on education. A number of household characteristics discussed in earlier sections are also subject to the external environment. Different aspects of the life situation such as seasonality, child work, migration, food crises, etc., are determined as much by the external environment as by the internal environment of the household. Even aspirations about children and interest in education are not always subject to individual parents' views and resolve alone. The social group to which they belong and the area where they live play an important role. This is not to say that everything that influences schooling participation is determined by the external environment, but that it has a significant influence. The external environment includes aspects of physical location and development, socio-economic conditions, and also customs, traditions and norms particular to a society. In a heterogeneous and stratified society like ours, it is not necessary that the external environment at any place has the same meaning for every individual family or group that lives there. Not only do customs, norms and traditions vary from one group to the other, but also the implications of having a particular physical location and infrastructural facilities may not be the same for different social and economic groups.

The next section containing five chapters attempts to understand the role of external as well as internal environments in education choices for different social groups as well as for girls. School functioning is also not independent of the general situation that exists in an area. The three dimensions of household, area and school, mentioned in the very first chapter, are looked at together in varying contexts. School participation decisions of children have been analysed for different groups in view of their life situations, including aspects of their own economic stability, social positioning, and school functioning.

NOTES

1. All references to children pertain to persons in the age group of 6 to 13 years (all children who have completed their six years but have not completed their fourteenth year) unless otherwise specified. This matches with the school-age definition for elementary education comprising eight years of schooling. All further references to enrolment rates, drop-out rates, etc., therefore, refer to age-specific enrolment rates. Age-specific enrolment rates are generally higher than the net enrolment ratios and lower than the gross enrolment ratios.
2. *Maqtabs* and madrasas are Muslim educational institutions. They are of different types and levels. These two terms have been used interchangeably in this and subsequent chapters. Please see Chapter 6 for a discussion of different types and levels of *maqtabs*/madrasas existing in the study villages.
3. All children who were reported as being enrolled and going to school were divided into three categories—regular, irregular and occasionally going—by the research team after ascertaining a number of things about them. This included the attendance patterns taken from the school register, the child's other engagements and responsibilities, etc.
4. Large-scale family migration (estimated to be about 60 per cent of the total households) takes place from Mahal village to sugarcane fields in other areas of Gujarat (mainly Surat) for about six months every year. It is common for children in the age group of 9-13 years to migrate along with others. The fieldwork was conducted during a season when about half the families were not present in the village and, therefore, it is likely that the actual number of out-of-school or irregular children is much higher than what is shown here.
5. Dalit was used in the 1930s as a Hindi and Marathi translation of Depressed

Classes, the term the British used for what are now called the Scheduled Castes. There have been two definitions of Dalit. The broad one includes the Scheduled Castes, the Scheduled Tribes, the landless, and poor peasants. The narrow one refers to the Scheduled Castes alone. The term has increasingly been used by the media and in common parlance to refer to the Scheduled Castes, especially by those who have been part of socio-political movements (Webster, 1999). We have used the terms Dalit and Scheduled Caste interchangeably in this report.

6. See Ahmad (1978) for a discussion of aspects of caste and social stratification among Muslims in India.
7. The distinction between upper and lower caste Muslims is based on the respondent's own reporting of the caste and its categorization as lower or upper caste.
8. *Anganwadis* are the early childhood care centres run under the Integrated Child Development Scheme of the Central Department of Women and Child Welfare. A local woman with the requisite minimum qualifications runs the centre with the support of a helper and provides nutrition as well as pre-school inputs. This also has elements of providing nutrition support to pregnant and lactating mothers.

4. The Schooling of Dalit Children: A Pandora's Box

BACKGROUND

The term 'scheduled caste' designates an official rather than a sociological category. It signifies a certain constitutional and legal status conferred upon a number of castes and communities, united by their position as 'untouchables' in the hierarchical caste structure of traditional Hindu society. The Constitution of India has conferred upon Scheduled Castes a kind of identity they did not have in the past. The innumerable castes and communities that make up the category had little knowledge of each other across the different regions of the country. Even within the same region, they were divided by modes of livelihood and social standing. The creation of a new all-India identity has not led to an effacing of the old identities based on membership of a particular caste or sub-caste (Béteille, 2000). These identities, as will be seen in further discussions, continue to have a role in sociological processes and also have an impact, among other things, upon schooling decisions.

The strictures of untouchability, of pollution and purity, on which the rigid caste structure is based also varies in different parts of the country and so do inequalities in the ownership, control and use of productive resources, including land and access to other means of mobility and an improved quality of life, such as education and health. However, the post-Independence period has witnessed many measures and changes that have directly or indirectly affected the situation and status of Dalits. The Constitution of India declared 'untouchability' illegal and introduced a number of positive discriminatory measures for the hitherto depressed classes, including the Scheduled Castes and Tribes. These involved an expansion of educational facilities and enhancement of employment opportunities. The access to and use of these opportunities has, however, varied across different regions and caste groups among the Dalits. The abolition of untouchability has not always meant an end to all such practices, it continues to exist in different forms and in varying degrees, impacting on social redundant relationships.

The ways and means of democratic polity have also affected the development of social groups and so have levels of economic and industrial development in different regions. The policy of universal adult franchise gave an equal right to all individuals to vote, and different social groups with numerical strength began to play important roles in contemporary politics. The level of economic development has been uneven in different states, affecting the expansion or stagnation of opportunities. The nature and implementation of measures such as land reforms, too, have not been uniform across the country. The history of political processes and social movements have also been varied in different parts of the country, reflected in conditions, identities and means of expression among backward classes, including Scheduled Castes and Tribes. Several of the study villages have a significant Dalit population who live under a range of conditions in terms of composition, economic development and socio-political processes. In this chapter, we discuss school participation patterns among Dalit children in the light of varying combinations of factors and try to discern those that have had an encouraging impact. The primary focus of the chapter is to understand the impact of caste-based discrimination, or that of being Dalit, in varying situations, on school participation patterns. Gender differentiation within Dalits, though of immense significance, has deliberately been left out and has been discussed in the chapter on girls.

DALIT VILLAGES: A FEW IMPORTANT DIMENSIONS

Twenty of the 37 study villages have significant Dalit populations, and the analysis here is based on the understanding of these twenty villages.[1] A few important features of these villages are given below:

Social Composition

Dalits, unlike STs, seldom live in single-caste villages, and hence all these villages have mixed populations. The proportion of Dalit households is half or more in seven villages, between one-fourth to half in four villages, and one-fourth or less in the remaining nine (Table 4.1). Dalits in these villages belong to different sub-castes and there is more than one sub-caste within one village in several cases, such as the villages in Sidhi (MP), Shravasti (UP) and West Godavari (AP). The social positioning of different sub-castes depends upon their traditional occupation and inter-relations, the livelihood choices they make, and their levels of dependence on other social groups.

Provisioning of Facilities and Work Opportunities

These villages are placed differently in terms of development and provisioning of facilities. While 60 per cent are poorly provided for [mainly in Araria (Bihar), Sidhi (MP) and Shravasti (UP)], a good number of them (40 per cent) are also well provided for in terms of facilities such as schools, transport, drinking water, etc. [mainly from West Godavari (AP), Chamrajnagar (Karnataka), Pune (Maharashtra) and Palamu (Jharkhand)]. Economic development also plays an important role, along with the accessibility of the village, in widening or restricting livelihood choices. The contexts of these villages also vary in terms of economic opportunities even within the same village. While villages with insufficient infrastructural provisioning are generally those with the lowest availability of work opportunities, the opposite is not always true. Some villages in Palamu (Jharkhand), though well connected, do not have sufficient work available within them.

Socio-political Processes

Socio-political processes varied in these villages in their nature and impact. In some villages of Sidhi (MP) and Shravasti (UP), the nature of state-level politics as well as access to power in the local panchayats seem to play an important role. The resonances of long histories of Dalit movements, even though not visible in any robust form within the villages, could be felt in some villages in Pune (Maharashtra) and Chamrajnagar (Karnataka) districts. No significant socio-political process was visible in several villages [like those in Araria (Bihar), Koraput (Orissa) or West Godavari (AP)]. The strong presence of Naxalite groups in Palamu (Jharkhand) presents a different kind of situation in terms of political awareness.

School Participation Patterns: Intra-group and Intra-village Differences

Intra-group Differences

Although Dalits emerge as one of the most educationally deprived social groups in terms of children's school participation, there exist large intra-group variations within them. At one end, in villages like Karandi in Maharashtra and Doddathupur in Karnataka, more than 90 per cent of Dalit children regularly attend school. At the other, in villages like Sultana in UP and Doriya in Bihar, barely 20 to 25 per cent of Dalit children attend school regularly. In fact, regularity is a far cry in many of these villages with more than half the Dalit children not even being enrolled in schools. This is the situation in Mudballa in Bihar and Sultana and Masahakalan in UP. In all, less than 30 per cent of Dalit children attend school regularly in 25 per cent villages, 30 to 50 per cent attend in another 45 per cent villages, and more than 50 per cent attend school regularly in only 30 per cent villages (Table 4.1).

Intra-village Differences

Participation rates for Dalit children are worse than those found in 60 per cent villages, better in the remaining 40 per cent villages. Enrolment rates for Dalit children are worse than those found in all villages in Araria (Bihar) and Shravasti (UP). Villages where enrolment rates are comparatively higher for Dalit children belong to different districts and states, namely Gavaravaram in West Godavari (AP), Naudhiya in Sidhi (MP), Doddathupur in Chamrajnagar (Karnataka), Karandi in Pune (Maharashtra), Ramraikuti

Table 4.1: Villages with Dalit Households: Background and Schooling Status

Sl. No.	Village name	Dev. category	Proportion of SC households (%)	Other social groups in the village	Main SC sub-Caste	Social group	Enrolled (%)	% within enrolled: Regular	% within enrolled: Irregular	% within enrolled: Occasional	Unenrolled	% within unenrolled: Drop Out	% within unenrolled: Never Enrolled	Madrasa	Regularly Going Col. 8 × 7/100
1		2	3	4	5	6	7	8	9	10	11	12	13	14	15
A.	*Villages with SC Population > 50 per cent*														
1.	Ayodhya Kolhua [Jharkhand]	C	88	UCH/ OBC	Bhuiya	SC	64.9	70.8	29.9	–	35.1	30.8	69.2	–	45.9
						Others									
2.	Lanka [Jharkhand]	B	80	ST/OBC/ UCH	Bhuiya, Chamar	SC	85.2	64.4	35.6	–	14.8	50.0	50.0	–	54.9
						Others									
3.	Kursa [MP]	C	65	ST/OBC/ UCH	Prajapati, Saket, Kori	SC	72.2	61.1	33.3	5.6	27.8	30.0	70.0	–	44.1
						Others	91.3	60.0	26.7	13.3	8.7	–	100.0	–	54.8
4.	Sultana [UP]	C	53	OBC	Khatik, Kori, Pasi	SC	30.6	66.7	20.0	13.3	69.4	11.8	88.2	–	20.4
						Others	63.7	66.7	33.3	–	36.3	–	100.0	–	42.5
5.	Gavaravaram [AP]	A	52	OBC/ UCH	Madiga, Mala	SC	67.6	68.2	31.8	–	32.4	28.6	71.4	–	46.1
						Others	63.6	71.4	28.6	–	36.4	50.0	50.0	–	45.4
6.	Doriya [Bihar]	D	51	OBC/ UCH	Mushar	SC	76.7	33.3	54.5	12.1	23.3	10.0	90.0	–	25.5
						Others									
7.	Balanagar Kodri [UP]	C	50	OBC/ UCH	Chamar, Kushwahia	SC	66.7	55.5	40.7	3.8	33.3	50.0	50.0	–	37.0
						Others									
B.	*Villages with < 50 per cent SC Population > 25 per cent*														
8.	Doddathupur [Karnataka]	A	47	UCH/ OBC	Adi Karnataka	SC	95.5	95.0	5.0	–	4.5	100.0	–	–	90.7
						Others	80.0	100.0	–	–	20.0	75.0	25.0	–	80.0
9.	Mudballa [Bihar]	C	32	Muslims	Mushar	SC	36.8	–	85.7	14.3	63.2	–	91.7	8.3	–
						Others	11.1	75.0	25.0	–	88.9	–	34.4	65.6	8.3
10.	Jogini [MP]	C	26	UCH/ OBC/ST	Saket	SC	61.1	60.0	30.0	10.0	38.9	28.6	71.4	–	36.7
						Others	64.7	45.5	40.9	13.6	35.3	50.0	50.0	–	29.4

11. Naudhiya [MP]	C	25	ST/UCH/	Saket	SC	90.9	50.0	35.0	15.0	9.1	100.0	–	–	45.5
			OBC	Basor	Others	72.5	34.5	58.6	6.9	27.5	36.4	63.6	–	25.0
C. *Villages with SC Population <25 per cent*														
12. Ramaraikuti	C	20	OBC/	Sheel	SC	87.5	42.9	14.2	42.9	12.5	100.0	–	–	37.5
[Assam]			UCH		Others	85.7	26.3	42.1	31.5	14.3	100.0	–	–	22.5
13. Bayyangaddam	A	18	OBC/	Mala,	SC	68.2	100.0	–	–	31.8	42.8	52.2	–	68.2
[AP]			UCH	Madiga	Others	76.0	94.7	5.3	–	24.0	83.3	16.7	–	72.7
14. Mulasar	C	12	OBC/ST	Chandala,	SC	54.5	25.0	50.0	25.0	45.5	50.0	50.0	–	13.7
[Orissa]				Ghasi	Others	44.8	30.8	53.8	15.4	55.2	43.8	56.2	–	13.8
15. Honnahalli	A	12	UCH/	Adi	SC	55.5	100.0	–	–	45.5	100.0	–	–	55.5
[Karnataka]			OBC	Karnataka	Others	65.1	96.0	–	4.0	34.9	53.3	46.7	–	62.4
16. Padheiguda		12	ST		SC	50.0	33.3	66.7	–	50.0	66.7	33.3	–	16.6
[Orissa]					Others	63.0	80.0	20.0	–	37.0	10.0	90.0	–	50.4
17. Karandi	B	11	UCH/	Mahar,	SC	100.0	100.0	–	–	–	–	–	–	100.0
[Maharashtra]			OBC	Matang	Others	63.3	100.0	–	–	36.7	81.8	18.2	–	72.0
18. Masaha Kalan	D	10	Muslim/	Chamar	SC	50.0	–	100.0	–	50.0	–	100.0	–	–
[UP]			OBC		Others	54.1	15.8	68.4	15.8	45.9	23.5	76.5	17.6	8.5
19 Ukamand	B	10	ST	Bhuiyan	SC	66.7	75.0	25.0	–	33.3	–	100.0	–	50.0
[Jharkhand]					Others	45.5	81.8	18.2	–	54.5	22.2	77.8	–	37.2
20 Kermeli [Orissa]	B	8	ST/OBC	Gonda	SC	100.0	85.7	14.3	–	–	–	–	–	85.7
					Others	85.3	93.1	6.9	–	14.7	60.0	40.0	–	79.4

NOTES: 1. Column 2 shows development category based on an index prepared by taking infrastructural facilities into account (see Appendix Table A.1).
2. Column 3 shows the approximate proportion of the population belonging to this social group.
3. Column 7 shows the enrolment of 6-13-year-old children against the total population of the age group.
4. Columns 8, 9 and 10 show the distribution of enrolled children [Column 7].
5. Column 12, 13 and 14 show the distribution of unenrolled children [Column 11].
6. Column 15 shows the population of regularly school-going children in the total age group children.
7. The schooling status data for the SC or other children have not been included for the villages where their proportion in the surveyed households is 20 per cent or less.

SOURCE: 1. Columns 3, 4 and 5 based on the Village Appraisal Report.
2. Remaining columns based on the Household Survey.

in Dhubri (Assam), Ukamad in Palamu (Jharkhand), Mulasar in Koraput (Orissa) and Kermili in Nuapara (Orissa). However, the same districts also include villages where the situation is the opposite and enrolment rates for Dalit children are lower than those for others. Dalits are generally ahead of only ST children in backward regions, but in economically advanced regions, they are also ahead of OBCs and upper caste Hindus.

Profile of Dalit Households

There has been a change in the status of Dalits since pre-Independence days, evident from their growing presence in politics, bureaucracy and educational institutions. The changing situation is also apparent from the increasing number of cases of conflict and assertion being reported from different parts of the country. However, the process of change has been rather slow, and even within poor families, Dalit families happen to be over-represented among the poorest, the landless, the low-earning, low-skilled wage earners and illiterates, categories that signify deprivation and vulnerability. We have seen earlier that schooling participation rates for children are negatively associated with these household characteristics, and now we see Dalits come across as the worst on many of these indicators.

About 38 per cent of Dalit families belong to the lower strata of BPL families against an average of about 32 per cent. Similarly, about half of the Dalit families are landless against an average of 40.5 per cent. The average land-holding size among the Dalits is very low at 1.25 acres, the lowest among all social groups (Table 4.2). Land is the most important asset in rural areas and possession of land not only signifies a better economic situation, it also means less dependence on others for earning one's livelihood. In terms of occupation, 'status change for the Dalits has largely been of a nature that has transported them from menial occupations in the caste-feudal structure to low-status, low-paying and low-skilled jobs in the modern occupation structure' (Velaskar, 1998). This is obvious from the fact that more than half of the household heads in Dalit families are engaged in low-skilled wage-work as their primary occupation. Their large representation in non-agricultural labour makes it obvious that even when they shift from agriculture to non-agriculture, it is mainly in the low-paying, unskilled jobs (Box 4.1).

Literacy and schooling of parents are positively linked with school participation patterns among children almost universally. Here too Dalits fare badly; an overwhelming majority of Dalit parents continue to be illiterate and in only 6.6 per cent Dalit families both parents were found to be literate. The average years of schooling is abysmally low at 1.03 years for Dalit adults as a whole; for males it is less than two years and for females less than one year. The average in terms of years of schooling for Dalits is much lower than that for upper caste Hindus, though comparable with

Table 4.2: Profile of Households in Different Social Groups

	UCH	OBC	SC	ST	UCM	LCM	Total
Proportion of EBPL in total households	12.3	24.4	38.7	34.6	32.7	40.0	31.9
Average family size	4.9	5.6	5.7	5.4	5.9	6.5	5.6
Proportion of landless in total households	37.0	41.9	49.6	29.0	49.1	41.8	40.5
Average landholding owned (acres)	4.40	1.86	1.25	2.19	1.27	2.99	2.03
Per cent of household heads in agricultural wage work*	31.3	31.2	30.1	16.0	25.0	16.4	24.4
Per cent of household heads in non-agri. (unskilled) labour*	2.4	9.1	20.1	15.6	17.3	10.9	14.3
Proportion of families with both parents illiterate	35.8	63.4	72.3	70.4	41.8	80.0	65.4
Proportion (per cent) of families with both parents literate	30.9	12.2	6.6	5.5	9.1	5.5	9.5
Average years of schooling for adults (total)	2.53	1.25	1.03	1.07	1.62	0.92	1.26
Average years of schooling for adults (male)	2.92	1.69	1.46	1.55	2.25	1.5	1.72
Average years of schooling for adults (female)	2.18	0.83	0.59	0.55	0.89	0.21	0.78
Proportion of most vulnerable families** (per cent)	7.4	14.0	17.6	6.6	3.6	10.9	11.2

NOTES: * These show the proportion of household heads in primary occupations.
** Based on an index taking food crisis, debt for food, working for wages, etc., into account.

SOURCE: Household Survey.

BOX 4.1: WE ARE KOPARIYAS: WHAT CAN WE DO?

Sudhri, the oldest among the six children of Ramnarayan and Nanhi, is 12 years old. She has never been to school. Nor have her younger brothers, Kunwarchand (8), Man Singh (7) and Ram Singh (6). The younger siblings, Jaimangal Singh (3) and Rani (4 months), are of course too young to go to school. The family is one among several Kopariyas (SC) families living in Kori Purba, a part of Sultana village in the Shravasti district of UP, who keep moving from one place to the other for about eight months every year. They usually migrate to cities in Punjab and other northern parts of the country during June-July and come back just before the Holi festival in March. From July to October they repair umbrellas and sell plastic flowerpots on pavements after which they start begging. While begging, they take on different faces, including those of the blind and the physically handicapped.

Sudhri and Kunwarchand actively help their parents in selling flowerpots and begging. Sudhri also helps her mother in household chores and shares the major responsibility in taking care of the younger children. Unlike children from other communities in the same village, Sudhri is articulate, talks to strangers without any hesitation, speaking fluent Hindi. This is true of Kunwarchand and other Koparia children as well.

The family lives in a semi-*pucca* house which they have built with savings from their visits. 'But it has no meaning. We spend the majority of our time in plastic tents amidst all kinds of filth and dirt,' says Nanhi. They also have about 1.5 acres of land which they use to cultivate paddy. Their earnings are sufficient to meet their basic needs, and they have no debts. In terms of economic condition, they are somewhat better placed than wage earners in the same village whose situation tends to be worse. They do not see any embarrassment in their occupation. 'Everybody in my family and community does this work. Somebody becomes blind, somebody crippled. This is what we all learn since childhood,' says Nanhi. 'And we are not thieves. Whoever gets involved in this kind of activity gets excommunicated by the group,' she adds. The caste panchayat is a very strong body and its decisions are final.

Nanhi does not like the fact that both she and her husband are illiterate. 'All children must be educated at least till class X', she says. But then why is she not sending her children to school? 'How can I? We are hardly ever there in the village,' and then 'Education hardly has any role in our profession,' adds Nanhi. She says that it is essential to involve children in begging as people tend to be more sympathetic towards them. Her husband Ramnarayan adds, 'Moreover, the village school is hardly functional. Teachers come and go as per their own choice. The government hardly has any control over them.' Like her mother, Sudhri, too, does not see any relevance of education in her life. 'What is the use of education in my life?' is her response to why she never went to school. This applies to her brothers as well. 'There is no difference between boy and girl. Both are equally important in our kind of work,' opines Nanhi, without any ambiguity.

Towards the end of our interaction, Nanhi says with a sad face that she would be happy to see her children carrying school bags but given her community's occupation, there is no way she can realize this dream. 'We are Kopariyas. What can we do?' she asks.

other caste groups. This reflects the fact that Dalits, denied access to formal education in traditional Hindu society, remain one of the most educationally deprived groups even after half a century of Independence.

VARIATIONS IN HOUSEHOLD PROFILES OF DALITS

Dalits, as mentioned earlier, are not homogeneous in all respects and a perusal of disaggregated information reveals that within a similar broad pattern, there exist wide inter-village and inter-community (within Dalits) differences in terms of land ownership, literacy and occupation. On the one hand, villages like Doriya in Araria (Bihar) and Naudhiya in Sidhi (MP) have all Dalit households landless and heavily dependent on low-skilled wage work. On the other, villages such as Sultana and Balanagar Kodi in Shravasti (UP) and Doddathupur in Chamrajnagar (Karnataka) have about one-fourth of Dalit households with more than 2.5 acres of land. However, many so-called landowning families have land because they have received redistributed land after Independence, though the quality of the land is so poor that they remain virtually landless. Poor SC families cannot afford the heavy investment needed to make these wastelands productive and hence continue to depend on daily wage work. This was reported to be the case for villages in Araria (Bihar), Palamu (Jharkhand), Shravasti (UP), Sidhi (MP) and Chamrajnagar (Karnataka) (Table 4.3).

Differences also exist in the main occupations of household heads. While agricultural wage work is the main occupation in more than 70 per cent of Dalit household heads in Doriya and Mudballa, it is more than 50 per cent in Gavaravaram, Bayyangudem, Doddathupur and Honnahalli, and the proportion is as low as 20-5 per cent at Balanagar Kodri and Mulasar. Disparities between different Dalit groups exist even in literacy levels (Table 4.3). However, despite disparities within Dalits across villages, their position is worse than others everywhere, with very few exceptions. This indicates that even at places where Dalits are ahead of their counterparts in other places, they remain worse than other social groups in their own areas. This is true not only for literacy levels but also for land ownership and representation in better-paid or high-status occupations. Despite years of reservations in government jobs, the representation of Dalits in salaried jobs is very low. With abysmally low levels of education in most cases, it is difficult for them to reap the benefits of reservations and other such provisions.

Regional differentiations between Dalit groups also need to be understood in the light of the fact that they consist of a large number of sub-castes which have had differentiated access to education and diverse occupations in the past. Dalits in these 20 study villages consist of 21 different sub-castes. Table 4.4 shows that literacy rates for different sub-caste groups in different states varied. Disparities can be seen even in the same group in different states. The Chamars in UP have a higher level of literacy than their counterparts in Jharkhand and the Koris in MP are better placed than those in UP. The Mushars of Bihar and the Bhuiyans of Jharkhand have less than 1 per cent women and less than 10 per cent men are literate among them. The Mahars in Maharashtra and the Koris in MP have the highest literacy rates among these groups. Education has been consciously pursued as a key strategy of socio-economic change by Dalits in Maharashtra. The Mahars, the largest group among the SC population in the state, 'right from the British days when they gained access to military services and opportunities in the urban economy and then under the powerful impact of Dr Ambedakar's clarion call to 'Educate, Organize, Agitate', have been at the forefront of educational pursuit' (Velaskar, 1988).

The discussion on profile of Dalit households helps in understanding low schooling participation patterns among them in general and also the intra-group or inter-village differences visible within Dalits. However, access to and use of resources and opportunities among Dalits depends a lot on the social, economic and political contexts in which they live. The social positioning of Dalits is linked to their sub-caste identity, the population

Table 4.3: Profile of Dalit Households in Selected Villages

S. No.	Village	Social Group	Landless	Land more than 2.5 acres	Male (14+)		Female (14+)		Main Occupation of the Household Head			
					Illiterate	Schooled	Illiterate	Schooled	Cultivator/ self-employed	Agri- labour	Non-agri. labour	Salaried
1.	A Kolhua [Jharkhand]	SC	70.0	10.0	58.8	26.5	96.4	3.6	15.8	00	84.2	00
2.	Lanka [Jharkhand]	SC	16.7	16.7	43.6	48.7	79.4	8.8	32.0	16.0	36.0	8.0
3.	Kursa [MP]	SC	7.1	57.2	84.2	10.5	94.7	5.3	85.7	00	7.1	00
		Others	11.1	66.7	50.0	42.9	64.3	35.7	72.7	00	9.1	00
4.	Sultana [UP]	SC	9.5	28.5	52.3	34.1	92.1	7.9	90.5	00	00	4.8
		Others	00	50.0	50.0	50.0	100.0	00	40.0	00	20.0	00
5.	Gavaravaram [AP]	SC	89.5	5.3	70.4	25.9	80.8	11.5	15.0	55.0	25.0	00
		Others	57.1	42.9	37.5	50.0	55.6	33.3	42.9	42.8	00	00
6.	Doriya [Bihar]	SC	100.0	00	81.5	11.1	100	00	4.8	80.9	9.5	00
7.	Balanagar Kodri [UP]	SC	25.0	29.2	75.7	18.9	89.7	10.3	66.7	20.8	12.5	00
		Others	00	100.0	50.0	50.0	100.0	00	100.0	00	00	00
8.	Doddathupur [Karnataka]	SC	46.2	23.1	47.8	52.2	59.1	36.4	46.2	53.8	00	00
		Others	66.6	8.3	70.6	23.5	63.2	31.6	41.7	58.3	00	00
9.	Mudballa [Bihar]	SC	72.7	00	46.2	30.8	92.3	00	9.1	72.7	9.1	00
		Others	57.1	28.6	45.8	16.7	84.2	5.3	46.7	26.7	6.7	6.7
10.	Jogini [MP]	SC	87.5	00	57.1	35.7	100.0	00	50.0	25.0	12.5	00
		Others	13.3	66.7	38.5	42.3	87.5	4.2	80.0	00	13.3	00
11.	Naudiya [MP]	SC	100.0	00	75.0	25.0	100.0	00	66.7	00	33.3	00
		Others	64.7	5.9	64.0	20.0	78.3	17.4	35.3	35.3	29.4	00
12.	Ramraikutti [Assam]	SC	60.0	00	50.0	00	100.0	00	60.0	40.0	00	00
		Others	52.9	5.9	29.6	40.7	33.3	47.6	35.3	47.1	5.9	5.9
13.	Bayyanagudem [AP]	SC	90.9	9.1	68.8	25.0	61.5	30.8	9.1	63.6	18.2	9.1
		Others	53.8	38.5	51.9	29.6	71.4	28.6	46.2	30.8	15.4	00
14.	Mulasar [Orissa]	SC	60.0	00	66.7	33.3	81.8	9.1	45.5	27.3	00	00
		Others	42.9	28.6	93.8	00	100.0	00	21.4	64.3	00	00

15.	Honnahalli [Karnataka]	SC	25.0	25.0	60.0	20.0	71.4	28.6	00	60.0	.00	00
		Others	19.0	52.4	75.0	17.9	85.7	11.9	50.0	45.5	4.5	00
16.	Padheiguda [Orissa]	SC	100.0	00	100.0	00	100.0	00	33.3	00	00	66.7
		Others	45.5	13.6	76.0	4.0	96.2	3.8	90.9	4.5	4.5	00
17.	Karandi [Maharashtra]	SC	20.0	00	80.0	20.0	33.3	66.7	20.0	00	60.0	00
		Others	60.0	15.0	17.9	67.9	35.7	46.4	42.9	38.1	00	9.5
18.	Masahakalan [UP]	SC	00	16.7	50.0	41.7	100.0	00	100.0	00	00	00
		Others	15.0	30.0	77.3	11.4	90.6	3.1	76.2	9.5	00	4.8
19.	Ukamand [Jharkhand]	SC	20.0	20.0	55.6	44.4	100.0	00	40.0	00	40.0	20.0
		Others	22.2	22.2	52.2	39.1	87.5	8.3	50.0	00	44.4	5.6
20.	Kermeli [Orissa]	SC	50.0	25.0	66.7	00	57.1	14.3	75.0	25.0	00	00
		Others	15.0	30.0	38.7	41.9	81.8	12.1	57.1	28.6	4.8	4.8

NOTES: 1. A person has been considered to be schooled if he/she has been to school for at least one year.
2. The data for 'others' not included if the number of households covered is 20 per cent or less in the total sample of households covered.
3. A person has been considered to be schooled if he/she has been to school for at least one year.
4. The data for 'others' not included if the number of households covered is 20 per cent or less in the total sample of households covered.

SOURCE: Household Survey.

composition and their inter-relations with other caste groups in the village. The dynamics of present inter-caste relations is determined both by the traditional hierarchical relationships they have had and the requirements of present-day survival strategies. The widening of economic opportunities and the contemporary history of political processes both have a role in determining the relative social positioning of Dalits. The diverse situations that exist in different study villages are being analysed here to understand the varying contexts and its impact on the schooling of children.

Table 4.4: Traditional Occupations and Literacy Rates for Major SC Groups Found in Study Villages

SC Sub-Caste [State]	Study Village/s Where Present	Dominant Occupations	Literacy Rate [1981]		
			Male	Female	Total
1 Adi-Karnataka [Karnataka]	Doddathupur, Honnahalli	Agr. labour, Carpenter	28.4	10.81	19.77
2 Basor [MP]	Naudhiya, Barambaba	Making baskets and drum-beating	21.11	13.24	4.76
3 Bhuiyan [Jharkhand]*	A. Kolhua, Lanka, Ukamand	Wage labour and bricklayers	7.72	0.77	4.3
4 Chamar [Jharkhand]*	Lanka	Leather work, agr. labour	20.51	2.36	11.52
5 Chamar [MP]	Barambaba agr. labour	Leather work,	NA	NA	NA
6 Chamar [UP]	B. Nagar Kodri, Masahakalan	Agr. and skin and hide work	26.6	3.92	15.98
7 Chandala [Orissa]	Mulasar	Cultivators, weavers and agr. labour	37.29	9.47	23.49
8 Damba [Orissa]	Mulasar	NA	NA	NA	NA
9 Ghasi [Orissa]	Mulasar labour	Scavenging and agr.	30.98	7.34	19.13
10 Gonda [Orissa]	Kermeli	NA	NA	NA	NA
11 Khatik [UP]	Sultana & poultry, agr. labour	Business in veg., fruit	27.98	6.52	17.9
12 Kori [MP]	Kursa labour	Weaving and agr.	38.64	12.5	26.33
13 Kori [MP]	Sultana	Weaving	24.75	4.51	15.24
14 Kushwahiyan [UP]	Balanagar Kodri	NA	NA	NA	NA
15 Madiga [AP]	Gavaravaram, Bayyanagudem	Leather work and making of footwear	15.93	6.53	11.31
16 Mahar [Maharashtra]	Karandi	Agr. and non-agr. wage labour	52.57	23.54	38.38
17 Mala [AP]	Gavaravaram, Bayyangedum	Agr. labour	29.72	12.51	21.23
18 Matang [Maharashtra]	Karandi	NA	NA	NA	NA

19	Mushars [Bihar]	Doriya, Mudballa	Wage labour and cultivator	4.01	0.32	2.2
20	Pasi [UP]	Sultana	Cultivator	17.96	1.71	10.17
21	Patharkat [UP]	Balanagar Kodri	NA	NA	NA	NA
22	Prajapati [MP]	Kursa	NA	NA	NA	NA
23	Saket [MP]	Kursa, Jogini, Naudhiya	NA	NA	NA	NA
24	Sheel [Assam]	Ramaraikutti	NA	NA	NA	NA

NOTES: *Jharkhand was carved out of Bihar in 2000 and became an independent state.
(i) The names of the sub-castes as reported by the people and as reported in the Village Appraisal Reports.
(ii) NA—Not Available from the same source.

SOURCE: Census of India, 1981; As given in S.K. Singh, *Scheduled Castes* (vol. II), New Delhi: Oxford University Press, 1995.

THE SEPARATED ONES

PHYSICAL SEPARATION

Dalits live in segregated clusters known by their caste. In Doriya and Mudballa (Bihar), it is Musahri for Mushars; it is Matanangvasti for Matangs in Karandi (Maharashtra); Kori Purba for Koris in Sultana (UP); and SC-Mala Peta and SC-Madiga Peta for Malas and Madigas in Gavaravaram (AP). This is true for all the villages irrespective of region or level of development. Although caste-based clusters are common for all caste groups in rural India, unlike other cases where mixed housing is also widespread, Dalits face complete segregation even today. These SC clusters often happen to be the more difficult localities in terms of access and facilities. If it is a low-lying area with no transportation in one village, it is located on a hilltop in another. This has serious implications for the daily lives of adults as well as children. They have to walk longer distances in search of water, fuelwood and work, and in some cases have to remain cut off for months together during the rains (Box 4.2).

These disadvantages are further deepened because of the discrimination faced in receiving government facilities under the different schemes. Localities with dominant caste populations tend to corner all the benefits of such schemes. For instance, there are only two hand pumps for the more than 140 households living in Musahri at Mudballa village in Araria district. Most hand pumps under government schemes are placed in the main Muslim locality, which happens to be the landowning dominant social group in this village. The case is similar in several other villages in all parts of the country. The location and functioning of the PDS outlet, usually in the hands of some influential person from the dominant caste of the area, is a problem for the lower castes in most places. These PDS outlets do not open regularly, rarely follow any routine, the supply is erratic, and hence poor people rarely find

BOX 4.2: BHAT IN KURSA (SIDHI, MP) AND MUSAHRI IN DORIYA (ARARIA, BIHAR)

Bhat, a *tola* of Kursa village situated in the middle of hilly terrain, is difficult to reach. Mainly inhabited by the Koris (SC), the houses are located at a distance from each other. Rich in forest resources, the land is difficult to cultivate with no irrigation facilities. People are not able to raise more than one crop in a year. Maize is the common crop cultivated and dependence on the forest is high. Despite being part of the same village, this *tola* does not have all the facilities available in Kursa. Bhat remains cut-off, does not have any electricity unlike the main *tolas*, faces acute shortage of water, and people have to walk up to 10-12 km. for their daily work. Life is tougher during the rains when they cannot even commute, and since it is also the period of illnesses, it is common for people here to die due to the inaccessibility of medical help.

The story is the same for the Musahri in Doriya village which remains cut-off for several months during the rains. There is no forest, hence no question of depending on it arises. People describe life during the rains as 'worse than hell'. With epidemics such as cholera and malaria common during the rains almost every year, there are many deaths. Poverty as well as physical inaccessibility make it next to impossible for them to access medical help.

them dependable. Those who survive on daily earnings find it difficult to wait for this PDS shop to open and generally have no choice but to buy essentials from the local shopkeepers, generally at higher prices.

PHYSICAL SEGREGATION AND ACCESS TO SCHOOL

Physical segregation adversely affects access to school, unless the school is located within the Dalit habitation. All study villages have a primary school[2] but not necessarily within Dalit habitations, and all-weather access remains an issue. At Balanagar Kodri (UP), the school is located in the Brahmin habitation, Balanagar Kodri Khas, away from Reharwa, Pakri and Dhobiyan Purva, the three main *tolas* housing the entire SC population of the village. There is a *nallah* cutting across the village which swells up during the rains and becomes intimidating, taking the shape of a violent river. It is impossible for children in Dhobiyan Purva, located on the other side of the *nallah*, to attend school for at least three months. The other two *tolas*, though located on the same side as the main *tola*, Balanagar Kodri Khas, are in the low-lying areas and the road leading to the school gets submerged. Hence, children from these locations are also unable to attend school during the monsoon. The story is not very different for flood-prone Mudballa (Bihar) where the school is located in the Mukhiya *tola*, the cluster of houses belonging to the 'important persons' of the village. This is not only far from Musahri, the Dalit cluster, but there is also a small canal in between and the connecting *kuchcha* road gets submerged during the rains (Box 4.3).

BOX 4.3: AMBEDKAR GRAM IN UTTAR PRADESH

In the late 1990s, during the regime of the Bahujan Samaj Party (BSP), a political party drawing its mass support mainly from among the Dalits, a new approach or scheme was launched to give greater attention to villages with very high Dalit populations. SC-dominated villages were declared Ambedkar Grams and a number of government development schemes were to converge to bring in overall improvement at one go. The two study villages, Balanagar Kodri and Sultana, were among those identified for the purpose. This generated a lot of interest and activities in the initial phase. It was common for officials from various departments to visit and discuss investment plans. Villages even now refer to that period quite nostalgically—'Those were the days one officer after the other used to visit us, ask us what we want and so on.' But hardly anything tangible and with a long-term impact happened. A new primary school was sanctioned but intra-village strife between different Dalit groups and indecision about its location led the authorities to shift it to some other village. Dalits, however, feel that powerful Brahmins had a role in inciting in-fights between different Dalit groups as they did not want a school to be located in any Dalit habitation. A mahila complex consisting of three toilets, three bathrooms, and one hand pump was built in one of the two main SC *purvas* at Balanagar Kodri. This still lies vacant, mostly unused. A panchayat bhavan was also built but has remained locked for years. Moreover, the government's interest in the whole concept of Ambedkar Gram died once the BSP ceased to be in power in the state.

SOCIAL SEGREGATION

The isolation of Dalits is not limited to physical segregation alone. Physical segregation has its roots in socio-cultural segregation, based on rules of purity and pollution, and reflected in the practice of untouchability. The practice is still present everywhere and varies only in its forms and degree of intensity. Inter-caste dining is a taboo everywhere. Water is not accepted from Dalit persons by any other communities in all these villages. Dalits are not allowed to enter the houses, especially kitchens, of all other castes. Some of their traditional occupations like pig rearing are looked down upon by others. Purity and pollution taboos exist not only among caste Hindus but also among tribes, considered 'higher' in the social hierarchy. The Gonds (ST) in Sidhi and Orissa villages maintain this against the Chamars and the other SC groups. It is also important here to add that all the villages also reported some diminution in the intensity of such practices over the last fifty years. However, basic social divisions exist everywhere and the acceptance of socially discriminatory practices by Dalits, even in circumstances where they have experienced a change in social or economic status, is persistent (Box 4.4).

The social dynamics of the village affects or at least is perceived to affect the location of schools and the posting of teachers to the disadvantage of Dalit communities. For instance, the Mushars in Mudballa village (Araria, Bihar) feel that the powerful Muslim landlords are not interested in allowing

BOX 4.4: TEA IN 'SPECIAL' MUG FOR DALIT EX-PRADHAN
(An Account given by the UP Study Team)

In one of the study villages in Shravasti district in UP, the serving gram pradhan (elected head) of the panchayat was a Brahmin when we went there for our fieldwork. The ex-gram-pradhan was, however, a Dalit, Chamar by caste. We had been interacting with them in the course of our stay in the village. One day, while we were sitting in front of the present pradhan's house and discussing various issues, the ex-pradhan happened to pass by. He stopped and joined us at the invitation of the pradhan. After some time, somebody served us tea from the pradhan's house but no tea was offered to the Dalit ex-pradhan. We noticed this but kept quiet. After a few minutes, the person reappeared with a glass of tea. Seeing him, the ex-pradhan immediately got up, went to one corner of the veranda, took out a mug kept in a shelf, and then the person poured the tea in that mug from a distance so that the glass and the mug did not touch each other. The pradhan caught us noticing this and started laughing. 'This is how things are in the villages. You people are from cities. You would not understand this,' he said.

Mushar children to be educated and hence make sure that school gets only Muslim teachers. They believe that Muslim landlords through their connections in the administration manage to get any Hindu teacher posted in this school transferred within a short period of time. Dalits in Balanagar Kodri (Shravasti, UP) blame Brahmins for the wrangling among different Dalit communities, which resulted in the shifting of a new school to be opened in the village to another one. The only school in the village, therefore, continues to be in the Brahmin locality. The location of a school is important not only to promote or prevent education but also to ensure which community gets to vote and apparently it is the use of schools as election booths which makes the issue of situating a school in a particular locality so crucial (Box 4.5).

BOX 4.5: SOCIAL SEGREGATION OF DALITS IN ORISSA VILLAGES

Dalits face social segregation and obvious discrimination from all other social groups at Mulasar village in Koraput district of Orissa. Untouchability is still practised in the form of the age-old tradition of not allowing the same ground well to be used. Dambas and Ghasis, Dalit caste groups in the village, are not allowed to draw water from ground wells. Though they are permitted to use water from tube-wells, the platforms of the tube-wells are washed before they are used by any other caste group. On some social occasions, if the Chandalas, another Dalit group, are offered food in the village, the platform on which the food is served is thoroughly washed before others are served. These practices are not unique to this village. They are very much prevalent in the area and do not draw any reprobation from any corner.

SOCIAL SEGREGATION AND ITS ECHOES IN SCHOOL

Social segregation, more often than not, extends itself to school in some form or the other. This gets expression mainly through an indifferent or negative attitude by teachers and hostile peer group behaviour. Dalit village experiences suggest that it is common, though not universal, for teachers belonging to Caste Hindu groups to discriminate against Dalit children. The social group to which the teacher belongs becomes important in this context. Only 29 per cent of schools (7 out of the 24 schools surveyed) in these 20 villages have a SC teacher. Five of these schools are located in the southern and western parts of the country, two at Gavaravaram (AP), one in Doddathupur and one in Honnahalli (Karnataka), and one at Karandi (Maharashtra). Other than these, only one school at Lanka (Jharkhand) and one at Kursa (MP) had one SC teacher each (Table 4.5). The larger representation of Dalits in teaching jobs in southern states could be due to the greater levels of literacy and a more rigorous implementation of the reservations policy. Discrimination faced by Dalit children at the hands of teachers takes many shapes. At some places, Dalit children are 'unnecessarily beaten, abused and harassed by upper caste teachers.' (FGD, Honnahalli, Karnataka) In some villages, the teacher asks lower caste children to do a number of personal tasks such as fetching firewood and if the children do not oblige, physical punishment is meted out to them. Sheer neglect of Dalit children by teachers by making them sit in the last row and excluding them from all activities is also common. In cases where all children belong to Dalit or other disadvantaged communities, it is common for teachers to absent themselves or come for fewer hours. No attention to and low expectations from Dalit children are common attitudes among teachers. Dalit children also face hostile peer behaviour as children belonging to the upper castes generally bully them and do not allow them to mix as equals. The general experience of Dalit children in school, therefore, is that of neglect and indifference, when not outright discrimination and rejection (Box 4.6).

BOX 4.6: SCHOOLING EXPERIENCES OF DALIT CHILDREN

Sidhi (MP): Dalit children reported facing discrimination both from teachers and peers at many places in Sidhi. SC families in Naudhiya village complained that despite the fact that the local government school is better than other government schools in the area, their children do not learn as much as they should given the lack of attention from teachers. Children from Thakur families always sit in front and do not allow others to come forward. At Kursa village, the SCs, especially the Prajapatis, were very critical of upper caste teachers' behaviour towards SC children. The Brahmin headmaster asks lower caste children to do a number of personal tasks such as fetching firewood and if the children do not oblige, they are punished. At Jogini village, the complaint was that both the teachers in the local government school are Brahmin and since the majority of the children belong to the lower castes, they do not seem interested in teaching. There is one Alternative Schooling Centre (now converted to an EGS) near Saket *basti*, which generally remains closed because the high caste teacher does not turn up. Local educational administrators agreed that upper caste teachers are biased against lower caste students.

Shravasti (UP): The situation in UP villages is no different from that seen in MP. Peer relations between different caste groups are tense in Balanagar Kodri village.

All the SC communities also reported that the teachers discriminate in favour of Brahmin and against SC children in terms of attention. Both the teachers belong to the higher caste, and Dalit children said that they are beaten frequently for no apparent reason.

Araria (Bihar): At Doriya village in Bihar, the school is located within the Mushar habitation but there is only one teacher who belongs to the upper caste. Though he comes regularly and the Mushars generally have a high regard for him, he does not have many expectations from Mushar children. Mushar women feel that the teacher is 'good' because he does not beat the children unnecessarily and once, 'when he took several children to his village for three days to work on his fields, he paid full wages and also allowed them to watch television'. It is obvious that discrimination is also felt, or reported, only after attaining a particular level of consciousness. Mushar women in Doriya seemed to believe that their children are not meant for higher education. 'What can teachers do? Mushar children are never known for their studies; education is meant for Brahmins,' they say. This statement was frequently repeated by Mushar women during their interactions.

Palamu (Jharkhand): At Ayodhya Kolhua village, Dalit children do not face any discrimination from their peer group simply because upper caste Rajput parents do not send their children to the local government primary school. This is because 'the school is located in the midst of SC houses' and they 'do not want their children to be like Bhuiyans.'

Koraput (Orissa): The most obvious form of discrimination was reported from Mulasar village in Orissa. In the local government primary school, seating of the children in the classes and during the midday meal is community based. This is a multi-caste village, and Khati happens to be a high caste from whom all other communities, except Brahmins, accept food. The woman who cooks in the school belongs to this community, so that there is no problem on this front. At Mohul Bhatta, another village in the same district, the children from the Mali community, supposed to be the highest caste in the village, do not accept food at the *anganwadi* as the worker belongs to a lower caste.

Chamrajnagar (Karṇataka): Dalit children 'are unnecessarily beaten, abused and harassed by the local Lingayat headmaster' at Honnahalli village, according to parents. All other teachers, including one SC teacher, come from outside and are not much interested in changing this scenario. The VEC is dominated by Lingayats and described by the Dalits as 'defunct'. The headmaster's lack of interest is blamed for this state of the VEC.

(Based on FGDs held with men's and women's groups in the field study villages.)

Physical segregation and social exclusion, obvious or subtle, do have an impact on the community's identity, self-image and aspirations. Poverty and its associated hardships get accentuated for Dalit families in a social context of physical and socio-cultural segregation. Together, these lead to a situation in which the Dalits tend to have a low self-image with very little hope of change in their status. They, too, start believing in the prevalent stereotyped view that education is not meant for them. The complete absence of positive role models from the community strengthens this outlook. Unfortunately, the school, instead of breaking this segregation, reinforces the subsidiary status of Dalit children in most cases. However, the situation is neither the

Table 4.5: Profiles of Schools and Teachers in Selected Villages with Dalit Households

S. No.	Villages	Physical Infrastructure rating* Pry.	Physical Infrastructure rating* U. Pry.	Student-classroom ratio	PTR	Social group of teachers	Sex M	Sex F
1.	Ayodhya Kolhua [Jharkhand]	V. Inade		81.0	40.5	1 Gen, 1 OBC	2	–
2.	Lanka	Inadequate		30.0	30.0	1 ST, 1 SC	2	–
3.	Kursa (EGS) [MP]	V. Inade		101.5	203.0	1 SC	1	–
	Kursa [MP]	Avg.	Avg.	92.0	61.3	3 Gen, 1 ST	3	1
4.	Sultana [UP]	Inadequate		265.0	132.5	1 ST, 1 OBC	2	–
5.	Gavaravaram (1) [AP]	Inadequate		130.5	65.2	1 Gen, 3 OBC, 2 SC	3	3
	Gavaravaram (2) [AP]	Inadequate		170.0	56.7	1 Gen, 1 OBC, 1 SC	2	1
6.	Doriya [Bihar]	Inadequate		81.0	81.0	1 Gen	1	–
7.	Balanagar Kodri [UP]	Inadequate		155.0	77.5	2 Gen	2	–
8.	Doddathapur [Karnataka]	Avg.	Avg.	48.5	24.6	1 Gen, 1 OBC, 1 SC	2	2
9.	Mudballa [Bihar]	Avg.		20.0	30.0	1 Muslim, 1 OBC	2	–
10.	Jogini [MP]	Avg.		–	22.5	4 Gen	4	–
	Jogini (Pvt.) [MP]	Avg.		47.6	71.5	2 Gen	1	–
11.	Naudhiya-[EGS] [MP]	V. Inade		–	61.0	1 Gen	1	–
	Naudhiya [MP]	Avg.	Avg.	58.3	58.3	2 Gen, 1 OBC	3	–
12.	Ramraikutti [Assam]	–		–	55.5	2 OBC	2	–
13.	Bayyanagudem (1) [AP]	Avg.		93.5	46.6	1 Gen, 2 ST, 1 OBC	4	–
	Bayyanagudem (2) [AP]	Inadequate		49.6	62.0	3 Gen, 1 ST	4	–
14.	Mulasar [Orissa]	Inadequate		70.5	41.0	3 Gen?	2	1
15.	Honahalli [Karnataka]	Avg.	Good	59.5	39.7	2 Gen, 2 SC, 1 OBC	4	1
16.	Padheguda [Orissa]	V. Inade		50.0	21.5	2 Gen	1	1
17.	Karandli [Maharashtra]	Good	Avg.	32.5	32.5	1 NT, 1 SC	2	–
18.	Mashakalan [UP]	Inadequate		83.5	167.0	1 Gen	1	–
19.	Ukamand [Jharkhand]	Inadequate		52.0	52.0	2 Gen	2	–
20.	Kermeli [Orissa]	Inadequate	V. Inade	58.0	29.0	2 ST	2	–

NOTES: * Based on assessment made by the research team, taking the number of rooms, condition of building and space availability as per enrolment into account.

EGS: Education Guarantee Scheme School. All schools not marked otherwise are Government Primary Schools

SOURCE: School Survey.

same nor static everywhere. Signs of change are visible in a variety of ways. Change is more evident in places where either political processes or economic development have provided greater opportunities to Dalits.

Expansion of Economic Opportunities and Shifts in Occupation Profiles

The arrival of new opportunities of employment, within rural areas and outside them, opens a path to change, especially in terms of the loosening up of traditional dependence on landlords. Opportunities within rural areas include a greater demand for labour due to increased investment and change in the nature of agriculture. This also means an upward push for wages and a somewhat more stable economic situation for Dalit labourers. This has also led to an increased interdependence between high caste landlords and Dalit laboureres as the stakes are high for the landlords and the supply of labour not abundant in the area. At certain places, high caste landlords have sold their land to new investors leading to a change in local equations between them and Dalit labourers as they do not remain the sole providers of work any more. New opportunities within villages also come in new forms of earning, e.g. contributing milk to dairies set up within the village (Chart 4.1).

Dalits are also making use of opportunities outside rural areas either by migrating to distant places or to neighbouring town areas for daily wage work. Something which started as a distress-coping mechanism has become a regular practice to add to income and break away from traditional dependence. The widening of opportunities has also helped in getting away from complete dependence on traditional, skill-based occupations for which enough demand does not exist any more. The groups that have been able to diversify, adopt multiple occupations and combine incomes from different sources are better placed than those solely dependent on their traditional occupations. As a result of migration and the broadening of opportunities, the incidence of attached labour, quite prevalent in Sidhi and Palamu villages, is on the decline. However, the practice is still widespread among groups or families who have not made use of such opportunities and continue to live on land provided by landlords (Boxes 4.7 and 4.8).

WIDENING OF OPPORTUNITIES AND SCHOOLING PARTICIPATION PATTERNS

Opportunities that help Dalit families increase their income and bring greater stability (e.g. greater work availability within villages) are more significant for increasing schooling participation among their children. The stability which comes from inter-dependence is different from total dependence on landlords in a feudal set-up. Despite the continuation of social exclusion in some sense, the changed economic dynamics mean greater self-respect among Dalits. Work opportunities outside villages, especially if it means the

Chart 4.1: Economic Opportunities and Impact on the Life Situation of Dalit Families

District (State)	Village	Signs of change: Economic opportunities	Impact on the life situation of Dalit families
West Godavari (AP)	Gavaravaram	Fertile land, assured irrigation, heavy investment by big landlords, high crop intensity, high demand for labour, high wages	Interdependence between high caste landlords and Dalit labourers, stability in the life of Dalits, better economic condition, High demand for labour, pushing children into wage work
Chamrajnagar (Karnataka)	Doddathupur	Local high caste Lingayat families sold their land to Tamils who invested in plantations, high demand for labour in plantations, cooperative dairy set up	Change of equation between Lingayats and Dalits; Lingayats no more providers of work Supply of milk to cooperative and alternative means of income, though controlled by Lingayats, depends on supply from all castes.
	Honnahalli	Alternative livelihood available in the form of work on farms owned by Tamil investors in neighbouring areas.	Dependence of Dalits on local landlords reduced but still exists in some manner
Araria (Bihar)	Doriya Mudballa	Migration to Punjab and Haryana for six to eight months every year	Reduced dependence of Dalits on debt from high caste families Homestead land still belongs to upper caste families, some exploitation continues, paid work among children continues New opportunities for children's work in urban areas open
Palamu (Jharkhand)	Ayodhya Kolhua, Lanka	Migration to central Bihar for agricultural work and to nearby towns and other areas for non-agricultural work	Reduction in the practice of attached labour Reduced food crisis
Shravasti (UP)	Balanagar Kodri, Sultana	Migration to different city areas to work as rickshaw pullers, other casual labour Shift from traditional occupation (e.g. Khatiks from vegetable growing to agricultural labour)	Additional income and reduced food crisis Break from dependence on traditional skill-linked occupation for Dalits meant greater ability to survive and cope
Sidhi (MP)	Naudhiya	To nearby towns for work as construction workers, white washing, etc. (mainly Saketo and Basora)	Reduction in the practice of attached labour Greater negotiating power with the local landlords due to reduced dependence and alternative sources of income available

BOX 4.7: NOT INTERESTED IN STUDIES?

Tagaram Ankali (44) and his wife Suramma (40) are landless like other Madiga (SC) families in Gavaravaram village of West Godavari district in AP. They work as agricultural labourers. They have five daughters, Neelavathi (24), Venkata Lakshmi (20), Maniamma (13), Gangarathnam (11) and Jaliyamma (9). Both husband and wife are illiterate and did not send Neelavathi to school because 'of ignorance'. The second daughter, Venkata Lakshmi, was admitted and completed Class V from the government primary school located in the village. Maniamma was not as lucky. She was admitted to school but had to be withdrawn after just one year as she was needed to help the family by working as a contract maid servant for a local landlord's family. Gangarathnam was never enrolled as she was required to take care of Jaliyamma and she herself was only four years old. Later, at the age of nine, she also started working as a contract maid servant in another landlord's family. Venkata Lakshmi was lucky that there was no immediate younger sibling. And the family's financial situation was not as bad then either.

The family is currently steeped in debt. Their economic situation became precarious at the time of Neelavathi's marriage. Ankali paid a dowry of Rs. 2,000 and spent another Rs. 3,000 on the marriage arrangements. He borrowed Rs. 4,000 from the local moneylender at an interest rate of 10 per cent per month. The entire amount was supposed to be paid in 10 weeks' time and there was a penalty for late payment. The family could repay the amount in 20 weeks. Venkata Lakshmi was married two years later, taking another loan of Rs. 4,000. This time the rate of interest was different, 5 per cent per month, i.e. 60 per cent per annum, plus putting Mariamma as a domestic servant in the landlord's (moneylender) house. He would not pay her any wages till this debt was fully repaid. The amount remains unpaid till now. Meanwhile, the family entered into another debt. About four years ago, they received a piece of land and Rs. 12,000 for house construction under the Indira Awas Yojna. Since this amount was not sufficient for constructing the house, they borrowed Rs. 1,000 from their son-in-law on no interest. The son-in-law also arranged for another Rs. 2,000 from the moneylender of his village at a lower rate of interest at 36 per cent per annum. All these debts have not been paid so far. Gangarathnam was given as a contract servant on an annual salary of Rs. 1,000 to add to the family's income so that the mounting debts could be repaid.

Mariamma and Gangarathnam work for 9-10 hours everyday. They do not like working in the landlord's house. 'It is tough, especially washing clothes,' they say. The youngest, Jaliyamma, is currently enrolled in school but hardly ever goes. All the elders in the family are busy throughout the day in their work and she roams around the village. 'Since she is not interested in studies, we are now thinking of putting her also as a contract domestic servant,' says Suramma, the mother.

absence of the father, or both parents, for substantial periods leads to instability in the family. The children in such families often have to share extra responsibilities during these periods, making regular attendance at school difficult. Nevertheless, better work opportunities for Dalit families, within or outside the village, improve their negotiation powers within the village. Changed equations with local landlords, reduced uncertainties and improved income are reflected in the shape of a positive change in aspirations, increased interest in schooling and school functioning.

BOX 4.8: RANJEET AND VEERENDRA: *CHARWAHI* IS THEIR FATE

Both Madhukar Sada (42) and his wife Guchki Devi (32) are agricultural wage workers. They belong to the Mushar (SC) caste and live in a Musahri *basti* in Doriya village of Araria district. Like all other Mushar families, Madhukar is also landless. He does not have any cattle either. This is his third marriage; the first wife deserted him and the second died after a brief illness. This is Guchki's second marriage; her first husband abandoned her. From his second marriage, Madhukar has two sons—Ranjeet (12) and Veerendra (8) and has two more sons—Viranchi (3) and Siranchi (1) from his third marriage. He refused to adopt Guchki's only daughter from her first marriage; the girl lives with Guchki's parents. Madhukar is very proud to have four sons and expects them to take care of him in his old age.

His village Doriya is far from town and the availability of wage work in and around the village is not very high. Many people from Doriya have been migrating to Punjab and Haryana to work in agricultural farms and rice mills in the last ten years. Madhukar has also been to Haryana three or four times to work as a construction labourer. It was four years ago that he went the last time and had brought back Rs. 3,000. He prefers to stay in the village and would migrate only if absolutely necessary. Though it is common for this family to take cereals on loan from landlords and return one-and-a-half times the amount after harvest, they have no other debt. The only outstanding debt is an IRDP loan of Rs. 3,500 which he had taken in 1994. He had paid Rs. 1,500 as bribe and managed to get Rs. 2,000 in cash instead of the cattle for which it was meant. He spent this money on his second wife's treatment. He does not even know the current amount of the loan and has no intention of returning this.

Madhukar and his wife, like the majority of other Mushars, are illiterate. Both feel very unhappy about this. 'My father put me into *charwahi* (full-time wage work for one family) when I was only 7; I used to get three meals a day and Rs. 200-300 per year,' complains Madhukar. However, as a father, Madhukar is doing the same to his children; both the older sons work as *charwahas.* Ranjeet started working when he was 9 and Veerendra when he was only 7. Ranjeet gets an annual payment of Rs. 1,700 and Veerendra Rs. 1,400 in addition to three meals a day. Both of them stay at their employers' places in the neighbouring village. Their responsibilities include tending cattle and taking them for grazing. They also do certain other sundry household chores. Veerendra is still very young and wants to go to school. The government primary school is located within Musahri and many of his friends are enrolled there. He basically wants to play with his friends. He manages this, too. He leaves his employer's cattle to graze on their own and comes to his own village for some time almost every day to play kabaddi with his friends.

Madhukar Sada collects the children's earnings directly from the landlord. The children do not get anything out of this. He uses this money to run his household. He feels that even if educated, there is no guarantee of getting a job and hence it is better that the children work as *charwahas.* 'At least they are getting proper meals and, in addition, a fair amount of cash is also coming in,' he says.

However, the impact on schooling decisions is not always positive. Increased demand for labour within the village also pushes children into work. Migrating families also tend to get to know about newer options for children's work leading to the migration of children, especially boys, for work in urban areas. None of these work opportunities demand any level of schooling and hence it is easier to withdraw children from schools and put them into work. Child labour among Dalits is anyway high in areas with feudal relations and in communities which still follow traditional occupations.

SOCIO-POLITICAL PROCESSES AND INTER-RELATIONSHIPS

The nature of politics both at the larger levels of state and nation and socio-political processes at local levels influence identity as well as the socio-economic positions of different social groups and sub-groups. This is specially so in the Indian set-up, characterized by a democratic polity of universal adult franchise and sharp social divisions based on caste. Socio-political processes, at times alone and at times in combination with economic changes, have had a role in shaping identity and influencing the social positions of Dalits in different parts of the country. Social positioning and political consciousness play critical roles in building a commitment to the schooling of children.

SOCIO-POLITICAL MOBILIZATION AND AWARENESS ABOUT SCHOOLING

Social and political mobilization among Dalits help in creating a consciousness about their identity and awareness about their own oppression. Wherever Dalit movements have been stronger, their participation in schooling has been higher, mainly because of greater emphasis on education as a means of breaking away from their past. The Dalit movement has been strong in Karnataka and Chamrajnagar district has the highest Dalit population in the state. Resonances of earlier Dalit movements were visible in the form of instances of increased assertion in the study villages as well. Dalits were vocal in their criticism of school functioning, but sent their children to school despite adverse situations. At Honnahalli village, a high proportion of Dalit children attend school regularly despite the fact that the head teacher in the local school openly discriminates against them. Schooling participation for Dalits is even higher at Doddathupur, the other village in the same district, where there is no discrimination at school and an NGO distributes textbooks and notebooks to very poor children regularly. Unlike Honnahalli, Dalits are not a minority and the Village Education Committee (VEC), with representation from both Dalits and upper castes, is very active at Doddathupur. In the course of time, the schooling of children becomes a norm at such places and every child is sent to school. The situation for Dalits in Karandi village (Pune, Maharashtra) is somewhat similar, they continue to be mostly dependent on wage work but have attained greater awareness and political space.

However, schooling is not always the focus in all forms of political mobilization. Several Naxalite groups have a strong presence in several districts in Jharkhand, including Palamu. The Naxalite movement has been instrumental in eradicating the practice of bonded and attached labour widely prevalent in the district. The level of awareness among Dalits and also other groups, especially STs, of their Constitutional rights relating to minimum wages and access to forest resources is visibly high in the villages in this district. But schooling of children as a necessary means of emancipation and empowerment has not been emphasised by Naxalites. However, there appears to be a shift in their approach in recent years with a greater emphasis on creating pressure for the better functioning of government schools. They have also started running several of their own schools for young children with an emphasis on creating an awareness of their rights and changes in the social order.

AFFINITY WITH POLITICAL PARTY, ACCESS TO POWER, AND SUPREMACY WITHIN DALITS

A common Dalit identity is more common in areas where the Dalit movement has been stronger and the community does not consist of many sub-castes. Sub-caste identities tend to conflict with the concept of a single Dalit identity and intra-Dalit tension is common, creating divides similar to inter-caste ones in their nature and ramifications. The dominant Dalit group in such situations seems to be much more aware and conscious about the schooling of their children in comparison to other Dalit groups. Other Dalit groups at times face similar opposition and obstacles in the schooling of their children as much from the dominant Dalit group as from caste Hindu groups.

The domination of one Dalit group over others has its roots in history as well as certain contemporary political developments. For instance, in UP, the Chamars form the most dominant, prosperous, and educated group among Dalits, feared and respected by others. They have had greater interactions with the upper castes, they were also the first to adopt Sanskritization and later political means to improve their position in the caste hierarchy. They played a central role in the former United Provinces and in the formation of both Republican Party of India and the Bahujan Samaj Party (Pai, 2000). The supremacy of Chamars among all SC groups was obvious in the study villages with mixed Dalit populations. At Balanagar Kodri village, they dominate the panchayats, do not accept water and food from other SC castes and have benefited most from the Indira Awas Yojna for housing. The other Dalit groups, the Kushbahiyas and Patharkatwas feel threatened by the Chamars. The Chamars are also much more vocal against the Brahmins, the local landlords, and question their supremacy vociferously albeit without confronting them directly. The identification with the Bahujan Samaj Party (BSP), a party at the forefront of state politics since the 1990s, makes them feel powerful during their regime. The school participation rate is high for Chamars as compared to other Dalit groups. Interestingly, the Chamars say that they do not send their girls to the school located in Brahmin *tola* for fear of eve-teasing at the hands of Brahmin boys, whereas Kushbahiyas and Patharkatwas children feel threatened by Chamar boys (Box 4.9).

BOX 4.9: INTRA-DALIT GROUP RELATIONS AT VILLAGES IN SIDHI DISTRICT (MP)

In Kursa village in MP, the Prajapatis are the most powerful among all Dalit groups. Potters by traditional occupation, they have been transferred to the Dalit list only in the recent past, and this has annoyed the Sakets, who were the most dominant among the Dalits in the village till the Prajapatis were given Dalit status. The Prajapatis have been more advanced in education and hence in a better position to benefit from government schemes. They are large in number, maintain good relations with Brahmin landlords, and have managed to gain political power by winning the post of sarpanch in the panchayat elections. This has also annoyed the Sahus, belonging to the OBC group, as they feel that the Prajapatis are similar to them, but unnecessarily getting advantages meant for Dalits. In this process, the Sakets and the ST groups such as the Kols and the Baigas are being left behind in all respects. Unlike Kursa, the control of the village panchayats continues to be in the hands of the dominant upper caste groups, Vaishyas in Jogini village and Chauhans in Naudhiya village. Although the Vaishyas are facing a challenge from the Yadavas at Jogini, the relationship between the Sakets and the Vaishyas remains, by and large, feudal in nature. It is obvious that only those Dalit groups are able to take advantage of government schemes which have already achieved some level of education and exposure.

Representation in local panchayats also signifies access to political power after the 73rd and 74th Constitutional Amendments were passed assigning a greater role to them. This is especially true for states like MP where district, block and village panchayats have been given an important role and commensurate powers in the areas of rural development, education and health. Although other caste groups still dominate the panchyats in many areas, including those where they are small in number, Dalits have captured power in places where the seats were reserved or they have come out of feudal relations. However, it has mainly been one Dalit group that has been more active in reaping these benefits and it dominates over other Dalit groups. The same Dalit sub-caste could be politically and socially weak in one village and strong in another, depending upon social composition and positioning. The inter-relationships between Dalit groups and their implications for schooling in this situation also remain the same as described earlier.

It appears that places where political processes at the local and state levels have been dynamic and the Dalits politically active, evidence of an emerging Dalit identity as an oppressed people reasserting their dignity against oppression is also more visible (Box 4.10). The emergence of political consciousness is a gradual process, and particular combinations of various

BOX 4.10: NAGAMMA: STRUGGLING TO EDUCATE HER CHILDREN DESPITE GREAT ODDS

Nagamma, now 32, was only 10 when she got married and only 12 when she came to her husband's house. During the initial years of marriage, her husband, Mahadevaiah, worked as an annual farm labourer against an annual contract in the neighbouring district of Tamil Nadu, and the family lived there. Annual wage contract is common in Honnahalli and the other neighbouring villages of Chamrajnagar district in Karnataka. The labourers are bound to provide service for all 365 days in a year in lieu of a fixed wage generally lower than the daily wages. They are also provided with a place to live within the farm area. Many wage workers opt for this due to assured employment and also, at times, because of the need for cash. They take their wages in advance and in return pledge their labour for the whole year.

The arrangement was working fine for Mahadevaiah and Nagamma while their children were young. They have two daughters, Savitha (14) and Jyothi (9), and one son, Madevaswami (11). When Savitha turned 4, the couple started worrying about her education. They are Dalits, and feel that education alone can help in changing their social status. There was no school at the farm where they lived and hence they decided to move to their village. Here, they began working for daily wages and managed to build one room for themselves after receiving support from the government under the Ashray Scheme. Unlike other SC families in the village, they have no land of their own. The village has an upper primary school where the couple enrolled all three children.

Last year, Savitha completed her Class VII and Madevaswami Class VI. Savitha was married off immediately after that. The couple needed 10,000 rupees for her wedding and hence Mahadevaiah took an advance and became an annual farm servant again. He had already completed seven months when we met them, and the family was expecting him back in three months' time. He does not receive any wage or food other than the advance of 10,000 rupees. Madevaswami has also discontinued his studies after Class VI and though Nagamma says he is staying with his sister and would be back in three months time, the neighbours say he has also become an annual farm servant and would be back after completing his one year.

Nagamma is the President of the local self-help group, and expresses complete faith in education. 'I did a mistake by marrying Savitha at a young age. I requested her in-laws to continue her education but they are not interested. I will not repeat the same mistake again. Next year, I will put Madevswami back in Class VII and after that I will send both him and Jyothi to Chamrajnagar for further studies.' She says she had to temporarily withdraw Madevswami due to a particularly bad financial situation; the family is surviving only on Nagamma's earnings. She remains ambiguous about how Madevswami's withdrawal helped her financially. 'From next year, there would not be any problem,' Nagamma states confidently. 'In case of any crisis, we will again take a loan and become farm servants. That is the only way we can raise money, but we are determined to educate our children,' she says. Some of her close relations in Chamrajnagar told them about SC/ST hostel facilities. 'There is a lot of discrimination from local students against us.I will now send them to a hostel,' she says. Jyothi, a student of Class I, has heard about Kiran Bedi and wants to become a police officer. Her mother, too, has high expectations from her and Madevswami—'Once educated, they will get jobs and free us from our bondage', she says confidently.

factors at particular historical junctures facilitate them. In states like Bihar and Orissa, where Mushars or Chandalas have not been part of any major political or social movement, not many signs of assertion are visible. They tend to accept subjugation more readily as compared to others who belong to groups which have been part of any active political or social resistance movement. This directly impacts on their views regarding education and the schooling of children.

Schooling of Dalit Children: Encouraging Factors and Processes

As discussed earlier, education demands a long-term commitment and it is not an easy choice for poor families living in constant insecurity to send their children to school continually for several years. It is even more difficult for Dalit families living in a state of social and economic marginalization. Nevertheless, this commitment is present in certain places and has come about due to several reasons such as increased access to educational facilities, expansion of economic opportunities, exposure to the benefits of education, and political or social mobilization. These factors act either independently of each other or in combination, depending on the circumstances. Their impact is best felt when they work in combination and in the same direction, reinforcing the effects of one another (Chart 4.2).

The availability of a school within a Dalit habitation appears to be one of the most important conditions for ensuring the enrolment of Dalit children. Having been denied access to education for centuries, school or education does not form part of the natural view of life of many Dalit groups even now; this is not true for communities that have already achieved high literacy rates and experienced educational advancement. The availability of school within their own habitations, therefore, assumes tremendous significance. The presence of a school before their eyes immediately makes it a 'possible' option. High enrolment in the villages in MP proves this; with the advent and implementation of the EGS scheme, most Dalit habitations in the state now have a primary school.

However, the presence of a school within their habitation does not necessarily ensure the regular attendance of Dalit children. The irregular functioning of schools and discrimination against Dalit children discourage them from attending school regularly. It is not easy for socially isolated and economically marginalized Dalit children, in most cases first-generation learners at school, to continue in the face of adverse teacher and peer attitudes. What helps in overcoming adverse situations in school and also on other fronts is a strong commitment to schooling which is based on several factors.

An increased level of exposure leads to an increased interest in children's schooling but often it is limited to the desire to develop some literacy and numerical skills. As a result, this interest finds expression only in terms of enrolment of children and that too only if school happens to be located

Chart 4.2: Categorization of Villages in Terms of Schooling Participation Status of Dalit Children

Schooling participation category	Names of the villages	Certain specific features
1. Low enrolment, low regularity (1 village)	Mudballa (Bihar)	School not within habitation, low work availability within village, some long-term migration, schooling not common even among dominant group (Muslims), school irregular and teacher disinterested in teaching Dalit children, no sign of socio-political mobilization
2. Medium enrolment, low regularity (4 villages)	Balanagar Kodri (UP), Masaha Kala (UP), Mulasar (Orissa), Padheiguda (Orissa)	School not accessible from all habitations, low work availability (except Mulasar), some short-term migration, obvious social discrimination against Dalits, Dalits either at the lowest rung and unquestioning or strong intra-Dalit tension, discrimination against Dalit children by teachers and hostile peer behaviour
3. High enrolment, low regularity (3 villages)	Doriya (Bihar), Naudhiya (MP), Ramraikutti (Assam)	School within habitation, long-term migration and work in neighbouring areas common, feudal past (except Ramraikuti) and some practices continue, children's engagement in work common, school somewhat irregular and teachers disinterested
4. Low enrolment, medium regularity (1 village)	Sultana (UP)	School in one tola but far from others, short-term migration and work in neighbouring areas common, long-term migration among particular sub-caste (Koparias), children's engagement in work common for Koparias, school somewhat irregular
5. Medium enrolment, medium regularity (4 villages)	Gavaravaram (AP), Jogini (MP), Ayodhya Kolhua (Jharkhand), Ukamad (Jharkhand)	School within habitation, high demand for labour within village (Gavaravaram), work in nearby towns common (Jogini and Ayodhya Kolhua), migration common (Ayodhya Kolhua), Children's engagement in work present, not very high, Naxalite influence present (Ukamad), School regular and SC teachers in position (Gavaravaram and Ukamad), irregular (Jogini and Ayodhya Kolhua)

(contd.)

Chart 4.2: (contd.)

Schooling participation category	Names of the villages	Certain specific features
6. High enrolment, medium regularity (2 villages)	Kursa (MP), Lanka (Jharkhand)	School within habitation, SC dominant villages, some Dalit groups asserting their identity (Kursa), Naxalite influence present (Lanka), some migration, schools irregular (Kursa), regular (Lanka)
7. Medium enrolment, high regularity (2 villages)	Honnahalli (Karnataka), Bayyanagudem (Andhra Pradesh)	School within habitation, work in close by areas common, schooling of children common for dominant (upper caste) social groups, strong Dalit identity (Honnahalli), well connected, upper-primary school present, school regular, teacher discriminates against Dalit children (Honnahalli)
8. High enrolment, high regularity (2 villages)	Doddathupur (Karnataka), Karandi (Maharashtra)	School within habitation, well connected, strong Dalit identity, schooling of children common for dominant/other social groups, work and income opportunities available, upper primary school present (Doddathupur), school regular, teachers interested, an NGO active in supporting poor children (Doddathupur), VEC active

NOTES: 1. High enrolment = 70 per cent and above, medium enrolment = 50 to 69 per cent, low enrolment = below 50 per cent.
2. High regularity = 80 per cent and above, medium regularity = 50 to 79 per cent, low regularity = below 50 per cent.
3. No village with Dalit population fell into the category of low enrolment, high regularity.

within the habitation. It does not translate itself into a sustained interest which makes parents pursue their children's education in terms of making them attend school regularly. Socio-political awareness or education in the family helps in creating a more permanent and long-term interest in education which helps in maintaining regularity and attaining completion. Prevailing social norms also play an important role. If most children from the community or the village go to school, then even those families whose own commitment may not be very high start sending their children. On the other hand, if most children are unenrolled or irregular, it affects even others whose personal situation is not really a barrier in enrolment or regularity.

Socio-political awareness and a belief in education as a means of effecting change in their position seem to play the most important role in building this commitment. Social or political awareness often helps in overcoming disadvantages caused by the lack of educational attainment or poor economic conditions in the family. Participation in political processes among Dalits helps in asserting their identity, brings hope for change and builds greater aspirations for children. This also acts against sending children to work for wages. However, it is also obvious that socio-political mobilization has also taken place among groups who have secured the minimum economic security and are not suffering from acute poverty. It is also clear that in absence of a common Dalit identity, the benefits of political assertion remain confined to more vocal and powerful sub-communities in villages with a mixed SC population.

Finally, it can be said that caste, through its correlations with poverty and social marginalization, does have a role in aggravating educational deprivation among Dalits. However, the scenario transforms with changes in economic opportunities, status, socio-political mobilization, general governance and the functioning of schools. The situation is best at places where all three factors—school functioning, improvement in the family's educational and economic status and the nature of political processes—operate in combination. Doddathupur in Chamrajnagar, Karnataka and Karandi in Pune, Maharashtra are two such examples. On the other hand, the situation is the worst in places like Mudballa where poverty is acute, levels of education low, inter-relationships feudal, social and physical exclusions marked, schools located away from the Dalit cluster and their functioning poor and discriminatory.

NOTES

1. This twenty does not include villages where the proportion of SC households was less than 5 per cent of the total number of households in the village. It also does not include villages where SC households did not constitute at least 20 per cent of the sample households surveyed, even if their representation in the total number of households was more than 5 per cent.
2. Includes EGS and AS centres of MP because these are designed to function for the full four hours.

5. Notes from the Margins: Tribal Children at School

Background

A large number of indigenous communities in India, speaking their own languages and following cultural practices relatively distinct from the mainstream, were categorized as aboriginals or tribes by colonial rulers in the nineteenth century. These communities were in the nature of individual ethnic groups, characterized by autonomous political and social organization, territoriality, and a consciousness of group identity. The labels 'tribe' and 'aborigines' signified the 'uncivilized' and created a new social category. They also gave diverse social groups an identity that extended beyond their own communities, blurring differences that existed between groups (Nambissan, 2000). This common identity was further strengthened after Independence with the granting of the status of 'Scheduled Tribe', which, as in the case of the Scheduled Castes, is an official rather than a sociological category. This common identity, again as in the case of the Scheduled Castes, has not meant an effacement of the original identities, although the original identities themselves have undergone a transformation due to a number of economic and cultural processes experienced over time.

Tribes were not part of the traditional Hindu caste structure. Physical isolation, a rather self-sufficient economy characterized by free access to and control of productive resources, especially the forest, have been the distinctive features of traditional tribal societies. However, the penetration of the colonial administration into tribal areas rich in forests and mineral resources led to increasing alienation from their traditional rights to forests and lands. It also left these communities vulnerable to exploitation by traders, moneylenders and merchants (Nambissan, 2000). This also meant an imposition of the norms and culture of mainstream society and the initiation of certain practices hitherto unknown to tribal societies. Therefore, the nature of the constitutional safeguards for the Scheduled Tribes is somewhat different from those for the Scheduled Castes in view of the basic qualitative differences in their positions. While for the SCs, these safeguards relate to (i) removal of disabilities thrust on them by nefarious traditions and (ii) provisions for positive discrimination in their favour to enable them to acquire an honourable position due to them in the national life, those for STs have been about ensuring that (i) the tribal people do not lose command over resources in the process of change and development, and (ii) while the tribal people are enabled to take full advantage of new advances in knowledge, the best in their tradition is not lost (GOI, 1988).

Based on these safeguards, specific provisions have been made for protection and positive discrimination in their favour. These measures, besides including some common to SCs, also encompass specific programmes and projects, the Tribal Sub-Plan being the most important among them. The interventions under these include special provisions for the spread of elementary education for tribal children. However, as the subsequent analysis will reveal, the tribes have, by and large, been marginalized both economically and culturally, and are at the bottom end in terms of school participation rates. While they have been deprived of their traditional rights to forests and other resources, they have not been able to reap the benefits of a 'modern' economy. At the same time, it is also true that large inter-regional variations exist and all tribes, as in the case of the SCs, cannot be treated as uniform. Depending upon the process of development and the nature of integration into mainstream society and economy, the status of STs varies from one place to the other. Many tribes were more dependent on forests and at most practised rudimentary agriculture with no individual control over land *per se*, while others had been in settled cultivation and individual control of land was not alien to them. The tribes who owned land emerged as economically better placed in a changed scenario because land, unlike state-controlled forests, continued to be an important productive resource controlled by private individuals.

The nature of social and political mobilization among the tribal population in post-Independent India has been different from what was experienced in the case of Dalits. Barring a few examples, tribals have not been at the forefront of the national polity. A number of small movements have been reported from several parts of the country, but their fights have mainly been struggles for survival in a system alien to them in its nature, culture and approach. The presences of Christian missionaries and non-governmental organizations (NGO) have also played a role in the spread of literacy and advancement in school participation among tribal children in certain pockets. The status of education is generally better at places where these forces have been active. As in the case of the Dalits, this chapter discusses schooling participation of tribal children in varying contexts.

TRIBAL VILLAGES: A FEW IMPORTANT DIMENSIONS

Eighteen study villages, distributed over the seven states of Orissa, MP, Jharkhand, Gujarat, Karnataka and Maharashtra, reported having an ST population in varying proportions. While STs constituted more than half of the total households in eleven villages, they were between 25 to 50 per cent in two and less than 25 per cent in five villages. It is common for STs, unlike Dalits, to live in a homogeneous set-up, and four out of eighteen villages are inhabited entirely by them. The character of mixed habitations with ST populations is also different. In ST-majority villages, there are generally no upper caste families, only SC or, at times, OBC families. The social composition of the village is important in determining the context because it has implications for access to resources, the nature of occupation and social relationships. Also important is the fact that some villages have only one ST group while others have more than one, and tribes living in the same village are also quite different from each other in terms of their origin, cultural practices and occupational profiles.

About half the villages are fairly placed in terms of connectivity and provisions of infrastructural facilities, the rest being quite poorly positioned. However, taking the village as a whole is misleading in many cases as it is common for a few tribal families to move and settle away from the main habitation. This aspect has been dealt with later in the chapter.

School Participation Patterns: Intra-Group and Intra-Village Differences

INTRA-GROUP DIFFERENCES

The present status of schooling participation among ST children is worse than that among Dalit children in certain respects. This despite the presence of a number of special initiatives and schemes for the education of STs. The proportion of children regularly going to school from the total children is as low as 7.7 per cent and 11.8 per cent at Bharwa Munda and Mulasar villages in Koraput in Orissa. Incidentally, the highest proportion of ST children going to school regularly has also been reported from a village, Kermili, in the same state, Orissa. Thus, there are significant differences even within a region. Sidhi in Madhya Pradesh also presents a similar picture ,with this proportion being high at 75 per cent in Kursa and quite low at about 29 per cent in Barambaba village. In general, out of the eighteen villages, the proportion of children regularly attending school is lower than 40 per cent in ten, between 40 per cent and 60 per cent in four, and above 60 per cent in only four villages.

The proportion of never-enrolled among out-of-school children was significantly higher than that of drop-outs in the case of Dalit children in almost all the villages, except four, whereas the trend is mixed in the case of ST children; drop-outs constitute the majority of out-of-school children in twelve out of eighteen villages. It is, therefore, important to understand the features of relatively higher irregularity and drop-out rates among tribal children in most places.

INTRA-VILLAGE DIFFERENCES

Participation patterns among tribal children are worse than others in about two-thirds of the villages where there is a mixed population. In fact, in the majority of the places where SCs could be seen as doing better than others, the 'others' mainly comprised STs. However, STs show a better participation rate than others in a few villages located in different states, including UP, Orissa and MP. But being better or worse off is not independent of the general level of schooling participation in the village. For instance, with a low enrolment rate of 50 per cent, STs in the village Kathkuiyan Kalan (UP) are better than others who have an enrolment rate of only 15 per cent. On the other hand, even with a high enrolment rate of 84 per cent, ST children are worse off than others (93.8 per cent) in Kermili in Orissa (Table 5.1).

Profile of ST Households

The marginalization of STs is obvious from their over-representation among BPL families. Though they constitute only about 8 to 9 per cent of the total population, they cover more than half the BPL population. Even among BPL families, they are over-represented among the lower section with more than one-third of the tribal families belonging to this category (see Table 4.2). Despite the fact that landlessness is not as high among STs as among Dalits, most tribal families live on the margins. Landed tribes are actually poor peasants, and those who do not have access to land survive mainly on wage work in agriculture and other low-paid sectors. Even those who cultivate their land generally supplement this with wage work either within the village or by migrating for short periods. Dependence on the forest continues to be high for many tribal groups, and with a substantial decline in their rights over forest produce and use life has generally become tough for them.

However, it is important to add that despite deprivation and poverty, STs are comparatively less vulnerable to food or other forms of crises due to their continued dependence on the forest. They manage to survive even lean periods by accessing fruits and roots for food and other produce for sale. Nevertheless, the not-so-high levels of landlessness and relatively low representation in wage work does not reflect control over their own lives; it actually reflects the lives of people who have failed to reap the benefits of development and opportunities after having been deprived of their traditional rights due to various reasons, including pressure from powerful groups and the claims of the state and hence continue to live on the periphery.

The level of parental literacy, which has a positive impact on children's schooling participation, is abysmally low for ST parents. The proportion of families with both partners literate is the lowest for STs among all social groups. Only lower caste Muslims are equal to STs in this respect. The average number of years of schooling for the ST adult is lower than that for the average poor family, also true for both men and women taken separately. The average number of years of schooling for tribal women is about half a year, which is higher than only one social group, lower caste Muslims (see Table 4.2). However, it may be added that in a situation where all deprived social groups—Dalits, STs, Muslims and even the OBCs—have such low

Table 5.1: Villages with Tribal Households: Background and Schooling Status

S. No.	Village name	Development category	ST (%) in Pop.	Other social groups in village	Name of the major tribe	Social group	Enrolled	% within enrolled			Un-enrolled	% within unenrolled		Regularly going Col. 8 × 7 / 100
								Regular	Irregular	Occasional		Drop-out	Never enrolled	
1	2	3	4	5	6	7	8	9	10	11	12	13	14	15
A. Villages with ST Population > 50 per cent														
1.	Ukamand	B	86	SC	Kharwar,	ST	45.5	81.8	18.2	–	54.5	22.2	77.8	37.2
				Korba	Others	66.7	75.0	25.0	–	33.3	–	100.0	50.0	
2.	Khurakhurd	C	100	None	Oraon	ST	45.5	38.9	61.1	–	54.5	12.5	87.5	17.7
3.	Mahal	B	100	None	Kunbi, Worli	ST	69.2	77.1	17.1	5.8	30.8	56.3	43.7	53.4
4.	Wakarya	B	100	None	Bhil, Konkani	ST	75.9	90.2	9.8	–	24.1	100.0	–	68.5
5.	Maddur Colony	B	100	None	Soliga, Jenukurbha	ST	64.7	100.0	–	–	35.3	100.0	–	64.7
6.	Barambaba	C	85	SC	Gond, Kol,	ST	68.4	42.1	52.6	5.3	31.6	61.1	38.9	28.8
				Baiga	Others	92.3	75.0	8.3	16.7	7.7	–	100.0	69.2	
7.	Kathkuian Kalan	C	89	OBC/ SC	Tharu	ST	50.0	41.7	50.0	8.3	50.0	–	100.0	20.9
						Others	15.0	66.7	33.3	–	85.0	–	100.0	10.0
8.	Kermeli	B	63	OBC/	Gond	ST	84.0	90.5	9.5	–	16.0	50.0	50.0	76.0
			SC		Others	93.8	93.3	6.7	–	6.2	100.0	–	87.6	
9.	Padheilguda	C	88	SC	Paroja	ST	63.0	80.0	20.0	–	37.0	10.0	90.0	50.4
						Others	50.0	33.3	66.7	–	50.0	66.7	33.3	16.7
10.	Cherichuan	D	100	None	Bhunjia	ST	51.4	100.0	–	–	48.6	70.6	29.4	51.4
11.	Bharwa Munda	C	72	OBC/ SC	Gond	ST	11.5	66.7	33.3	–	88.5	43.5	56.5	7.7
						Others	16.7	66.7	–	33.3	83.3	40.0	60.0	11.1

B. Villages with < 50 per cent ST Population > 25 per cent														
12. Mohul Bhatta	C	48	OBC/	Paroja	ST	45.5	60.0	20.0	20.0	54.5	58.3	41.7	27.3
		SC	Khanda	Others	85.7	66.7	33.3	–	14.3	50.0	50.0	57.2	
13. Mulasar	C	38	SC/	Bhumiya,	ST	47.0	25.0	62.5	12.5	53.0	44.4	55.6	11.8
		UCH	Paroja, Khanda	Others	50.0	29.4	47.1	23.5	50.0	47.0	53.0	14.7	
C. Villages with ST Population <25 per cent														
14. Kursa	D	20	SC/	Kol, Baiga	ST	100.0	75.0	–	25.0	–	–	–	75.0
		UCH		Others	77.8	58.6	34.5	6.9	22.2	25.0	75.0	45.6	
15. Jogini	B	14	SC/	Kol	ST	50.0	66.7	33.3	–	50.0	66.7	33.3	33.4
		UCH		Others	65.2	48.3	37.9	13.8	34.8	37.5	62.5	31.5	
16. Naudhiya	C	23	UCH/	Kol	ST	78.3	33.3	55.5	11.2	21.7	40.0	60.0	26.0
		SC		Others	79.5	45.2	45.2	9.6	20.5	50.0	50.0	35.9	
17. Karanci	C	07	UCH	Mahadev	ST	33.3	100.0	–	–	66.7	75.0	25.0	33.3
			Koli	Others	90.3	100.0	–	–	9.7	100.0	–	90.3	
18. Ratapalli	A	16	OBC/	Gond	ST	87.5	85.7	14.3	–	12.5	100.0	–	74.9
			UCH	Others	93.3	85.7	14.3	–	6.7	66.7	33.3	79.9	

NOTES: 1. Column 2 shows the development category based on an index prepared taking infrastructural facilities into account (See Appendix Table A.I).
2. Column 3 shows the approximate proportion of the population belonging to this social group.
3. Column 7 shows the enrolment of 6-13-year-olds against the total population of the age group.
4. Columns 8, 9 and 10 show the distribution of enrolled children [Column 7].
5. Columns 12, 13 and 14 show the distribution of unenrolled children [Column 11].
6. Column 14 shows the population of regularity going in total age group children.
7. The schooling status data for the ST or 'other' children have not been included for the villages where their proportion in the surveyed households is 20 per cent or less.

SOURCE: 1. Columns 3, 4 and 5 based on the Village Appraisal Report.
2. Remaining columns based on the Household Survey.

levels of average years of schooling for women, this kind of comparison can look absurd.

VARIATIONS WITHIN TRIBES

Table 5.2 shows that there are notable inter-village differences among STs in terms of land ownership, primary occupation and literacy levels. Patterns of land possession, occupation and literacy are also linked with their origin and the process of mainstreaming they have experienced. In Sidhi district in MP, landlessness is high (90 per cent) at Naudhiya village where only the Kols are found as compared to Barambaba where the Gonds live. The Gonds, numerically the most dominant tribe of India, have been a very prominent group which established their political power, founded states and exercised their influence far and wide. Agriculture and animal husbandry have been the basis of their economy. Individual ownership of land has been common among them, especially among the Rajgonds. Gonds have several sub-communities, the Rajgonds being one of them, and most Gond families in Sidhi belonged to this group. On the other hand, the Kols have always been mostly landless and survive mainly on agricultural wage work. The Baigas, the third tribe present in the study villages in Sidhi, have mainly been dependent on forests. It is only in recent times that they have begun cultivation and working as labourers. The literacy rates for the Baigas are lower than those for the Kols, and their rates are notably lower than those for the Gonds (Table 5.3).

The Gonds in Orissa are above the Kandhas, Bhunjias, Bhumiyas and Parojas, the other four tribes, in terms of literacy rates for both men and women. The Parojas are the poorest and the most deprived among these tribes found in villages in Orissa. Landlessness is also lower among STs at Kermili, Bharwa Munda, Cherichuan and Ratapalli, villages where the Gonds are one of the important constituents of the ST population, unlike Padheiguda and Mohul Bhatta where ST households consisted mainly of the Parojas (Tables 5.2 and 5.3). Landlessness is not so high among the Khandas, the Bhumiyas and the Bhunjias in Orissa. Among the Khandas, cow herding was a common traditional occupation. The Bhumiyas, found in Mulasar village in Koraput district, still depend on forest collections significantly though agricultural wage work is also common. The village Cherichuan in Nuapada district is mainly inhabited by the Bhunjias. Among the Bhunjias, though landlessness is not high, literacy rates are quite low, though higher than those for the Parojas.

The literacy rates for the tribes found in the study villages in Jharkhand have been relatively higher. This is especially true for Oraon men at Khurakhurd and Khairwar men at Ukamand. The Oraons in that region have been at the forefront of several social and political movements, the one led by Tana Bhagat being the most well known. Their dependence on forests

Table 5.2: Profile of Tribal Households in Selected Villages

S. No.	Village	Caste	Landless	More than 2.5	Male (14+)		Female (14+)		Main Occupation of the Household H ad			
					Illiterate	Schooled	Illiterate	Schooled	Cultivator own work	Agri labour	Non-agri labour	Sala[illegible]ed
1.	Ukamand	ST	22.2	22.2	52.2	39.1	87.5	8.3	40.0	—	40.0	20[illegible]
	Others	20.0	20.0	55.6	44.4	100.0	00	50.0	00	44.4	5.6	
2.	Khurdakhurd	ST	17.4	47.8	42.9	42.9	86.2	6.9	27.3	00	63.6	[illegible]
3.	Mahal	ST	20.8	37.5	39.4	30.3	67.6	20.6	58.3	29.2	4.2	8[illegible]
4.	Wakarya	ST	8.0	20.0	35.3	50.0	71.9	18.8	80.0	16.0	00	4[illegible]
5.	Maddur Colony	ST	48.0	20.0	61.0	36.6	62.5	28.1	44.4	28.0	00	12.[illegible]
6.	Barambaba	ST	00	80.0	63.4	26.8	87.5	6.3	76.2	9.5	00	4.[illegible]
	Others	00	50.0	33.3	16.7	50.0	50.0	75.0	00	00	00	
7.	Kathkuiyan Kalan	ST	00	8.3	50.0	35.0	95.2	4.8	100.0	00	00	0[illegible]
	Others	8.3	25.0	52.4	38.1	87.5	6.3	83.3	00	8.3	00	
8.	Kermeli	ST	6.7	33.4	28.0	52.0	81.8	13.6	68.8	12.5	6.3	6.[illegible]
	Others	44.4	22.2	77.8	00	72.2	11.1	44.4	55.5	00	00	
9.	Padheiguda	ST	45.5	13.6	76.0	4.0	96.2	3.8	90.1	4.5	4.5	0[illegible]
		Others	100.0	00	100.0	00	100.0	00	33.3	00	00	66.[illegible]
10.	Cherichuan	ST	53.3	20.0	59.1	22.7	86.4	00	80.0	00	6.7	0[illegible]
11.	Bharwa Munda	ST	27.8	33.3	48.1	22.2	95.5	00	23.5	29.4	47.0	0[illegible]
	Others	42.9	28.6	70.0	20.0	92.3	00	12.5	75.0	00	00	
12.	Mohul Bhatta	ST	58.3	00	91.7	8.3	100.0	00	69.2	23.0	00	0[illegible]
	Others	38.5	7.7	86.7	6.7	88.9	11.1	84.6	7.7	00	7.7	
13.	Mulasar	ST	22.2	44.4	90.9	00	100.0	00	33.3	44.4	00	00
	Others	66.7	00	75.0	25.0	88.9	5.5	31.3	50.0	00	00	
14.	Kursa	ST	00	50.0	66.7	33.3	66.7	33.3	66.7	00	00	00
		Others	4.8	61.9	70.0	23.3	83.3	16.7	81.8	00	9.1	00

(contd.)

Table 5.2 (contd.)

S. No.	Village	Caste	Landless	More than 2.5	Male (14+)		Female (14+)		Main Occupation of the Household Head			
					Illiterate	Schooled	Illiterate	Schooled	Cultivator own work	Agri labour	Non-agri labour	Salaried
15.	Jogini	ST	33.3	00	100.0	00	100.0	00	33.3	00	33.3	00
	Others	40.0	50.0	40.5	43.2	90.3	3.2	75.0	10.0	10.0	00	
16.	Naudhiya	ST	90.0	00	73.3	00	100.0	00	20.0	50.0	30.0	00
	Others	68.8	6.3	63.6	36.4	75.0	5.0	62.5	6.3	31.3	00	
17.	Karandi	ST	100.0	00	25.0	50.0	62.5	25.0	00	57.1	00	14.3
	Others	33.3	16.7	28.0	64.0	27.6	58.6	52.6	21.0	15.8	5.3	
18.	Ratapalli	ST	25.0	50.0	42.9	57.1	57.1	42.9	50.0	00	50.0	00
		Others	4.8	47.6	44.1	32.4	66.7	11.8	61.9	19.0	14.3	4.8

NOTES: 1. A person has been considered being schooled if he/she has been to school for at least one year.
2. The data for 'others' are not included if the number of households covered is 20 per cent or less in the total sample of households covered.

SOURCE: Household Survey.

has been considerably reduced and they are now mainly settled cultivators. This is also true for the Khairwars in Palamu district and individual possession of land is common among both these communities. The same is not true for the Korwas in Palamu, said to have migrated to this part from MP. Previously, they used to practice hunting, gathering and rudimentary agriculture, but now they mainly survive on wage work. The Tharus of UP, found in Kathkuiyan Kalan of Shravasti district, bordering Nepal, are a landholding community with individual proprietorship of land. This is reflected in the fact that not a single ST family in the village is landless (Table 5.2). In Karnataka, while landownership and settled cultivation is common among the Nayakas, it is not so for the Soligas and the Jenukurubhas, the main constituents of ST families surveyed at Maddur Colony in Chamrajnagar. Both Soligas and Jenukurnbhas depend mainly on agricultural wage work and forest collections even now.

The Kolis, also known as Mahadevs, in Maharashtra, have mainly been cattle keepers and labourers. Landlessness is high and not a single Koli family reported possessing any land at Karandi village in Pune district (Table 5.2). However, the literacy rates for the Kolis were among the highest among ST groups found in the study villages (Table 5.3). Literacy rates were also high and landlessness low in Wakarya village in Dangs district of Gujarat, mainly inhabited by Bhils. The Bhils are the second largest Scheduled Tribe in India and have been associated with many social movements and a number of historical events. Wage work in agriculture as well as non-agriculture is common among them now. Unlike them, most of the Kunbis, a tribe found in Mahal village in the same district, are small or marginal farmers though they supplement their income through occasional wage work. A number of persons from the Koli tribe in Maharashtra, the Nayakas in Karnataka, and the Bhils and the Kunbis in Gujarat, are also in salaried jobs as school teachers, forest guards, etc. This is reflected in the fact that the proportion of household heads in salaried jobs is the highest in Karandi, Maddur Colony, Mahal and Wakarya, the four villages where these tribes have been found (Table 5.2).

There are more than 450 tribes in India and those covered in this study's villages far from represent all the tribes found in the country. There are tribes, especially in the north-eastern parts of the country, educationally and economically much more advanced than many other groups and there are tribes that are still living in isolation, untouched by processes of 'development'. However, the tribal populations covered under the study's villages, though not falling in either extreme category, reflect the more common experiences encountered by STs in a variety of contexts. All these villages have tasted 'development' and 'mainstreaming' in varying degrees with significant bearing on their economic, social and cultural lives. These, in turn, have crucial influences on their children's schooling.

Table 5.3: Dominant Occupations and Literacy Rates for Major ST Groups found in Study Villages

S. No.	ST Sub-Caste [State]	Study village/s where Present	Dominant Occupations	Literacy Rate [1981] Male	Female	Total
1.	Oraon [Jharkhand]	Khurakhurd	Wage labour, cultivators	32.38	14.19	23.28
2.	Khairwar [Jharkhand]	Ukamand	Wage labour, hunting, cultivators,	28.70	5.31	17.22
3.	Lohra [Jharkhand]	Ukamand	Agr. labour, cultivators, hunting	21.01	4.08	12.71
4.	Korwa [Jharkhand]	Ukamand	Cultivators, agr. labour	10.37	1.90	6.14
5.	Kunbi [Gujarat]	Mahal	Cultivators, agr. labour, fishing	41.55	21.35	31.47
6.	Warli [Gujarat]	Mahal	Cultivators, agr. labour, forest collection	15.42	4.30	9.87
7.	Bhil [Gujarat]	Wakarya	Cultivators, wage labour	27.85	8.24	18.18
8.	Konkari [Gujarat]	Wakarya	NA	NA	NA	NA
9.	Gond [MP]	Barambaba, Kursa	Cultivators, agr. labour	21.04	3.98	12.46
10.	Kol [MP]	Barambaba Kursa, Jogini, Naudhiya	Cultivators, agr. labour	9.54	1.13	5.40
11.	Baiga [MP]	Barambaba, Kursa, Jogini	Cultivators, agr. labour, forest collection	6.71	0.50	3.62
12.	Tharu [UP]	Kathkuiyan Kalan	Cultivators, agr. labour	25.43	4.73	15.34
13.	Gond [Orissa]	Kermeli, Bharua Munda, Rattapalli	Cultivators, agr. labour	31.39	6.33	18.73
14.	Paroja [Orissa]	Padheiguda, Mohul Bhatta, Mulasar	Cultivators, agr. labour	8.60	1.04	4.76
15.	Kandha [Orissa]	Mulasar, Mohul Bhatta	Cultivators, agr. labour	24.22	4.54	14.44
16.	Bhunjia [Orissa]	Cherichuan	Cultivators, fishing, animal husbandry, wage	8.5		
17.	Bhumia [Orissa]	Mulasar	Cultivators, agr. labour	11.30	1.48	6.34
18.	Soliga [Karnataka]	Moddur Colony	Cultivators, agr. labour	12.27	5.04	8.74
19.	Jenurkurnbha [Karnataka]	Moddur Colony	Forest production collection, cultivators,			
20.	Bettakurubha [Karnataka]	Moddur Colony	Forest production collection, basket weaving			
21.	Nayaka [Karnataka]	Moddur Colony	Cultivators, agr. labour, wage labour, forestry	28.64	9.00	18.95
22.	Koli [Maharashtra]	Karandi	Agr. labour, wage labour, poultry farming	42.20	16.28	29.46

NOTE: * The Jharkhand state has been carved out of erstwhile Bihar.
SOURCE: Census of India, 1981, as given in S.K. Singh, *The Scheduled Tribes*, vol. III, New Delhi: Oxford University Press, 1995.

Remote and Scattered Habitations

The majority of tribal habitations are located in remote areas near forests and in hilly regions. Tribal habitations are typically characterized by the dispersed location of only a few households at one site, and often a number of small hamlets, situated at quite a distance from one another, together constitute one village. Tribal hamlets are, therefore, usually small in size and scattered and sparsely populated.

The remoteness of the location and the scattered nature of the habitation have several implications for their lives, livelihood and also schooling. The *anganwadi* or school located in one hamlet seldom attracts children from other hamlets. For instance, all the Orissa study villages, except Cherichuan and Padheiguda, have *anganwadis*, but the use, which is anyway limited because of poor functioning, is restricted only to the families living in the same hamlet. Although the village would be considered as having been provided for in government records, it is actually impractical to expect tribal women with heavy responsibilities at home and outside to travel a distance of 2-3 km to drop off their children at these institutions (Box 5.1).

BOX 5.1: SCATTERED HABITATIONS IN TRIBAL VILLAGES

Small and scattered habitations are typical of tribal villages. Often different parts of the same village are not adjacent to each other. For instance, the village Bharwa Munda in Nuapada district in Orissa consists of three hamlets, Bharwa Munda, Ghatipada, and Naikpara. Ghatipada is located 2 km away from the main hamlet and so is Naikpada. In Kermili, the other village in the same district, the four hamlets, Gauntipada, Kudapada, Naikpada, and Junapada, are located at good distances from one another. The villages in Koraput district, the other district of Orissa, also show similar patterns. Separate hamlets are inhabited largely by a single community or are divided into separate clusters of different communities. This is especially true for the remotest and the most interior hamlets. For example, in Mulasar village, Kandhiaguda, the hamlet located farthest from the main hamlet, is inhabited only by the Kandha families, and in Mohul Bhatta in the same district, the remotest hamlet Jinupada, also inhabited only by the Kandhas, is located about 3 km away from the main hamlet. While Jhaliaguda is separated from the main hamlet by a ravine, Gadiguda is located on a hill top and is separated by another ravine.

These features are not unique to Orissa. Four of the six hamlets in the Gond-dominated Barambaba village in Sidhi district (MP) are inhabited by the Gonds alone. The Baiga families of the village live in a separate hamlet located close to the forest, about 6 km away from the main hamlet. The majority of Kol families in Naudhiya village live in a separate cut-off *basti* known as Kolan. This is, however, to break away from their subservient relationship with the local Chauhans for whom they have been working as attached labourers for ages. Separate clusters are common at even those places where they are not living in separate hamlets. The Korwas do not live in the same clusters as the Khairwars in Ukamand village in Palamu district (Jharkhand) nor do the Warlis live with the Kunbis in Mahal in Dangs district (Gujarat).

The same is true for schools. Apart from the fact that the lack of the physical existence of a school in the habitation makes it difficult for poor parents to think about schooling their children, there are real problems of accessing schools located in other hamlets. It is actually very difficult for young children to cross ravines, hillocks and walk long distances to reach school everyday. This was reported to be the case in many villages, especially at Koraput district in Orissa. At Mulasar village, not a single child from Kandhaguda, the far-off hamlet, is enrolled in the primary school. Similarly, at Mohul Bhatta, the school is located in the main hamlet and no child from the other hamlets attends it. The school location in Wakarya village in Dangs district (Gujarat) is also a problem as it is situated close to the river and remains cut-off from the rest of the village during the rains. At Ukamand in Palamu district in Jharkhand, one cluster of houses is separated from the main habitation (where the school is located) by cultivated land and a railway track. Physical access to school is not an issue in Nuapara district in Orissa because of close location and the absence of barriers. Schools are present in almost all habitations of the Sidhi villages (MP) because of the EGS programme in operation.

TEACHER ABSENTEEISM

Teacher absenteeism is common in remote tribal areas. This was reported to be most widely prevalent in villages in Koraput (Orissa) and Sidhi (MP) districts. It is also common for teachers here to put the names of children on the rolls on their own and mark them present irrespective of their enrolment or presence. The level of absenteeism is not as high in Nuapara in Orissa and Palamu in Jharkhand. However, teachers are most regular in areas which are more developed and where the general level of governance is better. These are also better-connected areas and the levels of literacy and awareness are higher (for example, Dangs in Gujarat, Pune in Maharashtra). The functioning of all government service delivery institutions generally match each other's levels of functioning. Places where Primary Health Centres or the local outlet of the Public Distribution System are functioning better have better functioning schools and vice versa (Box 5.2).

BOX 5.2: ATTENDANCE RECORDS

On a casual visit to the local primary school in Mulasar village in Koraput district in Orissa, the research team found the school open and about four or five children playing. There was no teacher around. The children told the team that only the headmaster had come in the morning and had gone home after an hour. The other two teachers were absent. The registers were lying in the open and the attendance register showed 56 children present in the school on that day. Out of five subsequent visits to the school, the same scene was repeated on two more occasions—a few children playing outside the school, no teacher present, and the attendance filled for the day.

Cultural Identity, Language, and Community Living

Separate clusters and hamlets for separate tribes are based on separate cultural identities. A distinct cultural identity and a strong sense of exclusivity characterize most tribes. Most maintain these despite years of mixing and intermingling in the same village or area. Each tribe has its own sets of festivals, customs, beliefs, and deities. They also often differ in the ways in which they celebrate common festivals, and those with a sense of their past take great pride in this. This was especially visible among the Gonds in Sidhi villages and the Oraons in Khurakhurd. The intermingling of different tribes living in the same village is not common. Distinct cultural identities also get reflected in certain practices based on notions of purity and exclusivity from others. Certain tribes, especially those which have practised settled cultivation for long and own individual land, consider others 'inferior' to them. A notable feature is that those considered inferior also have their own notions of purity and pollution, reflected in practices where they exclude others. Different tribes often speak different languages and dialects exclusive to them (Box 5.3).

BOX 5.3: EXCLUSIVITY AMONG TRIBES

Different tribes, even if living in the same village, maintain exclusive identities. Socialization is also generally endogamous and they identify more with people belonging to their tribe rather than to those living in the same village or area. There is also a sense of being 'superior' to others in many tribes. For instance, the Gonds in Sidhi villages prefer to socialize only among their own community and do not consider the Kols and the Baigas as their equals. Similarly, the Bhumiyas in Mulasar village in Orissa look down upon the Parojas and the Kandhas, and the Kharwars in Ukamand village in Jharkhand do not treat the Korwas as equals. However, this seldom leads to any form of exploitation and cannot be compared with the practice of untouchability. This is more to do with an isolated existence and a sense of separate territoriality in the past. The Soligas in Maddur Colony consider themselves 'superior' to the Kurubhas, whereas the Jenukurubhas feel they are superior to 'others'. The Kunbis and the Warlis in Mahal village in Dangs district in Gujarat also consider each other 'different'.

Strong community ties are also reflected in practices linked with livelihood. Exchange labour was one of the most common practices found in several tribal villages. It is common for the Gonds in Barambaba (MP), Bhunjias in Cherichuan, Parojas in Padheiguda (Orissa), Kharwars in Ukamand and Oraons in Khurakhurd (Jharkhand) to work on each other's fields during agricultural seasons. Their participation in community-oriented development work in terms of providing free labour has also been quite high. They were reported as participating very enthusiastically in activities such as the construction of a check dam or watershed in some villages of Jharkhand, MP and Orissa. Tharu families in Kathkuiyan Kalan go to a hilly river located 10 12 km away for fishing and it is common for them to share fish with other families who could not go.

THE TEACHER AS PART OF THE 'COMMUNITY'

The acceptance of teachers by the community as one among them appeared to be critical to increasing schooling participation in tribal areas. An understanding of and respect for tribal cultures and practices is important for teachers to gain this acceptance. The presence of a tribal teacher, especially when he or she belonged to the same community, apparently makes it easier. Coming from the same community, it is believed that the teacher would understand and respect the culture and ethos with much greater sensitivity. This was experienced in varying degrees in all three villages where teachers belonged to the same community as the majority. Although tribal teachers are present in all except three (15 per cent) schools in tribal villages, they are not necessarily from the same community (Table 5.4). However, tribal teachers in general are more sensitive towards tribal children, though those from the same community extend themselves more. Non-tribal teachers, on the other hand, tend to judge tribal practices from the 'mainstream' cultural perspective and consider tribal children 'inferior'. This is manifested in discrimination in mixed villages and indifference and disinterest in others. The most glaring example is that of children from the Kol community in primary schools in the Sidhi district who face discrimination from teachers as well as their peer group in the same manner as Dalit children. The EGS school located at Kolan *basti* in Naudhiya village (Sidhi) often opens only for one to two hours as the upper caste teacher from the dominant Chauhan community is not interested in teaching, and the Kols neither have the same concept of time to monitor the number of hours nor the courage to question the teacher (Box 5.4).

BOX 5.4: TEACHER FROM THE SAME TRIBAL COMMUNITY

The primary school located in the Gond-dominated Tilwani hamlet of Barambaba village in Sidhi district has two Gond teachers. They visit children's houses frequently and talk to parents about enrolment and regular attendance. They are also much more regular as compared to the teachers in other schools in the same village. Similarly, at Kerimili in Nuapara district, again a Gond-dominated village, the headmaster is from the same community and lives in the village itself and takes a lot of interest in making the school regular and lively. The only teacher posted at Kathkuiyan Kalan in Shravasti district of UP belongs to the same Tharu community and hence people relate to him as one among them. The acceptance of the teacher by the community is much higher in these villages as compared to villages where the teachers belong to some other community.

MEDIUM OF INSTRUCTION AT SCHOOL

The language or medium of instruction at school has an important role in making children feel accepted and interested. An increasing amount of research strongly advocates the use of the mother tongue or home language as the medium of instruction in early education.[1] This assumes greater

Table 5.4: Profile of Schools and Teachers in Selected Villages with Tribal Households

S No.	Villages	Physical Infrastructure Rating*		Student–Classroom Ratio	PTR	Social Group of Teachers	Sex	
							M	F
1.	Ukamand	Inadequate		52.0	52.0	2 Gen	2	–
2.	Khurakhurd	Inadequate		56.5	113	1 OBC	1	–
3.	Mahal	Average	Average	27.2	40.6	3 ST, 1 Gen	4	–
4.	Wakarya	Average		16.0	16.0	1 ST	1	–
5.	Madlur Colony	Average		26.5	26.5	1 SC, 1 ST	2	–
6.	Barambaba-Tilwani	Inadequate		18.5	37.0	1 Gen	1	–
	Barambaba	Inadequate		36.7	110.0	2 ST	2	–
7.	Kathkuiyan Kalan	Inadequate		74.5	149.0	1 ST	1	–
8.	Kirmeli	Inadequate	V. inadequate	58.0	29.0	2 ST 1 General	3	–
9.	Padheiguda	V. inadequate		50.0	21.5	2 Gen	1	1
10.	Cheri Chuan			10.0	9.5	1 ST	1	–
11.	Bharwa Munda	Inadequate		40.0	32.5	2 Gen	2	
12.	Mohul Bhatta	V. inadequate		35.5	35.5	2 Gen	1	1
13.	Mulasar	Inadequate		70.5	41.0	3 Gen	2	1
14.	Kursa (EGS)	V. inadequate		101.5	203.0	1 SC	1	–
	Kursa	Average	Average	92.0	61.3	3 Gen, 1 ST	3	1
15.	Jogini	Average		–	22.5	4 Gen	4	–
	Jogini (Pvt.)	Average		47.6	71.5	2 Gen	1	–
16.	Naurya-[EGS]	V. inadequate		–	61.0	1 Gen	1	–
	Naurya	Average	Average	58.3	58.3	2 Gen, 1 OBC	3	–
17.	Karandi	Good	Average	32.5	32.5	1 NT, 1 SC	2	–
18.	Ratapalli	Inadequate		42.0	28.0	2 OBC	2	–

NOTES: * Based on assessment made by the research team, taking the number of rooms, condition of building, and space availability as per enrolment into account.

EGS: Education Guarantee Scheme school.

All schools not marked otherwise are government primary schools.

SOURCE: School Survey.

significance in the context of tribal children because of the fact that the majority of tribes have their own mother tongue, often quite distinct from the dominant state or regional languages. These children face problems wherever teachers do not speak their dialect at all. This was reported to be the case at Mulasar and Mohul Bhatta villages (Koraput) in Orissa, where the majority of the teachers, including tribal ones, came from other areas and did not know the local languages. However, other than Orissa, most tribal villages covered in this study have one common language used by everybody and if the teacher can interact in that, children do not face any problem. Hence, from the perspective of language, it is more important to have a local teacher than a tribal teacher.

LIMITED MEANS OF LIVELIHOOD AND DEPENDENCE ON FORESTS

Agriculture has been the main source of livelihood for tribal populations like most other social groups in rural India. The majority of tribal families are primarily either small or marginal farmers in all the villages except in the Paroja-dominated villages in Orissa (Padheiguda and Mohul Bhatta in Koraput district), the Kol-dominated village, Naudhiya in MP, and among the Jenukurubhas and the Bettukurubhas in Maddur Colony in Chamrajnagar district (Karnataka), where they depend mainly either on wage work or on collecting food and other materials from forests.

Cultivation in most tribal areas is characterized by a lack of irrigation facilities and the consequent dependence on rains or rivulets for irrigation, low productivity, single cropping, and extensive use of family labour. All family members, including children, participate in different agricultural activities on different occasions. It is more common for women and girls to participate in the activities of transplanting and weeding, and for men and boys in ploughing, carrying seedlings and harvested stock, and threshing. The use of HYV seeds or other such modern agricultural practices is not at all common in these villages. In some places, especially the villages in Koraput district in Orissa, the availability of cultivable land also declines due to rivulets and their changing courses. As such, agricultural produce is never adequate for the whole family throughout the year. This necessitates a dependence on alternative sources of livelihood (Box 5.5).

The forest is the most common and natural means of sustenance for tribal populations. It is a perennial source of raw materials, collection of saleable produce, and also consumables such as fruits, roots and vegetables. Animal husbandry and cattle keeping are common among tribes and the forest also serves as grazing grounds for their cattle. Cattle, especially a pair of bullocks, are very important for cultivating families to plough the land. For certain tribes, the forest continues to be the primary or only source of livelihood. The Bettukurubhas in Maddur Colony depend entirely on forests. Besides collecting fruits and vegetables for consumption, they meet all their

BOX 5.5: CIRCUMSTANCES, THE TEACHER AND VULNERABILITY

Like others from his community [the Bhuiyan (ST)] and his village (Lanka) in Palamu district of Jharkhand, Kail Ram has several occupations. He cultivates the 0.35 acre plot of land he has received from the government, labours as an agricultural wage worker within the village, migrates twice a year to work on the farms of big landlords in Bihar, makes and sells earthen tiles during lean agricultural seasons, and collects and sells *tendu* leaves from the adjacent forest once a year. Ever since their eldest son, Munna (15), started working in a hotel in the nearby town of Barwadeeh, his wife, Bimli Devi, has stopped working for wages. She does household chores and helps Kail Ram in making tiles as well as in farming.

Kail Ram and Bimli Devi have five children. Two more did not survive. The eldest daughter, Munni, was married off at the age of 12. The eldest son, Munna, started working in a hotel when he was 11 and did so for about three years. He used to work there for about 12-13 hours for a sum of 20 rupees and three meals a day. He stopped liking that work and has recently left to work as a casual labourer in Barwadeeh. He gets work for about 15-20 days per month and receives about Rs. 45 rupees per day. Like their parents, both Munna and Munni are illiterate. Kail and Bimli never thought of sending them to school.

At the time of Munni's wedding, Kail managed to get an IRDP loan of Rs. 1,500 in the form of cattle. He paid a bribe of Rs. 500 and took the remaining Rs. 1,000 in cash instead. He spent this money on Munni's wedding and other consumption purposes and has not repaid any part so far. He had to take another loan about two years ago when he fell seriously ill and treatment in the government hospital was not helping. He had to go to private doctors which was costlier. Bimli also went to the local *ojha* and spent about Rs. 200 in sacrificing one cock and giving liquor to the *ojha*. Although he sold his two goats, it was not sufficient and he had to borrow Rs. 600 at an interest rate of Rs. 20 per month. He cleared this debt in one and a half year's time with the support of his own and Munna's earnings. The family has not been able to earn anything through the collection and sale of *tendu* leaves because of the ongoing agitation for a revision of the rates for the procurement of these leaves.

Kail's younger children, Kuldeep (8) and Pratima (5), have started going to school this year and are enrolled in class I. The youngest daughter, Rani (3), is currently too young to go to school. 'Earlier nobody from our habitation was going to primary school, which is situated in another habitation of the same village at a distance of about one kilometre,' says Kail. He has enrolled Kuldeep and Pratima this year only after the new teacher in the village school insisted. Many other families from the habitation have also done so after the new teacher came. Almost all children from 5 to 12 from this *tola* are enrolled in Class I. 'The school had only one teacher so far who never used to go to anybody's place. The new teacher takes more interest and goes to people's houses,' says Bimli. 'I have also realized that education helps in dealing with others. We will try to educate Kuldeep as far as possible,' adds Kail. He hopes Kuldeep will get a government job after he completes his education and expects Pratima to get married to an educated person if she herself is educated. However, it is not certain how far this commitment will last. One incidence of illness in the family, one year of drought, or the transfer of the new teacher, anything can bring about a change in their circumstances and may mean the discontinuation in the schooling of these children

Chart 5.1: Levels of Dependence on the Forest for Livelihood and Survival

High dependence on forests (11 villages)	Moderate dependence on forests (3 villages)	Low dependence on forests (3 villages)	No dependence on forests (2 villages)
Ukamand (Jharkhand), Barambaba (MP), Kermili (Orissa), Mohul Bhatta (Orissa), Bharwa Munda (Orissa) Padheiguda (Orissa), Cherichuan (Orissa), Mahal (Gujarat), Wakarya (Gujarat), Maddur Colony (Karnataka)	Khurakhurd (Jharkhand), Mulasar (Orissa), Kursa (MP)	Kathkuiyan Kalan (UP), Bharwa Munda (Orissa), Jogini (MP)	Naudhiya (MP), Karandi (Maharashtra)

requirements for other essential goods by the sale of baskets made out of bamboo sticks collected from the forest. The Jenukurubhas in the same village have abandoned their traditional occupation of honey collection due to various laws and restrictions imposed by the government. Yet they depend on the forests for grazing their cattle and for the collection of fruit and tubers (Chart 5.1).

Dependence upon forests for cattle grazing and collection of minor forest produce (MFP) such as *tendu* leaves and *mahua* seeds is common to all tribal villages, except Naudhiya (MP) and Karandi (Maharashtra). While in certain villages like Jogini (MP), Bharwa Munda (Orissa) and Kathkuiyan Kalan (UP), the use is limited to collection of seasonal minor forest produce like *mahua* or *tendu* leaves and as cattle-grazing grounds, the level of dependence is much higher in certain other villages. A common practice among tribal peoples is to clear small pieces of forest land for cultivation. This was quite prevalent in a few study villages in Orissa. At Mahal and Wakarya in Gujarat, almost the entire population survives on fruit, herbs and tubers collected from thick forests during the lean season from June to September every year.

WOMEN AND CHILDREN PLAY CENTRAL ROLES IN FOREST-RELATED ACTIVITIES

The involvement of women and children in almost all earning and livelihood activities is characteristic of tribal life. While men, women and children participate in farming-related activities, it is often only women and children who are responsible for collection of fuelwood, dry leaves, fruit and tubers. The hard-working tribal women also undertake heavy jobs such as carrying headloads and walking tens of kilometres to sell fuelwood or other small products. The cutting and collection of fuelwood from forests and carrying it to towns for sale is common at Barambaba (MP), Kermili (Orissa) and

Mohul Bhatta (Orissa). At Kathkuiyan Kalan in UP, Tharu women accompany their men in equal number to fish; they dry the fish and save it for use during a lean season when nothing else is available for consumption.

Children are central to many tasks such as the collection of dry leaves, fuelwood, and fruits. One common responsibility of tribal children is to take their cattle to forests to graze. In fact, it is quite common to combine the two activities—grazing cattle and collecting essentials—from forests. This was reported from several villages, including Mahal and Wakarya in Gujarat, Maddur Colony in Karnataka, Kathkuiyan Kalan in UP, Mohul Bhatta in Orissa, and Barambaba in MP. Among the Gonds in Barambaba village, it is almost customary to keep one son exclusively for this purpose. The girls, apart from taking part in agricultural activities and collection from forests, are commonly engaged in sibling care. This was also reported from almost all the villages, though at certain places the incidence is high. The Gonds in Barambaba use at least one son in the family for cattle-grazing purposes. The practice of entrusting older children with the responsibility of taking care of younger children is also customary among the Parojas in Koraput district of Orissa. The involvement of children in livelihood activities makes it difficult for them to attend school (Box 5.6 and 5.7).

BOX 5.6: DEPENDENCE ON THE FOREST IN UKAMAND VILLAGE, PALAMU, JHARKHAND

Dry leaves collected from forests provide a livelihood to at least half the families in Ukamand village. They collect dry leaves from forests, make *donas* (small disposable balls) out of these leaves, and then carry them to the district headquarters for sale. It is mainly the children's responsibility to collect dry leaves and the women's to make *donas* and sell them. Children also help in the making of *donas*. Women generally go to sell these *donas* on alternate days, and a family manages to earn about 30 to 40 rupees per day through this activity. *Mahua* is another important item of forest collection that helps in survival. Almost all the families in the village collect *mahua* from the forest and brew it to make local wine mainly for self-consumption. However, about one-third of the families also earn money through this. Women go to different *haats* in nearby villages and sell the local brew. Besides, many women are also involved in cutting and collecting fuelwood from the forest, which they carry to the nearby towns for sale. This is often the most important source of livelihood in these families.

BOX 5.7: BABULAL AND HIS STICK

Babulal (9) can always be seen with a stick in his hands and a few heads of cattle. He leaves home early with his cattle and spends the day in the forest. He knows various parts of the forest quite well and loves to boast about his knowledge. In between his chores, he comes home once to have food. While in the forest, Babulal also collects firewood, fruit and roots, depending on the season. During the *mahua* season, his mother also accompanies him and together they collect and prepare *mahua*, for this is their main source of food during the rains. In the evening, when he comes home at about seven, he is too tired and generally sleeps early after having his second meal of the day. He is not fussy, and eats whatever leftovers his mother gives him. Evening is the time for his elder bother, Tilakraj, to study but by then Babulal is generally fast asleep. He rarely shows any overt interest in Tilakraj's studies, but makes it a point to tear his books and notebooks whenever they have a fight.

His parents, Rai Singh and Dhanwanti, cultivate three acres of land; they own two and have taken one on a sharecropping basis. This is their main source of livelihood. Since the land is not very fertile, the produce is not always sufficient to meet the family's requirements. They collect *mahua*, other fruits and roots from the forest during different seasons to supplement their diet. They also have one cow, one buffalo, two bullocks and three goats. Bullocks are crucial for farming and the cow is used for milk. Goats are sold whenever there is an urgent need for cash, during festivals or during any crisis. Last year during the rains, many in the village including Rai Singh, caught cholera and he sold one goat for 800 rupees. This was, however, not adequate and he borrowed 1,000 rupees from the local moneylender at the exorbitant rate of interest of 60 per cent per annum. Rai Singh also works for wages, but work is not readily available in this Gond village where every family owns small pieces of land.

Rai Singh and Dhanwanti have three sons, Tilakraj (10), Babulal (9) and Daddu Singh (3). Tilakraj studies in Class V in the local government primary school. Babulal was never enrolled in school. All Gond families have cattle, and it is almost like a tradition among Gonds to give one child the responsibility of cattle grazing. Rai Singh identified Babulal for this job. He asks, quite casually, 'Who will take these cattle for grazing if both of them go to school?' It is natural for him to send one child to school and keep the other for helping out in economic activities.

The local school is regular and both the teachers in the local primary school belong to the same community; they are Gond. They did try to influence Rai Singh to send Babulal to school. But he feels this is impossible as there is nobody else to take responsibility for the cattle. Both parents realize and appreciate Babulal's important role in supporting the family but do not feel there is anything wrong in not sending him to school. 'Babulal will continue to do cattle grazing and grow into a cultivator while Tilakraj will get educated and find a job for himself,' says Rai Singh about his aspirations for his sons. Babulal himself has the same view of his future: 'I will take cattle for grazing, what else?'

TOUGH LIFE, LOW EARNINGS, AND FIGHT FOR SURVIVAL

Despite hard work by women and children, tribal family earnings remain small. For instance, after walking up to 20 km. with heavy headloads, they earn the meagre sum of 15 or 20 rupees. Their earnings are reduced by about one-fourth, 5 to 10 rupees, as they have to bribe forest guards and officials at check posts, as felling of trees by the tribal population is illegal. This is especially difficult in areas where the forests have been declared part of sanctuaries and severe restrictions have been imposed. The tribal population also faces difficulties in many areas on account of encroaching on forest land for cultivation.

The reservation of forests during the British period, and the subsequent laws enacted during the post-Independence period restricting the entry of the tribal population into the forest and their using of its resources, have had serious implications for tribal life. A crucial distinguishing feature of tribal society is their association with a territory to which they belong and over which their command is sanctified by their tradition. During the initial phase of reservation, certain tribal rights were recognized which continued to be enjoyed for a long time without much interference. However, in the wake of the 'development' thrust, the demands on forest resources became manifold and multi-dimensional. They also became an easy source of augmenting revenue, particularly because the line between what could be deemed the using-up of the capital base and what is in the nature of harvesting merely the incremental is rather thin. The forests were ravaged by contractors in collusion with a variety of vested interests with disastrous consequences. Tribal populations have also been obliged to extend cultivation over forest land as in the past, the new laws against it notwithstanding. In fact, the pressure on their economy is still greater, both internal on account of population growth and external on account of intrusions by individuals, institutions and even the state. Consequently, they have no alternative but to 'encroach' to suppress the fire of hunger in a setting away from 'development', having as their lot nothing but unagreeable fallouts (GOI, 1988).

While environmental degradation is a real issue and local populations can be held responsible for some part of it, it is minimal as compared to what is done by contractors and other vested interests. The tribals also do not have any other means of survival. Uneducated and unexposed to the ways of 'development', they are constantly exploited by middlemen as well as government agencies. It was reported from many study villages that traders and middlemen buy certain MFP that command good prices in the market at throwaway prices from tribal people. Moreover, even the right to collect MFP, which was conceded as a right at the time of reservation, has become a concession with the passage of time. The price which the tribal population gets for MFP even in the cases of purchase by government agencies represents the return for the labour input for collecting the item and not the value of the product over which they have a right.[2] In many cases, as reported from villages in Orissa, tribals are unable to get even this price because of their need for immediate earnings and their inability to wait and go to government collection centres; they prefer to sell to traders and middlemen who come to their doorstep.

TENSION, UNREST AND ALIENATION

As a result of the laws restricting forest use by the tribal populations and the manner in which these are being implemented, many areas are experiencing tensions between local people and government agencies. Difficult livelihood situations, inability to find a place in the modern economy, exploitation by traders as well as government officials, and disregard for tribal traditions in the implementation of forest laws have led to further alienation among tribes. Alienation from the government makes them suspect state interventions, including schools, adding to the constraints caused by cultural and linguistic differences experienced at school (Box 5.8).

BOX 5.8: SOCIO-POLITICAL MOBILIZATION AND TENSION AND UNREST IN TRIBAL VILLAGES

During the fieldwork for the present study, we witnessed ongoing protests for tribal rights over forest produce in several villages. An agitation under the banner of the CPI (ML) was on at Ukamand village (Palamu, Jharkhand) against restrictions put on the collection of *tendu* leaves. The collection of *tendu* leaves and their sale is a month-long activity in which the entire family is involved and manages to earn about a 1,000 rupees every year. This is an important source of earning cash in all tribal areas, which can then be used to buy essentials such as clothes, etc. Similar protests were also observed in Orissa where an area containing 61 villages in Nuapada and Komna blocks had been declared a sanctuary (Sunabeda Sanctuary) by the government of Orissa. Chereichuan and Kermeli villages are located in this area. This would imply that a population of 22,000 from 5,660 households, 87 per cent of these being ST, is going to be deprived of their major source of livelihood, i.e. the forest. The people in this area have been put under great pressure to leave their villages. They reported harassment by forest department officials who periodically search their houses for any collection of MFP they might have made. People protested this move on several grounds, including the fact that the constitutional requirement of consulting the Palli and gram sabhas (73rd Constitutional Amendment) was not respected by the government. They demand the formation of a joint committee consisting of representatives from the government and the affected villages to manage the sanctuary, protecting the primordial rights of the people. They also demand rights on land that they have been cultivating for ages.

(Based on interactions and local newspaper reports collected during fieldwork.)

Alternative Means of Livelihood: Wage Labour

Low productivity in agriculture, insufficient produce to last the whole year, and the depletion of forests and restrictions on its use by the local population force poor tribals to look for alternative means of survival. The tribal subsistence economy does not offer any opportunity to earn cash, increasingly a necessity with greater interactions with the outside world and the disintegration of a barter-based economy. Local availability of wage work in agriculture is minimal in tribal villages, especially at places where almost everybody owns small pieces of land. As mentioned earlier, the use of family and exchange labour is more common among tribes. Even if there are a few families who employ hired labour, the requirement is very low. As such, the availability of wage work within the village is generally limited to government-sponsored development work carried out under various employment assurance and rural development schemes. Although most tribal villages reported having received some funds for such schemes, this is also rarely sufficient to provide adequate employment.

Wage work is important at places where there is little or no dependence on the forest and cultivation is either not remunerative or not an option at all. The Kolis in Karandi village in Maharashtra and the Kols of Naudhiya village in MP are completely dependent on wage work as they are located far from the forest and own no land. Despite the fact that the village has fertile land and wage work is available for maximum months during the year, the Kolis are the poorest social group at Karandi. The situation is worse for the Kols in Naudhiya due to the concentration of land in the hands of the Chauhans, low wages, and feudal relations (Box 5.9).

BOX 5.9: KOLS IN SIDHI (MP) VILLAGES

Kol families living in the villages of the Sidhi district in MP are supposed to have been brought there by Chauhan families to work in their fields, and the system of attached labour, known as *harwahi*, is still in practice. The Chauhans settled the Kols on their land and in return made the whole family work for low wages throughout the year. The 'attachment' passes from one generation to the next, and generations of Kol families have been serving the same Chauhan families. However, certain signs of the breaking down of this system are now visible. One such example is the decision of about 60 Kol families (of the total 300) in Naudhiya village to shift to a far off *tola* on the hills in order to break away from the attached labour system. However, though they are no more in *harwahi*, their dependence on Chauhan landlords continues for several reasons. The Chauhans continue to own about 75 per cent of cultivable land in the village. The wages are low and the Kols are never able to sustain themselves during the lean period of the monsoon, on their own. They are always forced to borrow from the Chauhans, and they do so often by pledging their labour in the future. In this way, their exploitation continues unabated. The Kols (the STs) of Sidhi district, unlike the Sakets and the Basors (the SCs), have not tried to develop new skills and seek to earn a living by working in nearby towns. The Kols are exploited in Kursa and Jogini villages as well, but the situation is slightly better because of their access to forests which provides them with an alternative form of livelihood during lean periods.

Though the practice of contract labour exists at other places as well, the terms are not as exploitative. For instance, at Kermili village in Nuapara district (Orissa), a few landless and marginal landowning families enter into contracts with large landowning families to work from June to September for a fixed payment, including cash and harvested paddy. The wages are comparable to prevalent rates and the contract is generally entirely voluntary and not against any loan. Moreover, both parties belong to the same tribe, the Gond, and no social exclusion is faced.

Mulasar in Koraput district (Orissa) is the only village with a tribal population where opportunities for wage work have expanded within the village since 1995, when the construction of a canal was completed. The availability of assured irrigation throughout the year has changed the character of agriculture, and apart from growing multiple crops, cashew cultivation has also begun. The involvement of children in wage work has also increased with this change. This practice is similar to what was seen for

Dalits in villages in Andhra Pradesh and Karnataka where the demand for labour is high because of assured irrigation and the farming of commercial crops.

SEASONAL MIGRATION: AN IMPORTANT COPING STRATEGY

The need for alternative means of livelihood is not limited to landless STs; even those engaged in cultivation find it increasingly difficult to sustain themselves for the entire year. This is especially true for areas where the quality of land is poor and the size of cultivable land is declining. With limited access to forest resources, it has become essential for them to have alternative means of survival. The availability of wage work within the village is generally low in tribal areas because of the dependence on rains and the smaller size and inferior quality of land. Seasonal migration to near and faraway locations has emerged as one common strategy in several places. Unlike the SCs, the practice of single migration and non-agricultural labour in nearby towns is not prevalent among the STs. Barring a few cases, migration among STs is typically characterized by family or sub-family-based labour for jobs where the wages are paid on the basis of quantity rather than the number of hours or days worked. This includes work in agriculture such as harvesting or sugar cane cutting and in non-agriculture such as work at brick kilns or stone quarries. The extent of migration was reported to be the highest from Bharwa Munda in Nuapara (Orissa) district, followed closely by Mahal as well as Wakarya in Dangs district (Gujarat) and Khurakhurd in Palamu district (Jharkhand) (Box 5.10).

BOX 5.10: JAYENDRABHAI: READY FOR HIS FUTURE

Mahendrabhai Bhotubhai Valvi (17), the elder son of Bhotubhai Valvi in Mahal village of Dangs district in Gujarat, has been going to sugarcane fields for the last nine years. His younger brother, Jayendrabhai (11), has started accompanying him for the last three years. They generally go to sugarcane fields in Surat district where they work as agricultural labour for about three months—January to March—every year. This is common in his village where either the entire family or at least two members from the majority of families migrate to sugarcane fields during harvesting season every year. Bhotubhai sends his sons and does not go himself because his sons are physically stronger. 'They are capable of doing the hard work required for sugarcane cutting,' he says. He stays back with his wife, Baijuben, to take care of his field and farm in the village.

He owns 1.5 acres of land and, till three years ago, used to get good produce from this. But due to drought during the last two years, the family, like many others, has been hit badly. Bhotubhai owned many cattle but two of the cows died and he had to sell the other two to pay debts. Now he owns only one buffalo. He is also forced to go to the neighbouring village in search of work because of the prevailing drought conditions. His own farming, however, still consumes the bulk of his time. Baijuben and both the sons help in farming activities whenever they are in the village. While Mahendrabhai is engaged in fishing most of the time, Jayendrabhai likes hunting in the forests. Fish and birds are part of their regular diet and help in survival even during adverse conditions. The brothers also help their mother in collecting *timur* leaves and other roots or fruits from the forest.

Both boys enjoy their life and except for sugarcane cutting, which is tough, they don't mind their responsibilities at all. Most of their friends from the same age group are involved in similar activities and, therefore, they are seldom alone. Both children were going to school till they started going to the sugarcane field. Bhotubhai feels it is important for children to know their environment, understand the forest, and learn the different aspects of farming rather than continue their studies. 'Educated people are sitting idle everywhere. Education has no use for us farmers,' he avers. Jayendrabhai agrees: 'I will be better prepared for my adulthood if I know more about cattle, forest and agriculture. I don't want to be like those who are educated but neither have any job nor do they know anything about farming'. Jayendrabhai's logic also stems from his love for the forest and the outdoors. He loves to hunt and roam around in the forest rather than be confined to the classroom and feels this is also true for all kids in his village. 'Even those children who are enrolled leave home for school, but don't really go to school. They keep playing by the riverside,' he reveals. The teachers, though regular, are generally not bothered about children's regular attendance. 'Teachers have no answer to the question about whether these children are going to get jobs after completing their education, and that is why they don't force us to send our children,' says Bhotubhai.

Seasonal migration has helped the tribal population to cope with severe food crises and also drought-like situations. However, this has rarely brought about any significant change in their basic lifestyle. The earnings are sufficient only for survival and even if there is a little extra, the tendency is to spend it on self-consumption. The families in Dangs district in Gujarat were reported to be spending on better food and brews for the period till the earnings from the sugarcane cutting last. Similar observations were reported from other villages as well. It is important to understand that for families living in a continued state of deprivation and recurrent food crises, it is natural to overspend on 'good' food and brews on days when it is possible. Moreover, the tribes are culturally more inclined to live in the 'present' rather than to think of the 'future'. Finally, there is no option available for any alternative investment in these places per se except at places where some NGOs have tried to build self-help groups or create other such opportunities (Box 5.11).

BOX 5.11: FAMILY MIGRATION FROM TRIBAL VILLAGES

Bharwa Munda is a drought-prone area and survival is often an issue. Seasonal migration to brick kilns in the neighbouring states of Andhra Pradesh and Madhya Pradesh started during the early 1990s. Over the years, some local labour contractors have established a network of brick kilns in neighbouring states, and they recruit labour in three-person units, the unit being know locally as a *patharia*. In most cases, this unit is made up of family members, including young children. They migrate in November after paddy harvesting and come back in June at the time of sowing. Each *patharia* is paid an advance of 4,000 to 5,000 rupees, generally used to buy grain and stored for consumption during the period between July and

October. Wage rates vary between 60 and 100 rupees for 1,000 bricks made and the difference between the advance and total wages is paid at the site. The wages they receive at the place of work are generally sufficient only for consumption and they rarely bring any savings. However, stored grains bought with the advance help to sustain them for the next 4 months. A few single migration cases also exist in the village. They also go to brick kilns but earn mainly through loading and not through brick-making. The extent of migration varies from year to year depending upon the crop; it increases during drought years and decreases if the crop has been good.

The pattern is similar at Mahal and Wakarya villages in the Dangs district of Gujarat, the extent of migration being higher in the former. While about 60 per cent of the total families migrate from Mahal, about 30-40 per cent of the families from Wakarya migrate to sugarcane fields for 3 to 6 months every year. The system operates through labour contractors; labour is hired in pairs or a unit of two persons known as a *koyta*. Children above 12 form part of the *koyta* and a group of about 25-30 *koytas* are commissioned together. Younger children also add to the income through the sale of sugarcane leaves in nearby markets. They are provided free bamboo huts and a family with one *koyta* and two children can earn 6,000 to 7,000 rupees at the end of the 6 month period.

The pattern of migration is slightly different in Palamu district. About 10-15 of the total 72 households in Khurakhurd village go to Rohtas and Sasaram, districts in central Bihar, for about 20-40 days thrice a year. During paddy and wheat harvesting, wages are a portion of the harvested grains which last for a number of months. Children also accompany their parents at the time of harvesting as they can add to the earnings by making bundles and collecting the grains that fall on the ground. Another five to six families go to Nainital in UP between November and June every year for sand mining. They are paid about 6 to 7 rupees per quintal of sand and one family manages to earn about 70 to 80 rupees a day. They make huts by the riverside and live there for about eight months. Another five to six families migrate to stone quarries in Haryana for the same period of eight months almost every year. Another 20-25 families also migrate to Rohtas district in Bihar for about four months during the rainy season, where they break stones and get paid on the basis of the number of lorries with broken stones. In all these cases, the children above 10 participate in work. Children 8-10-year-olds take care of younger siblings while the rest of the family is busy at work. The incidence of migration is low in Ukamand, though the pattern is similar except for the fact that a few individual males also migrate to Punjab and other places. Also, about 10 young boys in the age group of 8-12 years from Ukamand village work independently of their parents at hotels in nearby towns.

In contrast to the patterns seen above, the families in Maddur Colony in Karnataka do not migrate together in groups, nor does one entire household migrate at one point of time. While the male members go to Kerala plantations for almost the entire year, their families join them during peak season from January to April. Family migration is prevalent in about 50 per cent of the total households in the village. Most local families had cleared forest land for cultivation and the state government granted them ownership rights. However, most families sold their lands to big farmers from the neighbouring state, Kerala, at throwaway prices and became landless in the process. The village is surrounded by cashew plantation farms but almost no wage work is available within the village. Their dependence on migration to the Kerala plantations is quite high.

The Presence of NGOs and their Influence

Some villages have experienced the presence of non-governmental organizations (NGO) trying to influence the lives of the local population in some manner or the other. Three different NGOs working with the aim of developing literacy skills and micro finance activities were active in three villages (Chart 5.2). These organizations operate through local workers, to whom they provide training and support. They have succeeded in organizing women-based self-help groups that provide credit and promote self-employment opportunities. This is critical considering the high level of indebtedness among tribal populations. It is common for them to borrow during lean periods at exorbitant interest rates from local moneylenders and traders. Borrowing is also resorted to frequently to arrange resources for dowry or bride price, depending on which custom is more prevalent among which tribe, and for festivals and other rituals to be followed at the time of marriage or death. The SFGs in the three villages have been active and helped in reducing dependence on traders and moneylenders to some extent.

Chart 5.2: NGOs in Tribal Villages

Village	NGO Present	Areas of work
Mohul Bhatta, Koraput, Orissa	LEAD (Literacy Education and Agriculture Development)	Agriculture and literacy
Padheiguda, Koraput, Orissa	Sarvodaya	Literacy, micro finance
Khurakhurd, Palamu, Jharkhand	Sarvangeen Vikas Sansthan	Literacy, micro finance, empowerment
Maddur Colony Chamraj-nagar, Karnataka	VGKK (Vivekananda Girijana Kalyana Kendra)*	Education, empower-ment

NOTE: * The organization is located 100 km. away from the village but it works with the Soligas in many villages, including Maddur Colony.

SOURCE: Village Appraisal Reports.

The Soligas in Maddur Colony associate themselves with VGKK in Karnataka. A few Soliga children from Maddur Colony were also studying in a residential school being run by the organization. However, the other two tribes, the Jenukurubhas and the Bettukurubhas, did not identify themselves with this NGO. The presence of NGOs, therefore, was limited to very few villages and even within these villages, their reach and influence remained restricted to a few families. No example of an NGO significantly influencing the livelihood or attitudinal patterns among tribal populations was visible in any of the villages. Nonetheless, even small interventions and successes have made differences and it is important to take note of them.

Ashram Schools

In the context of the availability of and access to schools in tribal areas, ashram schools acquire significance. The concept of the ashram school is based on the Gandhian philosophy of self-reliance and the practice started with an experiment by Thakkar Bapa, a Gandhian, in Panchmahal district in Gujarat during pre-Independence days (Ananda, 1994). The Government of India has supported a centrally-sponsored scheme to establish ashram schools. Ashram schools are residential institutions built to serve tribal children from a cluster of villages by providing free boarding and lodging. The reasons behind the concept of the ashram school are many. First, the difficulty of establishing primary schools in small tribal habitations due to the rigidity of conventional norms. Second, to create a congenial atmosphere for teaching/learning as it is assumed that the tribal households do not provide such an environment. Third, the policy to develop the total personality of children by imparting vocational skills in order to help them get better occupational and employment opportunities (Sujatha, 2000). Ashram schools are present in or around the study villages in Jharkhand, Koraput, Nuapara, Dangs, Shravasti and Chamrajnagar districts, especially in tribal-dominated regions. However, the number is limited and very few children from the study villages were enrolled in ashram schools (2.7 per cent of the total enrolled children).

Ashram schools generally follow a rule of providing admission to children coming from at least a distance of 6 to 8 km, and if children from nearby villages are given admission, they are not provided with boarding. This is the reason why no child from the village was enrolled in the ashram schools located in the same village, Mahal in Dangs district (Gujarat) and Kathkuiyan Kalan in Shravasti district (UP). Of all the study villages, the highest number of children were in various ashram schools from Wakarya village in Dangs district. One reason is that the village had no local primary school till 1999.

The preference for ashram school was expressed by many parents in Jharkhand, Orissa and Gujarat. The reasons for this preference included 'free food, clothing, and boarding'. Unlike other places, the parents at Wakarya also mentioned that education imparted in an Ashram school is more relevant to their lives. Village reports suggest that the curriculum of the ashram schools include agriculture and other life-skills in addition to general subjects only in Gujarat. No such practices were visible in ashram schools visited elsewhere, i.e. Orissa, UP or Karnataka (Box 5.12). The parents at Wakarya as well as Bharwa Munda expressed that the fact that since children stay there, their education does not act as a constraint on seasonal migration. However, with very limited seats it is not easy to get admission in ashram schools, and people complained of interference and nepotism by influential persons in getting admission.

BOX 5.12: ASHRAM SCHOOL IN MADDUR COLONY, CHAMRAJNAGAR, KARNATAKA

The ashram school being run by the Social Welfare Department in Maddur Colony presents a different kind of case. Although it is an ashram school, it is not residential in nature. This is the only school available in the village and all the children in it are from the same village. The children are served meals three times a day and also get free clothes, textbooks and stationery from the school. There are two rooms of which one is being used by the headmaster (HM) as his personal residence. The HM frequently visits the taluka headquarter, Gundalpet, located at a distance of about 22 km., and the other teacher is often alone in teaching all the children. He is also not very regular and, according to people, the school does not open for more than three days in a week. Even when it opens, all the time goes in serving meals and hardly any teaching takes place. The HM is also reported to use foul language against tribal children. However, whenever the school opens, the attendance is good because of the meals being served.

ENCOURAGING AND DEPRESSING FACTORS AND PROCESSES

Formal education and schooling in its present shape and form are still not a very familiar concept for tribal populations in many parts of the country. The presence of an external force plays an important role in raising their interest in education and commitment to the schooling of children. Experience indicates that the external force can be in many forms; in some places it is an NGO working with the community for many years, elsewhere it is a motivated teacher, and at other places it is just close contact with the outside world. These external forces help in creating a need for schooling among parents. The level of interest in schooling is also higher at places, at times without any external force at work, where tribal families are landless and live in exploitative conditions. Their situation here is akin to that of Dalits, and they view education as one of the means of hope for changing their situation. However, the usual hopelessness about a child's future and weak employment linkages act as impediments in translating this interest into a stronger commitment.

The presence of a school within a habitation (including hamlets and *tolas/purbas*) is critical to all educationally backward social groups, at the bottom end of the socio-economic structure for ages. However, the presence of a school within the hamlet, though essential, does not necessarily ensure enrolment in tribal areas. The formal school approach and the curriculum with its rigidities also clash with the tribal ethos and culture. Many children who discontinued schooling stated that they did not like the emphasis on discipline and fixed routines in school. The school calendar also seldom takes note of the agricultural and forest produce-collection seasons when involvement of children in certain activities is unavoidable. Different tribes observe different festivals, generally celebrated for many days together, and no child attends school during the period. This is the case during Chaitl

Navratri in Sidhi villages, during Naukhai in Nuapara villages, during Chait in Koraput villages, and during Sarhul in Palamu villages. These festivals are an intrinsic part of socio-cultural identity and take precedence over all other needs. Tribal parents also often questioned the role of schooling in equipping children to manage their own lives. In areas where the tribal populations largely own small landholdings, and cultivation is their main occupation, parents raised the issue of relevance in relation to the need for including information related to sustainable agricultural practices and cattle keeping in the school curriculum. School functioning is also not very regular and reliable in most tribal areas. There are areas where tribal parents have shown interest by enrolling their children but feel disillusioned because of the schools' irregular functioning.

As discussed earlier, an active and motivated teacher helps to overcome some of the above-mentioned school-related problems. There is evidence of a clear upsurge in enrolment and attendance patterns in schools triggered by the work of committed teachers. However, this happens only when the teacher interacts closely with the parents and develops a social relationship with them. The serving of cooked meals also helps in raising enrolment. The hamlets in Orissa villages and the Maddur Colony in Karnataka provide such examples. But, as the evidence clearly indicates, even regular schools and active teachers do not lead to high participation in areas where the children's involvement in livelihood-related work responsibilities is high. The very nature of livelihood options is such that any adjustment is not easy (Box 5.13).

BOX 5.13: THERE ARE MANY MORE SITAUAS AND SONUS

Tall, dark and acutely anaemic, Sitaua (35) lives in Naudhiya village of Sidhi district (MP) with her husband Sukhlal (40), daughter Sonu (12) and sons Nandlal (10) and Brijlal (5). She works as an agricultural wage worker during the season and in landlords' houses during lean periods. Sukhram goes to Sidhi everyday in search of work. He works from 8 in the morning to 8 at night and earns about Rs. 25-30 in a day. Out of this, he spends about Rs. 20 on essentials and the rest on Sitaua's medicines. Though he himself had jaundice a few months ago and was advised complete rest, he could not take any. The family's financial situation worsened after their eldest son, Ravindra (15), died in a road accident. He was working in Sidhi in a shop for a monthly sum of Rs. 600 which was a big support for the family. They built their two rooms mainly from his earnings. The family belongs to the Kol tribe and lives in a Kol *basti* situated on a hill outside the main village. Kols were originally brought here by Thakur landlords who generally made them live on small pieces of land adjacent to their own houses. This meant working as attached labour and providing services for all kinds of sundry work on demand to that family. Though this arrangement continued for years, it was always resented by Kols, and about five years ago many of them shifted *en masse* to government land on the outskirts of the village. However, this has increased their hardships. For instance, there are only two handpumps for about 60 families and everyday it takes hours before Sonu manages to fill enough water for the day. Still, they 'prefer this independent status to that attached status'.

Sonu gets up at five in the morning and begins her day by cleaning the house. And then begin various rounds of water collection. She is used to this task and manages to do her cooking in between. She also manages to eat and feed her younger brothers in between her various rounds. Her parents leave home early for their work. After finishing all the morning chores, Sonu and her brothers run to their school. But on many occasions, she has to come back home after playing with her friends as the teacher does not come regularly. Even when he does, he generally does not stay for more than two hours. 'I keep thinking, how come hours are very long when we go for wage work and very short when children go to school?' asks Sitaua, who always thinks it is 11:00 a.m., even if children come back home at 9:00 a.m.

There was no school in the Kol *basti* initially. The village school was situated at a distance of 2-3 km and it was difficult to send small children there. When the EGS programme was launched in the state, the Kols also put in an application and were very happy when a centre was opened within their habitation. They saw this as another indicator of their independence from the top landlords. But there was no educated person within the community and, therefore, they proposed Devi Singh from the main village as their teacher. In fact, the teacher Devi Singh himself was very active in making the proposal for the EGS as this meant an easy source of employment within the village.

Both Sitaua and Sukhram want to educate their children. They say 'Education helps in understanding our environment better. Our eldest son was a Class V pass and he could take care of himself well. He was never cheated.' Sukhram is also aware of the fact that there are special provisions for ST children and once educated, his sons can get jobs. They want Sonu to be educated so that she becomes a good mother. But they, especially Sitaua, feel very frustrated by the school's irregularity. 'Although the cereal that children get in school is important, we want to send our children even if it is not given. But now slowly children have started going only on days when cereal is distributed. What to do? The school is never open,' she complains. She has confronted Devi Singh on this issue several times, but to no avail as 'he does not say anything but does not come regularly either', she says dourly. She cannot confront him beyond a point as he belongs to the powerful Chauhan community.

The tribal economy has been based on cooperation and this is visible not only at the level of the community but also at the level of the family. The entire family works together to earn or manage a living and children are integral to survival efforts. The practice of involving children in cultivation, cattle grazing, and forest produce collection has now been extended to the processing of forest produce for sale and participation in family-based wage labour. Although tribal families are not the only ones to be engaged in family-based labour activities, the incidence is much higher among them as compared to other groups. It is also obvious from the fact that employers from faraway places prefer to hire these families through local agents. The employers find family-based labour cheaper compared to individual labourers, and tribal families with their tradition of the entire family working as a unit are more suited to this. This phenomenon adversely affects both enrolment and regularity in schools (Chart 5.3).

The availability of residential ashram schools has helped in increasing the participation rates in areas from where seasonal family migration is

Chart 5.3: Categorization of Villages in Terms of the School Participation Status of ST Children

Category	Names of the Village	Certain Specific Features
1. Low enrolment, low regularity (2 villages)	Khurakhurd (Jharkhand), Mulasar (Orissa)	Khurakhurd—only ST, high migration (single & family), school within village, close toes with nearby town. Mulasar—mixed village, school within village but many habitations remain cut off, little migration but tradition of engaging children in own and wage work prevalent. Moderate dependence on forest in both villages.
2. Medium enrolment, low regularity (2 villages)	Barambaba (MP), Kathkuiyan Kala (UP)	Both ST dominated villages, mainly small cultivators, School within village and teacher belonging to the same Tribe present. Very incidence of engaging children in own work like cattle grazing, agricultural work, fishing, etc. High dependence on forest in Barambaba.
3. High enrolment, low regularity (1 village)	Naudhiya (MP)	Mixed village, Kols (ST) entirely landless, far from forest, high dependence on local UCH landlords and prevalence of attached labour system in the past, school within habitation but irregular and disinterested teacher.
4. Low enrolment, medium regularity (2 villages)	Bharwa Munda, Mohul Bhatta (Orissa)	High ST population, small cultivators, dependence on forest moderate to high, School within village but not easily accessible from all hamlets at Mohul Bhatta, Active VEC and regular school at Bharwa Munda, Very high family migration (Brick kilns) from Bharwa Munda.
5. Medium Enrolment, medium regularity (2 villages)	Mahal (Gujarat), Jogini (MP)	Mahal—only ST, high migration in pairs/ families, single crop rainfed agriculture, High dependence of forest, far from town; Jogini—low ST population, low dependence on forest, dependence on wage work/own cultivation; close to town, School within village (both villages)
6. High enrolment, medium regularity (1 village)	Kursa (MP)	High ST population, landless, wage-dependent Kols, heavy dependence on local landlords, far from town, no migration, moderate dependence on forest, school within habitation but irregular. Dalits asserting themselves but the same not so much visible among Kols.
7. Low enrolment, high regularity (2 villages)	Ukamand (Jharkhand), Karandi (Maharashtra)	Ukamand—very high ST population, small cultivators, high dependence on forest, high migration (single, in pairs, and family), school within habitation but not accessible to all habitations; Karandi—very low ST

			population, landless, mainly surviving on wage work, no dependence on forest, school within village.
8	Medium enrolment, high regularity (3 villages)	Maddur Colony (Karnataka), Fadheiguda, Cherichuan (Orissa)	All or very high ST population, dependence on forest high, own cultivation common, no migration (except Maddur Colony where the migration is high), school within habitation, accessible from all hamlets, cooked meals served in schools in all these villages
9	High enrolment, high regularity (3 villages)	Wakarya (Gujarat), Kermili, Ratapalli (Orissa)	Kermili—developed, big village, high ST population, and the STs well represented in panchayats, relatively large sizes of land and higher level of literacy, school regular and teacher from the same community; Wakarya—high ST population, work in neighbouring areas common, school recently opened but practice of sending children to Ashram schools prevalent. Ratapalli—developed, big village, mixed population, very small ST population, school regular, children from all communities generally go to school regularly

NOTES: 1. High enrolment = 70 per cent and above, medium enrolment = 50 to 69 per cent, low enrolment = below 50 per cent.
2. High regularity = 80 per cent and above, medium regularity = 50 to 79 per cent, low regularity = below 50 per cent.

common, e.g. Bharwa Munda (Orissa) and Wakarya (Gujarat). Although the rate of enrolment was low at Bharwa Munda, five out of six enrolled children were enrolled in an ashram school. At Wakarya as well, till two years ago, there was no local school and all enrolled children were going to ashram schools. Even now, about one-fourth of school-going children are enrolled in ashram schools. The demand for ashram schools was visible at many places, especially because it did not involve any direct cost and the parents become free from child care responsibilities. However, this demand was also visible mainly among those parents with some exposure to education and the outside world. School participation rates are higher in well-connected and developed areas where better employment avenues are available. Also, as seen in the beginning, a higher level of literacy in the village has a positive impact on school participation.

Finally, it can be said that the status of school participation among tribal children needs to be understood with reference to their traditions and cultural identities, and their continuous fight to survive in an alien system which does not always recognize their rights and respect their practices. The common practice of involving children in livelihood strategies is guided by the needs of survival, tradition and the low perceived value of schooling. Formal and rigid school processes coupled with teachers' attitudes add to divides that already exist. The relevance of school education assumes greater significance for tribal populations as the skills learnt in formal schools rarely contribute to their endeavours to survive and cope. The tradition of involving children in livelihood breaks down only with sustained efforts, often by external forces, to build a commitment to schooling. This is facilitated, on the one hand, by the economic or development processes that help in providing basic economic security, and, on the other, by the availability of a functional school. It is also important for the school to break its traditional ways of functioning and reach out to families and children by becoming institutions to which they feel they belong.

NOTES

1. Refer to Nambissan (2000) for a detailed discussion on the issue of language and schooling of tribal children.
2. Refer to GOI (1988); *Report of the Commissioner of the Scheduled Castes and the Scheduled Tribes: Twenty-Eighth Report* (*1986-87*) for details on access to forests and denial of basic rights to the tribal population. In the context of Minor Forest Produce (MFP), the state has a practice of levying royalties, on which the report says, 'The State has no right to levy royalty on a produce over which the tribal people had been given a right even though the circumstances may have changed and the produce may have become more valuable because of its diverse use and the extension of market economy in the tribal area. This is the part of the development process. If the tribal people are facing the backlash of development, denying them the benefits of the changing situation on technical grounds will be unfair.'

6. Surmounting Stalemates: Muslims and Schooling

BACKGROUND

According to Census Report 2001 Muslims constitute more than 12 per cent of India's population. The states of Assam, Uttar Pradesh, West Bengal, and Bihar have a higher proportion of Muslims than the country-wide average. Bihar, West Bengal, and Uttar Pradesh account for more than half the Muslim population in India. However, Muslims form a significant proportion of the population in many other states in the western and southern parts. Muslims generally lag behind other communities in most parts of the country both socially and economically. Disaggregated data on socio-economic and educational development among Muslims are not easy to come by.[1] The Census of India does not compile or publish data for Muslims as a category. Nevertheless, some sample surveys done in the last two decades provide useful comparative data on Muslims.[2]

The majority of Muslim households in rural areas are marginal agriculturalists, wage earners, and petty craftsmen or traders. Traditionally, they survived more on skill-based craftsmanship and, except for a few households in certain areas, did not possess much land. Today, with small landholdings and dwindling markets for their products, Muslims are economically worse off than most other communities. The NCAER (1999) has recorded lower household and per capita incomes among Muslim households compared to those belonging to other religions. Muslim representation in professional educational institutions and white-collar jobs has been very low. The growth of the middle class among Muslims has been much slower than in other religious communities.

Muslims are also educationally one of the most backward communities. They have apparently not taken to secular education in a big way even in the 1990s when there has been considerable expansion of school facilities and significant increases in enrolment. The literacy rate for Muslims is notably lower than that for Hindus and the differential becomes much wider when we look at the proportion of students completing the upper primary and secondary levels of schooling. The literacy rate for Muslims is significantly higher than those for the SCs and STs in the country as a whole, but even this does not hold true for states with a high concentration of Muslims. In West Bengal and UP, however, the literacy rates among Muslims are lower than the rates for the SCs (NCAER, 1999).

There are significant variations in the educational as well as economic status of Muslims across different states. In the southern states of Karnataka and Kerala, Muslims are much better off than in other parts of the country, rating better in some Human Development Indicators than other communities (NCAER, 1999). Muslims are not a monolithic entity with a common outlook, self-perception, and disposition towards economic, social, and educational development. In fact, the Muslim community consists of socially stratified groups and significant class distinctions based on disparities in income.

Social stratification and 'caste characteristics' among Muslims are complex, making it difficult to offer context-neutral generalizations. Although a clear caste identity exists among Muslims,[3] there has been very little sociological work on social stratification among Muslims. A set of micro studies on social stratification among Muslims in several parts of the country shows a varied picture in different regions but confirms the existence of largely endogamous, hierarchically ordered groups with some occupational specialization. However, inequalities of status do not seem to be because of any religious or ideological reasons or considerations of ritual purity and pollution, unlike the Hindu caste system. The social stratification of Muslim groups is based variously on descent (the upper most groups tracing their descent to Arab tribes), the original Hindu caste groups from which they were converted, occupation, etc.

While sociological work among Muslim communities has been scarce, there has been intense debate about the reasons for the continued socio-economic backwardness of Muslims. At one end is the viewpoint that Muslims are basically traditional and anti-modern in their outlook, inward-looking, and largely under the influence of religion and religious leaders. At the other end, a strong viewpoint that social, economic, and political processes in the past five decades have involved a degree of exclusion, if not the marginalization of Muslims. However, it is clear that political leadership, especially Muslim leadership, has continued to pursue issues of a communitarian nature, not recognizing that all Muslims may not be facing the same problems and a somewhat more differentiated strategy is necessary for dealing with problems that different sections or strata of Muslims face (Imtiaz Ahmed, 2001).

In this chapter, we attempt to understand schooling participation patterns among Muslim children in various contexts, trying to comprehend the reasons for low participation and also the factors that cause it. However, the analysis has one severe limitation. This is primarily based on the understanding drawn from five villages located in three states, Assam, Bihar, and Uttar Pradesh only, and all these villages happen to be Muslim-majority villages. The five study villages cannot be taken to represent all types of situations as Muslim households constituted at least 60 per cent of the total households in these villages. This implies that we will not be able to analyse contexts where Muslims are a minority, a critical aspect in understanding schooling-related decisions among them in India.

CERTAIN BASIC FEATURES OF THE MUSLIM STUDY VILLAGES

None of the five villages are well provided for in terms of road, transport, health and other infrastructural facilities (they are either in the C or D category of the infrastructural index, see Appendix, Table 2). The lack of facilities reflects a kind of powerlessness accompanying social backwardness and cultural isolation among Muslims, resulting in less investment in the areas where they are in a majority. In fact, all SC, ST, and Muslim-majority areas are not well developed unless they are also inhabited by landlords from other dominant social groups who could be few in number but influential in terms of the ownership of resources. Lack of access to facilities, as seen in previous chapters, affects the quality of lives adversely and adds to the general hardships faced by poor people belonging to any group.

Another important feature of these villages is a high rate of migration. While in the three villages in Bihar and UP the rate of single male migration is quite high, both villages in Assam have reported both single and family migration, this being higher in Tiapara as compared to Jhakuapara (Table 6.1). Single male migration from villages in Bihar follows a similar pattern to that seen for SCs in these areas. People go to nearby towns for casual work in the non-agricultural sector and to Punjab, Haryana, and Delhi for work in agriculture as well as other sectors. Family migration to brick kilns

Table 6.1: Selected Village Characteristics

S. No.	Name of village	Grade for infra facilities	Rate and type of migration	% pop. Muslim	Social group within Muslims*	Other social groups
1.	Jhakuapara (Dhubri, Assam)	C	Moderate (Single male + family)	100	Upper caste	2 more mixed habitations (OBC)
2.	Tiapara (Dhubri, Assam)	C	High (Single male + family)	100	Upper caste	No other group.
3.	Mudballa (Araria, Bihar)	C	High (Single male)	61	Lower caste**	SC (Musahars) constitute 32 %
4.	Kismat Khabaspur (Araria, Bihar)	D	High (Single male)	73	Upper and lower caste	UCH and OBCs constitute 27 %
5.	Masalia Kalan (Shravasti, UP)	D	High (Single male)	80	Lower caste**	SCs and OBCs constitute 20 %

NOTES: * This is based on the distribution seen for the households surveyed.
Lower caste Muslims [illegible] more than 85 per cent of the sample households.

SOURCE: Village Appraisal Reports, Household Survey.

is common from Tiapara in Dhubri district in Assam. In Jhakuapara, the availability of agricultural wage work is somewhat higher due to the cultivation of a special variety of paddy that can be grown twice a year.

School Participation Patterns: Intra-group and Intra-village Differences

The overall enrolment rate of Muslim children (51.6 per cent) is the lowest among all social groups (SC-66.9 per cent, ST-63.5 per cent). Also, only about 38 per cent of the enrolled children are reported to be regular. This proportion is much smaller than that observed for Dalit and ST children. In all, less than one-fifth (19.3 per cent) of Muslim children attend school regularly. A very large proportion of Muslim children (almost 25 per cent) are reported as attending school only occasionally. Including this group of children, 'virtual' drop-outs, the drop-out rate for Muslim children is also the highest among all social groups.

An important aspect of Muslim children's education is that about 18 per cent of them attend *maqtabs*/madrasas and not formal schools. This does not include a small proportion of children who attend both *maqtabs* (which run for a couple of hours in the morning and evening) and a regular school or children enrolled in a regular school, but actually attending *maqtabs* more regularly. Another notable point is that despite a fair proportion of Muslim children going to madrasas, the proportion of never-enrolled, not even in a madrasa, is as high as 22.8 per cent. This is as high a proportion for never-enrolled as seen for Dalits, and higher than that for all other social groups including STs. Madrasa-going children form about 38 per cent of the total out-of-school Muslim children. If those who go to *maqtabs* are treated as part of never-enrolled children, they cover about 44 per cent of the total never-enrolled children and together they constitute about 41 per cent of total Muslim children.[4]

Intra-group Differences

Large differences exist in enrolment rates for Muslim children in these five villages. However, these differences narrow significantly if one takes patterns of regular school attendance into account. However, the differences remain significantly high as only about 8 per cent of Muslim children attend school regularly in Masaha Kalan (UP) as compared to about 34 per cent in Jhakuapara (Assam). There is not much difference between the remaining four villages. The level of enrolment is generally higher in Assamese villages though the incidence of irregularity is as high as, if not higher than villages in UP and Bihar.

A significant proportion of out-of-school children go to *maqtabs* in all villages except at Jhakuapara, where there is no *maqtab* located within the

Table 6.2 (a): Schooling Participation Patterns of Muslim Children (per cent)

Village	Enrolment	Regular among enrolled	Out of school	% of out-of-school going to madrasa	Regularly going among total children
Mudballa (Araria, Bihar)	12.1	75.0	87.9	65.5	9.8
Khabaspur (Araria, Bihar)	40.0	34.6	60.0	31.8	13.7
Masaha Kalan (Shravasti, UP)	57.7	13.3	42.3	50.0	7.7
Jhakuapara (Dhubri, Assam)	80.9	41.9	19.1	0.0	33.9
Tiapara (Dhubri, Assam)	72.5	12.5	27.5	47.0	9.3

Table 6.2 (b): Schooling Participation Patterns of Muslim Children (per cent) (upper and lower caste)

Category	Enrolled		Drop-out		Never-enrolled		Going to madrasa	
	Boys	Girls	Boys	Girls	Boys	Girls	Boys	Girls
UCM	71.4	68.5	10.7	11.1	8.9	11.1	8.9	9.3
LCM	38.7	31.4	8.6	2.0	30.1	37.3	22.6	29.4
Total	51.0	50.5	9.5	6.7	22.1	23.8	17.4	19.4

Table 6.2 (c): Schooling Participation Patterns of Muslim and Other Children (per cent)

Village	Category	Enrolled	Drop-out	Never-enrolled	Going to madrasa
Mudballa (Bihar)	Others (SC)	36.8	–	57.9	5.3
	Muslim (LCM)	12.1	–	30.3	57.6
Masaha Kalan (UP)	Others (SC)	50.0	–	50.0	–
	Muslim (LCM)	57.7	3.8	19.2	23.0
Jhakuapara (Assam)	Others (OBC)	95.6	2.9	1.5	–
	Muslim (UCM)	80.9	12.4	9.0	–

NOTE: The brackets in the column II shows the dominant social group in the population in the respective categories.

SOURCE: Household Survey.

village. It is important to add that irregularity is reported to be as high in madrasas as in schools in these villages. Also significant is the fact that there are marked differences in the enrolment patterns of lower and upper caste Muslim children, it being significantly higher for the latter. The proportion of never-enrolled and those going to *maqtabs* are much higher for lower caste groups. Table 3.22 shows that 49.1 per cent of all upper caste as against only about 24 per cent of all lower caste Muslim households send all their children to school. The proportion of households not sending any child to school is the highest at 47.3 per cent for lower caste and the lowest for upper caste Muslim households (14.5 per cent) from among all social groups. The practice of sending one child to a government school and the other to a madrasa is also common in many lower caste Muslim families. However, it is important to mention that large proportions of sample households in Bihar and UP villages belonged to the lower caste, whereas all belonged to the upper caste in the Assamese villages.

INTRA-VILLAGE DIFFERENCES

A comparison between Muslim children and children of other groups in the 3 villages with a mixed population [Table 6.2 (c)] shows that while enrolment rates are lower for Muslim children in one Bihar village (Araria) and one village in Assam (Dhubri), it is similar to the SCs in the UP village. In both Dhubri and Araria, the difference in enrolment rates between Muslim and Dalit children is almost entirely on account of the proportion of children going to *maqtabs*/madrasas.

PROFILE OF MUSLIM HOUSEHOLDS

We have seen earlier that certain livelihood patterns and the literacy status of households have crucial linkages with schooling participation patterns among children. The profile of Muslim households based on selected indicators confirms their poor status. The proportion of LBPL among the lower caste Muslims at 40.0 per cent is higher than that among Dalits and STs. This proportion at 32.7 per cent is not very low for upper caste Muslims as well. In fact, the extent of landlessness as well as the incidence of dependence on wage work is higher for upper caste Muslims as compared to lower caste Muslims. About 42 per cent of lower caste and 49 per cent of upper caste Muslim families are landless. Both parents are illiterate in 80 per cent of lower caste Muslim households, the proportion being the highest among all social groups. Unlike landownership and dependence on wage work, there exist significant differences between lower and upper caste Muslims in terms of literacy levels and education. Lower caste Muslims are quite close to and, at times, worse than Dalits in terms of literacy status (see Table 4.2).

Since all the surveyed households in Assam belonged to the upper castes and a large proportion in Bihar and UP to lower caste Muslims, it is likely that there are some differences between the status of the two groups, on account of the different contexts in Assam, Bihar and UP. Socio-cultural factors are similar in Bihar and UP, and different in Assam (Table 6.3). In Assam, most 'original' Muslim residents of the state (as distinguished from later migrants from East Bengal/Bangladesh) are upper caste, and well integrated into the socio-cultural ethos of the state. However, there are notable differences between upper and lower caste Muslims that cannot be attributed entirely to differences in a cultural context. Also important is the fact that despite differences between upper and lower caste Muslims, even upper caste Muslims are not comparable to upper caste Hindus, either in

Table 6.3: Landownership, Literacy, and Schooling among Muslim Households

(in per cent)

Village	% landless	% pop. having less than 1 acre	% male illiteracy	% female illiteracy	% male schooled	% female schooled
Mudballa (Araria, Bihar)	64	70.0	44.0	68.0	41.6	4.3
Khabaspur (Araria, Bihar)	56	69.5	37.3	86.3	45.8	2.2
Masaha Kalan (Shravasti, UP)	11	57.0	84.6	96.5	2.56	4.5
Jhakuapara (Dhubri, Assam)	48	76.0	20.9	58.8	46.5	17.6
Tiapara (Dhubri, Assam)	52	72.0	36.8	55.2	26.3	18.4

SOURCE: Household Survey.

terms of education or economic indicators (see Table 4.2). They can, at best, be placed close to the OBCs, also in no way equal to upper caste Hindus (Box 6.1).

BOX 6.1: NO COOKED MEAL FROM MUSLIM LANDLORDS

Mudballa is a village in Araria district in Bihar. Muslims constitute about 60 per cent of the total population and Dalits about 30 per cent. While almost all Dalit families are poor, Muslims comprise both rich and poor. Some Muslim families are big landlords while others are very poor landless households depending entirely on wage work and sharecropping. Dalits complained of facing discrimination at the hands of Muslim landlords in getting land for cultivation on a sharecropping basis. They also made it clear that they do not accept cooked meals from Muslim landlords as part of the wages, otherwise a common practice in that area. Instead, they take dry cereals. Poor Muslim households which generally get preference in getting work or land for sharecropping from Muslim landlords, face a lot of hardships during lean agricultural seasons. The condition is especially bad during the rains. While Dalit families survive on fishing during this period, there is no such option available to Muslim families. Families whose members migrate are able to manage, but for the remaining households there is no alternative but to borrow money to feed their families.

LIVELIHOOD CHOICES AMONG MUSLIM HOUSEHOLDS

In general, the state of poor Muslim families in these villages is similar to those of poor families from any other social group. Poor Muslim families are mostly landless in four out of five villages and depend almost exclusively on casual wage labour earnings or share cropping. Sharecropping is common in villages in Bihar and UP. These three villages also have high disparities in economic levels among Muslim households. The poorest households are either landless or have very small uneconomic landholdings. Cultivation on very small landholdings is hardly remunerative especially in the absence of the required investment. About 10 per cent of Muslim households also engage in trade and petty businesses like tailoring, etc.

At least one adult male from a significant proportion of households (50-80 per cent) migrates to distant places for work, remaining away almost throughout the year. The economic situation of such households is improving, i.e. they are at least able to survive without facing a food crisis. Those with very small landholdings also face economic insecurity due to low agricultural productivity and the uncertainty of rains. The incidence of debt is also very high. Owing to the non-availability of good public health care facilities, most households have to incur considerable expenditure for the treatment of even routine illnesses (Box 6.2).

Poverty, deprivation, and vulnerability in individual households affect the schooling participation of Muslim children in the same manner as they do any other group. The difficult livelihood situation—poor agriculture, low agricultural wage rates, non-availability of agricultural work during lean seasons, a dependence on casual wage work, and a high incidence of long-duration migration—lead to an all-consuming concern to earn enough for basic needs among the poor and the extremely poor households of these villages. Households where 1-2 adult male members are regularly away to distant places are in a somewhat better economic position. But the absence of pressure from the father who is away and the additional burden of work

BOX 6.2: MONIUL'S LIFE IS NO DIFFERENT

Moniul (13) began working at the age of 10, as a labourer for a particular family when his father, Shamsuddin, started getting acute chest pains frequently and needed money for treatment. By making Moniul work for an annual wage of 2,000 rupees in a landlord's house, he managed to get some advance, which he used for his treatment. Due to illness, Shamsuddin can no longer work as hard as he used to, and therefore, Moniul's earnings are a great help in running the household. Moniul was enrolled in Class V when he had to discontinue school.

Due to some family altercations, Shamsuddin has left his own ancestral village and settled down in the neighbouring village where he does not have any land or other assets. He takes small pieces of land (about 1 to 2 acres) from local landlords on a sharecropping basis and produces paddy or jute. He and his wife also work as casual wage workers in agricultural seasons. During lean periods, he goes to nearby towns in search of non-agricultural labour. However, with his illness, he is not able to go to work all the time.

Shamsuddin has four more children—two daughters and two sons. Samida (9), the second child, is enrolled in Class III and likes to go to school. But she has loads of household responsibilities—cleaning the utensils, sweeping the entire house, helping her mother in cooking, taking care of three younger siblings, and so on. She misses school quite frequently. Her younger brother, Ainul (6), often accompanies Samida to school though Samida avoids taking him there as it affects her freedom. Shamsuddin and his wife, Malina Biwi, feel that though education is important, it would perhaps not be possible for them to educate their children. 'Economic hardship forced us to withdraw Moniul and let us see how far Samida continues', says Shamsuddin. The present's uncertainty also makes them unsure about their children's futures. 'I don't know what their futures are going to be,' he says.

on the woman and children of such households for cattle grazing and own farm work, or even wage work, adversely affect the regular participation of children in schools. The high level of irregularity seen among Muslim children is explained to a large extent by the high levels of migration among their parents.

Also, the large-scale migration of adult males to urban areas has made this a desirable, even glamorous, 'objective' among boys between 10-12 years. Children start preparing themselves for going to urban areas once they are 14-15, and hence this adversely impacts on their interest in continuing their education. None of the jobs undertaken by adult migrants require them to be educated. The hope of getting into jobs that require education is even bleaker among poor Muslim parents. Very low representation of Muslims in white collar jobs adds to the much-prevalent belief among the poor that formal education does not have much value for those who do not have the means to complete higher education and access to those who are powerful and control resources (Box 6.3).

BOX 6.3: LIFE IS GOING TO BE THE SAME, WHY EDUCATE THEM?

Dukhan Mansuri 52 years old, has eight children, four daughters and three sons. None of Dukhan's children has ever been to school. All of them are illiterate like their parents. The eldest son, Allauddin (29), is married and lives separately. The two eldest daughters, Marron (24) and Tazamia (22), were both married when they were about 12 years old. The second son, Salauddin (20), lives in Delhi and comes home only for 2-3 months every year. He works there as a rickshaw puller. He was married about three years ago to a 12-year-old girl from the same village, Kismat Khabaspur in Araria district of Bihar. Salauddin has been living in Delhi for several years and now does not send more than Rs. 1,000-2,000 every year to his father. The next son, Nuruddin (15), has also been working at a hotel in Delhi for the last five years, i.e. since the age of 10. Nuruddin was married at the age of 10 to a 5-year-old girl, Rabina, about five years ago. Though Dukhan had sent Nuruddin to Delhi expecting some financial contribution, the son does not keep in regular touch and does not send any money to his father.

The third son, Murtaza (12), lives in the village itself and takes the only cow that the family owns for grazing. He was married about three years ago, at the age of 9, to a 5-year-old girl. Murtaza still does not understand the meaning of marriage and is not aware of the fact that he already has a wife. He, like his brothers, wants to go to Delhi and earn money so that he too can have better clothes and shoes. He does not want to study; he has never even gone to a madrasa. Murtaza has two younger sisters, Momina (8) and Kausar (6). Momina has already started helping her mother in household chores and in taking care of Kausar.

Dukhan has many occupations—agricultural wage worker, cultivator, and small trader. He gets bangles, nail paint, *bindis*, etc., from a nearby town and his wife, Sakina, sells them in the village by going to people's houses. They manage to earn about Rs. 30 to 50 everyday. The couple managed to save about Rs. 15,000 through different means and have lent it against a mortgage of 2 acres of land. They cultivate this land and don't need to share the produce. The borrower does not pay them any interest and can take his land back by paying the principal amount of the loan. The family, therefore, manages to have enough for a basic living.

Dukhan and Sakina did not send their children to school because 'there is no use of education in their life. The boys need to learn to earn—earn through different kinds of wage work. For this, education is not required', says Dukhan. He feels that there is no other future for his boys other than leading a life similar to his own and he does not see education as having any role in that. For the girls, it is important to get married and go to their 'own' home. Parents hardly have any role other than to get them married, and, therefore, 'education has no meaning for them either'. Seeing other children of the village, Sakina at times desires to send her youngest son, Murtaza, to school, but feels he is too old to start now. She, too, does not see any value in educating daughters. 'What have we to do with them'? They have to go to their 'own homes'.

FUNCTIONING OF SCHOOLS

The government primary schools in all these five villages function irregularly, the difference being only of degree. Inadequate infrastructure characterizes them all, except the one in Mudballa in Araria district. Teachers are irregular at all these schools, more so at Tiapara in Assam and Khabaspur in Bihar. The PTRs are low because of low attendance and, in fact, all these schools function as single-teacher schools where all classes are held together. This happens even if more than one teacher is in position because only one teacher is present on most days. In the three villages in Bihar and UP, only 15-30 per cent of those enrolled were actually present in the classrooms on the days of the visits. The ratio of attendance was in the range of 50-60 per cent in the Assamese villages (Table 6.4).

The villagers of Khabaspur complained that the teachers are totally disinterested and the school remains closed very frequently (Box 6.4). A similar complaint is made by the villagers of Masaha Kalan in UP and Tiapara in Assam. In the Mudballa school, the head teacher takes no interest in the functioning of the school and takes greater interest in the *maqtabs* that are run within the primary school building. People also have a poor perception of the quality of teaching/learning in these schools. The unreliability of school functioning and the perception that little 'teaching-

Table 6.4: Schools in Muslim Villages

Village	Infrastructure rating	Attendance as % of enrolment	Classes held together	PTR	Enrolment share (%)		People's perception
					Boys	Girls	
Mudballa	Average	30	I to V	30	66.7	33.3	irregular
Khabaspur	Very inadequate	28	I to V	47	80.8	19.2	irregular
Masaha Kalan	Inadequate	14	I to V	167	65.9	34.1	irregular
Jhakuapara	Inadequate	NA	I to IV	NA	58	42	irregular
Tiapara	Very inadequate	NA	I to IV	NA	55	45	irregular

NOTE: NA: Not Available.

SOURCE: School Survey and Focus Group Discussions.

BOX 6.4: SCHOOL IS HARDLY FUNCTIONAL: WHERE DO WE SEND THEM?

Mohammad Naseem and Biwi Zahani send their son, Tanveer (12), and daughter, Yasmeen (8), to a *maktab* for religious education. The other two children, one son and one daughter, are presently too young at 4 and 2 respectively. Naseem works in a nursery in the neighbouring town on a monthly wage and hence does not generally face seasonal crises as is common in his village, Mudballa (Araria, Bihar). They also own 2 *bighas* of land and hence manage to sustain themselves without migrating or borrowing.

On the question of why they do not send their children to the local primary school, Biwi Zahani says, 'Schools are hardly functional. Where do we send them? The *maktab* is more regular. That is why we send the children there.' Tanveer wants to become a maulvi after completing his studies and Yasmeen a housewife like her mother.

learning' takes place are definitely important factors in depressing enrolment and discouraging the regular attendance of children. There is hardly anything in these schools to make poor parents, consumed by the primary concern to make both ends meet, see much benefit in schooling or change their views on education and the schooling of children.

Irregular and indifferent functioning of schools in areas inhabited by poor and socially marginalized families always reflects, among other things, the powerlessness of poor people. In this context, Mudballa village in Araria district in Bihar offers a significant insight. The village has a few Muslim landlords and a large number of landless or marginal landowning Muslim as well as landless Dalit families. Both lower caste Muslim and Dalit families depend on the landowning Muslim families for wage work and for getting land for cultivation on a sharecropping basis. The school is located in the main *tola,* known as Mukhiya *tola*, where the Muslim landlords live. Most children belonging to these landlords' families either go to private schools or higher-level madrasa in the nearby town. It appears that the landlords are not interested in the proper functioning of the local government school. While both Muslim and Dalit BPL families blame the irregular functioning of schools for the low levels of enrolment and regularity, Dalits also openly mention the role played by the Muslim landlords in getting Hindu teachers transferred and encouraging Muslim teachers to be irregular. Both poor Muslim and Dalit households have started migrating to places outside the state in large numbers, which has reduced their dependence on local landlords. The landlords, therefore, do not want to further lose their supply of labour by letting poor children be educated.

Religious Education and School Participation

There is no doubt that low school participation among Muslims is linked to low economic and educational status as also to the poor functioning of schools in these areas. However, this does not explain it fully, especially in the light of facts that the enrolment rates and regularity of Muslim children in these villages is lower than in the other villages with comparable situations, including SC villages where lower caste households face discrimination and a definite disadvantage in social and political processes within the village. The functioning of schools in most other villages in these districts is not much better and the economic condition of poor households is comparable. This difference, as mentioned earlier, finds an explanation in a fair proportion of children going to *maqtabs* and madrasas.

We have seen earlier that sending children to religious educational institutions is common for Muslims in all those villages that have this option available. Four out of five villages have one or more such centres present. Jhakuapara in Dhubri, Assam does not have any educational institution managed by a religious body. There is a *maktab* that offers part-time, rudimentary religious education in an adjoining village that does not attract many children from Jhakuapara. Mudballa in Bihar and Tiapara in Assam have bigger madrasas whereas Khabaspur (Bihar) and Masaha Kalan (UP) have lower level *maqtabs*. The proportion of children attending only madrasas is higher in the two villages with higher-level madrasas (Box 6.5).

BOX 6.5: TYPES OF *MAQTABS* AND MADRASAS

There are various kinds of educational institutions managed by religious bodies or community groups among Muslims. The nature of these institutions, the curriculum, and the levels of courses offered differ from state to state and are also specific to particular sects of Islam. There are three major categories of these religious institutions.

Maqtabs: Usually attached to mosques or functioning in the house of the local *munshi, maulvi* or *janab,* these are the primary religious educational institutions for young boys and girls of 4-8 years age that impart basic knowledge about the Koran *Sharif, namaaz,* and basic principles of Islamic theology. *Maqtabs* run generally for only 2-3 hours every day but many also run for 4 or more hours. There are no grades and each child learns at his/her pace. *Maqtabs* are located in almost every major Muslim village in the states of UP, Bihar, West Bengal and Assam. While in some states like UP and Assam, they are loosely affiliated to a state-level board (Assam State Deeni Shiksha Board, UP Deeni Talimi Council), there is hardly any supervision or standardization. In *maqtabs*, religious education is more in the form of memorizing and reciting the *Koran Sharif* in Arabic. Often, the teacher is untrained himself and does not follow the meaning of the Arabic texts being taught. There is little or no stress on literacy and numerical skills.

Madrasas (Primary level): These (also known as *maqtabs*) follow a primary level (4-5 year) religious curriculum often prescribed by a state-level council/board and function for 4-5 hours a day. In Assam, the main components of this 5-year curriculum are the *Koran Sharif, Akkaid Ketab, Deeniyat Tajweed,* and Islamic history. These also focus on the learning of the Arabic and Urdu alphabet, and basic numbers. However, this curriculum does not prepare children in any way to join mainstream education. They either continue to the next level of religious education or leave studies after the primary-level course. Some of these also include some teaching of the local regional language, e.g. Hindi.

Madrasas (Higher level): These are usually secondary-level institutions which begin at the upper primary level, i.e. 10-12 years of age (equivalent to Class VI) and continue for 9 years in two stages of 4 and 5 year durations. Some madrasas also offer education equivalent to the higher secondary, Bachelor's and Master's degrees. They also often have a primary section that offers a basic course on religious education.

Most madrasas, except a small proportion, offer only a religious curriculum that enables graduates to become religious teachers—*hafiz*, *munshi*, *maulana*, etc. There is no clear picture available about the number of madrasas in the country. According to one estimate, the total number of madrasas presently functional in the country is about 30,000 in the 1980s (GOI, 1988). In UP itself, the number is supposed to be more than 15,000. However, most madrasas are not affiliated to any centralized state/regional board. They are affiliated to various religious societies and trusts belonging to various Islamic schools of thought. For example, in UP, only about 870 *maqtabs*/madrasas out of the estimated 15,000 institutions are affiliated to the Arabic/Persian Examination Board. All others are privately run through registered societies. This is also the position in Bihar, West Bengal, and Assam. The *Deeni Talimi* Council of UP, which has about 15,000 madrasas attached to it is a non-examining supervisory organization. In Bihar and Assam too, there are such state-level voluntary associations for providing *Deeni* education. But the *maqtabs* and madrasas included in these councils have complete autonomy in managing the institutions, conducting examinations, and certifying students.

Madrasas also differ greatly in the size, viz., enrolment and infrastructure. Typically, the bigger ones have hostel facilities and attract students from surrounding areas. In the states of UP, Bihar, West Bengal, Orissa, MP, Assam, and Maharashtra, state-level madrasa Boards have been set up which are recognized by state governments and receive aid. A small proportion of madrasas are affiliated directly to the State Board of Secondary Education and the Higher Secondary Council. Teachers in madrasas do not receive any pre-service training and the curriculum has remained unchanged for ages. There has been little headway in changing the curriculum despite the recommendations of several groups and institutions (Siddiqui, 1988). Low enrolment of girls in higher-level madrasas and high drop-out rates are common. For example, in the Keranatia madrasa at Tiapara (Assam), there are 26 girls out of 76 students at the entry level and no girls at the seventh level. The enrolment at the first level (*farila e wal*) is 76 which is progressively reduced to only 7 at the seventh level (*Safela Chararun*).

(Based on personal consultations and Madrasa Education in India: A Study of Past and Present by Kuldeep Kaur; Centre for Research in Rural and Industrial Development, Chandigarh, 1990.)

RELIGIOUS EDUCATION: A SCHOOLING OPTION FOR LOWER CASTE MUSLIMS

Many Muslim parents perceive sending children to religious institutions as a schooling option. The common practice of sending one child to a madrasa and the other to a school reflects their view of madrasa as a schooling option (Box 6.6). That the madrasa is a schooling option is also clear from the fact that many non-poor families also send their children to madrasa, especially at Mudballa (Bihar) and Tiapara (Assam) where higher level madrasas are present (Table 6.5). In fact, the proportion of children going to madrasas is higher for APL families as compared to both strata of BPL families. The incidence of children remaining never-enrolled is much higher for poor families (Table 6.6). This shows that poverty and livelihood constraints prevent many Muslim households from sending children even to madrasas.

Table 6.5: Institutions Imparting Muslim Religious Education

S. No.	Village	Religious institutions	Enrolment	Teachers	Remarks
1.	Mudballa, Araria, Bihar	2 *maqtabs*	92 (both)	1 religious teacher each	1 *maqtab* functions inside the primary school
		1 madrasa	120	4 religious teachers and 1 for English/Hindi	Small hostel for 25-30 children
2.	Khabaspur, Araria, Bihar	1 madrasa (1 more in adjoining village)	40	1 religious teacher	Some children attend both school and madrasa
3.	Masaha Kalan, Shravasti, UP	1 *maqtab*	32	2 religious teachers	Irregular attendance in *maqtab*
4.	Tiapara, Dhubri, Assam	3 madrasas			Details are given in Chart 6.1

SOURCE: Village Appraisal & Interaction with *Maqtab*/Madrasa teachers.

Chart 6.1: Type of Madrasas at Tiapara, Dhubri, Assam

Name of institution	Nature of curriculum	Teachers	Scope for graduates
Hafizia Madrasa	Completely religious; 8 classes	Not available	Go for higher religious qualification, viz. maulana
Keramatia Madrasa	Mainly religious, but also offers primary level government curriculum	7 teachers. All with religious qualifications (maulana/hafiz). Only one under matriculate for all general subjects, viz., language, mathematics, science	General curriculum barely gets transacted; theoretically can take admission in upper primary schools; mainly for further religious qualification.
Pre-senior Madrasa (upper primary)	General education with special emphasis on Arabic	8 teachers with matriculation/high school qualifications	Affiliated to Assam High Madrasa Education Board. Graduates could go to senior madrasa and qualify as Arabic teachers.

BOX 6.6: ONE SON GOES TO MADRASA, ONE TO SCHOOL

Mohammad Baseeque and Biwi Zannati, a lower caste Muslim couple from Mudballa village, have three sons, Margoob, Matloob, and Mahboob. Margoob is 12, Matloob 9, and Mahboob 5 years old. Baseeque is 42 and his wife Zannati 38. They are landless and survive on wage work. Zannati does not go out to work in the field as no Muslim woman in the village goes out to work. Baseeque works as an agricultural labourer during the sowing and harvesting seasons and has started going to Punjab for the last two years to work in a rice mill there. Their financial condition has improved since then. However, they are still in debt. They had borrowed 2,000 rupees about five months ago for the treatment of their youngest son. He does not keep well even now. They can still barely manage two meals of plain bread with salt. Still it is better than it was before Baseeque started going to Punjab.

Both Baseeque and Zannati are illiterate but are interested in sending their children to school. Margoob is enrolled in the local *maqtab* and studies in Class II there. Matloob lives with his grandparents (mother's parents) in another village where he goes to school. He is in Class IV now. Mahboob is presently too young to go to school. The parents did not send the elder son, Margoob, to school because the school does not function regularly here, the *maqtab* does. After completing this education, he will be able to become at least a *maulvi*. They sent Matloob to the grandparents' village so that at least one son will be educated and change our lives by taking care of us in our old age.

Table 6.6: Enrolment Status for Muslim Children Across Economic Groups

Economic group	Enrolment status (per cent)			
	Enrolled in school	Drop-out	Never enrolled	Enrolled in madrasa
APL	49.2	8.5	13.6	28.8
UBPL	55.8	8.6	21.2	14.4
LBPL	46.2	7.6	30.8	15.4

SOURCE: Household Survey.

It is important to note that while there are notable differences in the schooling status of children belonging to lower and upper caste Muslim groups, the enrolment rates being higher for the latter, there is almost no difference between children in APL and BPL households. The only difference between APL and BPL groups is that of a high proportion of never-enrolled children in BPL households. This shows the significance of social positioning in decisions for or against schooling. The preference for schooling (through 'secular' educational institutions) in upper caste Muslim families is comparable to the similar trend seen for upper caste Hindu households. A norm of schooling children exists among upper caste Hindu as well as upper caste Muslim families and many poor households despite adverse financial circumstances continue to send their children. This also shows that the practice of viewing religious education as a schooling option is more prevalent among lower caste Muslim families. Almost all upper caste Muslim children in Khabaspur (Bihar), Mudballa (Bihar), and Masaha Kalan (UP) go to private schools imparting 'secular' education. Masaha Kalan has a private school up to the upper primary level within the village. Some of these private-school-going children receive some religious education at home.

HIGH PERCEIVED EMPLOYMENT LINKAGES

One of the clear reasons for preferring religious education, emerging from the village reports and discussions held with Muslim parents, is highly perceived employment linkages. Muslim parents, especially in Bihar-UP villages, are quite articulate in asserting that while formal school education does not provide any long-term benefits such as jobs, the scope for getting employment as a religious teacher (*hafiz/maulana*) on completion of religious education is good. This was also reflected in the children's own aspirations. In Araria district, several boys were studying in the madrasas and wanted to continue their education in reputed religious institutions outside the district.

This perception needs to be understood within the general context in which these families live. The instabilities and uncertainties of life situations make them as vulnerable to processes and factors beyond their control as they do in the case of any other poor family. The availability of work in rural and urban areas that does not need any schooling per se and, perceiving these kinds of low-paying low-status work as the only options available to them, is a major reason for the low commitment to schooling. The need for education, as different from religious education, in most cases remains limited to the development of literacy which in this case generally gets fulfilled by madrasa education. 'It is important to note that contrary to the general belief, madrasas are playing a role, though very little, in making Muslims, especially boys literate. 75 per cent of the literate Muslims, especially in Uttar Pradesh, Bihar and West Bengal are literate because of these *maqtabs* and madrasas.'[5] The fact that this education does not make them employable outside the religious institutions does not dissuade them because the kinds of work that they normally get do not require any schooling anyway.

IMPORTANCE OF RELIGIOUS EDUCATION

However, this logic does not hold true for sending girls to madrasas; they are usually given a religious rather than a formal education. Girls do not generally become religious teachers and hence the question of employment linkages does not arise in their case. In any case, employment linkages are seldom taken into account while deciding about girls' schooling in any social group. This logic is generally not even cited by parents to explain the sending of girls to madrasas. For girls, there is a strong feeling that rudimentary religious education, especially knowledge of *namaaz* and the Koran is absolutely necessary. Almost all parents expressed the opinion that, as far as possible, some religious education should be imparted to children to enable them to perform *namaaz* and *roza* with full devotion and correctness (Box 6.7). For girls, it is more important so that they can raise their children as 'good' Muslims. The issue of girls will be discussed at greater length later.

> BOX 6.7: THEY GO BOTH TO SCHOOL AND THE MADRASA
>
> Afsana (8), Naimur and Sarvar (6, they are twins) go to a madrasa everyday at 7.00 a.m., come back at about 9.00 a.m., and then again go to school at 10.00 a.m. Afsana is in class III while Naimur and Sarvar are in Class I. Their parents, Ekramul and Rashida, own half an acre of land, and Ekramul doubles up as a cultivator and wage worker to support his family. Rashida, like other Muslim women in the village, does not go out to work. Naimur wants to become a police officer when he grows up, but Afsana does not say anything when asked what she wants to do after growing up. Both Ekramul and Rashida feel that both religious and Hindi education are important, and that is why they are sending their children to both the madrasa and the school. In fact, many Muslim families in this village, Kismat Khabaspur (Araria, Bihar), send their children to both madrasa and school.

SCHOOL *VERSUS* MADRASA

There is a significant difference between the nature and the manner of functioning of schools and madrasas. As against indifferent and irregular government schools following rigid procedures and norms, madrasas, especially those present in large numbers imparting rudimentary religious education as also those providing primary-level education alone, are much more flexible and suit poor families. The absence of grades and fixed time-frames for completing the curriculum offers flexibility that suits parents. Children could be irregular in attendance and could also be withdrawn at any time.

There are two types of *maqtabs* available for children in the younger age group of 5-14. While the smaller *maqtabs*, found in large numbers and present in almost every Muslim village or urban locality, concentrate only on memorizing the Koran, primary-level madrasas follow a 4-5-years curriculum which is one complete level. This is different from the formal schooling system where the primary level (up to grade IV/V) is only the first step to higher educational qualifications. Gains or returns from the formal education system are perceived to flow, if at all, after the higher stages of education have been completed. This requires parents to take a long-term view and make a commitment to education, which does not come easily in the deprived contexts of abject poverty and a preoccupation with earning for survival. The fact that middle and secondary schools are usually not available within the village and involve much higher direct costs is another deterrent. In the religious system, even the primary level provides basic religious education, an important goal in itself.

The relationship between the community and religious educational institutions is also different from that between the community and government schools. Religious educational institutions are perceived as an important part of one's identity that need to be sustained, and, therefore, the Muslim communities actively support them. The *maulvis* or teachers in madrasas generally belong to the same village and inspire greater trust. This is an especially important consideration when sending girls. The *maqtabs* and madrasas in all four villages are run by local committees which collect funds in an institutionalised manner for payment to the maulvi and for infrastructure improvement. In Masaha Kalan (UP), there is a cess collected on the agricultural produce with every harvest, and contributions also come from people working outside who send remittances home. In addition, they also receive funds from external sources. In Tiapara (Assam), apart from grants coming in from external sources, the Keramatiya madrasa is supported by an annual contribution of 1 per cent of the earnings of each family sending its children there. The committee also collects donations and food grains for poor children from other villagers staying in the hostel. In sharp contrast, government primary schools do not receive any assistance from the community and are rarely perceived as their 'own' institutions.

INTRODUCTION OF GENERAL SUBJECTS IN MADRASAS

One approach adopted to ensure the imparting of 'secular' education to Muslim children has been to integrate the teaching of modern subjects and religious teaching in the same institution. The government initiated one centrally sponsored scheme, 'Modernization of Madrasas' with an aim to introduce secular subjects in madrasas, meant specifically for recognized madrasas that receive aid from the government. Many madrasas in states such as Bihar, UP, MP, Assam, and West Bengal get government aid and are affiliated to the Madrasa Education Board. State aid is common even in other states like Kerala and Maharashtra. However, the effort to introduce the teaching of general subjects in madrasas has not been very successful due to various reasons (Box 6.8).

The scheme is voluntary and dependent on the willingness of the religious trusts running the madrasas to decide whether to take up general education subjects. Moreover, the scheme and its implementation itself suffered from several limitations; there is provision for only one teacher at one institution to teach all the general subjects, an ad hoc introduction to the combination of subjects to be introduced as per the discretion of the madrasa management, delays in the release of funds, no training for the newly recruited teachers, etc.—making it almost certain that the initiative does not succeed. Moreover, it is also important to recognize that a full-time madrasa curriculum is itself quite heavy and that adding more subjects without proper planning and preparation makes it very difficult for children to cope. A

> **BOX 6.8: THE MODERNIZATION OF MADRASAS SCHEME**
>
> This scheme has the objective of encouraging traditional institutions like *maqtabs* and madrasas to introduce the teaching of science, mathematics, social studies, Hindi, and English so that the students of these institutions are able to acquire an education comparable to the national system. The process of modernization is entirely voluntary. It covers the elementary and secondary-level classes in madrasas and allows for: (a) 100 per cent assistance for the appointment of one teacher for the general subjects, (b) assistance for the establishment of a book bank and strengthening of libraries in madrasas for these subjects, (c) provision of science and mathematics kits and essential equipment to madrasas.
>
> A study conducted by the NCERT in Kerala, Madhya Pradesh, and Uttar Pradesh to analyse the curriculum of government-aided and unaided madrasas found that the scheme has not really achieved its objectives. In general, it was found that the coverage of modern subjects is very limited. The madrasas do not teach each subject in a grade-wise manner as prescribed in the state curriculum. Initially, the thrust is on religious education and some basic teaching of languages. The other subjects are introduced later. Since almost all the teachers are untrained in the teaching of modern subjects, the quality of teaching is abysmal. In most cases, the number of teachers assigned to the teaching of the general subjects is small compared to the enrolment. They are often under-qualified. The remuneration paid to madrasa teachers is also very low. The NCERT study also revealed that a majority of teachers felt that the major goal of education in madrasas is knowledge of religion and Islamic principles to be a good human being. In both UP and MP, analyses of the curriculum and the responses of the teachers in madrasas showed that the most important subjects were theology and moral education followed by languages like Urdu, Hindi and English. The madrasa management often complained of inordinate delays in the release of funds from the government to implement the scheme.

better alternative is to revise the whole curriculum and design it afresh taking general subjects into consideration. However, this is not possible without the active interest and initiative of both the Muslim intelligentsia and Muslim religious leadership. Also important is a true commitment to the goal of universalization and a genuine political will to integrate Muslims into the national mainstream without questioning and hurting their cultural identity.

IDENTITY, ISOLATION, AND THE SCHOOLING OF CHILDREN

The strong need to send children to madrasas/*maqtabs* also needs to be understood in the wider context of contemporary history, especially in the post-Independence period. Despite the adoption of a secular Constitution and the bestowing of equal rights on all citizens irrespective of caste and religion, Indian society, like almost all other half-literate, multi-ethnic, multi-religious societies, has remained deeply divided. The nature of politics and political mobilization, especially in Hindi-speaking areas with large Muslim populations, has been such that it has created a tendency towards cultural isolationism among Muslims. 'Feeling that the majority of Hindus are determined to destroy their cultural symbols and deprive them of their separate religio-cultural identity, they have despairingly turned in upon themselves and cling to their religious traditions. Somewhat rigid and narrow interpretations of Islam have reinforced this isolationism.'[6] Muslim religious leadership, by and large, has also failed to distinguish the issues of cultural and religious freedom from those inhibiting socio-economic development, and has tried to use the situation to further their narrow political agenda.

In a situation where one community feels culturally insecure, even seemingly small issues, if perceived to be affecting their identity, take on significant symbolic importance. The content of the curriculum and textbooks in some states was found to be objectionable to the sensitivities of the Muslim population. UP, Bihar, and certain other states had a well-developed system of Urdu education which, with a greater emphasis on Hindi and English education in post-Independent India, witnessed a decline. The use of Urdu in general has declined[7] and so has the number of schools with Urdu as the medium of instruction. Although Urdu education was never limited to Muslims, and a good number of Hindus also opted for it, its decline is perceived as a systematic effort to destroy Muslim symbols.[8] It is also true that the majority of the remaining Urdu-medium schools are mainly attended by Muslim children, and the availability of textbooks and teacher training is worse in these schools. In such situations, many acts have strong symbolic value, and for Muslims sending their children to religious education centres is also one of the ways of asserting their cultural identity. This was also evident in repeated references to assert the need for religious education for Muslims and also in silences on the question of why this is so.[9]

Deprivation, Identity, and Preference: Issues in the Schooling of Muslim Children

At one level, poverty and deprivation affect schooling participation adversely among Muslim children in the same manner as they do for any other poor social groups. The presence of a very high proportion of children in poor Muslim households who have never been enrolled in either schools or madrasas confirms this. The employment of children, especially boys, in work is as high among Muslims as among Dalits or STs. It is common for them to join wage work both within and outside their villages at a very young age. Girls are generally engaged in household chores and sibling care, as in other educationally disadvantaged social groups, since they are barely 7-8 years old. Livelihood constraints and vulnerability to crises act as major impediments in making the schooling of children a definite choice.

The irregular functioning of government schools further depresses the demand for schooling. People, including Muslim men's and women's groups in all five villages, were vocal and open in complaining about the functioning of schools. The presence of a functional school with active and motivated teachers is an important condition to ensure enrolment and the attendance of children from poor families in all educationally deprived social groups that face social and economic marginalization. This is as true for Muslims as for other groups such as Dalits and STs.

The importance of religious education in establishing the socio-cultural identity, and presence of madrasas as a schooling option, further reduces the interest of Muslim parents in general education. The flexibility in the functioning of a madrasa making it more of a community-owned institution, and the high perceived employment linkages also play a role in making it an acceptable option for schooling. The irregular functioning of government schools also contributes in making madrasas an alternative choice for schooling. However, it is also important to remember that only 18 per cent of all Muslim children in rural areas are going to madrasas. There are many more (23 per cent) who remained never-enrolled or who have dropped out (8 per cent) from government schools. The choice for religious education, at least in the case of boys, is also not absolute, as revealed by the fact that many households send one child to a madrasa and another to a government or private school. The high rates of irregularity and drop-outs observed in madrasas indicate that the commitment to religious education is not so strong among poor Muslim parents.

However, this is not to say that general education can be promoted among Muslims at the cost of religious education (Box 6.9). It is important to recognize that the need for religious education is integral to Muslim identity and any effort to undermine that to promote general education will only further isolate them and will not have the desired impact. The presence of a madrasa symbolizes the distinct religious identity of Muslims even if they do not regularly send their children there. The Constitution has bestowed on every citizen the right of religious freedom, including the right to worship, propagate, and practise one's religion, also assuring the state's non-interference in matters of religion. Collective minority rights also allow freedom to groups to establish religious, cultural, and educational institutions of their choice and such institutions qualify for state funding. The Constitution, however, is also committed to the universalization of at least elementary education which cannot be achieved without taking all Muslim children into the fold of general schooling. However, the goal needs to be achieved taking all the relevant factors into consideration without making them feel further insecure, and raising their confidence in the state in general.

Adding some general subjects to the madrasa curriculum has had very limited success in the past and does not appear to be an effective choice for promoting secular education among Muslims, especially in the long run. The experiences of the places where school participation rates are high among Muslim children show that this has happened only with an increase in demand from Muslim parents followed by adjustments made in the timings of madrasas to morning and evening hours. This ensures that there

BOX 6.9: EDUCATION OF MUSLIMS IN KERALA SINCE INDEPENDENCE

Muslims in Kerala were not at par with other communities at the time of independence. However, the state government of Kerala made sincere efforts to promote education among all communities, including Muslims, since the 1950s, and largely succeeded in reducing the disparities, at least at school-level education. While, on the one hand, special schemes were launched to improve the enrolment and attendance of Muslim girls in schools, on the other, seats were reserved for them in educational institutions imparting graduate and postgraduate-level courses, Preferential treatment was also given in the allocation of seats from the 'general pool' to the Malabar region from where the largest number of Muslims in the state came. Large-scale expansion of the education system combined with the liberal policy of inducement to educationally backward communities paid dividends.

Initiative from private individuals and leadership from the Muslim community also contributed significantly in raising the level of education and schooling among Muslim children in Kerala. Leaders like Vakkaom Abdul Khader Maulvi and C.H. Mahammad Koya exhorted the community to send their children to schools and initiated the growth of private schools and colleges. A number of associations and groups were formed which succeeded in demanding special interventions from the government and influenced the community to adopt general education in a big way. Religious institutions continued to function but the timings were changed so that there was no clash with school timings. However, despite the spread of education, the representation of Muslims in government jobs is relatively low. Muslims constitute 21 per cent of the state's total population but occupy only 8 per cent of the government jobs.

(Based mainly on a paper by the same title by A. Abdul Salam, in *Education and Muslims in India since Independence*, edited by Khan Qadri and Siddiqui, New Delhi: Institute of Objective Studies, 1988.)

is no clash between madrasa and school timings. However, these efforts have been more in evidence in the western and southern states such as Kerala and Maharashtra, places where the demand for schooling has been high among non-Muslim groups and a social norm of sending all children to school exists. The existence of such a norm itself must have had a role in promoting the demand for schooling among Muslims as well. Leadership within the community and a higher level of exposure played an important role. State governments also made concerted efforts to promote secular education among Muslims in these states. Also, the development processes in these states have been such that even poor households, barring certain specific pockets, have generally been able to have a basic minimum of economic security.

Without any external force or socio-political process, it is not easy to build a commitment to schooling among educationally deprived groups including Dalits, STs, and Muslims, in situations where a norm for schooling children is not strong and basic livelihood choices impose a number of constraints. It is all the more difficult in the case of Muslims because of their sense of cultural isolation, alienation, suspicion, and a perception that an alternative to schooling exists in the form of religious education. The problem is compounded by poor and indifferent governance in states, especially in areas where the rates for school participation are low for Muslims as well as other deprived communities.

Therefore, cultural isolation coupled with a fear of losing their identity, impedes the process of mainstreaming Muslims. Communal politics of both majority and minority which further aggravates and preys upon this fear, adding to the deprivation caused by poverty and social backwardness in keeping children away from formal school participation. It is also important to remember that a large proportion, almost about 63 per cent, of out-of-school Muslim children are not going to madrasas and hence the preference for religious education should not be seen as the only reason for low schooling participation among them. Social stratification within the Muslim community also plays a role, with its correlation between educational backwardness among low-caste Muslim adults and low aspirations for their children. As in the case of Dalits, and some tribal areas, the availability of jobs that require no schooling further depresses the need for schooling. The existence of generally low levels of school participation rates among other communities, especially the poor, and also of non-functional, irregular schools have a depressing effect as they fail to create any positive image of a viable alternative. Losing sight of any one of these aspects would result in a simplified reading of the problem and would not help in developing any long-term effective changes. An area-based approach which emphasizes the right to education and works on a sustained basis to build a consensus in favour of general education in the community and the socio-religious leadership would be required.

NOTES

1. There is almost a total absence of any databases on the participation levels of Muslim children in primary/elementary education. This information is not collected or published by national-level censuses/surveys. At the state and district levels as well, disaggregated information is generally not collected on Muslims. Even in projects like the DPEP, which aims at a time-bound universalization of primary education, we did not get information on the status of participation of Muslim children in any state except Assam. The result is a lack of clarity on the magnitude of the problem.
2. Some of the recent works that provide information about Muslims in India include
   (i) Report of High Powered Panel on Muslims, SC, ST and Weaker Sections constituted by the Ministry of Home Affairs headed by Dr Gopal Singh, 1983 (sample studies in 45 districts in 12 states).
   (ii) N.C. Saxena, 'Public Employment and Educational Backwardness among Muslims in India', in *Man and Development*, December 1983.
   (iii) *All India Survey* (1982-83) *of Muslim-managed Educational Institutions*, New Delhi: Hamdard Education Society, 1983.
   (iv) *Muslims in India: Their educational, demographic and socio-economic status with intercommunity comparison based on field survey conducted in 1991*,

New Delhi: Hamdard Education Society. The study was commissioned by the National Commission for Minorities.

(v) NSS 43rd Round 1987-88, Table 37.4 (pp. 582, 583)—General education status of different religious communities.

(vi) *India Human Development Report*, National Council of Applied Economic Research, New Delhi: Oxford University Press, 1999.

3. This is evident from the very fact that the respondents categorized themselves into lower and upper caste Muslims during the Household Survey. Also see Imtiaz Ahmad (ed.), *Caste and Social Stratification among Muslims in India*, New Delhi: Manohar, 1978.
4. Please refer to Chapter 3 for Tables on which these figures are based.
5. Kuldeep Kaur, *Madrasa Education in India: A Study of Past and Present*, Chandigardh: Centre for Research in Rural and Industrial Development, 1990.
6. Imtiaz Ahmad, 'Secularism, Hindus and Muslims', *The Hindu*, 24 May 2002.
7. The issue of Urdu as a medium of instruction or the need for Urdu language teaching was not raised in our fieldwork. Neither we nor the people raised this as an issue for discussion.
8. The importance of Urdu to Muslims in the UP-Bihar context is also evident from the fact that several Muslim families in Masaha Kalan village (UP) referred to Urdu as their mother tongue even if the language which they speak is Awadhi.
9. During fieldwork in villages in UP and Bihar with Muslim populations, we faced one limitation. There was no Muslim field investigator in our team. This affected the nature of our discussion, which could not be very open on certain issues.

7. Fuzzy Borders: The Otherness of 'Other' Caste Groups

Background

In the last three chapters we analysed the status of education among children belonging to different social groups considered educationally more backward. However, the understanding of the role of social positioning and contextual diversity cannot be complete without understanding the situation among those who broadly form the 'others' in all statistics and reports. This 'others' is not a homogeneous category and can be divided into two main sub-groups, Upper Caste Hindus (UCH) and Other Backward Castes (OBC). OBCs, together with SCs and STs, form the category Backward Classes.[1] As seen in the case of other social groups, UCH and OBCs also consist of a number of caste and sub-caste groups. OBC, like SC and ST, is an official category and enjoys certain benefits of reservations in educational institutions and employment in government or semi-government organizations. As pointed out by many sociologists, OBC is the least homogeneous and the most loosely defined of the three categories. Unlike SCs or STs, OBCs are a more nebulous category and is mentioned in the Constitution in only the most general terms. There is no all-India list for OBCs and they are not even enumerated separately in the Census.

Post-Independence land reform measures such as the abolition of zamindari and tenancy reforms, despite their lacklustre implementation, benefited OBCs the most as the majority of erstwhile tenants belonged to certain OBC castes such as Jat, Yadav, Kurmi, and Koeri. Thus, they consolidated their position as middle peasants, especially in areas like UP, Bihar, and Haryana. The 1960s and 1970s witnessed the emergence of agrarian-based politics largely dominated by OBCs. They far outnumbered the upper castes and the new alliances made them very important in electoral politics based on adult franchise. Although they did not suffer untouchability in the past, their social status had always been lower than that of the upper castes and the political assertion that came with access to power gave them a more dignified identity and sense of equality with the upper castes. However, unlike UCH, OBCs cover a wide spectrum of castes. At the lower end, there are castes quite close to Dalits in terms of their economic position and social status. At the other end, there are castes that are wealthy and powerful, Sanskritized and occupying high rungs on the ladder of social status.

The upper castes, comprising Brahmin, Rajput or Thakur, and a number of other castes, are at the top of the caste Hindu hierarchy. Besides enjoying the highest social positions, they have traditionally had greater access to land and other assets in all parts of the country. Above all, they enjoyed access to education even before the advent of the modern education system and then they were the first to reap the benefits of Western education in the nineteenth and the twentieth centuries. It was natural that most of the leadership came from this group at the time of the freedom struggle, and they formed the biggest group in the post-Independence bureaucracy. Although with the emergence of other power groups and changing socio-political dynamics, their traditional supremacy has undergone a change, they continue to be the single-most powerful group in terms of access to higher education and in making use of the newer opportunities to their advantage.

The acceptance of the Mandal Commission's recommendations during the late 1980s—extending the benefits of reservations in educational institutions and jobs controlled by the Central government to OBCs—led to large-scale opposition among upper caste groups. This was despite the fact that many state governments already had such laws and, in any case, the employment base of the government had either been stagnant or was shrinking due to liberalization and several other economic reform measures. Although it is difficult to substantiate in the absence of Census data, it is largely believed that OBCs are still educationally backward as compared to UCH and have a much lower representation in jobs in the organized sector. However, both these groups are generally better placed than SCs and STs in terms of educational as well as economic status. Nonetheless, the situation varies from one place to the other; local conditions, including the factors of access to land and other resources, political dynamics, and social positioning determine the relationships between these two social groups as well as their relationship with others such as SCs or STs.

In the present analysis, we attempt to understand school participation patterns among children belonging to OBC and UCH groups in diverse socio-political, economic, and cultural contexts. The study of gender differentiation within these social groups will be undertaken later while discussing the issue of girls. The large differences between these two groups, in fact, call for separate discussion, but the two have been clubbed for the sake of convenience, and also to highlight the differences. All government educational statistics tend to treat these two similarly as they are clubbed under the categories of 'others' or 'general', which tend to paper over the large differences that exist between these two distinct categories.

STUDY VILLAGES WITH UCH AND OBC POPULATIONS

Although a few UCH and OBC households live in many of the study villages, the present chapter is based primarily on analyses of situations in 15 villages where the proportion of these social groups is significant and the information available from different sources allow for such a discussion. Seven villages have no UCH population, two villages have no OBC population, and the remaining seven have both UCH and OBC populations. The social mix also varies as in some villages only these two groups are present, while in others the population consists of other social groups as well. Also, while only one OBC sub-caste is present in some villages, in others OBCs comprise several castes placed differently in the social hierarchy. The same is true for UCH. These 15 villages, located in different regions of the country, provide a mosaic of social and economic conditions. It is important to note that unlike villages with a substantial SC or ST population, none of these villages are very badly placed in terms of infrastructural provisions such as schools, transport, drinking water, etc. However, they are not placed equally, and while four villages fall in the A category and seven in the B category, the remaining five are poorly provided for and fall into the C category (Appendix Table A.1).

School Participation Patterns: Intra-Group and Intra-Village Differences

Aggregate patterns in enrolment and participation have shown that UCH and OBCs are ahead of the others in terms of enrolment. However, the rate of enrolment among OBC children, though higher than the rest, is lower than that for UCH, and the difference widens if the pattern for regularly attending children is taken in place of enrolment. In fact, OBCs come much closer to groups like Dalits, STs, and Muslims in terms of regularly attending children. The disaggregated picture at the village level also shows that school participation patterns for OBC children in four out of five villages are worse than those for UCH children, the difference in per cent points being very high at Rahatmina (Bihar), Kursa (MP), and Gavaravaram (AP), and not so high at Honnahalli (Karnataka). At Bayyanagudem (AP), the trend is reversed with the rates for enrolment and regularly attending students being higher for OBC children than for UCH children.

An interesting trend emerges from the fact that while the enrolment rates for children among OBCs are generally higher than, or similar to, those of SCs, STs, or Muslims taken as a whole in most villages, the pattern is reversed when seen for those attending regularly. This indicates that the incidence of irregularity is high among OBC children as compared to other socially disadvantaged groups in many villages. UCH, on the other hand, always show a higher rate of regularly attending children as compared to all other social groups, the difference being marginal in some villages and significant in others (Table 7.1).

Inter-village comparisons for the same group reveal that there are larger variations among OBC children as compared to UCH children in terms of the proportion attending school regularly. A very high proportion of children

Table 7.1: Villages with UCH and OBC Households: Background and Schooling Status

Village	Dev.cat.	Social group mix	Social group	Enrolled (%)	% within enrolled			Out of school	% within unenrolled		Regularly going Col. 6 x 5/ 100
					Regular	Irregular	Occasional		Drop-out	Never enrolled	
1	2	3	4	5	6	7	8	9	10	11	12
Chandukuttemole (Karnataka)	B	OBC	OBC	80.0	76.3	23.7	–	20.0	60.0	40.0	1.0
Ramraikutti	B	OBC/SC	OBC	84.0	29.4	35.3	35.3	16.0	100.0	–	24.7
(Assam)			SC/ST	87.5	42.9	14.3	42.8	12.5	100.0	–	37.5
Bhamunigaon (Assam)	B	UCH	SC/ST	100.0	–	100.0	–	0	–	–	–
Sultana	B	OBC/SC	OBC	63.3	66.7	33.3	–	36.4	–	100.0	42.4
(Uttar Pradesh)			SC/ST	30.6	66.7	20.0	13.3	69.4	11.8	88.2	20.4
Jogini	B	OBC/SC/	OBC	64.7	18.1	54.5	27.3	35.3	66.7	33.3	11.7
(Madhya Pradesh)		ST/UCH	SC/ST	58.3	61.5	30.8	7.7	41.7	40.0	60.0	35.9
Ratapalli	B	OBC/ST/	OBC	93.8	86.2	13.8	–	6.2	100.0	–	80.9
(Orissa)		UCH	SC/ST	87.5	85.7	14.3	–	12.5	100.0	–	75.0
Rahatmina	C	UCH/OBC	UCH	96.3	92.0	8.0	–	3.7	–	100.0	88.6
(Bihar)			OBC	25.0	80.0	20.0	–	75.0	13.3	86.7	20.0
Bayyanagudem	C	UCH/OBC/SC	UCH	63.8	100.0	–	–	31.2	80.0	20.0	68.8
(Andhra Pradesh)			OBC	100.0	83.3	16.7	–	0	–	–	83.3
			SC/ST	68.0	100.0	–	–	32.0	56.0	50.0	68.0
Honnahalli	C	UCH/OBC/SC	UCH	100.0	100.0	–	–	0	–	–	100.0
(Karnataka)			OBC	58.3	94.4	–	5.6	41.7	53.3	46.7	55.0
			SC/ST	55.6	100.0	–	–	44.5	100.0	–	55.6

Bursa (Madhya Pradesh)	C	UCH/OBC	OBC	84.6	37.5	50.0	12.5	15.4	–	100.0	31.7
			SC/ST	75.6	63.6	27.3	9.1	24.4	30.0	70.0	48.1
Malegaon (Maharashtra)	A	UCH	UCH	75.0	100.0	–	–	25.0	100.0	–	75.0
Mulasar (Orissa)	A	OBC/SC/ST	UCH	41.7	40.0	40.0	20.0	58.3	42.9	57.1	16.7
			SC/ST	51.3	25.0	55.0	20.0	48.7	47.4	52.6	12.8

NOTES: 1. Column 2 shows a development category based on an index prepared by taking infrastructural facilities into account (see Appendix Table 2).
2. Column 5 shows the enrolment of 6-13-year-old against the total population of the age group.
3. Columns 6, 7 and 8 show the distribution of enrolled children [Column 5].
4. Column 10 and11 show the distribution of un-enrolled children [Column 9].
5. Column 12 shows the population of regularly attending children as a proportion of total age group children.
6. The schooling status data for any group have not been included if the proportion in the surveyed households is 20 per cent or less.

SOURCE: Columns 3 and 4 based on the Village Appraisal Reports. The remaining columns based on the Household Survey.

from UCH families attend school regularly in all the villages. All other groups remain behind in all villages except two in Orissa, one in Karnataka, and one in AP, where all groups show similar patterns. It is especially significant because school participation rates for UCH are high even in districts like Sidhi in MP or Araria in Bihar where patterns are otherwise not encouraging. The proportion of OBC children attending school regularly, on the other hand, varies from as low as 11.7 per cent at Jogini in MP to as high as 83.3 per cent at Bayyanagudem in Andhra Pradesh, with many levels in between. However, what is notable is that nowhere is the rate as high as 100 per cent, seen for UCH in about half the villages.

Village-level segregation establishes the need to understand the same group in diverse contexts. It is obvious that the situation is not the same everywhere for any one social group. The macro picture indicates the larger picture but only deeper analyses of micro situations can help in understanding the roles of a variety of factors and their interplay in influencing education-related decisions. The following sections analyse the contexts, including family background, socio-economic positioning, the larger environment, and school situations in different places and relate these to the educational participation patterns among these specific groups.

A General Profile of OBC and UCH Households

Other Backward Castes (OBC) are closer to SCs rather than to UCH in many indicators of deprivation and socio-economic backwardness. This is especially true for educational indicators such as the proportion of families with both husband and wife illiterate and average years of schooling for both men and women. The average size of landholdings owned by OBC families is not only much smaller than UCH households, but it is also lower than those of ST and Muslim families. The average size of the landholding among UCH is two to four times larger than it is for other social groups. However, the proportion of landless families is also very high among UCH, higher even than among STs. This means that those who own land among UCH generally have large-sized landholdings, unlike STs or OBCs. It is also important to note that a substantial proportion of the households even among UCHs and OBCs are very poor, though this proportion, especially among UCH, is significantly smaller than that among the Dalits, STs, and Muslims (Table 4.2).

As seen for other groups, within a broad trend notable differences exist within these social groups across different areas and regions. There are places where the entire, or an overwhelming, proportion of OBC families is landless. This is true for Chandukotemole in Chamrajnagar district in Karnataka, Sultana in Shravasti district in UP, and two villages, Gavaravaram and Bayyanagudem in the West Godavari district in AP. In contrast, a small per centage of OBC families are landless in several other villages, including Ratapalli in Nuapara district of Orissa and Jogini village of Sidhi district in MP. The proportion of landless is also low for Kursa in Sidhi and Honnahalli in Chamrajnagar district. In other villages, about 30 to 50 per cent of households are landless. The proportion of OBC households owning more than 2.5 acres of land is generally low, with most families owning small pieces of land except in Jogini and Kursa in Sidhi district and in Sultana in Shravasti district. Landlessness is high among UCH families in only two villages, Doddathupur in Chamrajnagar and Rahatmina in Araria district in Bihar. The proportion of landless among UCH is, however, not so low even in the two villages in West Godavari district. In the rest of the villages, the significant majority of UCH families own more land than 2.5 acres (Table 7.2). By and large, it was reported from almost every village that the best quality or the majority of irrigated land belonged to UCH households everywhere.

Inter social group patterns in landownership also show wide variations among villages. While landlessness among OBC households is comparable to Dalit families in the five study villages (Ramraikutti in Dhubri district in Assam, Kursa in MP, Bayyanagudem and Gavaravaram in AP, and Honnahalli in Karnataka), it is significantly lower in comparison to Dalits in four villages, Sultana in UP, Rahatmina in Bihar, Kermili in Orissa, and Naudhiya and Jogini in MP. The proportion of landless families among UCH, even when it is high, is less than any other social group in all villages except in Mulasar in Koraput district of Orissa.

Cultivation on own land and sharecropping is quite common among OBCs in certain villages. Many OBC households are also involved in petty trade and other sundry business activities, especially true for the villages in Sidhi district in MP. Agricultural wage work is common among OBC households mainly in central parts of India. Non-agricultural wage work, especially in combination with cultivation, is more common for OBC families in other parts of the country. Among UCH, cultivation and other forms of self-employment are comparatively more common, though wage work is also found in many places. Intervillage variations in occupation patterns are more marked for OBCs as compared to UCH households.

Intra-group variations in occupation patterns show similar trends as seen in landownership and the proportion of household heads in wage work, both agricultural and non-agricultural, being higher than other social groups in some places and lower in others. Inter-village differences are notable within OBCs in terms of literacy levels as well, this being sharper for men than women. All OBC women of 14 years and above are illiterate in four villages, two in Sidhi district in MP and one each in Araria district in Bihar and Shravasti district in UP. The female illiteracy rate is more than 50 per cent in more than two-thirds of the villages with OBC populations. The differences are, however, wider among UCH with all being illiterate in Mulasar in Orissa, on the one hand, and only one-fifth being illiterate in

Table 7.2: Profile of UCH/OBC Households in Selected Villages

Village	Caste	Landless	More than 2.5	Male		Female		Main occupation of the household			
				Illiterate	Schooled	Illiterate	Schooled	Cultivator/ self-employed	Agri. labour	Non-agri. labour	Salaried
Chandukuttemole (Karnataka)	OBC	72.0	4.0	65.2	30.4	75.0	25.0	14.8	62.9	–	3.7
Ramoraikutti (Assam)	OBC	60.0	0	33.3	37.5	38.9	38.9	26.7	53.3	6.7	6.7
	SC/ST	60.0	0	50.0	–	100.0	–	60.0	40.0	–	–
Bhamunigaon (Assam)	OBC	47.8	21.7	27.3	60.6	57.6	27.3	56.5	17.4	8.7	–
Sultana (UP)	OBC	–	50.0	50.0	50.0	100.0	–	40.0	–	20.0	–
	SC/ST	9.5	28.5	52.3	34.1	92.1	7.9	90.5	–	–	4.8
Jogini (MP)	OBC	14.3	85.7	30.0	50.0	100.0	–	100.0	–	–	–
	SC/ST	72.7	–	64.7	29.4	100.0	–	45.5	18.2	18.2	–
Ratapalli (Orissa)	OBC	–	44.4	41.4	31.0	61.3	12.9	61.1	16.7	16.7	5.6
	SC/ST	25.0	50.0	42.9	57.1	57.1	42.9	100.0	–	–	–
Rahatmina (Bihar)	UCH	50.0	33.3	–	87.5	40.0	45.0	58.3	16.7	–	8.3
	OBC	66.7	11.1	50.0	30.0	100.0	–	44.4	11.1	44.4	–
Bayyanagudem (AP)	UCH	33.3	55.5	52.9	35.3	61.5	38.5	55.6	22.2	11.1	–
	SC/ST	91.7	8.3	70.0	25.0	66.7	26.7	16.7	58.3	16.7	8.3
Honnahalli (Karnataka)	UCH	–	100.0	85.7	14.3	80.0	20.0	60.0	40.0	–	–
	OBC	25.0	37.6	71.4	19.0	87.5	9.4	47.1	47.1	5.9	–
	SC/ST	25.0	25.0	60.0	20.0	71.4	28.6	–	60.0	–	–
Kursa (MP)	OBC	20.0	60.0	83.3	–	100.0	–	80.0	–	20.0	–
	SC/ST	6.3	56.3	81.8	13.6	90.9	9.1	82.4	–	5.9	–
Malegaon (Maharashtra)	UCH	30.8	23.1	13.0	65.2	55.2	41.4	69.2	15.4	7.7	–
Mulasar (Orissa)	UCH	80.0	–	100.0	–	100.0	–	–	100.0	–	–
	SC/ST	42.1	21.0	76.9	19.2	91.7	4.7	40.0	35.0	–	–

NOTES: 1. A person has been considered as being schooled if he/she has been to school for at least one year.
2. The data for any social group are not included separately if the number of households covered is 20 per cent or less in the total sample of households covered.

SOURCE: Household Survey.

Kursa in MP, on the other. It is important to note that a higher proportion of UCH women is schooled and a lower proportion illiterate in comparison to SC/ST women in three-fourths of the villages.

The particular caste or sub-caste to which the majority of households in a particular village or region belong, even within one broad social group, also determines their social, economic, and educational status.[2] While usually only one caste constitutes one group, in many other villages several castes together make one social group in the same village. These sub-castes themselves are differentiated in terms of social hierarchy and economic positioning. The profile of one group discussed for a particular village changes if this is further disaggregated for particular castes or sub-castes. In the following section, we include these aspects in our discussion of the socio-economic and political contexts of the villages from the perspective of UCH and OBC groups, later analysed to understand schooling patterns among children belonging to these groups.

It is obvious that UCH, even when poor, are generally not as vulnerable and are significantly better placed not only in comparison to more deprived groups like Dalits and tribals but also OBCs. They are especially ahead in educational indicators that have positive linkages with schooling participation of children. In contrast, OBCs, with high landlessness, ownership of small landholdings, high illiteracy, and a high incidence of multiple occupations are far more vulnerable, having a negative impact on schooling participation rates for children (Box 7.1). Also, among social groups, the

BOX 7.1: PAWAN'S STORY IS NOT VERY DIFFERENT

Pawan lives in Balanagar Kodri, a village in Shravasti district, UP. He is 13 but talks as if he is already an adult. He has three brothers and three sisters, three of them (one brother and two sisters) older than him and the remaining three younger. They belong to an OBC group, and own one acre of land and two bullocks. However, the financial situation of the family is deplorable. The eldest sister was married when she was hardly 10-11 years old. The family is in debt because of the expenses incurred for her wedding. The eldest brother is also married but lives separately with his wife and does not contribute anything to this family. Both his father and mother double up as cultivators and wage workers to somehow manage the household. The mother, in fact, 'triples' up because of heavy work at home, too. The sister, of course, is there to help the mother in domestic chores, but then she also takes the cattle to graze. The mother does not keep well and the family had also fallen into debt because of her illness.

Pawan used to go to school but stopped when he was in Class IV. Instead, he started working for wages in a nearby town. The family depends on his earnings in a very major way. They would not have anything to eat if he had not started earning. Pawan is committed to working for the family but misses school. 'If I had continued, I would have been in the middle school by now', he says ruefully. He also feels that education is important because 'it allows you to do what you want and nobody can cheat you'. He now realizes that he cannot study further but he wants to save, come back to his village, start some small business of his own, and educate his younger brothers.

OBCs have the highest variations across different sub-groups and regions, justifying the need for a disaggregated rather than a standardized analysis and approach.

Socio-economic and Political Positioning and the Process of Change: Implications for UCH

There are a number of castes and sub-castes within UCH, and numerous castes are together classified as OBC. Despite the fact that the study villages had representation of only a few of them, the analysis does provide insights into some common experiences of these social groups. UCH in the study villages represented seven different castes (Box 7.2).

BOX 7.2: UPPER CASTE HINDU HOUSEHOLDS IN THE STUDY VILLAGES

The number of UCH families among the poor is large only in a very few villages, Rahatmina in Bihar, Mulasar in Orissa, Bayyanagudem in AP, Malegaon in Pune district in Maharashtra, and Honnahalli and Doddathupur in Karnataka. UCH represents different castes in these villages: mainly Brahmins at Rahatmina, Khatris (goldsmiths) at Mulasar, Marathas at Malegaon, Vaishyas at Jogini, Kapus at Bayyanagudem, and Lingayats at Doddathupur and Honnahalli. The traditional roles and relations of these castes have been different from each other in the past and remain so even today. UCH are present in small numbers, though by no means in low positions, at Naudhiya (Thakurs), Kursa (Brahmins), and Jogini (Vaishyas) in MP, and at Gavaravaram (Khammas and Vaishyas) in AP.

SOCIO-ECONOMIC DOMINATION AND CHANGES

UCH are the most dominating caste in terms of landownership and traditional socio-political supremacy, especially in places where they are present in small numbers. However, this supremacy is being challenged by certain resurgent castes in some villages. The landowning upper castes, many of them absentee landlords, have survived for years by leasing out their land for sharecropping and depending on hired labour. Most hired labour has been in the nature of attached labour in the past, now changing due to a variety of reasons. Migration to urban areas or faraway places for agricultural work, though initially resorted to in times of distress, has opened up an alternative avenue for agricultural wage earners in eastern and central parts of the country, increased their income, and reduced their dependence on local landlords.

The infrastructural facilities for agriculture in areas such as Araria in Bihar and Sidhi in MP are not fully developed and even big landlords face cash crunches, especially in times of dire need such as their daughters' weddings. The prevalent system of dowry, the rates for which are highest among the upper castes, has forced many families to sell land. Sale of land is also the result of the fact that the richer among UCH are now investing in urban areas. The resurgent backward castes have taken advantage of the situation and invested their savings, usually earned through migration, in buying land. This is true of the Mandals (known as Kurmis) in Rahatmina village in Araria (Bihar) who have been buying land from Brahmin families with the money earned by migrating to distant places in Punjab and Haryana. This has, albeit in a very limited sense, changed social equations, and the backward classes are now becoming less vulnerable to exploitation at the hands of the upper castes in these villages. For instance, we have seen earlier that many Saket (SC) families in Naudhiya, traditionally the attached labour of the Thakurs, have bought land from them and have also started questioning their exploitation, and Dalits in Karnataka villages have started questioning the supremacy of the Lingayats. The Lingayats, traditionally landowning and the dominant caste, have sold their land to Tamil migrants for commercial plantations and many of them have started earning through wage work on these very plantations.

The case of the Marathas in Malegaon (Pune) in Maharashtra is different as they largely belong to the group known as Kunbi Maratha. They are considered inferior to the Marathas as such and, as a group, they have not owned much land or other assets. There has been a demand from them for OBC status so that they can access certain benefits of reservations in education and government jobs. Other UCH castes, such as the Vaishyas in Jogini (MP) or Gavaravaram (AP), have a different kind of relationship with backward castes or groups including OBCs, SCs, and even STs in some places. Though they are the landowning castes, their relationship with labour castes, such as the Sakets and the Kols in Jogini, is not the same as what the Thakurs have in Naudhiya. The relationship between the Thakurs and the Sakets in Naudhiya is guided by an extreme sense of superiority and power, and often involves the sexual harassment of Dalit women to establish that. In Jogini, the Vaishyas are as exploitative but they are mainly guided by their economic interests. The Vaishyas own almost all the irrigated land in the village and are mainly interested in ensuring that they get a regular labour supply at the cheapest possible rates. Although the Sakets have received some land from the government, it is largely barren, and hence they continue to depend on the Vaishyas for work. Increasing incidence of migration has led to some change, but it is not the same as in Naudhiya where the Sakets have started buying land from the Thakurs.

POLITICAL PROCESSES AND THE SHIFT IN UNQUESTIONED SUPREMACY

The supremacy of UCH is being questioned not only because of economic shifts but also, and perhaps more so, because of the nature of socio-political processes, already discussed in earlier chapters. Dalits in general, or some sub-castes in particular, have been resurgent and assertive in areas where political processes have been more active in giving them an identity not based on their traditional subordinate status. Socio-political processes can be either in the shape of Dalit movements or the rise of a national or regional party with its base and leadership from these groups. This has also determined the relationship between UCH and OBCs in certain parts of the country. For instance, in Bihar, the Yadavas and the Kurmis, both OBCs, have been in the forefront of state politics for the past two decades. The leadership of some national and regional parties comes from these castes and this has led to a great sense of pride among them. This confidence is reflected in many ways, including that of a positive self-image and hopes for their future. The Mandals (Kurmis) in Rahatmina village demonstrated this adequately in their interactions. The same is not true for the other OBC caste, the Amats, in the same village. Rahatmina is a Brahmin-dominated village both in terms of numbers as well as concentration of assets. Over the past two decades, the Mandals have become the most vocal politically and the most mobile economically. They have been traditionally small farmers and have now invested their incomes earned through wage work in urban areas or in distant Punjab and Haryana in agriculture and are optimistic about their future.

However, some sort of resurgence among the backward castes and a shift in landownership patterns should not be seen as a sign of decline in the status of UCH in general. Although a few UCH families have become poorer in this process, especially in places where they are large in number, as a group they remain the most influential and well networked. The evidences from all these villages make it clear that the socialization process of these families is very different from that of families belonging to the so-called lower castes, even if they have a similar economic status. The social respect that a Brahmin or a Thakur or a Khamma or a Maratha family commands, irrespective of the economic situation, is not matched by others. The non-poor of their own caste treat them as equals. The evidence from these villages shows that the resurgence of Dalits and OBCs is despised by UCH almost universally, even if political compulsions force them not to resort to direct confrontations.

THE CHANGING SOCIO-ECONOMIC SCENARIO AND THE NORM FOR SCHOOLING

The high social status of UCH has always been directly linked to their high educational status as compared to other social groups. The norm and tradition for schooling has always been strong, and in fact one of the reasons for their supremacy over others. With changing political equations and a shift in economic relations in rural areas, the need to school their children has become even more pronounced. They realize that education is the only means for survival in a changing world and that perhaps it also has the power to help them retain their status, prestige, and supremacy. Even poor

UCH families in the villages are articulate in expressing their commitment to education, reflecting a very high perceived value attached to schooling. Their high place in society and access to positions of power allow them to have a view of life very different from what is seen among Dalits, tribals' or Muslims (Box 7.3).

> BOX 7.3: PRIVATE SCHOOL IN GOVERNMENT SCHOOL?
>
> The government primary school located in Rahatmina village in Araria district in Bihar was disfunctional for many years when the villagers, mainly a few Brahmin families, decided to take matters into their own hands. There is only one teacher posted here, who is old and takes little interest. The villagers had been trying to get at least one more teacher posted for many years but nobody wants to come to this remote village. Three local educated but unemployed youths have now become teachers in the school, which has also started charging fees from students. Two separate registers are maintained, one for the government school and one for the private school, but there is actually only one school. It is not clear if this is a government or a private school! The old teacher comes and spends some time in the school but the reins are in the hands of the 'new' teachers. The Brahmin and Mandal families in the village are happy with the initiative but the poor Amat families are not very enthusiastic. The 'new' teachers claim that 'poor' children are not charged any fee but the Amat families contest this. Even if their children are allowed to come to school, they are neglected because they cannot afford to pay the fees and cannot even question the local Brahmin teachers who come from the same family that had donated land for the school in the past.

HIGH SOCIAL STATUS AND SCHOOL EXPERIENCES

The high social status enjoyed by UCH families is clearly seen in teachers' attitudes, expectations from children, and peer behaviour in school. The majority of teachers belong to high castes, and even when they do not, they have higher expectations from children belonging to upper-caste families. Research on the education system has clearly established the role of teachers' expectations in shaping children's performances. Children perform much better when teachers have high expectations from them. Low expectations from Dalit and tribal children is one of the major reasons for their low achievement levels. Teachers' day-to-day behaviour and attitudes revealed their bias in favour of upper-caste children in all villages. These children always sit in the front row, get greater attention, and are treated with affection. This is in sharp contrast to what is observed in the case of Dalit or tribal children, who sit in the back rows and get no attention from teachers.

Schools in UCH-majority areas (even if they are not the majority but if their children attend government school) are much more regular in comparison to schools attended only by Dalit or tribal children. This reflects a kind of 'power' that the upper castes still have in rural areas. This also reflects the fact that school functioning responds to people's pressure; it performs better in places where there is greater demand and greater pressure from 'powerful' sections. In other words, it responds rather than acts, and this is an important reason for the irregular and indifferent functioning of schools in areas where the commitment is ambiguous, people socially deprived and, therefore, less 'powerful' and undemanding.

Socio-Economic and Political Positioning and the Process of Change: Implications for OBCs

OBCs, unlike Dalits, have not faced untouchability and, unlike STs, have not had an isolated existence. They have been very much part of mainstream society, though they are lower rather than upper castes in the social hierarchy. However, as seen in the previous section, OBCs are not equal to UCH in matters of school participation patterns and the family's economic or educational profile[3] (Box 7.4).

> **BOX 7.4: OTHER BACKWARD CASTE (OBC) HOUSEHOLDS IN THE STUDY VILLAGES**
>
> OBCs found in the study villages comprised a number of different castes and sub-castes. They comprised mainly the Rajbhongis in Ramraikutti and Bhamunigaon in Assam, the Kurmi (Mandals) and Amat in Rahatmina in Bihar, the Gauda in Kermili and Ratapalli in Orissa, the Sahus at Kursa, the Yadavas at Jogini, and the Yadavas and a few others at Naudhiya in MP, the Kahars, Mauryas, and Yadavas at Sultana in UP, the Krubhas at Honnahalli and the Upparas at Chandukottemole in Karnataka, a mix of potters, Gauda and Athirajulu, at Gavaravaram, and many castes in small numbers, including the Yadavas at Bayyanagudem in AP.

Occupation and Children's Involvement in Work

One distinctive feature of OBCs in the past had been a homogeneity in occupation and economic status within the caste/sub-caste group. Although this is not true any more for all caste or sub-caste groups, this is more visible among them even now as compared to any other social group. Even if they have started participating in wage labour in agriculture and non-agricultural work in urban areas, they continue to do their own traditional occupation-related jobs as well. Ownership of small pieces of land is common among many OBC castes, except in AP and Karnataka villages. Cattle rearing is also very common and this is an important source of income for many families, especially in villages in Bihar, Orissa, UP and MP. Cattle is important for several reasons such as ploughing land, sale of milk, and also sale as animals in times of crisis. Both activities, cultivation and cattle rearing, have serious implications for children's lives and schooling.

As discussed earlier, farming on small landholdings is economical only if done through family labour. It has also been a tradition to engage children in different agricultural activities, essentially seasonal in character. Cattle grazing, on the other hand, is not even a seasonal activity, except in a few places where the animals are taken out for grazing only when there are standing crops in the field and are otherwise left free to roam and graze. A good number of OBC children are engaged in cattle grazing almost on a full-time basis.

POLITICAL RESURGENCE AND ASSERTION

The nature of the polity at different levels, starting from the national to the panchayat levels, also affects the social positioning and relationships between different social groups. Political processes at different levels are linked and affect each other significantly. Reflections of certain national- and state-level developments could be observed at the village level. The rise of certain backward castes to national and state-level politics in a number of eastern and central states has led to a greater sense of pride, assertion, and hope among them. They have started questioning the supremacy of the dominant castes, generally a particular UCH group. This is especially visible among castes which have not been at the bottom of the economic ladder and hence have been able to take advantage of changes in the economic scenario to consolidate their own positions. This is particularly true for the landowning castes such as the Kurmis and the Yadavas. Political access and economic mobility have strengthened each other and contributed to make them more assertive.

SOCIAL POSITIONING AND INTERRELATIONSHIPS

It is interesting to note that wherever these middle castes have land and have gained access to political power, they have begun exploiting other castes, generally Dalits or 'lower' OBC groups, in a manner similar to the way in which UCH landlords had exploited them in the past (Box 7.5). For instance,

BOX 7.5: THE YADAVAS AND THE MUSHARS IN DORIYA, ARARIA, BIHAR

The Yadavas are today the most dominant caste group in Doriya, a remote village in Araria district in Bihar. With about 150 families, they are large in number and own most of the land in the area. The Brahmins, traditional landlords in the area, are small in number and, having sold most of their land in the last two decades, do not exert the same power any more. The Mushars (Dalits) who had originally been brought here by Brahmin landlords are now working mainly for Yadava landlords. Most of the homestead land of the Mushars also belongs to the Yadavas and this gives Yadavas the main reason to exploit the Mushars. The Yadavas make the Mushars work on their land at a wage rate less than the prevalent market rate, also make them and their family members work for a few days without any wages, and threaten to throw them out of their homes if they protest. This continues despite a few Mushar families breaking away from this attached labour system and migrating every year to Punjab and Haryana to work at higher wages.

the Mandals in Rahatmina village (Araria, Bihar) did not see the landless Amats, also OBCs, as their equals in any manner. The same is true for the Krubhas in Karnataka villages who did not look at the Upparas as equals. Social divides are, however, getting blurred in villages inhabited by a variety of castes and located close to urban areas. This is seen clearly in Bayyanagudem (West Godavari, AP). Many OBC and also other caste groups live in this village, which offers enough opportunities for work both in agriculture and, due to its proximity to the town also, in non-agriculture sectors. Although clear caste identities exist, social inter-relationships are not divisive.

STRONG SOCIAL BONDING AND CASTE PANCHAYATS

Another important feature, though not so distinct as it is found commonly in a few Dalit and ST groups as well, is the crucial role of caste panchayats and affiliations in determining social beliefs, practices, and the very process of socialization. Although not found in equal measure and not equally important for all castes within the OBCs, this was found to play an important role in many OBC groups. Affiliation to the caste panchayats provides them a kind of support system needed in times of crisis. This, instead of becoming less important, has become stronger in certain areas and among certain groups due to social polarizations and changing equations. The stands taken by these bodies on issues such as girls' education are important influences on these groups (Box 7.6).

BOX 7.6: THE UPPARAS IN CHANDUKOTTEMOLE, CHAMRAJNAGAR, KARNATAKA

The Upparas, literally meaning 'those who sell salt', are generally recognized as one of the most socio-economically backward groups, found mostly in Chamrajnagar and adjoining districts of Karnataka. Their settlements are generally a little away from the main village, and caste panchayats are the most powerful bodies that determine many of their decisions. Caste panchayat decisions are final and binding on everyone. Those who disobey are excommunicated. This is feared as it means no work. The Upparas are mostly landless and survive on wage work. The decisions regarding excommunication are conveyed to landlords, who are asked not to hire particular persons and they follow the rulings because they do not want to lose their labour supply. Caste panchayat decisions also influence schooling as this body is instrumental in promoting beliefs such as girls should not be kept unmarried after puberty and so on.

SCHOOLING PARTICIPATION

A general change in the socio-economic and political positions among OBCs appeared to have led to positive changes in their perceptions of schooling as well. Most resurgent OBC groups send their children, especially boys, to school, at times to private schools, as these are perceived to be functioning better than government schools. The feeling that education is one weapon which gave UCH access to power in the past is seen among several of them, who now have the means to support sustained schooling participation. They do not want to remain behind on this front anymore. However, this commitment to education is generally limited to boys alone and they remain very conservative in their outlook towards girls. Also, this greater demand for schooling is limited only to those groups which have taken advantage of recent socio-political changes. The remaining OBC groups are still socially and economically deprived and do not show any obvious high interest in children's schooling. Nevertheless, changes can be seen at the individual family level even among those who, as a group, are not very progressive.

Deprivation, Social Status, Norm, and Schooling Participation

The above discussion makes it clear that in the Indian context, deprivation has a very different connotation for the upper castes in comparison to what it means to social groups such as Dalits, tribals, or, Muslims. Many individual upper caste families face economic deprivation, making them vulnerable to crises, but their situation is not as precarious because of strong social standing and support. This is especially significant in relation to a commitment to education. Education has always been important for the upper castes and has become all the more important in a changing world, where traditional economic relations have been eroded, new political equations are emerging, and old social hierarchies are being questioned. A strong social norm of sending children to school exists among the upper castes of all regions. Even if they do not see direct employment linkages, awareness of the larger benefits of education is higher among them (Box 7.7).

Most UCH families are generally keen on the schooling of their children and, except in situations of very difficult crises and economic hardship, they generally do not allow children to discontinue their education. The practice of engaging children, especially boys, in any work is almost non-existent among UCH. High parental aspirations are reinforced in schools in the shape of greater expectations and preferential treatment from teachers, and this creates a conducive environment for children's continued schooling.

As seen above, there is a lot of variation within OBCs in all respects and their attitude towards education depends upon their specific situations. In places where they have started asserting themselves and become interested in the schooling of their children, schools and teachers are also paying greater attention. On the other hand, in areas where they still do not hold any power and remain economically deprived, they face discrimination even in schools. Discrimination is not always evident in the form of teachers'

BOX 7.7: EDUCATION IS ALL IMPORTANT

Kashinath Jha, the son of a Brahmin cultivator and priest, could not complete his bachelor's degree course because of his father's sudden illness and death, which forced him to sell the family's only piece of land, about half an acre in size. The father had opened a small shop in the village to pay for Kashinath's education, which also remained unattended during his illness. After his father's death, Kashinath asked his younger brother, who had completed his matriculation, to look after the shop and left for Delhi to try his luck. He worked there in a factory for about a year and supported his family. After this, he went back and started taking land on a sharecropping basis for cultivation. This did not prove to be remunerative and he again went to Delhi to work in a factory. There he worked hard and sent money home to support the family and repay the debt taken at the time of his father's illness.

Kashinath was married off at the age of 19 and already had two daughters when his father died. In the village, there were family altercations after his brother's marriage and the family subdivided. Kashinath returned from Delhi as his mother, wife, and daughters could not live alone. He managed to get a loan of Rs 1000 from IRDP and started selling cereals during the season and vegetables during the off season. He continues with this occupation and works hard to earn for his family. His wife, Meera, is a class V pass and, being a Brahmin, does not go out to work. They have five daughters, Pinky (10), Preeti (7), Babli (4), Lovely (4), and Munchun (2). 'We wanted to have a son. That is how we got five daughters. Babli and Lovely are twins', informs Meera and adds, 'but now we are going to do our best to ensure that they are educated and made capable of facing this world'. Kashinath says that he has seen many ups and downs in life and knows that education alone secures one respect. The first four daughters are enrolled in a private school with a fee of Rs 30 per month for each child. 'Initially Pinky and Preeti were going to a government school but the teachers never used to come. That is why I shifted them', says Kashinath.

Although financially not very secure, the couple takes good care of their daughters. They are keen that the girls should get nutritious food with vegetables and milk. Since he deals in vegetables, it is not difficult to afford them and he wants to buy one cow to ensure that the girls get enough milk. Despite the long hours and the tough nature of his work, he takes out two hours every day to teach his daughters. He also wants to buy a transistor as 'it is a good source for a variety of information which is important for growing children'. Kashinath also plays Ludo and other games with his daughters and Pinky loves her father for that.

Pinky is very confident for her age and wants to study up to the graduation level. She does some light chores as her mother feels 'it is important for girls to know housework' but does not do any cooking or other major work. Her grandmother also helps her mother in taking care of the youngest sister, Munchun. At times Pinky also teaches her younger sisters. She wants to become a teacher. A local lady teacher is her role model.

behaviour but is also seen simply in the very irregular functioning of schools (Box 7.8). However, the number of teachers from the OBC community has also increased during the last two decades, changing the social composition of this group and thus having an impact on school environments.

BOX 7.8: EDUCATION IS NOT THAT IMPORTANT

Madevashetty (10) is enrolled in class III but rarely goes to school. Both his parents, Sidashetty (30) and Putamma (25), are landless agricultural wage workers and leave home early. He leaves the house as soon as his parents leave and along with his friends goes to all kinds of near and distant places. 'Why should I go to school? Sitting in the classroom is boring. I love to play with my friends and going to distant hills,' says Madevashetty without any hesitation. 'Once I grow up, I will start working for wages like my father. What is the use of education for that?' he retorts, when asked why he does not go to school. The parents are not overtly worried by this attitude. They feel they cannot force him to go to school. Once, when Sidashetty had beaten Madevashetty, he ran away and came home after two days. Now the parents prefer to keep quiet. 'He is our only son. I don't want to lose him. After all, education is not that important', says Putamma. She is also not worried about the fact that he keeps roaming around the whole village. However, she does not have the same attitude towards her 8-year-old daughter, Madevi. 'After all, she is a girl. She can't be left like that', says Putamma. Although Madevi is enrolled in class I, she goes to school only occasionally. In her mother's absence, she does all the household work and also takes care of her younger sister, Chikamma (5).

Putamma got married to Sidashetty when she was 9 years old. Sidashetty was 14 at the time. Two years after marriage, she attained puberty and came to her husband's house. At the age of 15, she had her first child, Madevashetty. Initially, they lived with Sidashetty's parents, but later separated and set up an independent house. Their lives, which were easy initially, became tougher and tougher with the arrival of more children. Successive pregnancies kept Putamma out of work and led to financial crises in the family. They had to survive on debt. Before Chikamma's birth, Putamma caught TB and was taken to Mysore for treatment. Sidashetty borrowed Rs. 10,000 and the entire family lived there in the hospital for four months. It took six years to repay that loan and it is only recently that they have become free from that burden. They resort to short-term loans every year during the rainy season. No wage work is available around the village from June to August, forcing them to take loans at exorbitant rates of interest, varying from 10 per cent per week to 20 per cent per month. Sidashetty migrates to neighbouring Tamil Nadu farms for one month during June-July and earns 100 rupees per day. He is generally able to save Rs. 1,000 and after coming back pays back this loan.

Sidashetty and Putamma are not worried about their children's education. Sidashetty says 'Education is useful in equipping one in communicating with officials and others coming from towns, and it also saves one from the embarrassment of putting your thumb on any paper.' But it does not have much relevance for poor people. 'Even those who have completed degrees are not getting employment. Whether educated or not, we have to work for wages. What is the sense in spending ten years and so much of money on it?' asks Sidashetty. Regarding his daughters, he says, 'Madevi and Chikamma will go to school up to Class V if they want. After that, they have to get married'. 'In our Uppara community, we cannot keep our daughters unmarried once they attain puberty. Even before that, if we need money we will have to send Madevi for wage work,' adds Putamma.

The livelihood situations are tough for many OBC groups, and engaging children in work is common, creating constraints on schooling. Strong affiliations to caste groups have led to a kind of insulation among many OBC groups which has a role in keeping them away from many progressive decisions. This is truer for more economically backward groups. Such affiliations provide a support system which they do not want to lose. On the whole, there are certain progressive OBC groups and a clear norm of sending children to school is getting established quickly. On the other hand, there are groups still living at the margins which do not view education as indispensable. Finally, at the cost of repetition, it is important to stress that there is a need to distinguish between the upper castes and the so-called other backward castes in educational data and anlayses for any meaningful understanding of the different social groups.

NOTES

1. See Béteille (1992) and Shah (1996) for discussions on the use of the term Backward Classes. The term OBC was widely used by British administrators as Other Backward Classes, but had come to mean 'Other Backward Castes' in administrative usage.
2. Unlike tribes and, to some extent, a few Dalit castes, different sub-castes among UCH and OBC have not been studied in such detail, and the Census also does not provide separate statistics. Therefore, the analysis in this regard is limited to field observations and general information available from other sources.
3. The fact that no large-scale survey or Census separates the two poses a severe limitation in this context.

8. Nature, Nurture, or Culture? Gender in Education

BACKGROUND

Gender differentials in education can be understood only in the wider context of female disadvantage in India. Despite impressive growth in several indicators of social change, in comparative terms, women still remain far behind men in all objective and material measures of well-being: economic self-sufficiency, education, nutrition, life expectancy, and mortality. Further, the daily experiences of most women still unfold against the backdrop of resiliently patriarchal social structures and cultural ideas. Gender bias pervades all spheres of life and society, and informs political decision making as well as intra-familial attitudes and values. Cultural representations of women are no less important than the constraints of the economy and the problem is further exacerbated when gender disadvantage is compounded by class, caste, region, and religion. The nature and intensity of this bias varies across economic systems and regions and over the life cycles of individuals within households. Gender then is a complex phenomenon, not amenable to simple analysis (Ray and Basu, 1991; Wazir, 2000).

By and large, irrespective of caste, religion, and overall socio-economic background, views on femininity and feminine roles often come into conflict with the goals of education: for their survival and unity, families build on the nurturant and docile aspects of femininity quite contrary to the ideal goals of learning, which stress a certain independence of thought, spirit of enquiry, and, at a more mundane level, relating to peers and developing non-familial loyalties (Karlekar, 2000). Socialization in the context of women seems to be heavily weighed in favour of tradition, and the social institutions of family, kinship, and marriage. It is closely intertwined with the process of role socialization of boys and girls, which eventually leads to the dichotomizing of masculine and feminine roles or to gender asymmetry. Social and cultural differences are based on biological differences and, therefore, viewed as 'natural'. In this way, the difference between the biological, the natural, and the social is obliterated through the process of value internalization within the sacred confines of family and kinship groups. These are further reinforced through religious ideology, myth, and ritual (Chanana, 1988).

Reports from the study villages provide detailed accounts of discrimination faced by girls in enrolling and attending school, because of economic, social, and cultural constraints. We have earlier seen that participation levels for girls in school education are much lower than that of boys, as reflected in lower rates of enrolment and higher rates of drop-out and non-enrolment. Girls comprise only 46.4 per cent of the total children population, while they constitute 53.4 per cent of out-of-school children. This, too, is only half the story, as enrolment or being in school alone does not ensure their regular participation; the gender bias also operates against them in regularly attending school. Girls clearly emerge as the most vulnerable and hence always the first to bear the brunt of the disadvantages arising out of poverty or social constraints, including caste and religion. In this chapter, we outline the constraints faced by girls and detail the processes whereby these constraints act together and reinforce each other in keeping girls away from school.

GIRLS' PARTICIPATION IN SCHOOL EDUCATION: THE WORSE HALF IN ALL GROUPS

We have seen earlier that barring Chamrajnagar (Karnataka) and Pune (Maharashtra), large gender differentials exist in all districts in school participation indicators. Gender differentials begin with girls' numbers itself being less than those for boys and are later widened in terms of enrolment and regularity. The girls are fewer in number than boys in all social groups except for UCH and OBC. Their share is lowest among Muslims; girls are only 41.3 per cent of the total population in the 6-13 age group. However, their share in enrolment is lower than their share in the population of all groups, including the OBCs and UCH. Among Muslims, the share of girls in enrolment is almost equal to the sex ratio in the age-group population (Table 8.1).

Significant gender gaps exist in school attendance regularity patterns among children enrolled from all social groups. The proportion of girls is higher than boys among those who attend school only occasionally and lower for those who attend school regularly in all social groups, barring Muslims. This includes the UCH, OBCs, SCs, and STs. The differential between boys and girls regularly attending school is the least for STs and the highest for Dalits. Taking both enrolment and regularity patterns into account, the picture of school participation is roughly the same for Dalit and tribal girls. In both social groups, about one-third of the girls are out of

Table 8.1: Share of Girls in Population and Enrolment

	% of girls in population (6-13 yrs)	% of girls in enrolment (6-13 yrs)
UCH	55.2	52.9
OBC	50.9	48.7
SC	44.7	41.0
ST	44.5	35.9
Muslims	41.3	41.1
Total	46.5	42.6

SOURCE: Household Survey.

school, another one-third going to school irregularly, and only the remaining one-third attend school regularly. The situation is only slightly better for the OBCs where about 44 per cent girls attend school regularly. The condition, however, is much better for upper caste girls since more than 72 per cent girls attend school regularly, even though this is significantly lower than the proportion of boys belonging to the same group.[1] In contrast, the situation is abysmal for Muslim girls; only 17 per cent of them regularly attend schools even though this is higher than the percentage of Muslim boys (Table 8.2).

Therefore, though gender disparities exist in varying degrees and forms for all social groups, girls in upper caste groups demonstrate significantly higher school participation rates than all other groups. We have seen earlier that sharp gender differentials exist in participation indicators for all economic groups—poor, very poor, and non-poor—the state of girls being the worst for the very poor. Only about 22 per cent girls in the lower segment of BPL families attend school regularly as against 33 per cent boys in their own group, 41 per cent girls in the upper segment of BPL families, and 53 per cent girls in APL households (Table 3.8). The discussion of the regional picture on gender gaps had shown that only 11 per cent girls were attending school regularly in Shravasti and only 21 per cent in Araria district as against 74 per cent in Pune and 67 per cent in Chamrajnagar district. Therefore, even at the cost of repetition, it is important to state that the issue of gender disparity is much more complex and everything—poverty levels, region, and social positioning—adds to the degree of gender disparity. This

Table 8.2: Schooling Participation Patterns for Boys and Girls in Different Social Groups

(in per cent)

Caste	Sex	Total	Enrolled			Dropout enrolled	Never	Madrasa
			Regular	Irregular	Occasional			
UCH	Male	100	91.07	8.93	–	7.80	4.70	–
	Female	100	90.47	7.95	1.58	13.92	6.51	[illegible]
OBC	Male	100	65.00	29.16	5.84	12.90	13.50	–
	Female	100	64.91	28.94	6.15	14.80	17.80	–
SC	Male	100	67.15	28.43	4.42	10.20	17.60	0.35
	Female	100	55.63	36.61	7.74	9.21	29.15	–
ST	Male	100	71.93	25.12	2.95	19.40	11.60	–
	Female	100	71.92	22.80	5.26	19.50	32.20	–
UCM	Male	100	22.50	42.50	35.00	10.70	8.92	8.92
	Female	100	32.43	35.14	32.43	11.10	11.10	9.30
LCM	Male	100	33.33	52.78	13.89	8.06	30.10	22.60
	Female	100	37.50	50.00	12.50	2.00	37.30	29.40
Total	Male	100	65.80	27.90	6.30	13.40	14.70	2.80
	Female	04.1	27.00	8.70	13.50	25.05	2.40	[illegible]

SOURCE: Household Survey.

makes girls belonging to socially marginalized groups such as STs, SCs, and Muslims in the poorest families and living in economically backward regions, the most deprived educational groups. At the same time, it is also important to reiterate that girls are worse off than boys in comparative terms in all situations and groups including the non-poor upper castes and those living in advanced regions.

FAMILY'S SURVIVAL: CRITICAL CONTRIBUTIONS MADE BY GIRLS

Girls, especially among poor and very poor families, play a very critical role in the survival and coping mechanisms of the household. Their contributions range from earning wages to participation in own farm or forest collection activities, on the one hand, to responsibilities of household chores and child-care, on the other. We have seen earlier that almost all out of school girls and about one-third in-school girls are engaged in some work for substantial hours during the day (Chapters 2 and 3). Engagement in work affects schooling participation adversely, especially after the age of 9 years or so. We have seen earlier that the regularity in attending school goes down for girls in the 9-11 age group, and it can be seen that the incidence of engagement in work is also very high for girls in this age group (Box 8.1).

Life situation are tough in poorly provided for villages in the districts of Bihar, Jharkhand, MP, and UP. Even the collection of drinking water takes a few hours everyday at several places. This is especially true for physically separated Dalit clusters and scattered tribal hamlets mostly located in difficult terrain. The workload of tribal women is very heavy in areas where dependence on forests is high. In other areas like Chamrajnagar in Karnataka and West Godavari in AP, the participation rates of women in wage work is high. A tough daily life and the engagement of women in various kinds of jobs as well as high participation in wage work forces somebody else to play a supporting role in domestic chores and child care, and daughters fulfill this responsibility. This is often precipitated due to the ill-health of mothers in rural areas. In any case, it is common for school-going children to have at least one non-school-going sister at home, doing household chores and looking after younger siblings. Such incidences are common in all regions and districts and among all social groups without exception.

However, it would be simplistic to believe that girls' engagement in work emanates only from difficult livelihood or general life situations. The secondary status of women in all walks of life, and patriarchal practices and cultural beliefs which make people view girls as liabilities, contribute also to the very casual treatment of girls' schooling. Parental aspirations regarding girls mostly revolve around marrying them off and fulfilling their 'responsibility' (see Table 3.24). Poverty and deprived life situations only add to these conditions to make the situation worse for girls in poorer groups. However, at the same time it is also true that poverty and related

BOX 8.1: GUDDU: THE PILLAR OF THE FAMILY

Guddu (12) is the third among five sisters and three brothers. Though her mother, Ramrati, had given birth to ten children and is pregnant with the eleventh child, two children did not survive. Her father, Daddi, belongs to the Sahu (OBC) caste and is a cultivator with five acres of land. Daddi works hard to support his family and arrange money for the daughters' weddings. Whenever he is free of working on his own field, he goes to the nearest town, Sidhi, in search of wage work. At the age of 40, he looks at least 70.

The eldest daughter, Nirmala (17), was married at the age of 12 and is already pregnant with her first child. The second daughter, Shyamkali (15), was also married at the same age. Guddu, like her elder sisters, has never been to school. But she loves to see her younger sister, Ramwati, in school uniform. Ramwati (11) is studying in Class VI in the middle school in the nearby town. The eldest son, Rambhavaran, also goes to the same school, while the second son, Rajkumar, goes to the local school. Guddu has taken over all major responsibilities at home, apart from helping her father in the fields so that her younger sister and brothers can go to school regularly. Despite this, she also nurses a desire to become literate and devotes some time in the evening to studying when Ramwati teaches her the alphabet and numbers using the *kuchcha* floor and pebbles.

The village Naudhiya, where Daddi lives with his family, is about 6 km. away from the district headquarters, Sidhi. The village has a middle school and is inhabited mainly by the upper caste, landed Thakur community and, therefore, there is generally a norm of sending everybody to school, especially among upper caste and OBC families. But Guddu cannot go to school because of her responsibilities. There are many more Guddus in the village. Her day starts at 5.00 a.m. She finishes her chores—cleaning their four rooms and courtyard besides the utensils—before other members of the family get up. Then she goes to collect water. She takes about 10-12 rounds of the 2 km. stretch to collect enough water for eight family members and eight animals. Milking cows and cooking for her school-going siblings comes next. Getting the younger brothers ready for school follows.

The parents have a lot of hopes from their eldest son, Rambhavaran, and therefore give special attention to him. Guddu is also expected to take special care of her brothers while serving meals and getting them ready for school. 'This is the most painful part of the day. I keep thinking, why do I not go to school? Why did my parents not send me to school?' says Guddu showing restlessness on an otherwise calm face. 'I could never ask this because nobody ever had any time for me. Slowly, I have understood that I am required for the family and I don't despise this,' she adds. Fully supportive of Ramwati's education Guddu at times also envies her. 'Why could I not have the same fate?' she wonders. Apart from working in the fields almost everyday, Guddu has the full responsibility of looking after the youngest siblings, Manoj (3) and Lata (1). The mother, Ramrati, is too weak because of frequent pregnancies and child-births. Still, both mother and daughter do a lot of work together inside and outside the home. There does not seem to be any other option. 'Girls have to accept their fate', feels Ramrati.

disadvantages, especially among social groups such as Dalits, tribes, and Muslims, deprive girls of even minimum opportunities available to girls from non-poor and non-deprived social groups.

Socialization, Socio-cultural Practices, and the Roles of Girls

The social practices and cultural beliefs which restrict girls' participation in schooling were found prevalent in all parts of the country and among all social groups, varying only in the degree of oppression and ramifications on different aspects of their lives. The unquestioning belief in the 'natural' role of girls to fulfil their 'feminine' responsibilities is present everywhere. The sexual bias in the distribution of functions within the home is only one of the ways in which the gendered role of girls is perpetuated.

GIRLS BELONG TO SOME OTHER FAMILY

The feeling and belief that 'girls belong to some other family' is universal among all parents. There is virtually no difference in this outlook and is seen in all regions, social groups, and economic groups. This has serious implications when it comes to decisions about the schooling of daughters. We have seen that schooling is not an easy option for poor parents in rural areas with unstable life situations and precarious economic conditions. A decision for schooling has direct and indirect implications for the survival of the family. Poor families, which in any case do not perceive schooling as very relevant or beneficial, view it as of even less use for girls who are not even going to be living with them after marriage. If at all any benefit will accrue, it will prove advantageous for those families into which these girls are going to be married, and not to the parents' family, and, therefore, is definitely low on their priority list. The low priority accorded to girls' schooling was obvious not only from the real depicted low preference in terms of enrolment and regularity, but also from the views expressed during discussions held in the villages (Box 8.2).

This belief that boys belong to the parents' family and hence investing in their education will yield returns later is more of a perception than a reality. The fact that the majority of grown-up married sons, especially in the poor and very poor families, separate soon after marriage and rarely stay together to look after their parents does not form part of the collective understanding of the situation. It is also clear from the views expressed on girls' education that society, which could be the village or the small social group constituting a particular religion or caste/sub-caste, has a role in determining the outlook towards the schooling of girls. The majority of parents when talking about girls' education refer to social practices prevalent within their caste or religion that act as constraints. However, in most cases, they accept these unquestioningly, and it is implicit that neither can anything be done about the situation nor do these restrictions require any change. There is a societal angle even in the better schooling status of girls seen for certain groups such as the UCH, despite holding the belief that 'girls belong to some other

BOX 8.2: VIEWS ON GIRLS' EDUCATION

The common view expressed in more than 90 per cent FGDs carried out separately with men and women in all the villages was that it 'does not make a difference if a girl is not educated because she has to get married and go to her "own" home'. The only variation was that of language. An additional statement was 'not very important because they do not have to go out and do a job, and when boys are not getting jobs, who will allow girls to go out and work'. The prevalent opinion was that 'a girl's job is to learn household jobs, support her mother and parents in other home-related work; sending her to school has no advantages'.

Some FGDs also revealed a difference of opinion among the participants. A few thought that education is important for girls. This view was based mostly on the rationale that 'they can write letters to their parents after marriage'. When asked why certain families send their girls to school if it is so unimportant, the answer was, 'the parents are sending their girls because of the money which the government gives,' or 'girls belonging to better-off and higher caste families who have no work at home are sent to school'.

One statement made by a poor Dalit woman in a village in MP was different 'It is very important to educate girls because in practical life, they are the ones who take care of the house and take care of the finances as well. It becomes important that girls are empowered enough to take care of their family and finances.'

(Based on Focus Group Discussions (FGDs) with men's and women's groups.)

family'. There exists a social norm of educating girls up to a certain level in those castes and this is also important for marriages. This is discussed in more detail later.

EARLY MARRIAGE

One of the prevalent social practices restricting girls' access to education is early marriage. Early marriage of girls is still prevalent among most communities, especially Dalits and a few tribal groups in economically poorer sections, in most of the regions. In some districts, the practice of child or early marriage is common for all social groups, while in others it is limited to particular groups. From all the study villages, the practice is most widespread in Sidhi district (MP), where child marriage is common among most tribal and all Dalit groups (Box 8.3).

BOX 8.3: EARLY MARRIAGE OF GIRLS

The practice of child marriage is most widely prevalent in Sidhi from among all the districts in this study. In Sidhi, this is common among the tribal groups of the Gonds and the Kols, as well as in all Dalit groups. The majority of girls are married between the age of eight and twelve years in Sidhi. In this district, child marriage is also commonly practised among the Muslims and the Yadavas, whereas in upper caste families, girls are married off at the age of 15-16 years. In Shravasti district in UP, the age of marriage is extremely low among specific communities, e.g. among the Patharkatwas, a SC group, children are married at the very early age of two to four years even now. The Tharus in the same district marry their daughters by the age of 12. The girls are married between the ages of 8 and 14 in both SC and Muslim families in most villages in this district. In Araria district in Bihar, most girls, especially those belonging to Dalit and Muslim households, are married between the ages of 12 and 14.

The Dalit and tribal population of Koraput and Nuapara districts in Orissa and Palamu in Jharkhand are no exception. Barring specific groups, girls are married by the age of 15. In Dhubri district in Assam, the age of marriage is not so low among most social groups, but Muslim girls in Tiapara village are married around the age of 14 to 15 years. The practice is also widespread in Chamrajnagar district in Karnataka where the average age of marriage appeared to be around 12 years in all villages, this being more common among SCs and OBCs. Among the Lingayats, an upper caste, the average age of marriage is around 15 to 16 years. The situation is slightly different in the Dangs district in Gujarat and the Pune district in Maharashtra. Though early marriage was prevalent among the tribal population in the Dangs till a decade ago, it is on the decline now and the majority of the girls are married after the age of 18. Girls are not married before the age of 16 even among the poorer families in Pune.

MORALITY, FEAR OF SEXUAL HARASSMENT, AND DOWRY

The practice of early marriage has its origins in several deep-rooted cultural beliefs, social situations, and economic compulsions. For instance, a very strong belief that girls should not be sent to school or kept unmarried after puberty is present among most communities in Chamrajnagar. This is particularly true for SCs and OBCs. Even in a village like Doddathupur,—where the school is functioning well, the community is happy with teachers, an NGO is helping in the distribution of learning materials to poor students, the social equilibrium is such that no community faces any discrimination at school and almost all children in the age group of 6-13 are going to school—all girls belonging to the Adi Karnataka (SC) and Krubha (OBC) castes drop out after completing class VII. The same is true for other villages in this district. It is ironic that despite the high participation of women in work in these areas, the cultural environment is so conservative that school attendance by adolescent girl is associated with immorality (Box 8.4 and 8.5).

The association between school attendance by girls and immorality is one of the reasons for the early marriage of their girls and withdrawal from school even without marriage in many parts of the country. Early marriage means restrictions on the free movement of girls. Interestingly enough, even when the marriage is not real, the impact remains the same. Among the Bhunjia tribe of Cherichuan (Nuapara, Orissa), girls are symbolically married to arrows around the age of 10-12 years. After this symbolic marriage, they are made to avoid male company till the time they actually get married to boys, and hence no question of going to school or any other such engagement arises.

BOX 8.4: SUBHADRA STILL WANTS TO GO TO SCHOOL

Parsu Jagat is one of the Gonda (SC) families in Kermili which is mainly inhabited by STs. Gonda is one of the lowest castes in the social hierarchy and these families face discrimination in using certain public utility services. Parsu's family of seven members lives along with other families of the same caste in a cluster at the outskirts of the village Kermili in Nuapara district of Orissa. He has five children—four daughters and one son. The two eldest daughters, Yashoda Bai (15) and Subhadra (14), work as grazers for others. Yashoda was withdrawn from school when she was in Class II. Subhadra was withdrawn a year later, when she too was in class II, after the birth of the third daughter, essentially to help her mother. Now that the younger siblings are slightly grown up and go to school, Subhadra has also started working as a grazer.

Landless Parsu and his wife work as wage labourers but the forest is their main source of sustenance. Work availability has gone down in the last two three years after a few neighbouring villages, which had landowning families, got submerged in the course of the construction of a dam. This has worsened the economic condition of the families which solely depend on wage work, and has resulted in a greater dependence on forest produce for their survival. Parsu Jagat's family is no exception. In different seasons, they collect different types of tubers: *Kitsan Kanda, Pita Kanda, Kulia Kanda, Kuin Kanda*, and leaves: mango, *tendu, kerma*, and survive on these. The forest is also a source for other produce which is collected and sold. These include *mahua* flowers and seeds, *char* seeds, *amla,* and many other medicinal herbs, and firewood. All family members get involved in the collection of this forest produce. The family, like others of their caste, faces hunger and acute food crises for major parts of the year. Except for the paddy harvesting season, there is never enough to eat for everybody in the family.

Subhadra is still interested in studying and despite the fact that several years have passed since her withdrawal from school, she knows how to write the alphabet and numbers. She blames Parsu for not showing any interest in educating her. She feels her father could have sent her, too, to an ashram school like a few others from her village. Parsu accepts that he does not see any value in educating girls. The only value he sees in sending children to school is the daily cooked meal which is served in school. 'Children get at least one proper meal,' he says drily. The wife differs. She says that circumstances forced her to withdraw the older children, but she will try her best to complete the education of the younger children. She sees education as a means of getting out of their drudgery but does not know whether they will be successful in educating even one of their children. Both husband and wife are already worried about Yashoda's marriage. 'She has already crossed 14. She should have been married by now as per community customs,' they point out. This would mean arranging money from somewhere, which is not easy. 'Even loans are not easily available if you don't have any assets,' they say.

In the feudal set-up of Sidhi in MP, the practice of early marriage arises also from the fear of sexual harassment. Sexual exploitation is undoubtedly the worst form of exploitation and is linked with the notion of the dominance of a social group. Sexual harassment of Dalit girls at the hands of upper caste men is widespread. Although with the increasing assertion of the SCs and changing political conditions, the practice has waned over time, the fear still

BOX 8.5: A GIRL IS A GIRL

Geetha's day starts at 6 in the morning and ends at 9 at night. She is always doing some work or the other—cooking, cleaning utensils, sweeping the floor, washing clothes, taking care of her younger sisters Indira (8) and Ramya (3), or doing something else. One rarely finds her free. 'I don't play any games, nor do I like to play,' says Geetha, all of 12 years herself. She was going to school till three years ago. 'I was in Class IV then. I would have been in Class VII now,' she says. She stopped going to school when the family decided to migrate for wage work. Every year they migrate from June to February from their village Honnahalli in Chamrajnagar district of Karnataka to a neighbouring district in Kerala. All three sisters accompany their parents, Madde Gowda and Kalamma, a Dalit couple, to Kerala.

Madde Gowda does not own any land and lives in a rented, one-room *kuchcha* house which was earlier a cowshed. He separated from his brother after several altercations and has not received any share in the house. It was not so difficult initially as they had only one daughter and could manage with whatever wages both husband and wife were getting within the village. However, with the arrival of more children, Kalamma started finding it difficult to go for wage work. Geetha and Indira were going to school, and therefore the mother had to be at home to take care of the younger children. This meant less income and economic hardship. Many other families from the village were migrating to Kerala plantations where work was assured and wages high. Madde Gowda also decided to go but since he was not on good terms with his brother, he could not leave his children behind. In Kerala, both husband and wife work for wages, and Geetha does all the household work. Kalamma says that their financial situation has improved after they started going to Kerala. She as well as the children have at least basic clothes now, she points out.

Indira was also studying in class II when the family withdrew them from school and began going to Kerala for about five-six months every year. 'The girls cannot go to school in either of the places. When we come back from Kerala in February, only two months are left in the school session and if we send them to school in Kerala, they would miss their examinations. In any case, there they teach Malayalam which has no use for us,' says Madde Gowda. Kalamma adds, 'what is the use of girls' education anyway? Geetha has to be married and we will send her to the in-laws' place in the coming two-three years. More education would mean more dowry, we cannot afford that.'

The couple seems unhappy about the fact that they have only daughters and no son. 'The daughters will get married and go to their in-laws' places. There will not be anybody to take care of us,' feels Madde Gowda. 'And on top of that we have to work hard and earn more. To get them married is our responsibility; we cannot shy away from that.'

exists quite strongly, especially among those groups which have not been able to reap the benefits of development. The Sakets (SC) in Sidhi villages, especially the women among them, expressed this fear quite often. The fear of sexual harassment in schools at the hands of boys from relatively higher and dominant castes acts as a deterrent to girls' participation in schooling, especially because the educational institutions happen to be co-educational.

Balanagar Kodri in Shravasti district of UP presents one such example, where the Chamars (SC) expressed this fear about Brahmin boys, while the Kushbahiyas, the less dominant among the SCs, were scared of Chamar boys teasing their girls at school.

The practice of early marriage is also linked in some sense with preserving the morality of girls, as any form of interaction with boys is perceived to make girls 'impure'. The early marriage of girls is, as expressed by many men's groups in study villages, also a matter of social prestige for most communities. If the girl is not married early, the chances of her being 'immoral' are high, which would mean loss of face in society and must be avoided. Though this sense of maintaining the purity of girls exists quite strongly even among upper caste groups, this does not act so much against girls' schooling at the elementary or secondary stage because of two reasons. One reason is obvious; they are generally the dominant social group and hence the social positioning operates in their favour. The second reason is the growing demand for 'educated girls' as brides by boys from upper castes and higher classes. In a predominantly patriarchal society, the groom's side dictates the terms of the marriage and the girls' parents adopt anything that facilitates the easy marriage of girls at the 'right' age. Although this practice does not arise from a progressive outlook towards girls' education, it does lead to a positive outcome—that of increased girls' participation in schooling, which creates its own, intended and unintended, influences on their lives.

The practice of dowry is customary in many parts of the country. It is practised in varying forms among all Hindu groups, including Dalits in all the study villages. It has now been adopted even by those communities among whom this had not been a traditional custom. Dowry was not common among tribal groups in any part of the country. A more common custom among them has been that of bride price paid by the groom and his family at the time of marriage. The root of this practice is traced to the hard-working and bread-earning role of women in tribal societies. However, though many groups still practice bride price, dowry is now common among many of them, especially those who have land and have been engaged in settled cultivation for long. It has also become common for those living along with or close to Hindus for long. The adoption of many Hindu customs, including dowry, have been part of the sanskritization process. Dowry was found to be prevalent among the Gonds and the Kols in Sidhi (MP) and the Oraons in Khurakhurd (Jharkhand).

The custom of dowry acts against girls' education, especially for poor families. In India, husbands are expected to be more educated than their wives in all communities. The rate of dowry is generally linked with the level of education. The higher the level of education, the higher is the amount of dowry. This means that parents have to arrange for higher dowry if they educate their daughters. It is, therefore, natural for poor families, living from day-to-day basis to regard education as highly demanding and unaffordable, especially in a cultural milieu where girls' independence is not only not valued but is also considered an undesirable trait. The trend of demanding less dowry from an educated woman, seen nowadays in the urban middle class, is yet not visible in rural areas, definitely not among poorer families. The reason perhaps lies in the clear linkages with earnings; while the urban middle-class woman is seen as a long-term asset with her higher earning capacity, this is not so in the case of a rural, half-educated girl, who would earn only as much as any other uneducated woman.

INTRA-HOUSEHOLD BIASES

The low value attached to girls' education is also obvious from intra-household biases. Whenever a family finds it difficult to send all their children to school due to various needs both at home and outside, and face a choice of prioritizing between sending a girl or a boy, there is rarely any hesitation involved. It is taken for granted that it will be the boy who will go to school and the girl are kept at home to take on domestic responsibilities. This is not uncommon even in those families which show a strong interest in educating their children despite poverty and are ready to make adjustments, but this interest and readiness is often limited to the schooling of boys and the same consideration is not extended to girls. It is the usual practice to keep at least one girl at home to support the mother in household work and child care. As mentioned earlier, the majority of school-going boys and even girls have at least one non-school-going sister at home, taking care of responsibilities and making it possible for them to attend school. Even when both girls and boys are sent to school, it is more difficult for girls as they also have greater responsibilities at home and do not really get any time for following up their studies (Boxes 8.6 and 8.7).

BOX 8.6 BUYING A BUFFALO IS MUCH MORE IMPORTANT

Sunadhar (13) is a student of Class VII in an ashram school in Ambagda village, where he gets all the facilities of boarding, lodging, textbooks, etc., free of cost. He wants to finish his school and go to college. He aspires to become a teacher and buy a motorbike, exactly the same one his teacher owns. His father, Krupa Harijan, a landless SC wage worker in Mulasar village of Koraput district, also wants his son to finish his education and get a government job. He says he will do his best to ensure Sunadhar's continued schooling. His younger son, Balaram (8), the youngest of five siblings, is also enrolled in class I in the village school. Krupa is worried about him as he does not show much interest in studies.

Krupa has three daughters, too—Sumri (17), Sukri (11), and Tulsa (10). Sumri is already married but continues to live with her parents. Both Sukri and Tulsa were enrolled in the local primary school but stopped going in Class III and II respectively. Both work in cashew-seed preparation on a wage and manage to earn about Rs. 4,000 each in a year. Krupa says he cannot continue their schooling as he can't bear the expenses. He would rather have them work so that they can take care of themselves and also add to the family's income. Krupa suffers from chronic stomach pains and cannot work the entire day. He gets Rs. 20 for half a day's work. He has only one buffalo at present and if he buys one more, he will be able to earn 35 rupees for the same amount of time. The rate is higher for those who bring their own pair of animals for ploughing. He expects to buy one more buffalo with the support of Sukri's and Tulsa's earnings. The availability of work is not a problem in the village. It is a canal-irrigated village and agricultural wage work is available during major parts of the year.

Regarding Sukri's and Tulsa's withdrawal from school, Krupa adds that the girls were not interested in studies. However, the girls explain this differently. Sukri says, 'I was interested in studies but the teacher never used to teach. Most of the time, I used to remain idle. At home, there is a problem of money and hence whenever the work is available, we go.' Tulsa says she would still like to go if other girls of her age do as well. She adds that many girls of her age do not go to school. She would not mind going to an ashram school either if others from the village also came along. She adds that, unlike her brother, her father was never interested in sending her to an ashram school. Both Sukri and Tulsa are also responsible for washing clothes, cleaning the house and utensils, and collecting water. Neither has any time for play. Tulsa can't name any game. On the other hand, Balaram can cite many: *bati,* kabaddi and more.

When queried about his perceptions or aspirations for the girls' future, Krupa has no specific answer. He really can't think of anything. His wife Sita feels that it is important for girls to learn household chores but then currently the most important thing is to buy one more buffalo so that the wage rate for her husband goes up. The couple feels that this is their first priority and cannot think of their daughters' education or any such other thing. They add that it is quite common for girls of this age in this village to work in cashew-processing units.

BOX 8.7: NORMS ARE DIFFERENT FOR VIMALESH AND KIRAN

Both Rajendra Oraon (33) and his wife Munia Devi (30) are illiterate. They were married at a young age and had their first child when Rajendra was 18 and Munia 15. They have one son, Vimalesh (15) and two daughters, Kiran (8) and Tara (2). They want to have one more son but are scared of getting another daughter instead. Vimalesh is studying in Class IX in the nearby town, Barwadeeh. He completed his Class V from the village school. The village does not have any upper primary school. They have 2.5 acres of land but only about one acre is cultivable. They have no cattle and have to take bulls on rent for ploughing. Munia does not go outside the village because she has a small child to look after. Earlier, Rajendra also used to work in the village itself. But the needs of the family increased, especially since Vimalesh entered high school and started going to Daltanganj, the district headquarters, to work as a rickshaw puller. He manages to earn about Rs. 40 to 50 everyday there.

Both husband and wife are totally committed to Vimalesh's education. They have full faith that 'once educated, he will definitely have a job and our days of poverty will come to an end.' Rajendra has taken a loan of Rs. 600 from the local self-help group to buy textbooks for his son. He has to buy bulls as well but textbooks were the first priority. His wife saves five rupees per day exclusively reserve for Vimalesh's educational needs. Vimalesh knows that his parents are working hard to provide him with an education. He is serious about his studies and wants to fulfil their expectations. He is always seen in the school uniform of blue shorts and white shirt, even on holidays. 'My mother gets me only these stitched as it serves both purposes,' he grins. He does not have any friend in the village. A boy from the neighbouring village is a friend, who takes him to school everyday on his bicycle. Vimalesh helps his father during the season, though the father does not want him to as he would prefer that he 'concentrate on his studies.' There is only one graduate in the village who teaches in a private school. Vimalesh takes his help in mathematics and other subjects whenever he feels the need.

Regarding girls, the couple feels that they can study at most up to the primary level in the village school. Presently, Kiran is not even enrolled in the local school, though she does go there at times. Munia feels it would not be safe to send them to a faraway school at that age. 'Moreover, what is the use of their education? Some basic education is enough for them,' she says. Rajendra echoes a similar view when he says, 'they will get married and go to their own homes.' Vimalesh, however, feels differently. He says that once he gets a job, he will take his sisters to a town and educate them properly.

Relevance of Schooling for Girls

RELEVANCE OF SCHOOLING FOR TRIBAL GIRLS

The relevance of education, an issue among tribals and Muslims, becomes more pronounced when it comes to girls' schooling. However, the belief that education is not relevant for girls has very different rationales in these two social groups. Tribal societies are generally known for greater freedom for girls. However, in a situation when most tribes are struggling to maintain their identity and survival, life has become tougher for tribal women. They have always done as much as their male counterparts, in fact, usually working much harder than men to support and sustain the family, and have traditionally shouldered greater responsibilities. The experiences in most tribal villages suggest that women tend to play the main role of breadwinner of the family, though not always recognized as such, and this has implications for girls as well. Girls are expected to follow in the foot-steps of their mothers and hence start participating in work at quite an early age. Schooling has hardly any role in this scheme of things. Therefore, the notion of gender equality existing in tribal societies does not extend to the participation of girls in schooling; it mainly remains confined to equal participation in work (Box 8.8).

It is important to add that the very equality of participation in work at times also becomes exploitative for girls in specific contexts. An extreme example comes from Arunachal Pradesh, a state with a very high incidence of hunger, poverty, and tough life situations. The system of bride price exists among the Nyshis, an important tribe, but instead of reflecting a higher status of women in society, it, in fact, leads to their commodification.

BOX 8.8: BRIDE PRICE AND GIRLS' POSITION: THE NYSHIS OF ARUNACHAL PRADESH

The custom of bride price prevalent among the Nyshis of Arunachal Pradesh finds mention in many anthropological works. The practice continues and in reality leads to the commodification of girls. Bride price is often determined by a series of intense bargains between the two families with the assistance of a go-between. Poor parents accept bride price for newly-born girls, or at times even before birth after some crude assessment of the pregnant mother which ascertains that the yet-to-be-born child is a girl. Once the negotiation is settled and the bride price paid, the girl becomes the property of her husband and his family. The girl continues to stay with her parents till the husband or his family actually take her. She generally goes to her husband's home at a very young age, child marriage being common. And she could very well be only one of many wives as polygamy is common among the Nyshis. Of course, only those who can afford to pay bride prices for more than one girl practise it. Once the girl goes to her husband's place, she is expected to perform all sorts of household and outside chores and live like a bought slave. Any violation of the given norm can cause the infliction of the harshest cruelties. Local newspapers are often full of reports of Nyshi women being shackled to blocks of wood as punishment to restrict their movement.

RELEVANCE OF SCHOOLING FOR MUSLIM GIRLS

It is not that Muslim girls do not work hard, but the genesis of the feeling among Muslim parents that schooling is not relevant for girls also has to do with their separate identity reinforcing the belief that religious teaching as opposed to secular education is more relevant for them. They generally attach more importance to girls getting religious education so that as wives and mothers they can look after their family and children in a righteous manner. The fact that it is less common for Muslim women to go out to work also makes schooling less important for them. They question the relevance of teaching girls Hindi and mathematics when girls are not ever supposed to go out and interact with the world. Boys' education still has some relevance because 'they have to work and interact with the world outside'. Among Muslims, there is also hesitation about sending girls to regular schools with male teachers, even at the primary level. However, all the study's *maktabs* and madrasas are co-educational and the teachers all male. Still, maulvis, by virtue of their religious standing, command respect and trust in the community, which non-religious schools seldom do (Box 8.9).

BOX 8.9: IF ONLY CIRCUMSTANCES AND COMMUNITY WOULD PERMIT!

Life was relatively simpler when Samid Ansari (50) and Biwi Amna Khatun (40) started their independent married life in Khabaspur village of Araria district in Bihar about fourteen years ago. Samid was working as a helper in a bus and Amna used to provide some support in processing harvested crops in the households of some big cultivators. They had only one son, Murshid, and they could support the family easily. Samid then managed to get a bus conductor's job which improved their financial condition. Meanwhile, they had another son, Mushtadeer. Both Murshid and Mushtadeer were admitted to a local government-run primary school after reaching the age of admission. By then, the couple also had two more children—daughters—Khatoon and Rokhat. Once, Mushtadeer fell seriously ill and the family had to spend a lot of money on private doctors. Samid could not attend his duty for several days, lost his wages, and had to take a loan from informal sources at a high rate of interest. This sudden crisis led to such a deterioration in the family's economic situation that Murshid was withdrawn from school and put to work for wages. Amna also stopped working for others because she had to look after the small children at home.

Murshid was 9 when he was withdrawn from school. He started working for wages but the payments were low in the village. So a year later, at the age of 10, he was sent to Delhi with his uncle where he started working in a hotel for a monthly payment of 400 rupees and food. Out of this 400 rupees, he used to send 300 to his parents. This did help Samid in repaying the debt. Using his employer's influence, Samid also managed to get a bank loan of 6,000 rupees, which he invested in taking the contract of a bus stand and buying goats. This improved his daily earnings to about 100 rupees per day. In the meantime, Samid and Amna had three more children—Pappu, Mumtaj and Danis. In Delhi, Murshid left his hotel job and started working in a leather factory for a daily wage of 50 rupees. Mushtadeer proved to be good in his studies. After completing the primary level, he started going to the upper primary school in Pategana, a nearby village.

Everything seemed to be going right when Samid, following an altercation, got entangled in a police case and was jailed. Murshid came back from Delhi and arranged for legal advice in order to manage bail for his father. It was not easy to meet the cost of litigation and support the family at the same time. Mushtadeer left school and joined his brother. Both brothers started working as porters at a bus stand in Pategana. But even then the earnings were not enough and they had to borrow heavily, especially because of litigation expenses. Finally, Samid was released from jail without any charge. But by then the family was already in heavy debt. Murshid decided to go back to Delhi and took Mushtadeer along. Both brothers currently work in a leather factory and send the better part of their earnings to Samid to repay the debts. Mushtadeer still nurses a desire to study further. The parents also feel very guilty for the fact that Mushtadeer had to interrupt his education for the family's sake, but feel helpless in view of the need to repay the outstanding debt.

Khatoon was never enrolled in school as she took care of the younger siblings from the tender age of four. Her younger sister, Rokhat, studies in class III. Pappu has also started going to school and is studying in class I. Both attend quite regularly and the parents are determined to get the other two also enrolled once they reach the appropriate age. Now that the younger siblings are a little older, Khatoon can attend school but she feels shy in going with younger children.

Both Samid and Amna are illiterate. But they consider education very important. They want their younger sons, Pappu and Danis, to study up to very high levels. 'We are ready to take all the burden. Our two older sons are also interested in educating their brothers,' says Samid. They are interested in educating their daughters as well but not up to very high levels. 'Although we don't differentiate between boys and girls, Rokhat can be sent at the most up to the middle level. Our community won't permit us to educate her beyond that age. She has to get married after that and the same thing applies to Mumtaj,' says Amna.

It is important to add two points here. First, the issue of relevance of schooling among tribals or Muslims is not specific to girls, but has greater meaning in their case. The difference between boys and girls in terms of enrolment is highest among tribals, which reflects the fact that the perceived relevance of schooling is even lower for girls. In the case of Muslims, it works differently. Although there is not much difference between boys' and girls' enrolment rates in schools as well as in madrasas, the primary reasons for sending them to madrasas are different. While boys are sent more for higher perceived employment linkages in comparison to those offered by secular education, girls are sent because of the role they have to play in managing their families and raising their children in the proper manner. This is the reason why very few girls are enrolled in higher-level madrasas and even when they are, they drop out much more quickly. Second, relevance, as discussed in preceding paragraphs, is only one factor, and not the only one, that impedes girls' schooling in these communities. General apathy towards girls' education, the custom of married girls ultimately staying with their husbands' families, and not with their parents, gender roles and socialization, poverty and its related constraints, all play a role.

School Facilities and Processes: A Reflection of Societal Norms

School Facilities

The significance of the availability of schools within one's own habitation, especially among educationally deprived groups like Dalits, tribes, and Muslims, has been discussed earlier. For obvious reasons, it is all the more important for girls. The availability of women teachers, who inspire confidence in parents and provide role models for girls who otherwise rarely come across any other educated woman in their own contexts, is abysmally low in rural schools. Only one-fourth of the schools in the study villages had a woman teacher present. Not a single woman teacher was found in any school in the villages located in Dhubri (Assam), Araria (Bihar), Nuapara (Orissa), Koraput (Orissa), Sidhi (MP), except one in an EGS School, Shravasti (UP), and Dangs (Gujarat). This means that women teachers were present only in the three districts of Chamrajnagar (Karnataka), West Godavari (AP), and Pune (Maharashtra). The absence of women teachers in rural areas in these states can be traced to several factors such as the absence of clear policy guidelines for recruitment and placement, very poor transportation facilities, lack of basic facilities in schools, and the absence of an orientation among women teachers to take up the challenges of teaching in rural areas.

We have seen that the level of girls' participation in schooling goes down further at the upper primary level. This is partially to do with the lower value attached to girls' education and social practices such as early marriage, but low availability of upper primary schools within their own habitation or at short distances also has a role to play. Even in areas where it is fairly common to send girls to school, many girls discontinue after the primary level because it is difficult to cover distances. Security is an issue and lack of good transport systems add to this problem. Moreover, it becomes costlier to send girls to upper primary level schools which many poor parents find difficult to afford.

SCHOOL PROCESSES

It is well known that the existing curricula in schools reinforce rather than question the prevailing societal values and gender relations. This has important implications in the long run as it helps in perpetuating the same attitudes towards girls' education. However, teachers' attitudes, which also reinforce aspects of feminine socialization and established gender roles, have a more immediate impact in influencing girls' own interest in schooling. But it is also important to add that girls' participation in schooling in rural areas is rarely subject to their own interests alone; mostly parents take the decisions. Girls who get the opportunity enjoy coming to school, if for nothing else then 'for peer interaction and time away from hard work at home' (FGD). Peer influence has even a greater role in the continuation of schooling. The increase in the number of girls attending school leads to a further increase because it generates greater interest among girls themselves and also because it becomes socially more acceptable.

SCHOOLING OF GIRLS IN POOR FAMILIES: MILES TO GO

Getting girls from poor and deprived families to enroll in school and making them continue and complete their education is one of the biggest challenges. The constraints that keep them away range from deep-rooted socio-cultural beliefs and notions of unquestioned, established caste and gender roles, on the one hand, and tough life situations and a very low perceived value or relevance of schooling for girls, on the other. Traditions of schooling, generally weak among many Dalit, tribal, and other deprived social groups, are harder to build for girls. The ways the schools, represent and reinforce, rather than question, the existing social and gender divides makes it more difficult to break the vicious circle that keeps girls from poor families away from school. Poverty and a vulnerable life situation add to prevalent social practices in keeping girls in no-win situations.

The social norm—whether or not to send girls to school—plays a very critical role. The norm in most UCH groups is to send them and that is why even if they are poor, they send their girls to schools. Similarly, this norm exists in certain areas in southern and western parts of the country, and socially disadvantaged groups send their girls to schools trying to overcome economic disadvantages. However, this norm itself is strengthened over time due to the interplay of a number of factors. It is important to understand these factors and processes if the vicious cycle in other parts is to be broken. It is also important to recognize that beneath a similar approach and view towards girls' education there are different kinds of logic and explanations working for different groups and regions. These finer differences also become crucial in building an understanding and initiating action.

NOTE

1. The number of upper-caste households in our sample is small and comprises only two castes, Brahmin and Lingayat. Very few children from the remaining castes found in the study villages such as Thakurs and Marathas are present in this sample, and hence the results need to be interpreted with caution.

9. Nowhere to Belong: Schooling in Urban Neighbourhood Slums

BACKGROUND

There has been a consistent increase in the urban population in India which has already crossed the 300 million mark. A large proportion of the population in urban areas continues to live in clearly identifiable low-income neighbourhoods, a significant proportion of which are not yet notified as slums. The quality of life in these slums, notified or unnotified (especially in the latter), is recognized as being abysmal on counts of the dismal position of sanitation, health, and education facilities. The urban poor, especially children, do not live in slums only; they also live on pavements, in makeshift tents, at railway stations, and virtually on the street. However, for various reasons in our fieldwork, we have covered only those living in slums. This means that only children living with families get covered in this study. In this chapter, we follow the same pattern and approach as those adopted for the study of rural areas. The larger context of children in terms of living in slums, family background, and the nature of school availability and functioning have been analysed first, followed by an assessment of schooling status. The patterns in schooling participation are then viewed in the light of specific contexts, and inferences are drawn regarding factors and processes that facilitate or restrict children's participation in schooling.

LIVING IN A LOW-INCOME NEIGHBOURHOOD AREA: WHAT DOES IT MEAN?

ORIGIN AND GROWTH OF SLUMS

Migration from Rural Areas

The origin and growth of urban slums in India are essentially linked with the issue of the migration of people from rural or semi-urban areas in search of livelihood. Shrinking opportunities in rural areas, and agriculture becoming less remunerative in rural areas, force people to migrate for short or long periods in search of livelihood or to supplement their family's income. The fifteen study slums, especially the newer ones, are also inhabited by immigrant residents from near and distant places; while the majority still has ties to their native places, many older migrants no longer have any such links. The migration was more from neighbouring places in the past, while in recent years, cities, especially metropolitans, have been receiving a larger number of people from areas where the pace of growth of employment opportunities has been slow and the economy has remained static or is less diversified. The largest number of residents in the slums of Delhi, Kanpur, and Malda are from Bihar. A substantial number also comes from neighbouring UP to Delhi. A small number of residents in Delhi and Kanpur belonged to different states, including MP and Assam. Kanpur, Warangal, and Parbhani have a good number of people from their own states. Malda in West Bengal is not a big city but it attracts people from neighbouring Bihar due to certain past linkages and the employment opportunities that exist there.

Temporary Settlement, Relocation, and Recognition

The age of the slum does not always mean that the residents have been living in that city or town for only those many years (Table 9.1). Some households in old slums could be those of recent migrants while families in newer slums might have shifted from some other locality in the same city. For instance, the Haiderpur slum in Delhi came into being when the Delhi Development Authority (DDA) allotted land to these families formerly living in another area on government land which had to be evacuated for new constructions. Similarly, the local municipality relocated residents now living in Coolipara in Malda by allotting land, as they had to be shifted to facilitate the building of a flyover. People coming to urban areas in search of livelihood with no or little income and an insecure future rarely have any other option but to settle in neighbourhood areas which, in the course of time, come to be known as unauthorized slums. It is common for people to initially settle down in unauthorized areas adjacent to an existing slum or fallow government land. Once those settlements grow in size, the residents expect the government to

Table 9.1: Years of Existence of Slums

Age of Slum	More than 50 years old	30-50 years old	10-30 years old	Less than 10 years old
Number of Slums	2	5	6	2
Name of Slum	1. Mirzapur (Malda) 2. Juhi Bumruiya, (Kanpur)	1. Rakhi Mandi (Kanpur) 2. Ramashray Nagar (Kanpur) 3. Manohar Nagar (Kanpur) 4. Zakhira 1 (Delhi) 5. Dakshin Baluchar (Malda)	1. Zakhira 2 (Delhi) 2. Haiderpur (Delhi) 3. Mehrauli (Delhi) 4. Sanjay Gandhi Nagar (Parbhani) 5. Bharat Nagar (Parbhani) 6. Coolipara (Malda)	1. Garib Nagar (Warangal) 2. Giri Prasad Nagar (Warangal)

SOURCE: Slum Appraisal Reports.

either authorize their residency rights or relocate them somewhere else with legal rights.

Both the slums in Parbhani have been regularized only in the recent past by the state government. However, Sanjay Gandhi Nagar is older than Bharat Nagar. Both the study slums in Warangal are not yet notified and are fighting for recognition. The Zakhira slums in Delhi are located on railway land and, therefore, cannot be notified as slums. However, the residents are hoping that the government would relocate them soon. The area is surrounded by railway tracks on three sides and though inhabited for more than 30 years, is not safe for residence purposes. The same is true of Dakshin Baluchar in Malda, which is located on the banks of the Mahananda river and remains flooded for almost three to four months every year, forcing people to live on pavements. Manohar Nagar in Kanpur, situated on a cliff close to the Ganga, is also dangerous and the people are resigned to the fact that they could face eviction at any time and be asked to move elsewhere. Although relocation is generally welcomed in unauthorized colonies, it also means living constantly in uncertainty and insecurity. Relocation or regularization is easier in areas where the pressure on land and space is still not very high but is very difficult in metropolitan cities. Ironically, the pace of expansion of job opportunities is higher in metropolitans.

The pressure of population on existing slums also grows with time and particular events lead to sudden jumps. For instance, a number of construction projects (big buildings, flyovers, stadiums, etc.) were undertaken in Delhi during the early 1980s to host the Asian Games of 1982. The demand for labour was high, and the workers came from neighbouring as well as distant places and continued to live in the city even after the projects for which they had been hired were completed. The population in many slums including Zakhira was reported to have gone up significantly after 1982. Similarly, Bharat Nagar in Parbhani, situated next to the Jayakwadi Canal, came into existence when people working on the canal project settled there after the construction of the project. Recognized slums also gradually keep growing and include portions that are not recognized. Haiderpur slum in Delhi has six camps, out of which three are new and occupancy rights not recognized. Ramashray Nagar in Kanpur originated as the lateral expansion of a series of recognized slums and, though the exact status is not clear there is no threat of eviction. There is also a section of floating population in many slums in all cities which comprises seasonal migrants.

The oldest among all of the study's slums, Mirzapur in Malda and Juhi Bamruiya in Kanpur, have slightly different histories. The origin of Mirzapur is interesting as the residents are Muslim refugees who migrated here from other parts of West Bengal at the time of Partition, taking it to be part of Pakistan. However, this remained part of India and they continued to live here. Juhi Bumruiya in Kanpur is mainly occupied by the ex-workers of the Swadeshi Cotton Mill. The mill is closed now and residents have taken to different occupations. Most residents have got rights over land in both these slums and do not face any threat of eviction. One important feature of slum dwelling is that a substantial proportion of families (22 per cent) live on rent even in unrecognized slums where nobody has any right of residency or ownership. Apart from places like the Mehrauli slum in Delhi and Rakhi Mandi in Kanpur where some influential persons have taken possession of land and then rented it to others, it is also common for people to invest and buy encroached upon land to build shanties so that at the time of relocation, their residency here is recognized. The better off amongst them build more rooms and rent them out to others.

Feeders to Particular Trades

Some slums have originated more as feeders to some particular trade or occupational practice. The Mehrauli slum of rag pickers in Delhi and Rakhi Mandi in Kanpur are two such examples. This particular slum in Mehrauli is inhabited almost entirely by illegal migrants from Bangladesh settled here by local garbage contractors. The government land, in the illegal possession of local landlords, has been rented out to the garbage contractors who have settled rag pickers on certain terms and who also have their garbage godowns located here. The rag pickers live under the constant threat of eviction and have already faced demolition a number of times. The houses are built of cardboard and polythene and are rebuilt after the phase of demolition gets over. Similarly, Rakhi Mandi, initially a coal yard, is also a mix of workplace and residence for labourers settled by contractors dealing in waste or half-burnt coal bought from nearby industries. The contractors have made make shift sheds and *kuchcha* houses for labourers mainly coming from neighbouring areas in UP. There is a constant threat of eviction as the land belongs to the Kanpur Development Authority (KDA) and is in the possession of some influential person who has rented it to the contractors.

Harassment, Political Affiliations, and Protection

It is common for slum dwellers to face harassment at the hands of civic authorities as well as the police due to the illegal status of their residence in unrecognized slums. Slum dwellers generally owe allegiance to some political force in their search to gain strength and legitimacy. In some cases, this happens to be the local wings of national parties, and in others some local political organizations (e.g. the Communist Party of India-Marxist (CPI-M), the Congress, the Bahujan Samaj Party (BSP), or the Dalit Sangharsh Samiti). However, these allegiances were more visible and effective in smaller cities. In Delhi and Kanpur, these were not as effective, and allegiances to some local powerful leaders were more common. These affiliations helped in getting relief from constant threats and harassment in varying degrees at all the places.

Size, and Social and Linguistic Composition

Dalits and Muslims are the Majority of Slum Dwellers

The size of the slums in terms of population and number of households varied. The majority of the slums housed 200 to 500 families, while some slums were bigger. The most noticeable feature of the social composition of the slum population is that there is an over-representation of Dalits and Muslims. Dalits, who constitute about 13 per cent of the total population, make up more than 43 per cent of the slum population. Similarly, Muslims, occupying about 12 per cent of the total population, make up about 38 per cent of the total slum population. One of the reasons for this could be the fact that these two social groups have traditionally not been landowning at most places, and hence the rate of migration has been higher among them. Muslims have primarily been artisans and the slackening of the demand for such handmade goods rendered them jobless. A general decrease in the demand for skill-based jobs has affected several Dalit groups which had been dependent on such occupations in the past. These two communities also face greater discrimination and isolation in rural areas. Movement away from rural areas helps Dalits break away from dependence on rural landlords and the trend has been increasing in the 1980s and 1990s.

It is important to note that the tribal population is almost non-existent in the slums. It is more common for them to migrate to other rural areas or to workstations such as brick kilns or stone quarries. It appears that even when they migrate to urban areas for work, they do not settle down in slums. It is more common for them to live together in temporary sheds and move together in groups. No communal tension was visible or reported in any mixed-religion slum. Although caste or community is not a big issue, region-based affiliations and discrimination were visible. Socialization was guided more by the state or the region of the state from where the families had emigrated. Nonetheless, upper caste Hindu and OBC families were definitely better placed in terms of the nature of jobs if not income levels as compared to SCs and Muslims.

Linguistic Composition

The majority of slum dwellers speak the main language spoken in that area or city. However, this is not the case in four slums in Malda and Parbhani. The residents of Coolipada in Malda, primarily having come from Bihar, speak Hindi. The same is true of those hailing from the same state in Dakshin Baluchar, though second-generation migrants speak the local language, Bengali, quite comfortably. The residents of the Mehrauli slum in Delhi do not speak Hindi, their mother tongue being Bengali. At Sanjay Gandhi Nagar in Parbhani, a number of Muslim families speak Urdu and not Marathi, the state language (Table 9.2). The population belonging to linguistic minorities faces problems on this count in several respects, including availability of jobs and the education of children.

Table 9.2: Size, Social and Linguistic Composition of Slum Populations

City	Slum	No. of families in slum*	Composition—Entire Slum	
			Caste/Social*	Linguistic
Malda	Mirzapur	1,000-1,500	All lower caste Muslims	Bengali
	Coolipara	356	70 % UCH, 20 % SC, 10 % OBC	95 % Hindi 5 % Bengali
	Bablaghat	100	50 % UCH, 25 % SC, 25 % OBC	90 % Hindi 10 % Bengali
Kanpur	Ramashray Nagar	400	95 % SC, 5 % OBC	Hindi
	Juhi Bumruiya	700	All SC	Hindi
	Rakhi Mandi	480	90 % SC	Hindi
	Manohar Nagar	300	Almost all Muslims, very few Hindu families	Hindi, Urdu
Delhi	Zakhira 1	15	90 % Muslims, 10 % mixed Hindu	Hindi, Maithili
	Zakhira 2	300	70 % SC, 30 % Muslims	Rajasthani Hindi
	Mehrauli	400-500	Bangladeshi migrants (Muslims)	Mainly Bengali
	Haiderpur	8,000-8,500	80 % Hindus (mixed) 20 % Muslims	Hindi
Parbhani	Bharat Nagar	250	50 % Muslims 50 % SC	Marathi
	Sanjay Gandhi Nagar	1,100	70 % Muslims 20 % SC, 10 % OBC	Urdu, Marathi
Warangal	Giri Prasad Nagar	194	40 % Muslims 60 % mixed Hindu	Urdu Telugu
	Garib Nagar	350	40 % OBC, 40 % SC 20 % Muslims	Telugu Urdu

NOTE: * Approximate.

SOURCE: Slum Appraisal.

OCCUPATION AND INCOME LEVELS

Casual Work in the Unorganized Sector

The vast majority of people living in urban slums are engaged in low-paid, unorganized sector jobs. This is true not only for recent migrants but also for those who have been living in urban areas for many years. The growing supply of labour both due to emigration and growth of population has meant the availability of labour for work at low wage rates in different fields including industry, trade, construction, etc., and there has been a growing casualization of work, especially in the private sector. The lack of schooling and specialized skills among this group of people makes it more difficult for them to demand better wages or greater social security. There is virtually no security in the majority of jobs being undertaken by poor slum dwellers and the fear of losing existing jobs or not getting any work in the future looms large. In some slum most people are engaged in similar trade or work while the nature of occupations is mixed in others. However, everybody associated with one trade or industry is not necessarily engaged in the same or similar work, nor do they have similar incomes (Table 9.3).

Three of the study slums have people engaged mainly in only one trade or industry; these are Mehrauli in Delhi and Rakhi Mandi and Manohar Nagar in Kanpur. In the Mehrauli slum in Delhi, the contractors, who have settled a group of rag pickers, have this understanding that the rag pickers would sell all the collected garbage to particular contractors. The rag pickers agree to this arrangement as they are assured of a buyer for their garbage. The contractors, though belonging to the same community and living in the same slum, are better off than the rag pickers. Similar economics work at Rakhi Mandi in Kanpur, where a number of people coming from neighbouring areas are settled by contractors and are engaged in the heavy work of loading and unloading coal. Local labour is used for the lighter work of sorting and separating the coal into different grades and selling it. In either case, there is no security, and even if the person has been working for a particular contractor for years, he does not get anything for the day he does not work. There is no concession even for illness or any other contingency. The workers are, however, provided loans or advances at times of acute need. The system is comparable to that of attached labour in rural areas where a patron-client relationship exists and workers are exploited in terms of not having the freedom to work elsewhere.

The situation is not very different in semi-organized industries. At Manohar Nagar in Kanpur, men are involved in different kinds of skilled

Table 9.3: Nature of Occupation among Slum Dwellers

Nature of Occupation	Distribution of those who are working (%)	
	Male	Female
Casual wage work (daily)	39.5	31.1
Contracted wage work	24.8	37.7
Self-employed	25.5	23.0
Piece-rated wage work	4.4	6.6
Regular salaried	3.6	–
Others	2.2	1.6

NOTE: Daily wage work on a casual basis includes loading, rickshaw pulling (rickshaw taken on rent and not owned), working in factories, construction and white washing, and helping others in selling small articles, etc. Contract wage work includes skilled, semi-skilled, and unskilled work; it may mean working in factories, shops, or upper-class households under varying capacities such as watchman, technician, skilled or unskilled worker, etc. Rag picking through a contractor, though poorly paid, has been included in this category because of its nature. Self-employment included running small tea-*pakoda-chaat* shop, selling vegetables, rickshaw pulling if the rickshaw is self-owned, tailor, etc.

SOURCE: Household Survey.

and semi-skilled work of processing leather and making different parts of the final products such as bags, shoes, belts, etc. The wages vary and even though a person may work for years, the nature of employment remains temporary. The ongoing slump and recent regulations to check pollution have affected the industry. Many tanneries not following the specified norms have been closed, leading to the loss of jobs; many cases of salaries being halved were reported. Those who have lost their jobs are taking to different kinds of occupations, including rickshaw pulling and selling small articles. Women in this slum do not go to the tanneries for work, but take up home-based leather work, mainly hunter making on piece-rate payments.

The occupations and their nature are more varied in other slums. Taking all the slums together, about 92 per cent of the men above 14 years participate in work. The work participation rate is lower among women as only 52 per cent of women in the same age group are engaged in earning-related activities, household chores not taken into account. Of the working men, around 40 per cent earn their livelihood through casual wage work on a daily basis and another 25 per cent is engaged in contract wage work. This can be said to be slightly better than casual work, even if the wages are not necessarily higher; these provide greater security of work. Salaried work is not common and very few persons in selected slums have such jobs. Even those who earlier had salaried jobs are now doing either contract or casual wage work.

Among women, the proportion of those working on casual wage work is smaller and of those working on contracted wage work is higher than males. Working as domestic help is the most common form of contract wage work among women. Going outside the home to work for wages is more common in Malda, Parbhani, and Kanpur. Working for wages is less common among Muslim and non-SC Hindu women as compared to SC women. Working as domestic help is particularly looked down upon as it involves cleaning the dirty/used utensils of other families, and is avoided by women belonging to caste Hindu households even in times of serious financial crises. Both husband and wife are engaged in earning activities in about 40 per cent of households, this proportion being the highest in Warangal.

Self-employment is also common among both men and women. In many cases, these are run as family enterprises and the entire family gets involved. This has implications for children's schooling. Although it is not always true, self-employment means lesser dependence on others for earning a livelihood even if the income is not necessarily higher. Working on piece rate is also prevalent, especially among women. This suits them as they are not required to go out of the house. Common jobs taken on piece-rate payments are *beedi*-making, hunter-making, *bindi*-making, assembling of electric switches, etc.

Low Wages, Meagre Incomes

Payments for most jobs are meagre and less than the prescribed minimum everywhere. Daily earnings vary between Rs. 50 to 120, depending upon the job. Those in rag picking cannot earn more than Rs. 50-70 a day and during the rains they are not able to earn anything. However, if the entire family is involved in rag picking, the income goes up. Those in construction-related or other semi-skilled or skilled work earn more. The wages for daily work are higher in Delhi, Kanpur, and Warangal as compared to Malda and Parbhani. Pig rearing, common only among some communities, is profitable due to diversified use (leather, meat, etc.) and high demand. Those in contracted wage work also earn on an average roughly similar amounts annually, their monthly earnings varying between Rs. 1,500 to 3,000. Wages are lower for those kinds of work more commonly performed by women. Wages are the lowest for piece-rate work, at times a very low rate of Rs. 10-12 a day is paid. Hunter making or embroidery work performed usually by Muslim women in Kanpur is one such example. Even when it is not so low, it does not go beyond Rs. 30-40 a day, and that too when several hands work together in the family. Women working as domestic help manage to earn around Rs. 1,000-1,200 per month in Malda and Rs. 1,500-2,500 in Delhi.

Poor payments are reflected in low levels of average annual income. About one-fourth of the total households earn Rs. 1,000 per month or less, and another one-fourth earn between Rs. 1,000 and 1,500 per month. About 85 per cent of the total households have a monthly income of Rs. 3,000 or less, the majority falling in the category of between Rs. 1,000 to 3,000 per month (Table 9.4). Apart from low payments, insecurity of jobs is the biggest problem. The irregular or insecure nature of work has been cited as the main work problem by both men and women. Health disorders or illness, occurring due to work or even otherwise, are cited as another major problem associated with work and earnings. Poor health and frequent illness forces them to be away from work, leading to a loss in earnings. Moreover, public

Table 9.4: Levels of Income in Urban Slums

Income Group (in Rs. per annum)*	% of households in this income group
Below 3,500	8.3
3,501-6,000	3.6
6,001-12,000	11.1
12,001-18,000	24.3
18,001-24,000	14.2
24,001-36,000	24.3
36,001-48,000	5.9
48,001-60,000	4.1
Above 60,000	4.1

NOTE: *The monthly income for a household has been estimated by taking into account the approximate income being earned by all working members as well as income accruing from any other source, e.g. rent, etc.

SOURCE: Household Survey.

health care facilities being poor, a good amount of expenditure is on private doctors and medicines.

LIVING CONDITIONS AND CIVIC AMENITIES AND PROVISIONS

Congested, Filthy, and Overcrowded

Living conditions in most slums are appalling and, in some cases, sub-human. Small houses built without any planning, lack of sewage, open drains which overflow during the rains and also on any day in many cases, stagnant water, garbage dumped on the roads and narrow pathways characterize all the slums. The situation is slightly better in Parbhani and Warangal where some open space is available. The majority of houses are *kuchcha* in all the slums, except at Haiderpur where half the families live in *pucca* houses (Table 9.5). The houses consist of one small room for the majority of families in most slums and more than 80 per cent of the households do not have a separate kitchen. The condition of the houses is also far from good in most cases. In mixed localities, the condition is worse for recent migrants living in the newer areas. The situation is worst in the Mehrauli and Zakhira slums in Delhi, and in Dakshin Baluchar in Malda. In Rakhi Mandi in Kanpur, the entire atmosphere is pervaded by coal dust all the time.

Unsafe Water, Inadequate Toilet Facilities, and Costly Electricity

The availability of safe drinking water is an issue in almost all the slums. Although hand pumps are available in all the slums, except the Mehrauli slum in Delhi, and is the main source of water in the majority of the places, the number is inadequate and the quality unsafe. It is common for residents to pay for the tampering of pipes or the use of 'private' hand pumps which a few individuals in the slums have. The poor quality of water leads to ill-

Table 9.5: Housing, Water and Sanitation in Urban Slums

S. No.		Distribution of households (%)		
1.	Type of house	*Kuchcha* 72.8	*Partially pucca* 18.3	*Pucca* 8.9
2.	Number of rooms	1 Room 55.6	2 Rooms 21.9	3 or more Rooms 27.5
3.	Condition of house	Good 15.4	Bad 59.2	Dilapidated 25.4
4.	Source of water	Hand pump 59.2	Pipe water 26.0	Others 14.8
5.	Distance of water source	Within 20 metres 74.4	20-100 metres 12.4	More than 100 metres 13.2
6.	Kind of toilet	Open space 59.2	Common flush 29.6	Others 11.1

SOURCE: Household Survey.

health and diseases. The situation is worse so far as availability of toilet facilities are concerned. Overall, more than 59 per cent families reported using open spaces for defecation. Even where some common public toilets are available, the number is grossly inadequate and the use remains limited to those living closeby. Moreover, many families cannot afford to use Sulabh Shauchalayas, which require payments of one to two rupees everyday. The availability of open space itself being limited in urban areas, people do not go very far for defecation; this results in a lot of filth and dirt all around, leading to various infections and diseases. Lack of civic amenities was cited as the biggest problem faced by residents in slums.

About two-thirds of the families in these slums have access to electricity, which is not available at all in Coolipada and Dakshin Baluchar (Malda). However, only very few of these slums have a legal electricity supply. In most other slums, people have taken illegal connections by paying monthly 'rents' to somebody from the electricity department or the police or both. This system generally operates through a local tout who works in connivance with government functionaries. It is also common for a few families with legal connections to sell electricity to others in the same locality. The availability of Public Distribution System (PDS) outlets is also limited and even at places where they are available, they are not reliable because of their irregular functioning. Moreover, the majority of residents have only 'yellow cards' that entitle them to receive only kerosene and sugar, and not other items. On the whole, the PDS is not a reliable option available to slum dwellers for their supply of essentials.

Poor Hygiene Conditions, Health Hazards in Occupation, and Frequent Illnesses

Illnesses as a result of poor sanitation and poor quality drinking water are common to all slums. People commonly complained of getting diahorrea, gastroenteritis, dysentery, malaria, fungal infections, tuberculosis, etc. Specific occupational practices led to specific diseases in at least six slums, this being true for all four slums in the industrial town of Kanpur. At Manohar Nagar, where the majority of the people—men, women, and children—either work in tanneries or are engaged in leather-related work at home, people commonly suffer from skin diseases and burns. Bronchial congestions and skin diseases due to coal dust are common at Rakhi Mandi. Children working in garages, common at Ramashray Nagar and Juhi Bumruiya, handle heavy objects and suffer minor injuries quite commonly. Children engaged in rag picking, common among a few families in Ramashray Nagar, pick up articles buried deep and sustain injuries, besides being vulnerable to harmful gases in the process of garbage collection. Rag pickers at the Mehrauli slum in Delhi are also vulnerable to skin diseases, high-risk infections, and respiratory disorders due to constant exposure to garbage, rubbish, and rags from all sources including homes, industrial dumps, hospitals, municipalities, open sewers, etc. At Garib Nagar in Warangal, people working in cotton mills have breathing problems as dust gets into their lungs.

The poor hygiene situation is worsened because of poor health care facilities. It is common to go to private practitioners located either within the slum or in nearby colonies, many of them quacks. Considering the poor state of health care and the meagre incomes among the majority of slum dwellers, this is a huge burden on them. The public health care system either does not exist or does not function properly. The health centres existing in slums in Kanpur were closed down suddenly, apparently to initiate a joint plan for slum development bringing together all departments and agencies dealing with these issues. However, people living in slums do not have any knowledge as to why this fund was withdrawn. These slums also had anganwadis, but these too were closed down suddenly without any communication to the community.

On the whole, the provision of civic amenities is poor in most slums, and this coupled with the lack of hygiene and over crowded housing makes the living situation quite pathetic. The situation is worse in unrecognized slums which are not even eligible for such provisions. In certain respects, all residents of slums are not equal, the better-off being located close to areas with larger and better provisions. Recent migrants being late entrants are generally in the worst state because of adverse location, lack of access to basic provisions, and a preoccupation with seeking a means of survival.

LITERACY, GENERAL SLUM ENVIRONMENT, AND SOCIAL PRACTICES

Low Level of Literacy among Parents

The levels of education among slum dwellers, though better than rural areas, is quite poor in general. Both partners are illiterate in the majority of households. Both husband and wife are illiterate in 52.5 per cent households and both are literate only in 11.2 per cent households. Either husband or wife is literate in the remaining 36.3 per cent households. The situation is best in Manohar Nagar in Kanpur with both partners being literate in one-fourth of the families and both being illiterate only in one-fourth of the cases, the rest of the households have at least one literate partner. The worst state exists at Ramashray Nagar in the same city, Kanpur, with both partners being illiterate in 83 per cent of the households and no household having both partners literate (Table 9.6).

General Slum Environment and Influence on Children

The general slum environment in terms of social relations and practices is not healthy or enabling. Alcoholism and gambling among males has been reported as a major problem in all the slums except at Mirzapur in Malda. This has severe implications for the family in several ways, one of the most

Table 9.6: Parental Literacy Status and General Problems in Urban Slums

	Distribution of households (per cent)			
Literacy status of parents	Both illiterate 52.4		One literate 36.3	Both literate 11.3
Biggest problem in slum	Sanitation and other amenities 64.7	Tension, gambling, etc. 17.7	Threat of eviction/flood 13.5	No school within the slum 4.1

SOURCE: Household Survey.

important repercussions being the diversion of male income for this purpose. The income of women, though less than their spouses, contributes more towards supporting the family. Alcoholism also leads to many illnesses including tuberculosis common in most slums. One of the most crucial and long-term impacts is that such practices create negative role models for children, especially boys. As a result, drinking and addiction to tobacco, *ganja,* and hashish is quite common among teenage boys. Delinquency in different forms is also reported to be common in this age group. The presence of illicit liquor shops coupled with drug trafficking and different forms of delinquency makes it easier for the police to enter and harass the residents, justifiably and unjustifiably. The police also provides cover to many such crimes and takes bribes for looking the other way (Box 9.1).

BOX 9.1: CHILDREN OF SEX WORKERS AND CHILD SEX WORKERS

The education of sex workers' children is an issue primarily because of the stigma attached to the profession of prostitution and its societal unacceptability. A survey sponsored by the Central Social Welfare Board (CSWB), in 1991, in six metropolitan cities of India indicated that the population of women and children in this trade would be between 70,000 and 100,000. About 30 per cent of them are reported to be below 18 years of age. According to another estimate, there are about 1.5 million sex workers in India, 20 per cent minor. One of the National Commission for Women studies says that about 60 per cent of prostitutes in Delhi are children below 15 years. Apart from known metropolitan centres like Mumbai, Delhi, and Kolkata, there are many smaller known centres in non-metropolitan cities like Varanasi, Murshidabad, Muzaffarpur, Nagpur, etc. In addition, the practice exists in practically all parts of the country and it is difficult to estimate the exact number of sex workers. The existing literature suggests strong tendencies among sex workers to produce children.

Most sex workers belong to lower or low middle class backgrounds. Indebtedness is common among them. They often access an informal system of indebtedness within their social circle. The interest rates are very high and often take the shape of bonded labour where particular sex workers are bound to work for a particular brothel keeper/pimp on specified, generally adverse, terms. This also impinges on children, especially daughters, who are made to join their mothers' occupation. Most child prostitutes are brought to big cities in the name of jobs in a household and then sold to brothel owners. Crisis situations, such as drought, lead families to send children to towns/cities in search of work. However, it is also not uncommon for them to have faced child abuse within the family and a father/uncle selling them off. They are also often exposed to drugs. Drug addiction keeps them under the control of their owners.

The children in such circumstances typically encounter the problems faced by a single-parent family, such as lack of a monitoring environment to provide security, care, and guidance, increasing responsibilities on the mother for the maintenance of the children, economic hardship, and lack of facilities to meet basic minimum needs. Being the children of prostitutes, they face some specific problems:

- — Unknown identity of fathers and often also separation from the mother, social abuse
- — Mothers either Indulgent or apathetic
- — Social non-acceptance, loneliness, and isolation in case the mother's occupation is known
- — Duality of personality caused by tendencies to keep secrets
- — Uncertainty and insecurity with regard to day-to-day existence
- — Neglect, feeling of deprivation and rejection
- — Affliction with some disease also suffered by the mother
- — Exposure to the world of prostitution

It is not easy to bring these children to school and sustain their education. The experiences of health projects (i.e. the Sonagachi project in Kolkata) show that the use of sex workers themselves as change agents and as peer teachers/trainers helps in outreach and impact. The children, when they come to school and get exposed to a world different from their own, generally react in two ways. One response is that they start hating themselves, their own likes, and develop a low self-image. They want to get out of their circumstances but do not know how. The second response is that they feel insecure and alien in this new environment and feel safe and secure in their own familiar setting. They withdraw and prefer to live on their own, especially if they happen to face any humiliation from others. A feeling of 'us versus them' is common because of several reasons. There is actual separation in some cases, i.e. there are separate classes for children of prostitutes in some municipality-run schools in Mumbai. One NGO in Navi Mumbai reported having faced strong public protests from parents over the inclusion of sex workers' children in the general class. In case of day schools, children get to spend only a few hours in the schools and, therefore, they are part of the nightlife of their mothers, which influences and affects them. Some NGOs also provide night shelters in the same place after running schools during the day. NGO experiences show that only concerted efforts and a mix of strategies succeed in ensuring their schooling.

Social Practices

The system of dowry is present in some form everywhere and causes a lot of problems among girls' parents. Early marriage for girls is prevalent but the age of marriage varies from one place to the other, being as low as about 10-12 years in the slums in Malda and around 16-17 years in the slums of Parbhani and Kanpur. The age of marriage for girls varies between 13 to 16 in the Delhi and Warangal slums. Concern for the safety of growing girls is the reason for early marriage in slums, besides this being customary among certain communities. However, it is interesting to note that neither alcoholism nor fear of sexual abuse of their own daughters is accepted to exist within families; it is discussed always in the context of 'others' and the general slum environment.

Life of Poverty, Insecurity, and Vulnerability

It is clear that life for poor families in low-income neighbourhoods or so-called slums in cities is actually a life of poverty, deprivation, and insecurity. The usual illegal status of residence makes them constantly uncertain of their residence, irrespective of the number of years they have been living in that particular area. They view any new person coming to the area with suspicion and hope—suspicion that the person is there to get the place evacuated, and hope that this would perhaps mean relocation and a legal right of residence. The work situation, with its irregular nature, adds to this uncertainty. Pathetic living conditions and the lack of civic amenities make living almost sub-human. Health hazards created both because of occupations and poor hygienic conditions make them more vulnerable. An illness not only means the draining of existing savings but also a reduction in future income. There is simply no concept of any leave, compensation, or any other social security provision in any of the jobs that these people do. Widespread alcoholism and gambling among males add to these conditions and make the environment more difficult for women and children.

SCHOOLS IN SLUM AREAS: AVAILABILITY, ACCESSIBILITY, AND FUNCTIONING

AVAILABILITY OF AND ACCESS TO SCHOOLS

None of the slums in any of the five urban centres, except one in Kanpur, has a government school within the slum premises. Juhi Bumruiya, the oldest of all, has a school as it was originally inhabited mainly by workers of an important public sector textile company. One slum, Coolipada in Malda, has a Hindi-medium community school running within the slum, and the two slums in Parbhani have an Urdu-medium private school within each of them. All slums, except one in Kanpur, have either government or private schools within a distance of 1 km. However, access to schools, especially for young children from poor and deprived communities, is not subject to the availability of schools at a manageable distance alone. It involves the larger issue of the school being physically accessible, socially or linguistically inclusive, and economically affordable. The procedures for admission also have to be sensitive to the lives and conditions of the poor and marginalized, and facilitative in character. In many cases, the schools available to slum children do not fulfil these conditions.

Procedural Problems in Government Schools

The requirement of a birth certificate at the time of admission is a major constraint faced by slum dwellers in Malda, Delhi and Kanpur. This is especially problematic for families which still follow the practice of going to their native places for child birth. It is quite common among first-generation migrants, and in many cases even second-generation migrants. The practice of getting birth certificates is not common in rural areas and in many cases, children are delivered at home and not at a hospital, making it all the more difficult. The necessity of a transfer certificate for the admission of a child going to a school in a rural area or in some other town earlier is also an obstacle. Poor uneducated parents do not usually have any clear long-term picture before them when they decide to come to urban areas in search of work. Once they come and find some work, they continue to live there and then if they decide to admit their children to school, the need for birth and transfer certificates is baffling and discouraging to them. They fail to fulfil these requirements and drop the idea of schooling their children. Also, most government schools located in the vicinity of slums cater mainly to lower middle class families living in the colonies in which the schools are located. Therefore, the target group children and the school's orientation regarding this is more important than distance in ensuring access to children living in slum areas.

Physical and Language Barriers

Physical and language barriers add to these procedural problems. Railway tracks and highways act as barriers to children on their way to school. Language is a bigger issue faced by those who have migrated outside their state. They have found a solution by setting up community and private schools. The residents of Coolipada, Malda, mainly from Bihar, want their children to get a Hindi-medium education. They started a community school with two teachers in 1986, with Hindi as the medium of instruction. The school runs on contributions from the community, and faces a lot of problems. There is only one Hindi-medium secondary school in the city located at a distance of about 8 km. from this slum. Urdu is the mother tongue of Muslim residents in the Parbhani slums and they face similar problems. Private schools running inside the slums impart instruction in Urdu but there is only one Urdu-medium school, located very far, for the upper primary level. Bengali-speaking children living in the Mehrauli slum in Delhi find it difficult to get admission due to a variety of reasons, language and the unclear legal status of their residence being the most important ones. They, therefore, remain out of school despite the fact that government schools exist in the vicinity (Table 9.7).

Private Schools

Private schools play an important role in providing schooling facilities to

Table 9.7: Access to Schools in Slums

Slum	School within slum	Whether Public School within 1 km	Whether Pvt. School within 1 km	Any major physical barrier between school and the slum	Problems in admission due to procedure	Other institutions present
Mirzapur (Malda)	No	Yes	No	None	Not mentioned specifically	Madrasa, ECCE, Vocational
Coolipada (Malda)	Yes (community)	Yes	No	Highway, railway track	Due to requirement of birth and other certificates	None
Dakshin Baluchar (Malda)	No	Yes	No	None	Due to requirement of birth and other certificates	None
Ramashray Nagar (Kanpur)	No	No	No	None	Due to requirement of birth and other certificates	NFE (World Vision)
Juhi Bumruiya (Kanpur)	Yes	Yes	Yes	None	Not mentioned specifically	NGO school
Rakhi Mandi (Kanpur)	No	Yes 2	Yes	None	Not mentioned specifically	None
Manohar Nagar (Kanpur)	No	No	Yes	Highway	Requirement of transfer certificate	Madrasa
Zakhira 1 (Delhi)	No	Yes	No	Railway track	Requirement of ration card	Madrasa
Zakhira 2 (Delhi)	No	Yes	No	Railway track	Requirement of ration card	Tuition centre
Mehrauli (Delhi)	No	Yes	No	None	Requirement of birth certificate and ration card	NFE (NGO)
Haiderpur (Delhi)	No	Yes	No	None	Requirement of birth and other certificates	PEEP

Bharat Nagar	Yes	No	Yes	None	Language at post-primary level	NFE (NGO) Madrasa
S.G. Nagar (Parbhani)	Yes (private)	No	Yes	Railway track	Language at post-primary level	Madrasa
G.P. Nagar (Warangal)	No	Yes	Yes	None	Not mentioned specifically	NCLP (NGO run)
Garib Nagar (Warangal)	No	No	Yes	None	Not mentioned specifically	NCLP (NGO run)

NOTES: NCLP: National Child Labour Project, supported by the Central Department of Labour, establishes schools for working children and provides various incentives including a monthly stipend as compensation.

These schools are generally up to the primary level, but in several places like Sanjay Gandhi Nagar, Dakshin Baluchar, Bharat Nagar, Zakhira, Mehrauli, Haiderpur, etc., there are middle and high schools in the neighbourhood as well. However, upper primary schools, though in the vicinity of the slums, cater primarily to the neighbouring colonies and usually serve non-slum settlements.

SOURCE: Slum Appraisal, Household Interviews and Case Studies

slum dwellers in Kanpur, Parbhani, and Warangal. These private schools have been opened to target children living in these slums, and compete among themselves to get more admissions. As such, they try to make admission procedures simple and do not ask for documents that are not available easily. Teachers maintain regular interaction with parents to secure and sustain admissions of more and more children. All these schools charge admission as well as tuition fees, and some poor parents find it difficult to arrange this on a regular basis. On the other hand, government schools always insist on certificates and documents for admissions which parents find intimidating.

Madrasas and Other Educational Institutions

Five out of the fifteen slums in this study also have madrasas. As discussed earlier in detail, Muslims view religious education as a vital part of their tradition and culture. This education for girls, according to parents in slums, also helps in getting them married into good families without much dowry. Religious education is associated with gaining greater social respect among Muslims everywhere, including in urban areas. The madrasas located in the Parbhani slums operate for two hours in the morning and evening and focus only on teaching the Koran. The madrasa in the Manohar Nagar slum in Kanpur has been operational for many years but teaching was confined to the Koran, Arabic, Hindi and Urdu till 2000. Since 2000, the maulvis have started teaching other regular subjects being taught in primary classes such as mathematics and environmental studies to attract more children. In contrast, the madrasa located at the Zakhira slum in Delhi follows the primary level of the Islamic curriculum considered to be the equivalent to Classes I to V, and is linked to higher-level Islamic institutions existing in cities like Allahabad, Patna and Aligarh. This madrasa runs in three shifts, 7.00-9.30 a.m., 2.30-5.00 p.m. and 7.00-9.30 p.m. The one located in the Mirzapur slum in Malda does not function regularly.

The availability of *anganwadis* or any other early childhood care facilities is very poor in slums. Among all the study's slums, Mirzapur at Malda is the only slum with a functional Early Childhood Care and Education (ECCE) centre being run with the support of the Integrated Child Development Scheme (ICDS). Although this functions regularly, the services, especially those related to early education, are poor. Non-formal centres run by different NGOs are found in the three slums in Kanpur. Although these centres run regularly, their role is limited to either providing supplementary teaching or basic literacy and numerical skills. Both slums in Warangal had schools supported by the National Child Labour Project (NCLP). These are full-time schools meant to bring working children to school and provide a monthly scholarship of Rs. 100 to each student. However, in reality they have become attractive options because of the stipend and have now started admitting any child from poor families, perhaps because of the problem of distinguishing working from non-working children. But seats are limited and, therefore, they usually cannot cater to all families living in that area.

PROVISIONING AND FUNCTIONING OF SCHOOLS

Physical Infrastructure and Teacher-Pupil Ratio

Private schools are better placed as compared to government schools in terms of physical infrastructure. Not only is the state of buildings better at private schools, but they also have the basic facilities considered important by parents, including separate classrooms for different classes, drinking water facilities, and toilets. This despite the fact that they are generally housed in smaller buildings. The only private school which does not have adequate space and only minimum facilities is the Urdu-medium primary school located at Sanjay Gandhi Nagar in Parbhani. Most government schools in urban areas are housed in old buildings that require repair, renovation or regular maintenance, and the space is generally not adequate to house the respective enrolments. None of the schools in Kanpur and Malda have the basic facilities of drinking water and toilets. Unlike rural areas, these are important in cities as children face security hazards in arranging for these needs. For instance, children in one school cross busy city roads to get water, and in another they request neighbouring houses to let them have water. The absence of toilets makes it difficult, especially for women teachers and older girls. Though the buildings for government schools in Warangal and Delhi are not always adequate *vis-à-vis* the number of children, these are relatively better placed in terms of facilities (Table 9.8).

In sharp contrast to rural areas, government schools in urban areas have favourable teacher-pupil ratios, not higher than 1:50 for any school, this being as low as 1:10 in one school. This shows that almost all schools in urban areas are adequately staffed, some over-staffed. This reflects the well-known phenomenon of school teachers 'managing' postings in urban areas, leading to the skewed distribution of teachers to the disadvantage of rural areas. This ratio is not very high even for private schools, though not always as low as government schools. Unlike the common practice of forced multi-grade teaching being followed by rural teachers, the availability of an adequate number of teachers means classes are generally held separately in urban areas. This is important because parents perceive this as a sign of good teaching practice. It may be added that the actual number of teachers present in government schools do not often match the number of teachers in position. However, this does not affect teaching as badly as it does in rural areas because of the larger number of teachers in position.

Parents' Perceptions

The general perception among parents regarding the functioning of government schools is very poor in urban areas as well. Although the schools

Table 9.8: School Provisioning in Urban Slums

Slum	Infrastructure Government	Private	Number of Teachers and PTR* Ratio		Class Organization	
			Government	Private	Government	Private
Mirzapur (1 govt. school)	Very inadequate. Roofs about to collapse. No toilet. No drinking water.		13 (27)		Separate classes for each class	
Coolipada (1 com. school)	Inadequate. No toilet. No drinking water.		5 (53)		1 and 2 together Rest separate	
Dakshin Baluchar (3 govt. schools)	1 school average, 1 poor. No toilet. No drinking water in either 1 good, all basic facilities available.		5 (15) 4 (10) 6 (24)		1 and 2 together Rest separate (both schools) All separate	
Ramashray Nagar (1 govt./1 pvt. school)	Very inadequate. Dilapidated. No basic facility. Classes held in the open.	Inadequate. Small rooms. Drinking water, toilets, fans available.	5 (30)	NA	Separate classes	Separate classes
Juhi Bumbruiya/ Rakhi Mandi (2 govt. / 2 pvt. schools)	1. Very inadequate (both). 2. No toilet. No drinking water in either.	1. Inadequate. Drinking water, toilet available. 2. Good. All basic facilities available.	1 (101) 2 (43)	5 (47) 4 (60)	All classes together 1, 2, 3 and 4, 5 together.	All classes separate All classes separate
Manohar Nagar (1 pvt. school)		Average. All basic facilities (toilets, drinking water, etc., available).		5 (19)		Class I separate; 2 and 3, and 4 and 5 together

Zakhira 1 (1 govt. school)	Inadequate. Drinking water available. No toilet.		6 (47)		All classes separate	
Zakhira 2 (1 govt. school)	Inadequate. Toilet available. Drinking water not available.		5 (48)		All classes separate	
Haiderpur (1 govt. school)	Good. All basic facilities available.		33 (42)		All classes separate	
Bharat Nagar (2 govt. aided schools)		1. (aided, primary) Inadequate. Water pump available. No toilet		4 (31)		All classes separate
		2. (aided, upper primary and secondary) Good. All basic facilities available.				All classes separate
Sanjay Gandhi Nagar (2 aided schools)		1. Marathi medium (aided) Good. All basic facilities available.		8 (63)		All classes separate
		2. Urdu medium (aided). Inadequate. Basic facilities not available.		9 (82)		All classes separate
Giri Prasad Nagar (1 govt./ 1 pvt. school	Inadequate. All basic facilities (toilets, drinking water available).	Average. All basic facilities (toilets, drinking water available).	5 (44)	5 (26.5)	All classes separate	All classes separate
Garib Nagar (1 govt. school)	Average. Drinking water available, No toilet.		6 (46)		All classes separate	

NOTE: *Pupil-Teacher Ratio (PTR) is shown in bracket.
SOURCE: School Survey.

were reported to be opening regularly everywhere, teachers, sincerity, interest, and involvement are questioned. A common complaint against teachers in government schools was that they are more interested in their personal work and do not take their job seriously because they are not accountable to anyone. The lack of discipline is another common complaint that parents have against government schools. Private schools are considered more disciplined and teachers accountable to students and parents because their jobs are not permanent. The biggest attraction of private schools is English teaching, but they are also perceived as providing greater attention to the individual child and better monitoring of his/her progress. The fact that teachers from private schools come to their doorstep for admission is also appreciated. However, the low salaries of teachers in private schools leading to their resignation and the consequent destablizing effects on school functioning were cited as negative elements of private schools. Another common complaint against private schools is that the teachers insist on private tuitions and harass those students who do not opt for this. The fee in private schools is high and many poor families said they cannot afford such payments. Nevertheless, despite certain complaints, the general perception is that private schools are better than government schools (Table 9.9).

Discipline Please

Parents from slums attach a lot of importance to 'discipline' in school, even if it is attained through corporal punishment or similar means. As mentioned earlier, the lack of discipline, or its presence, was considered an important distinguishing factor between government and private schools. However, interactions with children reflected a very different perspective. They were clear and articulate in expressing their dislike for teachers who beat children unnecessarily, punish them for minor lapses, make children do errands, give assignments they cannot understand, read from books without explaining, and do not appreciate their work. Most slum children also said that they like going to school because it gives them opportunities to play with peers, make friends, and to be away from household responsibilities. In many cases, parents and children varied in their opinions about particular schools. While parents perceived the school as not leading to any desirable progress in their children, the children liked going to school for a variety of reasons, the company of peers being the most important one.

Poor Support and Monitoring of Government Schools

Teachers from government schools feel constrained because of their involvement in too many non-teaching responsibilities including the census, polio camps, checking ration cards and voters' lists, etc. Teachers also complained about the poor infrastructure and lack of adequate physical facilities, and the government's indifference towards these aspects. They felt that the government is not serious about education and even if they do good

Table 9.9: School Provisioning and Functioning in Urban Slums: Parents' Perceptions

Slum (City)	School Infrastructure, Functioning and Other Issues	
	Government School	Private School
Mirzapur (Malda)	Teachers regular. Do not take much interest.	Better organized. Teachers pay more attention.
Collipada (Malda)	Teachers do not bother as they have fixed income.	Better organized. Pay individual attention and are responsible for children's performance. Better discipline.
Dakshin Baluchar (Malda)	Teachers friendly and considerate but lazy and irregular. Do not bother as they have fixed income.	Better discipline. More attention on co-curricular activities. But difficult to afford.
Ramashray Nagar (Kanpur)	No classroom functional; books supply delayed. Teachers busy eating, doing personal chores. Not interested in teaching. Children promoted on the basis of attendance, shown present even when absent.	All basic facilities provided. Teachers come home to ask parents to enrol their children. Children neglected here as well, not much better than government school. Teachers insist on tuitions.
Juhi Bumruiya/Rakhi Mandi (Kanpur)	Most basic facilities missing. Teachers busy in various other duties. Teachers sympathetic to children but old and lazy; not interested in teaching well. Children passed only on the basis of attendance. Do not learn anything.	All basic facilities provided. Expensive but no option if children have to be taught. Teachers maintain ties with parents to seek and sustain admission. Teachers take interest but insist on tuitions. Children discriminated against if they do not take private tuitions. Teachers paid less, therefore they leave jobs frequently leading to a high turnover.
Manohar Nagar (Kanpur)	Poorly maintained infrastructure. Teachers not interested.	Better maintained infrastructure. Expensive but better teaching. But teachers emphasize the need to take tuitions, families cannot afford.
Zakhira 1 (Delhi)	No clear perception	No clear perception
Zakhira 2 (Delhi)	Regular in opening. Children do not learn. Children play around and teachers keep gossiping.	Better because English is taught. Teachers take individual care of students.

(contd.)

Table 9.9: (contd.)

Slum (City)	School Infrastructure, Functioning and Other Issues	
	Government School	Private School
Haiderpur (Delhi)	Good infrastructure but no discipline. Teachers do not take interest; no discipline; children not learning anything.	Better discipline. Anything is good if it helps in maintaining discipline. Children learn English. Better monitoring of children's progress.
Bharat Nagar (Parbhani)		Irregular. Teachers not adequately qualified. Do not teach properly. Important because English is taught.
Sanjay Gandhi Nagar (Parbhani)		Regular. Teaching not good. As bad as government schools.
Giri Prasad Nagar (Warangal)	Regular. Good. Teachers pay attention.	Regular. Better because it teaches English. But difficult to afford because of high fees.
Garib Nagar (Warangal)	Building is about to collapse. Teachers not sufficient. Does not teach English.	Teachers inexperienced and indifferent. Charge high fees, only aim to make money.

SOURCE: Focus Group Discussions with Men's and Women's Groups in Slums.

work, they do not get the proper appreciation. Supervisors and administrators are not regular in visiting schools and even when they visit, they are interested only in checking the registers and records and not at all keen to know the progress of children or understand any problems that the teachers might be facing in running the schools. Headmasters are often involved in a number of meetings with no connection with the actual teaching in the schools.

Teachers' Understanding of Slum Situations

Almost all teachers, in private or government schools, showed some understanding of slum situations and the problems faced by slum children. These were identified and listed as: no support from parents, negative slum environment, requirement for girls to take care of younger siblings, weak financial situations, etc. However, this understanding was seldom translated into taking responsibility and the sensitive handling of children. Rather, it translated into negative opinions about the ability and sincerity of students coming from poor families living in slums. While a few teachers blamed lack of persuasion and follow-up action at home for the irregular attendance, and therefore, poor learning achievements, the majority of them believed that these children are not intelligent enough to learn and it is useless to spend time educating them. A few teachers also expressed their aversion to their dirty surroundings and expressed helplessness in having come to such 'dirty' places because of the need for a job. They seemed oblivious to the fact that their negative opinions and attitudes lead to very low or no expectations from these children, and this itself contributes to developing a low self-image and below-average performance among children.

Government schools in urban areas are different from those in rural areas in several ways. Unlike schools in rural areas, schools in urban areas open regularly and generally function for the prescribed hours, and they have an adequate, at times more than adequate, number of teachers. However, they are similar to schools in rural areas in two respects: poor infrastructure, which becomes more crucial here, and, more importantly, insensitive and indifferent teachers. Teachers' attitudes, and the willingness and competence to deal with children coming from poor and deprived backgrounds are crucial in rural as well as urban areas, and this is what is generally missing everywhere. Private schools in urban areas, if for nothing else but their very survival, are better as they try to extend themselves and reach out to poor parents rather than wait for them to come to schools.

School Participation Patterns

INTER-CITY AND INTER-SLUM DIFFERENCES

School participation patterns for children belonging to poor families in urban slums are only slightly better than those seen in rural areas. Only about two-thirds of the children in the 6-13 age group attend school. However, unlike rural areas, out-of-school children in urban areas are almost equally divided between drop-outs and never-enrolled. This means that the share of the ever-enrolled is higher in urban areas than in rural areas. A minuscule proportion of non-school-going children are enrolled in NFE or tuition centres. Inter-city variations are large and, more importantly, inter-slum variations within a city are also very large. The proportion of enrolled children is highest in Malda at 82.1 per cent and the lowest in Delhi at 42.3 per cent. With about three-fourth of the children enrolled, the proportion of enrolled children is also relatively high in Parbhani and Warangal. In Kanpur, the share of enrolled children is about 65 per cent, which is close to the overall national average for urban areas (Table 9.10).

The proportion of enrolled children is greater than 80 per cent in three (20 per cent) slums, this proportion being between 60 to 80 per cent in eight (53 per cent) slums. These include all slums in Malda, Parbhani, and Warangal, and all but one in Kanpur. The share of in-school children is very low and that of out-of-school children very high in the remaining four slums, three in Delhi (Zakhira 1 and 2, and Mehrauli) and one in Kanpur (Ramashray Nagar). The inter-slum difference in the proportion of in-school

Table 9.10: School Participation Patterns for Children in Urban Slums (per cent)

City	Slum	Enrolled	Drop-outs	Never-enrolled	*Angan-wadi*	Madrasa	NFE/ Tuition
Malda	Mirzapur	77.8	18.5	3.7	–	–	–
	Coolipada	91.7	4.2	4.2	–	–	–
	Bablaghat	75.0	18.8	6.3	–	–	–
	Total	82.1	13.5	4.5	–	–	–
Kanpur	Ramashray Nagar	42.3	23.1	11.5	–	–	23.0
	Juhi Bumruiya	75.0	7.1	3.6	14.3	–	–
	Rakhi Mandi	72.7	18.2	9.1	–	–	–
	Manohar Nagar	70.0	3.3	10.0	–	16.7	–
	Total	65.1	12.3	8.5	3.8	4.7	13.7
Delhi	Zakhira 1	36.4	9.0	31.8	–	22.7	–
	Zakhira 2	50.0	22.2	16.6	–	–	–
	Mehrauli	16.7	33.3	45.8	4.2	–	–
	Haiderpur	85.7	7.1	7.1	–	–	–
	Total	42.3	19.2	28.2	1.3	6.4	2.6
Parbhani	Bharat Nagar	74.1	25.9	–	–	–	–
	S.G. Nagar	76.7	16.7	6.7	–	–	–
	Total	75.4	21.1	3.5	–	–	–
Warangal	G.P. Nagar	87.5	8.3	4.2	–	–	–
	Garib Nagar	62.5	–	18.8	–	6.3	–
	Total	77.5	5.0	10.0	–	2.5	–
Total		66.4	14.6	11.5	1.4	3.2	2.3

SOURCE: Household Survey.

children within one city in terms of per cent points is the widest for Delhi (69 per cent points) and the narrowest for Parbhani (2.6 per cent points). The difference is high in Delhi slums, even if the case of Mehrauli is ignored as extraordinarily low.

GENDER DIFFERENTIALS

The gender differentials are not very high in schooling participation indicators in urban slums. In fact, the proportion of enrolled girls in the total population of 6-13 years is higher (69 per cent) than that for boys (64 per cent). The gender disparities in drop-outs and never-enrolled figures are also only marginal. The slum-wise picture presents a mixed trend with the proportion of enrolled students being higher for girls in certain areas and the opposite being true in certain others. However, it is more meaningful to compare the enrolment proportions in view of the ratios that exist for the respective populations.

Among 6-13-year-old children, school participation patterns vary for different age brackets. The proportion of enrolled is lower for girls and that for drop-outs and never-enrolled is higher in comparison to boys in the lower age group (6-8 years). However, the status changes in the next age group (9-11 years) where the proportion of enrolled is higher and that of drop-outs is lower for girls. In the higher age group, the proportion of enrolled as well as drop-outs is again higher for girls. It appears that though a smaller proportion of girls is admitted at the initial stage, they continue for a longer period as compared to boys. The boys start dropping out after the age of 8 for various reasons, including engagement in earning activities and the influences of the slum environment such as alcoholism, drug addiction, aimless roaming around, etc., whereas girls discontinue at a slightly later age when they are required for work at home or for marriage. This is also obvious from the fact that the share of enrolled-but-not-attending is higher for boys (Tables 9.11 and 9.12).

INTER-SOCIAL GROUP DIFFERENCES

The inter-social group differences in school participation rates exist even among slum dwellers though the differences are not always as sharp as seen in the case of rural areas. Although the number of the upper caste families itself is very low among slum dwellers, the proportion of enrolled children is the highest for them. This is followed by OBCs, SCs, and Muslims. Muslims have the lowest proportion amongst all social groups. Nonetheless, the proportion of enrolled children among Muslims in urban areas is significantly higher than in rural areas, this difference not being as significant for other groups. The proportion of families sending all children to school is also the highest for upper caste Hindu families with every household sending

Table 9.11: Gender Differentials in School Participation Patterns in Urban Slums (%)

Slum	Enrolled		Drop-outs		Never-enrolled		*Anganwadi*		Madrasa		NFE/Tuition centre	
	B*	G*	B	G	B	G	B	G	B	G	B	G
Malda												
Mirzapur	61.5	92.9	38.5	–	–	7.1	–	–	–	–	–	–
Coolipada	16.7	83.3	12.5	25.0	–	8.3		–	–	–	–	–
Bablag	75.0	75.0	12.5	25.0	12.5	–	–	–	–	–	–	–
Total	78.8	85.3	18.2	8.8	3.0	5.9	–	–	–	–	–	–
Kanpur												
Ramashray Nagar	57.1	25.0	14.3	33.3	7.1	16.7	–	–	–	–	21.4	25.0
Juhi Bumruiya	75.0	75.0	–	12.5	8.3	–	16.7	12.5	–	–	–	–
Rakhi Mandi	66.7	80.0	25.0	10.0	8.3	10.0	–	–	–	–	–	–
Manohar Nagar	62.5	78.6	–	7.1	18.8	–	–	–	18.8	14.3	–	–
Total	64.8	65.4	9.3	15.4	11.1	5.8	3.7	3.8	5.6	3.8	5.6	5.7
Delhi												
Zakhira 1	33.3	38.5	22.2	–	11.1	46.1	–	–	33.3	15.4	–	–
Zakhira 2	57.1	45.4	14.3	27.3	14.3	18.2	–	–	–	–	–	9.1
Mehrauli	8.3	25.0	41.7	27.3	50.0	41.7	8.3	–	–	–	–	–
Haiderpur	80.0	88.9	20.0	–	–	11.1	–	–	–	–	–	–
Total	36.4	46.7	27.2	13.3	24.2	31.1	–	2.2	9.1	4.4	–	2.2
Parbhani												
Bharat Nagar	81.3	63.6	27.9	27.3	–	–	–	–	–	–	–	–
S.G. Nagar	64.3	87.5	21.4	12.5	14.3	–	–	–	–	–	–	–
Total	73.3	77.8	23.7	18.5	6.7	–	–	–	–	–	–	–
Warangal												
Giri Prasad Nagar	81.3	100	12.5	–	6.3	–	–	–	–	–	–	–
Garib Nagar	33.3	80.0	–	–	33.3	10.0	–	–	16.7	–	–	–
Total	68.2	88.9	9.1	–	13.6	5.6	–	–	4.5	–	–	–
Total	63.9	68.8	15.3	13.1	11.6	11.4	1.2	1.7	4.1	2.3	3.3	2.8

NOTE: B: Boys, G: Girls.

Table 9.12: Schooling Participation Patterns for Different Age-groups of Children (%)

Gender	Age group	Enrolled	Drop-out	Never-enrolled	*Anganwadi*	Madrasa	NFE/Tuition centre
Male	6 to 8	74.2	1.6	11.3	1.6	6.5	4.8
	9 to 11	63.9	18.0	9.8	1.6	3.3	3.3
	12 to 13	51.0	32.7	14.3	–	2.0	–
	Total	64.0	16.3	11.6	1.2	4.1	2.3
Female	6 to 8	69.1	7.4	16.2	2.9	1.5	3.0
	9 to 11	73.4	7.8	9.4	1.6	4.7	3.2
	12 to 13	61.4	29.5	6.8	–		2.3
	Total	68.8	13.1	11.4	1.7	2.3	2.7

at least one child to school. On the other hand, more than one-fifth of OBCs and SCs, and more than one-fourth of the Muslim families do not send any child to school. Although the proportion of enrolled children is higher for OBCs in comparison to SCs, thc proportion of families sending all their children is higher for the latter as compared to the former (Table 9.13).

Table 9.13: Schooling Participation Patterns for Different Social Groups of Children (%)

Social Group	Enrolled	Drop-outs	Never-enrolled	Anganwadi	Madrasa	NFE/Tuition centre
UCH	93.3	6.7				
OBC	71.9	15.6	6.3	6.3		
SC	68.8	13.2	11.1	2.8	4.1	
Muslims	60.5	15.6	14.0	0.6	7.0	1.3
Total	66.4	14.6	11.5	1.4	3.2	2.3

SOURCE: For Tables 9.11, 9.12 and 9.13: Household Survey.

SCHOOL PARTICIPATION PATTERNS BY HOUSEHOLD

As seen in rural areas, the proportion of school-going children does not necessarily reveal the proportion of families sending all their children to school. Out of all families, only 56.7 per cent send all their children to school, while 22 per cent do not send any child to school. At least one child attends school from the remaining 21.3 per cent families. The proportion of families sending all their children to school is the highest for Haiderpur (87.5 per cent) in Delhi followed by Rakhi Mandi (83.3 per cent) in Kanpur and Coolipada (83.3 per cent) in Malda. The practice of not sending any child to school appears to be most common in Ramashray Nagar (41.7 per cent) households with no child in school) in Kanpur and Mehrauli (81.8 per cent). In Garib Nagar in Warangal, it appears to be common to send a child/ some children to school and keep some, mostly girls, away as the proportion of such households is the highest (44.4 per cent) there (Table 9.14).

HIGH REGULARITY

Unlike rural areas, irregularity does not appear to be as high among enrolled children in urban slums. About 90 per cent of the total enrolled children attend school fairly regularly. The proportion of occasionally attending children among the enrolled is also very low (1.4 per cent). Again, unlike rural areas, irregularity is higher among boys as compared to girls; only 6.4 per cent of the enrolled girls were perceived to be irregular in attending school as against about 14 per cent of boys. No enrolled girl was reported to be attending school only occasionally. All occasionally attending children from slums are boys (Table 9.15).

Table 9.14: Distribution of Households according to Children's Schooling Participation Status (%)

City	Slum	All in schools (%)	Some in, some out (%)	None in school (%)
Malda	Mirzapur	58.3	25.0	16.7
	Coolipada	83.3	8.3	8.3
	Bablaghat	63.6	18.2	18.2
	Total	68.6	17.1	14.3
Kanpur	Ramashray Nagar	25.0	33.3	41.7
	Juhi Bumruiya	66.7	16.7	16.7
	Rakhi Mandi	83.3	8.3	8.3
	Manohar Nagar	58.3	25.0	16.7
	Total	58.3	20.8	20.8
Delhi	Zakhira 1	33.3	33.3	33.3
	Zakhira 2	37.5	25.0	37.5
	Mehrauli	18.2	-	81.8
	Haiderpur	87.5	–	12.5
	Total	41.7	13.9	44.4
Parbhani	Bharat Nagar	58.3	25.0	16.7
	Sanjay Gandhi Nagar	50.0	33.3	16.7
	Total	54.2	29.2	16.7
Warangal	Giri Prasad Nagar	75.0	25.0	–
	Garib Nagar	44.4	44.4	11.1
	Total	61.9	33.3	4.8
Total		56.7	21.3	22.0

SOURCE: Household Survey.

Table 9.15: Regularity of Enrolled Children in Attending School

Distribution of enrolled children (%)	Male	Female	Total
Regular	86.1	93.6	89.9
Irregular	11.1	6.4	8.7
Occasional	2.8	–	1.4

SOURCE: Research Team's Perception.

GOVERNMENT AND PRIVATE SCHOOLS

Government schools remain the single largest provider of education at the primary and upper primary levels in urban areas as well, albeit the proportion of those enrolled in private schools is much higher as compared to that in rural areas. Thirty-seven per cent of school-going children are enrolled in government schools, 27 per cent in unaided private schools, and 26 per cent in aided private schools. It may be mentioned that though aided schools are privately managed, they receive substantial financial support, almost up to 90-5 per cent of the total recurrent expenditure, from government sources and hence should be seen separately from unaided private schools. The

Table 9.16: Type of School where Children are Enrolled

	Distribution of enrolled children according to management of school (%)					
	Government	Private unaided	Private aided	NGO	NCLP	Other
Boys	32.5	32.5	23.9	–	1.7	9.2
Girls	41.02	21.37	27.29	0.8	1.7	8.4
Total	36.75	26.92	25.6	0.4	1.7	8.8

NOTE: NCLP: National Child Labour Project.
SOURCE: Household Survey.

proportion of children attending government schools goes up to 38 per cent if children attending NCLP schools are added. It is important to note that the proportion of girls going to government schools is significantly higher than that for boys, the opposite being true for private schools. The proportion of girls enrolled in private schools is lower than that for boys in case of both aided and unaided schools (Table 9.16).

REASONS FOR NON-PARTICIPATION

As discussed in the context of non-participation in rural areas, children from poor families do not go to school for a variety of reasons and the decision, which in such families is often not even a well-thought-out decision but happens on its own, is a result of the complex interplay of a number of factors. When asked about the reason for a particular child being out of school, parents in a substantial number of cases (12 per cent for boys and about 10 per cent for girls) could not cite any specific reason. As discussed earlier, parents' responses to the question about the reasons for the child's schooling status have limitations, yet provide important insights (Table 9.17).

Table 9.17: Reasons for Being Out-of-School: Parents' Perceptions (per cent)

	Reasons	Boys	Girls
Child-related	Does not like to go to school	32.00	15.69
	Handicapped	6.00	3.92
Family situation-related	Household chores/sibling care	2.00	3.92
	Due to migration	0.00	3.92
	Family problems/illness	4.00	7.84
	Cost/poverty	24.00	25.49
School related	Failure	4.00	0.00
	School far off	2.00	5.88
	School is not good	6.00	3.92
	Procedural reasons	6.00	9.80
Others	No use of education	0.00	5.88
	No specific reason	2.00	3.92
	No response	12.00	9.80

SOURCE: Household Survey.

The child's lack of interest was cited as the reason in the case of 32 per cent of out-of-school boys as compared to only 16 per cent of out-of-school girls. It is quite common for boys living in slums to be independent and on their own at an early age. The fathers' preoccupation with looking for work and spending leisure time mostly drinking and gambling means the absence or near absence of any close monitoring of boys by older males. Mothers, even if they are not working, remain busy in various other chores and are unable to keep a close watch on young boys, who spend maximum time with their peers. The need to start earning from an early age also creates its own pressure on boys. The situation is different for girls. Despite the fact that they also start earning early, girls remain in much closer contact with their families, especially mothers. Outside influences, including coming in contact with educated women outside the slum, lead to higher aspirations and draw them towards seeking an education. Those who get a chance to enrol and continue for the initial two-three years want to continue further despite constraints. They do not always get an opportunity to fulfil this desire due to various reasons including the practice of early marriage found in every slum in varying degrees.

Poverty-related factors, including the high direct cost of education, are the second most frequently cited (24 per cent) reason for boys and the most commonly cited (26 per cent) reasons for girls. Other family situation-related constraints including one's own or somebody else's illness, frequent changes of residence like going to one's home town and staying there for months, and the need for support at home for household chores and sibling care, kept 20 per cent girls and 12 per cent boys out of school in that state. As compared to rural areas, school-related reasons get more prominence in urban areas. School-related reasons including distance, poor functioning, failure, and procedural problems were cited for 20 per cent girls and 18 per cent boys out of school.

OUT-OF-SCHOOL CHILDREN'S ENGAGEMENTS

In the context of the reasons for children remaining out of school, it becomes important to understand and analyse the patterns of engagement of out-of-school children in slum areas. About one-third of out-of-school children are engaged directly in earning activities, either working independently for wages or working with their parents in family-based work. Family-based work includes contracted work on piece-rate payments and working in small shops or other establishments, including selling sundry goods on *thelas*. More than one-fourth of out-of-school children, mainly girls, are primarily engaged in household chores or taking care of younger siblings. An interesting point is that a substantial proportion, more than one-fourth, of out-of-school children is not engaged in any particular work either in or outside the home. This share is very high for boys, confirming the hypothesis that boys in urban slums tend to be on their own and, even without any

Table 9.18: Major Engagements of Out-of-School Children (per cent)

Major Engagements* of Out-of-School Children	Boys	Girls	Total
Children mainly engaged in independent earning work	27.6	19.2	23.6
Children accompanying/helping their parents in earning activities**	10.1	5.8	7.2
Children mainly engaged in household chores/sibling care	8.7	38.5	25.4
Children going to madrasa/NFE/tuition centre	17.2	17.3	17.3
Children not engaged in any particular work for substantial hours	32.8	19.2	26.4

NOTES: * A major engagement is defined as something that keeps the child busy for at least four-five hours during the day.

** Includes vendors, small shops, piece-rate wage work

SOURCE: Household Interview and Profiling

compelling reasons, do not attend school. This also reflects the lack of perseverance in the schooling of children by parents.

There is a major difference between urban and rural areas in terms of the engagement of children in work. Even though the proportion of out-of-school children engaged in work is high (64 per cent for girls and 46 per cent for boys), these proportions are substantially lower than those seen in the case of children in rural areas. Almost all girls and 85 per cent of boys not in school are engaged in some economic activity in rural areas. Unlike rural areas, in-school children in urban areas rarely have any major responsibility preventing them from attending school more regularly (Table 9.18).

More than 80 per cent of children engaged in paid economic activities earn less than Rs. 1,000 per month (Table 9.19). However, the importance of these earnings for the survival of the family varies from family to family and cannot be understood unless seen from that perspective. Another important point is the very high rate of engagement in paid economic activities for children in the 14-17 years age group. About 96 per cent of children in this group are working, the proportion being almost the same for both boys and girls. Even if they are not engaged in work before the age of 14, the facts that they are going to join the work force at about 13-14 years and that the work does not require any schooling per se operate as factors discouraging the sending of children to school.

Table 9.19: Monthly Earnings of Working Children

Monthly income of children engaged in paid economic activities (Rs.)	Per cent distribution of working children in different income groups
Below 200	25.72
200-400	37.13
450-900	20.00
1,000 and above	17.15

SOURCE: Household Survey.

UNDERESTIMATION OF CHILDREN AT WORK

It is important to point out that any estimation of out-of-school and working children in urban areas, or for that matter even in rural areas, based on a sample household survey is bound to be an underestimation. This is so because it does not cover the large number of children living on the streets or working in establishments, who are almost all working and out-of-school. It also does not include children working as full-time domestic workers and living in the employers' households. The only way to capture these children is perhaps to do a child census covering all households, establishments, and 'streets' (Box 9.1). A recent survey conducted with the support of UNICEF in Guwahati city in Assam shows that there are about 14,000 out-of-school children (7-14 years) in the city. This also is considered an underestimation because of non-cooperation of the household heads employing young girls as domestic help.

BOX 9.1: STREET CHILDREN

Street children include two types of children:

Children on the street: Children who live in slums but spend most of their time on the streets. They form the largest component. Many work. Maintain regular contact with their families.

Children of the street: Children who live on the street/pavement. Tenuous ties with their families.

There are varying estimates of the total street children in the country. According to one estimate, there are about 11.5 million street children in India. City-wise estimates for a few selected cities show that the number is large. More than one lakh street children are estimated to be living in Kolkata and another one lakh in Delhi. Also 25,000 to 50,000 street children are estimated to be living in cities like Hyderabad and Bangalore.

Different estimates of street children show that:

- Clear estimates are not available for street children in most cities. The proportion of street children staying with parents or other family members varies between 55 to 90 per cent in different cities.
- The number of boys is much higher than the number of girls among street children, except in Kolkata where the difference is not high.
- In terms of age distribution, 70 per cent of street children are in the 11-15 year age group. A majority of street children are illiterate.

Street children face certain specific problems that children with close connections generally do not face. A number of studies have identified these as below:

- Most street children work. Many are self-employed as porters, vendors, shoeshine boys, newspaper sellers, rag pickers, helpers, etc. In Kolkata, more than 30 per cent of them are employed in shops and establishments. A significant proportion does a variety of odd jobs and scavenges or begs for food.
- Children working in shops, *dhabas*, etc. have to work hard for long hours, often without periods of rest, and for meagre amounts.

- Poor nutrition, unhygienic eating habits, eating leftover food or scavenging from garbage dumps, etc., leads to ill-health and diarrhoea, jaundice, gastroenteritis, etc. Other diseases result from the lack of water to bathe, sharing of blankets, exposure to infection during rag picking, tobacco intake, constant exposure to pollution, and low immunity levels.
- Drug abuse is a major problem. The intake of *gutka*, and the smoking of *beedis* and cigarettes start at an early age. Older children also get addicted to drugs. This results in oral health problems and respiratory infections.
- Street children are often harassed by the police.
- Street children lack emotional security. The most vulnerable are those without parents and homes.

Household Characteristics and Schooling Participation

It is apparent from discussions about reasons for non-participation that, among other things, it is also associated with certain features of the family, including the nature of parental occupation, household income, literacy levels or education, and parental perceptions about education. It is obvious that parental interest plays an important role in school participation patterns among children. Parents with a high interest in education tend to send all their children to school whereas the proportion of households with all children in school is lowest for those families where parents have not expressed any particular interest in education. Similar direct linkages exist between school participation patterns and the importance given to the education of the child. However, parental interest or a positive view of education itself is linked with certain household characteristics such as parental occupation, level of income, and literacy.

It can be seen that the levels of income as well as the nature of occupation among parents have a significant influence on schooling participation patterns among children. Although the number of fathers in salaried jobs is low, the rate of enrolment is high among children in such families. Eighty per cent of households with fathers in salaried jobs send all their children to school. The proportion of households sending all their children to school is lower for families surviving on daily wages or piece-rated work, this being the lowest for the families involved in running small shops or selling small articles on *thelas* or earning their livelihood through some sort of contract wage arrangement. This could be due to the fact that the involvement of children in livelihood-related activities is high in piece-rated work or self-employment. It is also possible that such engagements are not even perceived or reported as an engagement in paid activity. The schooling participation rate appears to be low for households where both parents are working, in many of these households the mothers run small shops/*thelas* (Table 9.20).

The nature of mothers' work has an interesting relationship with enrolment patterns among children. It is noteworthy that more than 70 per cent of households with mothers in contract wage work, which mainly consists of working as domestic help for middle class households, send all their children to school. This reflects the positive influence of coming in

Table 9.20: Households' Attributes and Children's School Participation Patterns

Category	% distribution of households across children's schooling status		
	All children in school	At least one child in school	No child in school
Nature of father's job			
Daily wage	65.45	20.00	14.55
Contracted wage	50.00	31.20	18.80
Self-employed	51.11	24.44	24.44
Piece rate	57.14	0.00	42.86
Regular salary	80.00	0.00	20.00
Nature of mother's job			
Daily wage	47.37	31.58	21.05
Contracted wage	71.43	0.00	28.57
Self-employed	35.29	29.41	35.29
Piece rate	60.00	30.00	10.00
Non-working	58.30	23.80	17.90
Family income			
Upto 6,000	31.60	15.80	52.60
6,001 to 12,000	57.90	26.30	15.80
12,001 to 18,000	61.00	24.40	14.60
18,001 to 36,000	62.50	20.00	17.50
Above 36,000	54.50	22.70	22.70
Both working	51.47	22.06	26.47
Literacy status			
Both illiterate	48.30	28.70	23.00
One literate	63.80	10.30	25.90
Both literate	72.20	22.20	5.60
Social Group			
Upper Caste Hindu	90.90	9.10	–
Other Backward Castes	57.90	21.10	21.10
Scheduled Castes	62.50	15.30	22.20
Upper Caste Muslims	37.50	25.00	37.50
Lower Caste Muslims	50.00	36.70	13.30
Parents' views on schools			
Very good	70.70	22.40	6.90
Good	67.70	27.80	4.50
Average	65.60	27.50	6.90
Bad	53.00	19.30	27.70
No response	17.60	18.50	63.90
Parents' interest in education			
No interest	36.90	28.40	34.80
Some interest	64.50	30.00	5.50
High interest	73.90	24.40	1.70
Total	56.70	21.30	22.00

SOURCE: Household Survey.

close contact with households where the education of children commands greater value. As against this, the proportion of households sending all their children to school is much lower for families where mothers go out to work for a casual wage or are engaged in running shops. The proportion of households with all children in school is roughly similar for families with non-working mothers and families with mothers engaged in piece-rated work.

The level of the family's income and schooling participation rates for children are positively associated up to a particular level, after which the nature of the association changes. Only about 32 per cent of households with an annual income of Rs. 6,000 or below send all their children to school; more than half of the households in this income category do not send even one child to school. With an increase in income, the proportion of households sending all their children goes up initially, and thereafter the proportion of households sending all their children shrinks and the proportion of households not sending even one child as well as households keeping at least one child out of school increases. It is possible that the increased income in the higher income group household is due to contributions made by children not going to school.

Literacy or education among parents emerged as one of the important factors having positive linkages with schooling participation patterns among children. Parental literacy helps in realizing the positive benefits of education, leading to greater commitment and adjustment among poor parents to the schooling of children. More than 72 per cent of families with both parents literate send all their children to school, another 22 per cent send at least one child to school, and only 5.6 per cent do not send any child to school. As against this, only 48 per cent of those families where both parents are illiterate send all their children to school. The proportion is higher even for those families where at least one parent is literate.

School participation patterns show direct linkages between parental perceptions of school functioning and teacher performance, indicating that the participation of children in school depends on this factor as well. However, it is important to mention that the majority of parents with no child in school did not express any opinion about schools or teachers, reflecting an indifference to or ignorance of these aspects. This shows that many parents who do not send their children to school are not even aware of the state of the school functioning in their area. Parental interest in education also influences school participation among children. We have tried to understand the level of parental interest by classifying their statements and views on education and the future of their children. As seen in rural areas, a high level of parental interest in education helps them overcome other constraints relating to their own livelihood, economic condition, etc. However, as mentioned earlier, parental interest itself emanates from a basic minimum level of economic security, and exposure to benefits of education.

IS EDUCATION IMPORTANT?

The value attached to education by parents as well as by the society in which the family lives becomes very important in ultimate decisions about the schooling of children. The situation in this respect is not very different for poor people living in urban areas from what is seen in rural areas. The insecurities and uncertainties of life are the same. There is no major difference in the views of education as objective conditions are not very different. As in rural areas, education is viewed as beneficial if it helps directly in improving employability and facilitates economic mobility. The availability of jobs with little requirement for schooling leads to a low perception of the value of education among poor households. However, the importance of certain basic literacy and mathematical skills is more visible in urban areas leading to a higher rate of ever-enrolment. But a number of other factors related to livelihood, school, social background, dwelling status, general life in the slum, etc., play a role and influence children's continuation in schooling adversely. The following section tries to understand school participation patterns in view of the larger contexts of children living in slums.

CHILDREN'S SCHOOLING IN URBAN SLUMS: ENCOURAGING AND DEPRESSING FACTORS AND PROCESSES

Living constantly in uncertain, insecure, and deprived situations, along with neighbourhoods of 'plenty' that exist in urban areas, has its own impact on a number of processes including the demand for education as revealed in school participation patterns. Unlike rural areas, the city or town does not belong to everyone nor does everyone belong to the city or town. This either alienates or challenges those who remain relatively deprived, and are made to feel that all the time. Despite a broad similarity in the contexts in which slum dwellers live in different cities, there are variations. How different families live in or respond to their situations determines a number of aspects of their lives, including children's schooling participation. What is more striking is the fact that the basic parameters that influence the level of commitment to schooling of children in urban areas remain largely the same as in rural areas.

UNCERTAIN AND VULNERABLE STATUS

Schooling emerges as a priority in areas where some basic stability in terms of dwelling as well as work availability exists. It is not coincidental that the highest level of school participation, more than 80 per cent of children having been enrolled, are reported from those slums where the status of residence is more certain, with the majority of families living in that city for many years. The availability of jobs is not a major issue for the majority of residents in these slums. Though the work remains temporary, it is available throughout the year, giving a sense of permanence to the slum dwellers. School participation rates are usually high in those slums where the majority of families have been living for many years and have a regular source of income.

In contrast, the uncertain state of living, the insecure nature of jobs in which parents are engaged, and the sub-human conditions of slums in terms of physical facilities make the issue of survival a major one. This is especially true for families vulnerable due to other reasons. They could be recent migrants to the city or to the slum with a very insecure job status such as rag pickers in Ramashray Nagar (Kanpur). They could be vulnerable because of their unclear legal status as is the case of Bengali residents in the Mehrauli (Delhi) slum, and so on. Parents in jobs that require assistance from children also adversely affect schooling participation (Boxes 9.2 and 9.3).

BOX 9.2: THE MEHRAULI SLUM: ENGAGEMENT WITH THE 'PRESENT' AND THE STRUGGLE FOR SURVIVAL

Almost one-fourth of the total children in Mehrauli are fully engaged in earning activities along with their parents. The children face hostility in the area, the school not being an exception, because of their unclear status; and language, too, is a major barrier. In any case, they have migrated here with an aim to fight the unbearable poverty back home and, despite missing the home environment, consider their present status 'definitely better' than what it was at home. The fact that they are managing to get food three times a day is a major relief and they do not appear to be in a position to undertake any long-term thinking about the future of their children.

BOX 9.3: GARIB NAGAR: CHILDREN WORKING IN THE *BEEDI* AND COTTON INDUSTRIES

Garib Nagar in Warangal presents a situation where the living conditions are not as bad, yet enrolment rates are relatively low. The slum, though not under the municipality and hence not recognized, is planned and has basic facilities. The social composition is mixed with the majority being Hindu (consisting of OBC and SC) but a good number of Muslim and a few Christian families as well. The men are in different occupations, the most common being that of *hamaali*, or casual wage earner, and the women are mainly engaged in *beedi* making. Work is available throughout the year and payments are regular. Childrens' engagement in *beedi* making and working in cotton mills is common in this slum. The rate of enrolment is very low for children in the 9+ age group. Younger children are being enrolled in the NCLP school, which offers monetary compensation, but older children continue to work.

SOCIAL BACKGROUND, OCCUPATION, AND EMPLOYMENT PROSPECTS

The process of urbanization has not really led to the effacement of caste or religious identities and affiliations. This also has connotations for social practices, occupations, and decisions about schooling. The desire to break away from traditional identity, which comes with connotations of hierarchy, discrimination, and isolation, is strong among certain groups. This desire leads to varying kinds of influences on the demand for schooling. While it finds expression in greater commitment to the schooling of children in some cases, it dissuades people from schooling their children in others. If education means entry into a job with caste connotations, it is not welcome even if it comes with greater stability. Ramashray Nagar in Kanpur presents one such example. On the other hand, Dakshin Baluchar in Malda provides another where schooling is seen as a means of getting out of the present unequal socio-economic set-up (Boxes 9.4 and 9.5).

BOX 9.4: DAKSHIN BALUCHAR IN MALDA: HIGH ASPIRATIONS FOR CHILDREN

Life is tough in Dakshin Baluchar in Malda with yearly floods and consequent shifting to pavements, irregular work and uncertain incomes. The living situation is bad, with very small shanties and almost non-existent civic amenities. However, three-fourths of the children attend school, the proportion being higher than that found in many other slums. The high demand for education in adverse circumstances could be ascribed to several factors. About half of the slum's population belongs to the upper castes, the tradition of education being strong among them. They send their children to school, facing all adversities. The majority of the non-upper caste women in this slum are engaged as domestic help in middle-class localities, creating strong influences regarding sending of the children to school. They have high aspirations for their children and view education as an important means to realize those aspirations. In addition to all these, the presence of schools in close proximity, including one with Hindi as the medium of instruction as it is spoken by about half of the population, also plays a major role in keeping enrolment high in this slum.

BOX 9.5: RAMASHRAY NAGAR IN KANPUR: BREAKING AWAY FROM THE 'SWEEPER' TAG

Ramashray Nagar in Kanpur mainly comprises Dalit households. Many residents work as sweepers in government and private set-ups. The attraction of earning money through work rather than spending years on education and then getting the lowest-ranked job of sweeper seemed to be present both among parents and children, especially boys. Kanpur, an industrial city, does offer a number of employment and earning opportunities in garages and factories, and boys from this locality are particularly attracted towards jobs in this field. The job of sweeper, though fairly well paid and secure, comes with a certain stigma, with caste connotations not really acceptable to the younger generation.

The high level of alcoholism present among adult males in the slum also provides a negative role model to younger boys. The value attached to girls' education is really low in the slum, as revealed during interactions and reflected in statements such as, 'They have to be married early and sent to their homes'. A high proportion of women are engaged in earning activities, working as sweepers and also in pig rearing, thereby leading to a high rate of drop-outs among girls, who are required for sibling care, household chores, and help in home-based earning activities. With no family where both parents are literate and more than 83 per cent families with both parents illiterate, the level of interest in education is low in this slum.

SCHOOL INCLUSIVENESS AND VIEWS ON SCHOOL FUNCTIONING

School availability does not even arouse the same interest in urban areas as it does in rural habitations. This is because the schools are generally not meant exclusively for slum residents. In this context, the 'inclusive' nature of school functioning plays a major role. The experiences of the unaided private schools in the Kanpur slums indicate this. The extension efforts by teachers to enrol children also play a major role in creating and enhancing the demand for education. The fact that these schools, unlike most government and aided schools located outside the slums, cater almost entirely to children from slums makes parents and children more comfortable. These schools do not seem as formidable as government schools with their rigid procedures. The negative image formed by teachers and their low expectations from slum children often lead to unjust comparisons and the marginalization of these children at school. A low representation of children from the slums or poor families further isolates them, causing a large number of drop-outs, especially among boys.

Children's school participation patterns do not match directly with people's negative or not-so-positive opinions about schools and teachers. It is not even necessary that it should be so; what is more significant is that people have views about schools and teachers. The expression of even negative views reveals a positive interest in education and awareness of the school's position and functioning. Situations where more people have no view on school functioning are more worrisome as that reveals an indifference towards education and a disinterest in the functioning of schools. This situation exists in most slums with very low enrolment rates including the Zakhira and Mehrauli slums in Delhi and Ramashray Nagar in Kanpur.

It is important to point out that the opening of schools, especially unaided private schools, is also a part of the prevailing demand for education in that area. In this age of the mushrooming of unaided English-medium private primary schools in many areas including slums and villages, especially in northern India, if no school has so far been opened in or around these slums, it does reveal a depressed demand for education. Zakhira 1 and 2 in Delhi and Ramashray Nagar in Kanpur are two such examples where despite the slums having been established for many years, no private school exists.

THE FRAGILE SOCIAL NORM

The patterns of enrolment also indicate that the social norm of sending children to school is very important. If a large number of children from a slum attend school, it influences others, including those who have come recently or who are economically more vulnerable, to send their children to school. However, the social norm itself remains fragile in certain cases, especially when it concerns girls. For instance, a girl from Zakhira 2 in Delhi experienced sexual harassment while leaving her school, leading to her withdrawal, followed by the withdrawal of many other girls. Despite the fact that there was a consensus and many girls were going to school from the locality, no force acted against the withdrawal of girls. Children from slums form a negligible percentage of the total students located in lower middle class colonies, and their withdrawal does not get noticed or missed by teachers who, in any case, remain oblivious to the problems faced by children.

SCHOOL PARTICIPATION AMONG MUSLIM CHILDREN IN URBAN SLUMS

In view of the notable difference in school participation rates observed for Muslim children in urban areas in comparison to rural areas, the issue of why this is so deserves interrogation. The rates of school participation among Muslim children are high, though varying, in five out of six slums where they live in substantial numbers. The analysis shows that three factors—stability in life situations, presence of a strong norm of sending children to school even among other communities, and a belief in the 'benefits' of education—have played a crucial role. The most crucial is the presence of a high perceived value attached to education and schooling. The need for religious education exists, but not as a schooling option. This is more as a part of righteous upbringing. These slums in Parbhani, Warangal, and Malda reflect the presence of a clear commitment to schooling of children among all communities, including Muslims. There is a definite demand for education with views such as the following being articulated: 'It makes all the difference in others' attitudes towards a person'; 'Educated persons are more respected and better equipped to handle things including fending for themselves wherever they go'; and 'Understanding monetary transactions and making better use of government programmes.' Their views also reveal that they are able to relate the schooling to their own lives and their children's futures. The demand for education exists for both boys and girls but the majority of girls go to government schools whereas the majority of boys go to private schools, perceived to be better and more useful. This, too, is a conscious decision as the education of boys is seen as an investment whereas that of girls is seen as a requirement to provide basic literacy and knowledge of numbers.

Life situations are more stable in these slums. Most Muslim residents in Malda, Parbhani, and Warangal have been living in these cities for many years and do not remain jobless. At Manohar Nagar in Kanpur, the majority of men work in tanneries which, despite being temporary, offer regular wages. The jobs were also better paid until at least the recent recession in the world market and certain other difficulties faced by the industry due to pollution-related regulations had an adverse impact. There is virtually no major disparity in income and almost all families have been assessed as living close to the poverty line, nobody being much below this or very poor. Work in the export-oriented leather industry for years has exposed them to the many benefits of education. Now even when some of them have shifted to other less-respected occupations such as daily wage work or rickshaw pulling, their aspirations for their children remain high and education is seen as one of the essential avenues of upward mobility. This is reflected in their preference for general education despite a full-time madrasa being present in the vicinity.

A noteworthy observation about all slums with high school participation rates for Muslim children, except Manohar Nagar in Kanpur, is that they have active and strong affiliations to one or the other major national political parties. The one in Warangal has links with the CPI-M, those in Parbhani are attached to the BSP, DSS and the Congress, and the one in Malda is allied with the Congress. It is likely that these active associations with political parties have played a role in creating awareness about educating children and drawing attention to the perceived benefits of schooling. Muslim children in these slums in Warangal, Malda and Kanpur do not regularly go to any madrasa; those in Parbhani go either before or after school hours.

However, the low demand for education in Zakhira 1, the only slum among all the slums in this study with a high Muslim population and a very low school participation rate, is partially due to the slum dwellers' preference for religious education, which, unlike formal education, is readily available within the slum at convenient hours. Religious education is attached to prestige, duty, and also better job prospects—becoming a hafiz—as against formal education, which is not perceived as being beneficial in either imparting values or assuring any employment opportunities. An important observation is that while a good proportion of boys go in for religious education, a good proportion of girls are never enrolled; they do not go even to a madrasa. This is contrary to the usual belief that more girls attend madrasas than boys.

Therefore, it is clear that the regularity of income, positive influences and role models, political awareness, high aspirations, and a norm of educating children among other communities, all play important roles in creating the demand for and a commitment to formal general education among poor Muslims families, as they do in the case of other groups. Religious education is not perceived as competing with, but complementing, secular education.

It is clear that enrolment rates go up with basic stability of living conditions, certainty of work opportunities, availability and functioning of schools, high aspirations for children, and a social norm of sending children to school. Low aspirations for children, unstable living conditions, uncertain livelihood status and the engagement of children in survival efforts, the 'non-inclusive' nature of schools, and indifferent attitudes of teachers depress the demand for schooling and participation rates among children. One important distinguishing element for urban areas is the influence of the negative slum environment on children, especially boys, which tends to act counter to all positive factors and processes and brings down schooling participation rates. The presence of positive role models for girls, on the other hand, is one positive element which acts in favour of girls' continuation in schooling. In general, the perceived utility of education is not high, but higher than what is seen among the rural poor, perhaps due to a greater exposure to the world of the educated. Finally, it can be said that the basic constraints faced by poor families remain largely the same in rural and urban areas, though the nature and manifestations of these constraints vary significantly.

10. Known Truths and Home Truths: The Ways Forward

School Participation Status: Far from Universalization

School participation status in terms of regular attendance is much lower than enrolment, which itself is far from universal. Only about 42 per cent of children in the 6-13 years age group attend school regularly in rural areas, the proportion being as low as about 28 per cent for the very poor. It is obvious that effective attendance in schools or regular school participation is much lower among poorer groups and they have a disproportionately high representation from among socially disadvantaged groups. As such, out-of-school children mainly comprise girls, children belonging to disadvantaged social groups such as Dalits, STs, Muslims and, in some areas, OBCs. The situation in urban areas is also similar, though somewhat better than rural areas; about 59 per cent children in this age group attend school regularly. There is also a regional dimension as the majority of non-school-attending children are concentrated in the eastern and central parts of the country. It is important to add that there are certain other groups, not directly covered under the study, such as the children of sex workers,[1] street children, children with special abilities, etc., who largely remain outside the ambit of school education, and deserve focused attention and efforts if the universalization of elementary education is the goal.

In this chapter, we conclude the study by first summarizing the understanding regarding schooling-related decision-making processes in poor families through a process chart and then examining macro-level responses in the light of the critical issues that have emerged. State policies and programmes have been examined first, followed by analyses of several NGO initiatives. Although the government remains responsible for ensuring the universalization of elementary education and is the largest provider of educational services, a number of NGOs have also intervened in this area and their experiences are particularly valid for understanding the approach necessary to reach vulnerable groups. This is followed by discussing the implications for policy and action for ensuring the effective schooling of children from marginalized groups.

Micro-level Decision-making Processes

The schooling status of a child reveals the parents' decision or demand for education. A revealed demand for education or a conscious decision in favour of schooling is definitely low among poor parents both in absolute and relative terms. The varied levels of schooling status for children belonging to the same economic and social groups across different areas, and also across different families within the same village, basically show that there is no uniform trend regarding the demand for education among poor and deprived groups. The demand for education in a household primarily reflects parental commitment to the schooling of children, which, in turn, is based on the perceived relevance or benefits of education. A commitment to education, as mentioned earlier, denotes a stage where children's education becomes a priority leading to a demonstrated or revealed demand for education. This is a parameter or boundary which defines parental resolve to educate their children given the contexts in which they live. The higher the level of that commitment, the higher is the chance of the child's admission, attendance and continuation in school. A higher level of commitment leads parents to make adjustments even in the face of adversities to send their children to school. On the other hand, a low level of commitment leads to non-participation of children in schooling, even if the circumstances are not debilitating.

A commitment to education depends directly on the parental aspirations for children and the perceived relevance or value of education *vis-à-vis* parental aspirations. However, parental aspirations and the perceived benefits or relevance of education are not independent of external factors and processes, and, in fact, depend a great deal on the three dimensions we have been discussing: the socio-economic context, the household situation or characteristics, and school availability and functioning. These three dimensions are themselves interconnected but they also act independently, and in either case have a strong influence on the commitment to education. As such, a commitment to education is not a static phenomenon and shifts with a change in the perceived relevance or benefits (Chart 10.1).

SOCIO-ECONOMIC CONTEXTS

Social Positioning

The social context has four main dimensions: social positioning, economic opportunities, socio-political processes, and cultural beliefs and practices. Social positioning and interrelationships, which in the Indian context are largely determined by caste or religious status, play a very critical role in raising or depressing parental aspirations for children. In that sense, social positioning has a group or collective dimension; families belonging to the same caste or religious group have similar social positioning. Dalits, STs, Muslims and, in some cases, certain OBC groups are the obvious disadvantaged groups in this respect. Low social positioning adversely influences the perceived value or relevance of schooling.

Dalits, who have faced untouchability in the past and continue to face

Chart 10.1: Schooling-related Decision-making Processes at the Household Level

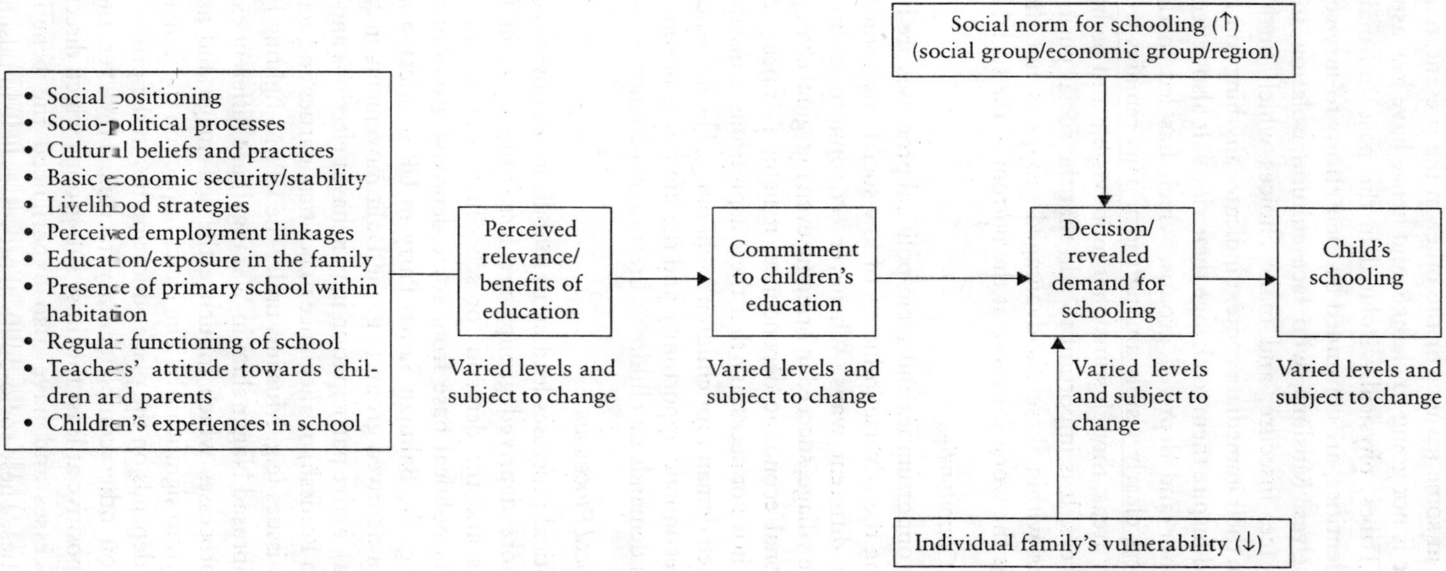

exclusion in some manner or the other in the present, tend to believe that their place is not going to change, and hence have low aspirations for their children. Tribes, physically isolated in the past and maintaining distinct cultural identities, are consumed by their efforts to survive and find a place for themselves. Muslims, who face cultural isolation and adverse social relations, feel insecure, and make choices which further isolate them. Nothing in their immediate context indicates anything contrary to this reality that would inspire them to change their views. It also reflects the powerlessness of poor and deprived groups, which has led to the deep sense of hopelessness clearly visible among them. This remains true for both rural and urban areas, though somewhat more visible and perhaps also stronger in rural areas. It is important to add that the social positioning of various sub-groups within these disadvantaged groups is not the same, and the situation is the worst for those at the bottom of the social hierarchy.

Economic Opportunities

Economic opportunities and socio-political processes are both instrumental in changing the adverse influence of low social positioning, and operate in somewhat different ways. Whenever economic opportunities, within or outside the village, succeed in bringing even marginal changes in the patterns of traditional economic dependence, it helps in raising their aspirations. However, it is not necessary that these aspirations translate themselves into an enhanced demand for children's schooling. The influence depends on the nature of economic opportunity and the kind of exposure it generates, and also on its demands on children's life and involvement in work.

Socio-political Processes

Socio-political processes leading to mobilization, obvious or subtle, among one or more deprived groups are less ambiguous in their impact on aspirations and the demand for schooling. The rise of a political party drawing its political base from some deprived group in national or state politics (e.g. the Bahujan Samaj Party in UP politics), a social movement involving a deprived group (e.g. the Dalit movements in Maharashtra and Karnataka), active participation in panchayat elections and activities (e.g. as in Madhya Pradesh) or allegiance to political parties and active participation on certain issues (e.g. Muslims under the CPI-M fighting for various rights in the Giriprasad Nagar slum in Warangal) are different examples of socio-political processes which influence the self-image and aspirations of the relevant group significantly. The exact impact on the demand for children's schooling depends on the place education has in the process of mobilization and also on other complementary factors. However, the influences are generally positive at least for those sub-groups which directly participate in these processes and have also experienced the benefits of economic opportunities. These socio-political processes help in raising confidence and overcoming the negative influences of exclusion, isolation and insecurity.

Socio-cultural Beliefs and Practices

Deep-rooted patriarchal values reflected in several socio-cultural beliefs and practices play an important role in depressing the demand for education, especially for girls. Although the disadvantage of being a girl operates at various levels and deep-rooted patriarchal values influence many decisions including that of schooling girls in all social and economic groups, this gets sharpened and becomes much more obvious among the poorer and socially disadvantaged groups. Some practices with direct linkages to schooling (e.g. early marriage of girls) are also more common in these groups. Socio-cultural beliefs also play an important role among groups which have maintained a distinct cultural identity or remained culturally isolated. Among several tribes, the involvement of children in livelihood activities such as cattle grazing or forest collection has been part of their culture, and they do not consider schooling in its present form relevant enough to abandon these practices. The preference for religious education among some Muslim families is also partially a cultural issue. Many of these cultural practices, however, also have significant social, economic and political dimensions in the context of poor families and need to be understood from that perspective as well.

HOUSEHOLDS—THE SECOND DIMENSION

Insecure Livelihoods and Unstable Life Situations

This brings up the issue of livelihood insecurity, poor financial conditions, and the tough life faced by poor families. Livelihood options available to poor families are typically characterized by low wages if it is paid labour and low returns if it is cultivation or any other form of self-employment. What makes the situation worse is the non-availability of work in all seasons. This means very low income and vulnerability to any crisis, leading to indebtedness at exorbitant interest rates or some other survival strategy on unequal terms. A common coping mechanism is to put children to work. The implication in rural areas is an unstable life characterized by changing livelihood options as determined by seasonality, lean agricultural periods, and alternative opportunities available. Most people are forced to have a mix of occupations combining wage work within and outside their own villages and, if they also own land, cultivation. The situation is not very different in urban areas, where poor households are mostly engaged in casual wage work which does not offer any security whatsoever. In their struggle for daily survival, it is only natural for poor households to have a short-term view of life, where immediate gains or comforts are valued more. The schooling of children demands continuous care and long-term commitment, which is a difficult proposition for households living in a context of continued insecurity and uncertainty.

Children's Involvement in Work

The engaging of children in livelihood-related activities for substantial periods of time in a year is fairly common among poor households. Upper caste Hindu households are the only exceptions where children are generally not sent to work outside the household, even if they happen to be poor. This is explained by the fact that manual labour has been traditionally a taboo for this social group. Children's engagement in work includes all sorts of chores for own farming, forest collection, sibling care, household activities, and also paid activities for others. Children engaged in paid labour generally work for long hours throughout the year.

The engagement of children in work is a complex phenomenon and needs to be understood at various levels. Although the involvement of children in work is both a cultural and survival issue in most cases, the culture has developed mainly out of economic necessity and the absence of any alternative norm which makes schooling the first priority for children. The livelihood options available to poor people in rural areas are those that necessarily require either the direct or indirect support of children. However, this also reflects the fact that they do not really perceive the schooling of children to be relevant or beneficial. The strong feeling that their children also have to lead a life similar to theirs, which does not really require schooling, coupled with the current concern with the issue of survival by adopting whatever livelihood opportunity is available, makes it difficult for them to develop a different perspective. Their adverse social positioning adds to their state of hopelessness about any change in the future.

The highest incidence of children in paid work in rural areas occurs in regions where poverty is widespread and work availability within villages is low. In these areas, children work at very low wages for local landlords and also migrate to other places. Migration with parents as well as with other children in a similar age group is common. A demand for children's work in places such as hotels, *dhabas,* small establishments, as also in brick kilns or similar units where family-based contracts are given, is one important reason which promotes their migration from rural areas. Children in such families make significant contributions to the family's earnings and survival.

The practice of children in paid work is also common in areas where the level of poverty is not so acute and work is available throughout the year, but land distribution is highly unequal. The demand for labour, including that of children, is high and though the wages are substantially higher than in other low work-availability areas, wages for children's work is lower than that of adults and, therefore, in demand. The culture of having children as full-time servants and grazers among the landowning class also leads to this demand. The immediate possibility of additional income by putting a child to work, even if it is not a survival issue, is resorted to for various reasons and reflects two things: one, that parental aspirations relate more to tangible aspects of life—to have a *pucca* house, to buy gold for a daughter's wedding—than to long-term goals and, two, that they do not see education as bringing about any tangible benefits.

Weak Employment Linkages

The employment linkages of education, considered to be the most tangible benefit by poor parents, are perceived to be very weak and, in some cases, non-existent. Two factors contribute to this perception. One, all jobs, or *naukri,* in government and public sectors require at least secondary-level education. Most poor families feel that they cannot afford the substantial investment of money and time required for this. A very high rate of failure at the secondary-level examinations further dampens their motivation. The second factor is the widespread unemployment among educated youth, too visible to be ignored, making the message loud and clear—education in itself does not lead to a *naukri.* The public and government sectors are facing virtual stagnation, if not already shrinking. There is stiff competition for the limited jobs available and poor families do not have the resources to break the hegemony of those who have everything—access to power, money to pay bribes, and political visibility to make themselves heard. The options available to poor families are petty menial jobs which do not require education. This is true for both rural and urban areas and is a major reason for the depressing commitment to education and demand for schooling.

It is obvious from the above discussion that the household or family dimensions of the commitment to education are not entirely independent of the social or societal dimensions. However, one particular family characteristic, which independently influences commitment to education quite significantly, is the literacy or the schooling levels of parents. Parental education, particularly the mother's level of education, matters a great deal in shaping the family's commitment to education. The exposure of parents, especially mothers, to the educated class also has a similar impact, building their commitment to schooling of children. This is particularly visible in urban areas where women work as household help for the middle and upper middle classes and come in contact with educated women.

SCHOOL—THE THIRD DIMENSION

The Presence of a School within One's own Habitation

School, the third dimension of the external environment which influences households' commitment to education and decisions about schooling, is no less important than the other two. The very presence of a school within the habitation raises people's interest in schooling. This is particularly valid for uneducated and poor parents who live in segregated or isolated habitations, and have traditionally not been participating in schooling. Schooling their children enters into the realm of possibility for parents only when a school is physically present in the locality.

The Functioning of the School

The mere presence of a school, however, does not ensure the regular schooling of children either; at most it inspires people to admit their children to school in the initial phase. School functioning is more critical in sustaining this interest, leading to the continuation of children in school. In fact, school functioning and processes have the capacity to work as a countervailing force to the constraints created by social and family situations. The regular functioning of school for the prescribed hours is the first requirement for an interest in schooling. The experiences at school in terms of teachers' attitudes are critical for children coming from socially and economically marginalized backgrounds. Positive and encouraging experiences help in building confidence in children and inspire parents to continue schooling. The nature of peer interaction is also important in this respect and so are the teachers' attitudes to parents. The impression of uneducated and poor parents about school functioning is synonymous with their impression of teachers. Teachers who extend themselves and try to identify with marginalized groups gain their respect and acceptance, which has a role in building a commitment towards schooling. Perceptions about the management of incentive schemes and children's learning are also important in forming opinions about teachers and school, which in turn influence the perceived value of education.

The existing situation in terms of school functioning is far from satisfactory in the eastern and central parts of the country. The situation is somewhat better in the western and southern parts of the country. In general, schools located in areas inhabited mainly by one or the other disadvantaged groups either remain closed quite commonly or function for less than the prescribed hours. In areas inhabited by mixed social groups, the situation is the same if children from dominant social and economic groups are not attending the government school. Wherever the option is available, dominant groups have begun sending their children to private paid schools. School functioning is better, though not necessarily so, in areas where the children from dominant groups attend the government schools. This too reflects the powerlessness of disadvantaged groups and a lack of commitment on the part of government institutions to change the situation.

The fact that the functioning of schools is better in the southern and western parts of the country, at least in terms of being regular if not in terms of practicing no discrimination, indicates two things. One, it reflects better governance, which is also obvious from the relatively better functioning of other institutions such as health centres, hospitals, etc. Two, it shows that school functioning improves even in areas inhabited by deprived communities if there is greater socio-political consciousness and awareness of the need for education. In these areas, the extent and incidence of deep poverty is also significantly lower and this, combined with socio-political processes, has lent deprived social groups some voice, but this is generally not the case in other areas. The centrality of education as a means of change in socio-political processes experienced in these areas, e.g. the Dalit movement, is also one reason for a higher level of commitment and the better functioning of schools.

School Accountability

Barring a small proportion of schools where teachers are motivated and take an active interest, schools do not function as motivated, responsible institutions, accountable for the learning of all children. Better functioning of schools in areas where children from influential sections attend school shows that they respond only when there is an obvious pressure for minimal performance. Schools are part of a government system typically characterized by accountability to the level above. The educational administration at no level demands accountability from the school to ensure the regular attendance of children. Schooling of children belonging to marginalized groups requires more sensitive and responsible functioning which could break barriers created by social positioning and economic disadvantage. Instead, schools in their functioning tend to maintain and reinforce social divides and disparities.

One of the initiatives to increase the involvement of local people in school management and to ensure accountability of schools to the people has been the constitution of the Village Education Committees (VEC) or its variants such as School Management Committees. However, these committees have also been largely dysfunctional, barring a few isolated examples. The teacher, who happens to be the member-secretary, manages the show in most cases just by maintaining a record of the meetings. The devolution of power to panchayats in some states is a recent phenomenon and the impact has yet to be seen. However, the issue of school accountability cannot be seen in isolation from the functioning of the entire schooling system. The schooling system is part of the larger system which is bureaucratic and hierarchical. Adherence to rules, procedures, and orders from above define the sense of accountability at all the levels. Rigid and vertical linkages leading to a hierarchical chain of decision making and reporting are typical features of the schooling system. Horizontal linkages and a problem-solving approach are not encouraged, which hampers initiative at lower levels. There is little commitment to a rights-based approach to children's education in the education system. Transparency and accountability to people are largely absent.

Distribution of Incentives

The administration of incentive schemes at the school level assumes significance in view of the high cost of schooling and the continuous financial crises faced by poor families. It is well known that so-called 'free education' is not free[1] and parents spend substantial amounts on textbooks, notebooks, clothes, etc. It becomes difficult for poor parents, especially in cash-starved rural areas, to arrange for these requirements on time. Different incentive schemes meant to support parents in this respect are managed poorly wherever they are in operation. For instance, in the case of the free textbook scheme, textbooks seldom reach the schools on time and the number is not adequate for all the children in the target group. The coverage of other schemes such as attendance scholarships or free uniforms is very limited as they cover only a small fraction of the target group such as girls or SC and ST children. The midday meal scheme is not operational at all the places, and even where it is dry cereals are provided in place of cooked meals except in selected states. This clashes with one of the important purposes for which the scheme was initiated—to provide nutritious meals to children who otherwise cannot afford to get such food. In view of the recent Supreme Court guideline[2] to the government to provide cooked meals in all primary schools, most state governments have shown their inability to shift from dry cereals to cooked meals due to the cost involved, unless the financial burden is taken up by the Union government. The distribution of even dry cereals is not timely and is beset with corruption at several levels.

The three dimensions of school, family, and society act in isolation and in combination, and help in building parental views and a commitment towards education, which in turn translates itself into a revealed demand for schooling. The nature of the combination varies and so does the impact on the demand for schooling. Depending upon the particular context, people's perception of the benefits or relevance of education varies, leading to different levels of commitment to education among parents. However, there are two important processes that impact on schooling decisions irrespective of an individual family's commitment. One is the social norm for schooling and the other is an individual household's vulnerability to different forms of crises. While the presence of a strong social norm of sending all children to school at least up to a particular stage acts in favour of schooling, and forces even parents with not a very strong commitment to education to send their children to school, the crisis faced by an individual family in terms of illness, death, sudden need for money, etc., forces many to keep their children, or a particular child, away from school even if the parents are committed to education. Although these two processes are part of the social and household context, they at times act independently of all other factors and influence schooling participation even without really impacting an individual parent's commitment to education.

Critical Issues

Several critical issues emerge from the analyses of the different contexts and understandings of schooling-related, micro-level decision making processes in poor families. Four major issues that are responsible for the fragile commitment to schooling are:

- Adverse socio-political positioning of the poor, making them vulnerable,
- Deep-rooted patriarchal values and socio-cultural practices,
- Basic livelihood insecurity and uncertainty, and children's engagement in work,
- Unaccountability of schools and the schooling system to people in general and to the issue of ensured schooling participation of children from marginalized groups in particular.

It is obvious that issues that influence the creation of commitment among parents to schooling of children is not limited to the accountability of the schooling system alone, and includes wider social and economic aspects. However, it is important that a state committed to the goal of the universalization of elementary education recognizes the issues, formulates policies, and guides action to address these in a forceful and unambiguous manner. It is possible, though not easy, to build a perspective and guide all efforts in that direction if the commitment is serious. The study has established that this has not happened so far. The following section attempts to identify the gaps in policies, programmes, and functioning of the schooling system so as to arrive at implications for policy formulation and action in the future.

State Policies and Initiatives

In the light of the issues that emerge from the analyses of the micro-situations of the participation of children in schooling from the perspective of poor and deprived families in varying contexts, we now proceed to understand and analyse how the state has responded, or has failed to respond, to these issues, as evident from policy documents, the formulation and implementation of schemes and programmes in elementary education, and the functioning of the entire schooling system. The focus is on analysis of policy approaches and programme initiatives in the last two decades, i.e. the 1980s and the 1990s, as the first three decades were more focused on establishing a system for mass education.

BACKGROUND

Education, especially school education, was considered the primary responsibility of state governments, and not the union government, during the early years of Independence. Education was a state subject till 1976 when it was put under the Concurrent List by the 42nd Constitutional Amendment. A new policy, known as the National Policy on Education (NPE), 1986 replaced the National Policy of 1968 which highlighted the need for a partnership between the central and the state governments. In

1990, a committee was instituted under the chairmanship of Acharya Ramamurti to review the NPE, 1986 and the Programme of Action (POA) based on the 1986 policy. In 1990, the committee submitted its report based on a number of specially commissioned research studies and wide consultations across different sections of society and recommended several alterations in the policy. In 1991, a Central Advisory Board on Education (CABE) Committee considered the recommendations of the Ramamurti Committee report and opined that while very little of the NPE, 1986 required reformulation, the POA needed to be revised considerably. The POA was subsequently revised and the revised POA, 1992 along with the NPE, 1986 remain the guiding policy documents till today.

The implementation of national policies has its own limitations in a federal set-up. This is especially true for subjects not exclusively union subjects. The NPE serves as a guiding principle for all the states but does not compel them to act on all the aspects it covers. It is largely the state governments' decision to choose what they want to act upon. Given the varying contexts and situations in all states, it is also justified to leave the choice to them. However, it also promotes inaction and does not make states accountable for even essential measures. The union government generally acts through Centrally Sponsored Schemes (CSS), whose number and presence increased substantially after the transfer of education to the Concurrent List in 1977.

The active involvement of the Union government in the elementary education sector, especially in the efforts to expand and improve the system was a major departure witnessed during the 1980s and the 1990s. The trends in expenditure in elementary education[3] during the last two decades reveal that though the major burden had been shared by state governments, the expenses have been mainly on account of the maintenance of the system. The maintenance of the system, too, is mainly limited to the payment of salaries to teachers as this alone accounts for about 90 to 95 per cent of annual expenditure in the sub-sector in all the states. Therefore, the Central Government's interventions, mainly in the form of CSS, remained the only source for developmental interventions and have been crucial in initiating and supporting states' efforts towards universalization. However, it also meant a greater dependence on the part of state governments on Union initiatives and assistance for any expansion or development in the sector.

The major schemes sponsored by the centre in the elementary education sector that begun during the late 1970s and the 1980s are Non-Formal Education (NFE), Operation Blackboard (OB), Teacher Education Programme, and the District Institute of Education and Training (DIET) scheme. DIETS were established to give a fillip to the quality of pre-service and in-service training to teachers teaching at the elementary stage by providing an exclusive institution at the district level. The realization of the limitations of a schematic approach led to the designing of new programmes with an area approach which emphasized decentralized planning taking all aspects of expansion, school improvement, and teachers' training together in designated areas. The late 1980s and the early 1990s saw the initiation of programmes such as the Andhra Pradesh Primary Education Project (APPEP), the Bihar Education Project (BEP), Lok Jumbish (LJ), and the Uttar Pradesh Basic Education Project (UPBEP) all designed specially for specific states and implemented in selected districts/blocks. This was followed by the District Primary Education Programme (DPEP), a nation-wide initiative, being implemented in more than 200 districts across different states. Janshala, a block-based programme based on similar principles and covering a few non-DPEP blocks, and the Sarva Shiksha Abhiyan (SSA) which has set the goal of achieving the universalization of elementary education by 2010. These two programmes are currently in operation and are expected to play major roles in efforts towards universalization.

An analysis of Union government initiatives shows that gaps exist at various levels, between the recommendations of the committees and the policy documents supposedly based on these committee reports, between policy statements and schematic formulations, between schematic formulations and implementation. The direction and quality of implementation vary from state to state. The scope of any CSS remains limited, and implementation depends a great deal on the functioning of the schooling system in particular states. Policy measures which can influence school functioning are mainly in the hands of state governments. Barring a few states, governments have not taken any major initiative to improve the functioning of the schooling system whether taking a cue from the national policy documents or on their own. The policies, programmes, and implementation for certain specific issues critical for ensuring the participation of children from marginalized groups are being examined here.

ENSURING AVAILABILITY OF SCHOOLS

Locating New Schools

The POA, 1992 directive to give priority to the needs of SC/ST habitations and hamlets in opening schools has remained largely meaningless in view of the fact that in the post-1980s period the growth of primary schools has slowed down drastically and there has been near stagnation in the case of upper-primary schools.[4] The fiscal positions of different states began deteriorating in this period and investment in education from state governments slowed down significantly. Andhra Pradesh and Uttar Pradesh were the only two major states investing significantly in opening the new schools in the 1990s. However, most states did not develop any firm criteria based on objective considerations to direct the location of the new schools. The majority of uncovered habitations are those inhabited by Dalits, tribals and other disadvantaged groups. Although recent data on the availability of schools within Dalit/ST habitations are still not available,[5] the field experiences clearly suggested that in the absence of firm criteria, vested interests play a role and new schools are not always located in habitations where they are needed most.

Non-Formal Education

The Central Government launched the Non-Formal Education (NFE) scheme during 1979-80 to provide schooling facilities to remote and school-less habitations. The NFE was run for a fewer number of hours by local teachers, known as volunteers, who were paid meagre sums as an honorarium. In practice, a large number of schools were opened in villages where the schools already existed. Later the focus was shifted to working children. The implementation of the scheme came under severe criticism for the right reasons. One major critique was for 'envisaging complete primary level of schooling for under-privileged children in two years through part-time instructions imparted by under-equipped and low-paid teachers'.[6] A good number of centres remained non-functional. The NPE, 1986 did mention the need to develop a systematic programme of the NFE with necessary inputs for education of comparable quality. However, in reality, the nature and functioning of NFE centres did not change much. The scheme continued for almost twenty years, till 1999-2000, when the more comprehensive scheme of Education Guarantee Scheme & Alternative and Innovative Education (EGS & AIE) replaced it.[7]

Education Guarantee Scheme

The Education Guarantee Scheme (EGS), a scheme launched by the Madhya Pradesh government in 1997, is now taken as a model for future expansion by many other states. EGS in MP is conceptualized as a demand-based initiative which makes provisioning, as defined by the scheme, an enforceable right. Under EGS, the village panchayat puts forward the demand and the government is bound to provide an 'EGS centre' within a fixed time-frame provided the given norms are fulfilled. There has been a lot of debate on the merits and demerits of this scheme on various counts,[8] but the fact remains that about 26,000 centres were opened in the state within two years and school provisioning was extended to remote and isolated habitations which at times did not even figure as separate habitations in any government record. This led to an unprecedented upsurge in enrolments in the state. However, the functioning in terms of teachers' interest and the regularity of classes being held is not uniform, and the regular attendance of children remains an issue as much as it does in the case of formal schools. This is especially true for feudal areas where the teachers come from the landowning dominant social groups and the children from marginalized Dalit or ST communities.

Alternative Schools

Meanwhile, the concept of alternative schooling, as distinct from non-formal education, emerged as an experiment for the schooling of those children who live in remote areas, or who face other constraints prompted by poverty, livelihood choices of parents, socio-religious barriers, and an inflexible formal school approach. The concept derived significantly from several on-going NGO initiatives and several alternative schooling experiments were initiated under programmes such as Lok Jumbish. The DPEP undertook the experiment on a larger basis and introduced the element of flexibility in the sense that various concepts of Alternative Schools (AS) came up depending upon the specific problems faced by different areas. Maharashtra and Gujarat tried to develop special models for migrant children, and Andhra Pradesh focused on mainstreaming by organizing short-term bridge courses. Many states also opened AS centre in school-less habitations.[9] Although the coverage of these programmes has been limited, and the feedback on the implementation and effectiveness varied, the experiences demonstrated that a variety of strategies are required to ensure schooling of children in difficult circumstances.

It is obvious that though availability and accessibility of schools remain a concern, the expansion of formal schools has almost stopped. The situation in terms of the availability of upper-primary schools is worse, which deters people from sending their children even to primary schools. The states which need to expand the facilities most, also face greater financial crunches. The EGS and EGS-like schemes have been the only means of large expansion in recent past. But any attempts at expansion through schemes such as the EGS need to be cautious about not becoming another NFE. The essential provisions of a good school need to be defined and a distinction made between essentials with which schools are to start and essentials that have to be ensured within an acceptable timeframe. Institutional mechanisms must be built for effective monitoring to ensure accountability to people, on the one hand, and sustaining teachers' interest and motivation, on the other. It is important to add that these measures are required in the formal system as much as in any alternative system.

MOBILIZATION AND AWARENESS BUILDING

The need for mobilizing parents and raising the level of awareness has been recognized by the policy and has also been emphasized by the programme formulations. Although this existed in some form of enrolment drive at the start of the school session, the practice had almost died out in most places when it was revived again by the POA, 1992 and the new programmes, such as the DPEP, included this as an important strategy. The focus, however, remained on using the campaign mode with the objective of enrolling all children, and not on building the commitment of people to schooling. Successful experiences in using traditional media in the Total Literacy Campaign (TLC) also influenced the policy and action in this respect. Schooling requires much greater and long-term commitment from parents, which cannot be built through campaigns alone. Campaigns are usually merely events that have a temporary impact and remain inadequate to challenge barriers created by years of segregation, exclusion, and isolation.

The strong need for social mobilization and opinion building in favour of schooling is a clear need in groups traditionally excluded or isolated and which face severe livelihood constraints. However, this has yet to find clear expression in any programmatic formulation initiated by the government. There has been a general tendency to avoid references to complex societal issues. The experiences of NGOs, discussed later, shows that intensive, long-term work with these communities is a pre-requisite to enable them to reap the benefits of education and build their commitment. The experiences also reveal the need for an external agent, either in the shape of political or community groups or a committed NGO, in initiating and sustaining such processes. It is not easy for government machinery with a typical orientation to implement such intensive opinion-building programmes. Committed NGOs or other organizations which can work intensively with communities are not present in most such areas where there is a need. However, this should not prevent the government from recognizing this and taking the necessary steps to initiate change in government-functioning and promoting social action.

CONDITION OF PHYSICAL INFRASTRUCTURE AND ADEQUACY OF TEACHERS

The improvement of physical infrastructure and the provision for the additional teachers in rural schools has remained the focus of many CSSs. The OB was launched with this specific purpose, and the DPEP also emphasized this considerably. However, even years of OB implementation, the very presence of poor and inadequate provisioning in most places including districts covered by the DPEP, shows the need for additional investment. Apart from investment, this involves the issue of prioritizing and targeting. Most states do not have any objective and firm criteria to direct investments in areas where they are needed most. The absence of objective criteria leaves room for vested interests to determine the direction of investment. In the case of teachers, even if they are initially posted at places where they are needed, they can easily seek and 'arrange' transfers. Despite the skewed positioning of teachers in remote and difficult rural areas adversely placed in most states, only a few southern states like Karnataka and Andhra Pradesh have developed new recruitment and transfer policies based on objective criteria. Otherwise, it remains ad hoc and is guided mainly by vested interests that often go against needs and equity considerations.

In order to address the issue of inadequacy of teachers, several states have adopted the so-called para teacher scheme providing additional teachers in formal schools (e.g. Vidya volunteers in Andhra Pradesh and Shikshakarmi in Madhya Pradesh). These are appointed for the particular school and hence cannot be transferred in normal circumstances. However, these teachers are not paid salaries equal to those of formal school teachers. In the long run, a dual system within the same sub-sector is bound to create dissatisfaction and to friction. It is important to look for institutional solutions before the situation gets out of hand. Though the need to address the issue of the non-availability of teachers in backward and remote areas and make arrangements to retain already present teachers is justified, it should not prevent reform in the recruitment and transfer policy for regular teachers. It is also important to have a policy regarding the physical infrastructure of schools. This should apply to all institutions providing schooling services irrespective of their origin. The requirement for adequate space for learning is basic, and even if the expansion is more important in the short run, there has to be a policy for providing basic infrastructure in the long run.

HIGH COST OF SCHOOLING AND INCENTIVES

In recognition of the fact that families belonging to SC, ST, and other backward sections require special motivation and are also more needy, the government has been implementing various schemes to provide incentives. The education policy also lays special emphasis on the need to provide incentives for girls' education, especially 'those coming from SC and ST communities' (POA, 1992). However, except for the midday meal and textbooks where the coverage is fairly wide, the existence of these incentive schemes is more theoretical than real. The coverage is so small that a large number of enrolled children belonging to these communities never get any of these incentives.

The issue of poor management and distribution of incentives has not received any attention in terms of policy or action. Incentives are critical for poor families facing financial crises and the problems associated with their management need greater attention. Some incentives lose their meaning if not implemented in the same spirit in which they were designed. For instance, if the attendance scholarship for girls meant for a particular period is distributed a year later, it fails t o generate any momentum for actual attendance. At the same time, it is important to realize that incentives alone cannot build a long-term commitment to schooling and it is necessary to combine this with other measures of intensive mobilization and opinion building. The problem lies in the fact that each input is implemented in isolation of the other. Also, the whole process is input driven where the implementation of a scheme becomes a means in itself rather than leading to a purpose.

GIRLS' EDUCATION

The issue of girls' education has received emphasis in all policy documents and programmatic formulations. In terms of real efforts, the interventions have largely been limited to the implementation of incentive schemes, the organization of special campaigns, and the training of teachers on gender sensitization. The issue of building positive gender images has been one of the important aspects in the revision of textbooks undertaken by several states during the last decade. These measures have been mainly initiated by the DPEP, and hence the implementation has not covered all districts in all states and they also varied in their character and impact from one state to the other. The evidence and experiences suggest that these efforts have influenced the classroom environment, now usually more gender sensitive or at least not overtly gender insensitive.[10] However, these measures do not influence parental commitment significantly.

The POA, 1992 mentions an increase in the number of women teachers in the rural areas to a half-way mark as one strategy to increase girls' participation and promote 'education for women's equality'. Under OB, half of the teachers recruited had to be women but the teachers recruited formed only a small proportion of all teachers. An increase in the number of women teachers in rural areas needs greater participation of girls from rural areas in secondary education and also a change in recruitment and training patterns. It also requires a change in working conditions and the provision of certain essential facilities in schools. Although the POA, 1992 did mention the need to make 'special efforts to recruit women teachers and augment teacher-training facilities for women', this did not receive the required thrust from the state governments. This remained a directive in the category of 'as far as possible', and though some states made concrete attempts to facilitate this most states did not take any serious step to make it happen.[11]

The expansion and strengthening of Early Childhood Care (ECE) centres was suggested by POA, 1992 in recognition of the 'work they have to do related with fuel, fodder, water, sibling care'. It did mention that the provision of these services should be seen as an integral part of elementary schools. However, in reality we have seen that the provisions of pre-school facilities and functioning are highly inadequate. The timings do not match with school timings so as to allow them to address the issue of sibling care. This was tried out under the DPEP in some states but the number of centres covered remained miniscule. The ECE centres are largely being run by the Department of Women and Child Welfare, under the ICDS programme. They have different norms for expansion and functioning, and despite efforts made under the DPEP, no real convergence has occurred. It is obvious that though the policy recognizes most issues, actions which require much more concerted efforts and fundamental changes in the direction and functioning of the government functioning are generally avoided.

Mahila Samakhya (MS), a programme started by the Department of Education in the late 1980s and operational in selected villages of several states, is the only government initiative that recognizes the need for acting on wider issues that impact on girls' education and attempts to address them by organizing women's groups and mobilizes them to act for themselves. The programme made a visible impact in raising the commitment of mothers towards girls' education but the implementation has remained limited to very small areas in each state. The argument in favour of slow expansion is that rapid spreading out hampers the quality of processes critical to the success of such programmes.

TEACHERS' ATTITUDES AND TEACHING QUALITY

The quality of teaching was raised as an important area of concern during the 1980s and the post NPE, 1986 period saw a lot of emphasis being placed on the regular training of teachers. Starting with the Teachers' Education scheme in the late 1980s, all programmes formulated in the 1990s included regular in-service teacher training as an important intervention. Under DPEP, all teachers are being provided annual in-service training, a practice not common on such a large scale till then. The focus of these programmes has largely been on introducing activity-based teaching. The field experiences suggest that in areas where school functioning has been more regular, teachers saw these programmes as relevant. In the areas where the functioning is poor, teachers did not perceive these as useful.

The training programmes did not deal adequately with the issue of attitudes, especially in the context of discrimination faced by children coming from poor and socially deprived groups. Unlike the issue of gender equity, the issue of social divides and implications for teachers remained neglected. Even if the issue of teachers' attitudes was addressed, it remained peripheral in nature. A short programme without much follow-up cannot be expected to change attitudes as 'attitudes take a long time to be internalized'.[12] This is especially true if it involves breaking the deeply entrenched values and practices with which the individuals have grown up. In this context, it may be mentioned that the Ramamurti Committee Report did highlight the need for teachers to acquir the 'right' attitudes along with knowledge and skills and also the need to inculcate this through long-term experiential processes—'attitudes towards work, towards children of different ages, towards women, towards different cultures, towards society, and towards others are hardest to build up. They can never be taught by direct instruction but are acquired through various processes such as exposure to role models, imitation of role models, peer attitude and other socialisation modes.' Although the POA,

1992 did realize the need for 'an inculcation of an understanding among teachers and students about the richness of the cultures of SCs/STs and of their contribution to culture and economy', this was not translated into any emphasis on the aspect of building teachers' attitudes.

TEACHERS' MOTIVATION, MONITORING AND ACCOUNTABILITY

The poor working conditions of teachers and the lack of suitable redressal mechanisms are considered the major reasons for the poor motivation among teachers, leading to absenteeism and disinterest. In order to improve the working conditions of teachers and the functioning of the system, the POA had envisaged states developing 'their own POAs with regard to matters like pay and allowances to teachers, other working conditions, norms for transfers and postings, removal of grievances, participation of teachers in the educational process, recruitment of teachers and the role of teachers' associations'[13]. However, very few states have acted on these issues and these processes continue to remain archaic, inefficient, and ineffective in most states. There is no internal mechanism to redress grievances; instead, elaborate rules and complicated procedures exist, the main cause for a large number of ever-mounting legal cases. The POA also recommended the computerization of records to facilitate effective and speedy grievance redressal. Barring a few states, the records are still maintained manually, leading to a large number of anomalies and consuming a lot of time.[14]

The issue of teachers' accountability was also mentioned in the POA, 1992 in terms of norms to be laid down for good performance and non-performance and to be used for monitoring. Evidence from the field does not suggest any evidence of objective criteria being in place for monitoring the performance of teachers. There have been some efforts towards building accountability to local people and institutions by creating a role for VECs or SMCs. The origin, nature, and constitution of bodies such as the VECs and SMCs vary in different states. At some places, these are statutory bodies created by an Act, while in others merely by administrative orders. Representation has been given to women and socially disadvantaged groups in these bodies in all states. However, their role is limited and they have not been given any control or say in core school management issues. In reality, in most places, they have failed to emerge as interested public bodies, and teachers are not accountable to them in any formal manner.

Taking a cue from the 73rd and 74th Constitutional Amendments, many state governments have devolved powers relating to school management to gram panchayats. However, the MP government has attempted to go one step ahead and make teachers accountable to gram panchayats. The salary of the teacher is released only after signatures from the *sarpanch* and one more member of the panchayat. Even if the transfer of powers to local panchayats does not lead to an immediate change in the situation everywhere, especially in areas where the panchayat itself is dominated by the feudal landlord classes, it has merits as a long-term strategy. Meanwhile, specific political and administrative measures may be required to facilitate their work. For instance, allowing a greater space for the gram sabha,[15] or the entire adult population, in the local panchayat decisions in MP may help in initiating a process of people's mobilization required to build their commitment to education and break the hegemony of vested interests. However, simultaneous administrative measures are also needed to create a climate for the accountability of state institutions—norms, guidelines, work culture, and responsiveness to people—to go alongside a decentralization of powers and responsibilities.

DECENTRALIZED PLANNING AND IMPLEMENTATION

Decentralized planning and implementation are important for building accountability and to allow space for addressing specific issues in different contexts. This has been the starting point for all programmatic initiatives in the last decade, the 1990s. However, experiences suggest that there is a fundamental problem in the shape of the wide gap that exists between the programme's philosophy and the norms or mechanisms developed to implement the programme. This can be best explained by taking the example of the Sarva Shiksha Abhiyan (SSA), the main vehicle to attain the universalization of the elementary education in the country.

The SSA framework issued by the Central government stresses a clear timeframe for achieving UEE, the provision of quality basic education, the promotion of social justice through basic education, the effective involvement of panchayati raj institutions, school managing committees, village education committees, PTAs, etc. The SSA framework also mentions some strategies considered crucial to the SSA programme, including institutional reforms to improve the efficiency of the delivering system, improving the functioning of mainstream educational administration, community-based monitoring and habitation-based planning for formulating district plans, and prioritizing the education of girls and a focus on special groups. However, the directives received for implementation do not appreciate the fact that these measures require fundamental changes in the school functioning system calling for strong policy decisions. The process of change is bound to be slow and painstaking and would require strong conviction, commitment, and perseverance.

Any improvement in the functioning of the mainstream educational administration which involves administrative reforms and restructuring, creating a climate of responsibility and accountability, and capacity building of functionaries and institutions would require a variety of measures and a long time frame. A focus on, and priority to, disadvantaged areas and groups would require planning and implementation processes and strategies that ensure a preferential allocation of funds, personnel, and attention to such deprived pockets. This would mean the establishment of a culture of and thrust for equity, the development of databases to identify such areas/groups clearly, and a set of norms to ensure that criteria-based, positive discrimination operates in favour of resource allocation to these disadvantaged areas/groups. These issues are mentioned only in the framework and have not been put at the forefront of the programme-implementation process in the initial stages of SSA as prerequisites for UEE, especially in educationally backward states and regions. Instead, the SSA planning, appraisal, and monitoring processes have stressed quantitative targets and speedy utilization of funds. The message clearly seems to be that additional spending alone can achieve universalization of elementary education. This detracts attention from the more crucial issues which are more difficult to address. But the constraints in achieving UEE are far more deep-rooted. A paradigm shift is required from the traditional system of planning and implementing a pre-defined set of interventions to a process where specific problems of deprived areas and disadvantaged groups are addressed through appropriate interventions and context-specific planning.

The discussion of government policies and actions makes it obvious that education policy and programming in the elementary education sector has covered a long distance and the last decade, the 1990s, has certainly witnessed an increased focus, a change in the discourse, and some efforts towards making it more inclusive.[16] However, it is also clear that though there is awareness about most issues that act as constraints in the participation of children from marginalized groups and that these are recognized in the policy documents, the measures adopted are generally easy to standardize and implement. The fundamental issues of raising the accountability of the school system as a whole require radical changes in the policies, power distribution, and ways of functioning. These are bound to affect existing vested interests adversely and hence are not easy decisions to implement. The ease of implementing simple solutions has prevailed in the choice of policies to address equity issues which have been over simplified, ignoring the complexities that characterize them.

The state governments, where the real responsibility for reforms lies, also face genuine dilemmas on several counts. The choices between expanding the system through formal schools or flexible alternative schools, between placing local teachers expected to be more sensitive to local parents and children but who may not be pre-trained and teachers who may not know the local language but who may be pre-trained, between large-scale campaigns and process-oriented, small-scale people's mobilization programmes, and so on are not easy choices. However, what is worrying is that the choices are not made based on a long-term vision but generally on short-term considerations, and are hence guided by immediate concerns. Also, many of the real constraints faced by poor and marginalized groups are really difficult to address by means of the education policy alone. However, they are not outside the realm of the state policies as a whole.

NGO Interventions

A common feature of almost all the NGO interventions in the area of education is the centrality of intensive work with the community, parents, children, panchayat institutions, other leaders, school teachers, etc. Appendix 3 provides a list of some well-known organizations and a summary of their approach, strategies and learning. This intensive mobilization, termed 'societal mobilization', has been achieved, in most cases, through the work of committed activists or volunteers over a period of time. Most of the programmes have been guided by a well-articulated philosophy, e.g. abolition of child labour or rights of the child or a more general principle of working with the most deprived children. Through their intensive work, many of these programmes have demonstrated that poor parents have made adjustments for the education of their children, wherever the mobilization has resulted in creating a commitment for schooling. The efforts are also guided to sensitize and strengthen the formal school system to ensure that these children continue to learn at schools. However, most programmes have achieved only limited success in ensuring the accountability of teachers and the school to the local community, and the sensitization of teachers and educational administrators to make the school system more 'inclusive'.

Several of these programmes hold the view that compulsory schooling is the only long-term solution to the problem of the low participation of disadvantaged children in education. However, almost all of them have worked through 'preparatory' strategies such as bridge courses, residential camps, half-way homes, preparatory centres, etc., prior to attempting the mainstreaming of children into formal schools. The inclusion of the 'hardest to reach' children—bonded child labourers, older street children, beggers, rag pickers, and even adolescent girls—has often involved the withdrawal of children from their environments and education through long-duration residential camps. Many such measures, such as residential camps, have high per-child costs. Many urban programmes have underlined the importance of 'pre-school' or early childhood educational institutions as a key strategy to ensure universal enrolment at the primary stage. For difficult groups such as children who migrate, bonded child labour, and street children, these organizations normally undertake a number of schemes of preparatory work, including a detailed family-wise planning and contact programmes, surveys to identify children, studies of patterns of migration or daily routines of street children, studies to identify and contact influential leaders, etc. This shows that compulsory education alone is not the solution. It involves the development of an understanding about specific groups, strategizing, undertaking preparatory work, intensive implementation and follow-up.

Clearly, non-governmental organizations which have worked for several years with particular kinds of deprived children are best placed to work at achieving universal education among these specific groups. However, large parts of cities and towns, areas from where families regularly migrate in search of work, interior forest areas, areas where caste or land-based exploitation is rampant, or areas inhabited by groups ethnically/culturally discriminated against, do not have a significant presence of NGOs or other people's movements which can take on these responsibilities. Mobilization in such areas is anyway a big challenge, and appears almost impossible in the absence of a movement of change. Government programmes have limitations in reaching out to the most difficult groups. The absence of a committed volunteer cadre constrains the working towards the goal of 'social mobilization'. Under programmes like the DPEP, the large number of tasks and the many dimensions of work also inhibit the intensive work required with such groups. Often, large programmes are not able to provide the flexibility and the scope for diversity necessary for the education of the 'hardest to reach'.

Implications for Policy and Action

Redefine the Universalization of Elementary Education

The inclusion of children from poor and deprived groups into the fold of sustained schooling can be achieved only with a fundamental change in the approach and functioning of the schooling system, on the one hand, and the socio-political empowerment of the poor and the deprived, on the other. A fundamental change in the approach and functioning of the schooling system, and efforts that would facilitate the empowerment of poor and deprived groups, demands an unambiguous commitment by the Central as well as the state governments reflected in concrete measures. A basic need in this context is to redefine the univeralization of elementary education to include universal enrolment, regular attendance, and sustained participation. The thrust on ensuring the enrolment of children by the end of 2003 has resulted in a lopsided approach in the field where the thrust is mainly on ensuring admission of children by entering their names in school records. This concept of UEE needs to be clearly articulated at different levels—state, district and sub-district—and communicated through all possible means—policy statements, programming, target-setting criteria, and monitoring indicators or processes.

A Long-Term Vision is Important

A serious commitment to the goal would also mean taking all aspects into consideration, such as specific contexts and requirements, likely constraints in implementation, likely opposition by vested interests, and developing a preparedness to deal with those. It is also important to differentiate between a long-term vision and short-term measures. Short-term measures are required but they, too, need to be designed and implemented in a manner that is consistent with, and which leads to, the long-term vision. A number of isolated short-term measures do not lead to much gain. A documented long-term vision is also crucial to ensure that there is a consistent policy of educational reform that does not get destabilized with a change of government or key personnel. Education reforms requiring major shifts in work culture, norms, and processes would require a long time frame. A long-term vision would also help in getting away from sub-sectoral thinking. Many aspects in elementary education are linked with secondary and higher education, and it is important to keep them in view. For instance, the quality of teachers in elementary education depends upon the quality of higher education, and the number of women teachers in rural areas cannot be increased without promoting secondary education among rural girls.

A CLEAR POLICY ON THE EXPANSION OF THE SCHOOLING SYSTEM TO MAKE IT INCLUSIVE

There are certain aspects that need greater attention for policy formulation and action from the perspective of including children from poor and marginalized groups. For instance, a clear policy needs to be developed for the expansion of the system in states where this is still one of the most important issues. The policy must take specific problems faced by different groups into account. These include the issue of locating the school in a particular *tola* or *basti* in the case of Dalit villages and the issue of isolated and dispersed habitations in the case of tribal populations. To cater to the needs of some groups of children, a shift in the whole concept of providing schooling facilities at least in the interim period is also required. These specific groups include migrating children, street children, child sex workers, the children of sex workers, etc. These groups live in specific circumstances where the life situation is far from conventional. This necessitates redefining school and schooling requirements taking their special circumstances into consideration. The specific requirement may vary from one group to the other and can be developed only after clearly understanding the problems they face.

NGO experiences suggest that the strategies to ensure access to schooling for such children would need to include different approaches such as intensive, short-term, condensed courses for older girls, residential/non-residential bridge courses for preparing the never-enrolled as well as drop-out children for admission in age-specific classes, seasonal hostels for children whose parents migrate, drop-in centres for children of sex-workers or street children, outreach contact programmes, residential schools, etc. It is important that such strategies are recognized as essential components of the UEE effort. Many of these interventions cost much more than just providing a school and hence governments need to recognize the need for higher investments for these children in difficult circumstances. It is also important that the implementing agencies get out of the NFE mode and not treat the alternatives as necessarily cheaper and inferior quality substitutes. This needs to be aggressively stated and communicated through all possible means. It is also important to recognize that the strategies for such groups require intensive preparatory work and follow-up with the community. Often strategies like bridge courses get picked up in government programmes as mechanistic interventions without a corresponding emphasis on the more difficult aspects like sustained mobilization of the community, changing attitudes at the school level, and providing support to such children after they are admitted to formal schools.

The inadequacy of upper-primary schools and the higher costs of this stage depress the commitment to schooling even at the primary stage. Many parents argue that since they are unable to bear the cost at a later stage, and the primary stage in itself has no 'benefit', they will not send their children to school even at the primary stage. This has been a major issue in many states and needs greater attention. The limited spread of ECCE facilities is also an issue. However, a greater cause of concern is the fact that though perceived as something which facilitates girls' participation in school by taking care of younger siblings, the functioning of the ECCE centres is not in coordination with primary schools even at places where they are present. It is important to decide in view of specific situations whether or not this is a relevant strategy, and in case it is perceived to be one, a clear policy must be developed in this regard.

MAKING SCHOOLS INCLUSIVE

Schools are currently not inclusive in the sense that children from all social and economic groups, or those with any other disadvantage, do not receive treatment which would attract them and their parents to schooling. The dimensions and nuances of these school-level problems vary, and it is important to develop a disaggregated understanding of school situations and then allow space for choosing priorities for school improvement. The simple issue of allowing the school calendar and timings to be determined by the local people based on the character of seasonality has been highlighted repeatedly by research as well as policy documents, but is not in practice in the formal system, except in a few states.

This also means that there is a need to redefine quality and follow a differentiated approach in view of the varying contexts. A largely undifferentiated approach to quality improvement has been pursued so far. Programmes like the DPEP have largely interpreted quality as the implementation of elaborate activity-based teaching-learning processes in classrooms. A differentiated approach to 'quality', based on school/social situations, would mean that in deprived areas, with inadequate 'learning conditions', the stress should be on establishing 'prerequisites of quality' before attempting formidable pedagogic improvement programmes. These would include ensuring basic infrastructure facilities, adequate teachers and textbooks, and midday meal programme.

The centrality of the context in designing appropriate pedagogic interventions may mean having a very different focus from the present practice of mass-training programmes. The focus cannot be the same for areas where the home language of children is very different from the medium of instruction or areas where social divides are sharp and so on. Neither the prevalent pre-service teacher-training courses nor the in-service training programmes have ever focused on issues of social exploitation, language disadvantage, relevance of education, marginalization faced by children in school, child work, etc. Even teacher educators or educational administrators are never required to delve into these issues. Issues of caste, language, religion, and ethnicity are politically and socially more sensitive and get neglected in favour of interventions which are apparently simpler, non-controversial, and easier to implement.

The monitoring of school improvement also needs to be in line with the definition of quality. Many indicators presently in use are only input/infrastructure based. Outcome- and process-based indicators, for example, those that assess in-class attention to the more vulnerable and irregularly attending children, teachers' attitudes towards lower caste and tribal children, assessment of children's learning on a regular basis, and school-community relations should at least supplement these input-based indicators. However, outcome- or process-based indicators are generally avoided because they are difficult to develop, quantify, and monitor.

SHIFT IN ACCOUNTABILITY, DECENTRALIZATION AND DEVOLUTION OF POWER

A shift in the accountability of the school system to assure learning by all children and their progression across grades, rather than to rules, procedures, and orders from above, is critical for a change in functioning. Unless an accountability framework can be put in place, only inputs in the form of teacher training, textbook development, and academic support will have a limited impact. The decentralization of power as well as responsibilities, both in political and administrative streams, is crucial to facilitate a shift in the accountability of the system. The transfer of power to local bodies giving them a definite role, on the one hand, and decentralizing administrative decision making processes, on the other, are likely to enable the shift in accountability. It is also important that decentralization or the devolution of power does not remain tokenistic in nature and creates space for genuine action at different levels. It is not easy to implement measures of decentralization involving real shifts in power, and the states will need to determine the ways in which it can be done. All actions need to be directed towards ensuring accountability to people. This would also involve a redefinition of the school-community relationship through a sustained effort. People, especially the marginalized, have to be the focus of this process. The challenge is to ensure that the most marginalized need representation and are given in voice in the processes evolved for enhancing and strengthening the school-community relationship.

SOCIAL MOBILIZATION AND SOCIO-POLITICAL ACTION

Social mobilization is critical to generate confidence, raise hope, help build a commitment to education, and enable people to demand functional, good-quality schools. This is especially relevant for groups which face exclusion and isolation, on the one hand, and an unstable livelihood situation, on the other. The nature of social mobilization has to be such that it generates social-political action from within the community. The process should be such that it helps people in realizing their rights to education and other aspects of life, enlarging their opportunities, leading them to demand quality education and other services from the state. There could be several strategies leading to this empowerment and the correct mix could be chosen depending upon the particular context.

Social action on the part of groups and organizations, and even concerned individuals, are important along with state-sponsored social mobilization initiatives. Experiences clearly indicate that socio-political processes, generated by actions and leadership from a group outside the government, are more successful in creating interest, building confidence, and bringing about change. Political parties, civil society organizations, elected local bodies, activists, all these and more have a responsibility to initiate processes which would lead to confidence building and empowerment among all groups which are marginalized, socially and economically. This also necessitates a recognition of the goal of universalization of elementary education as an active agenda by all political parties and concerned social organizations. Political parties, though mentioning this in some context or the other, have so far not really taken up this as a priority. Vested interests, which play the dominant role in decisions making, act at several levels to hinder initiatives likely to question the *status quo* or those perceived as leading to little political gains. Without a clear and unambiguous commitment by political parties, in and outside the government, it is difficult to bring about radical shifts in the functioning of schooling systems and the positioning of poor and marginalized families.

WORKING CHILDREN

We have seen earlier that child work is not a homogeneous category. With variations in the nature of the work, the number of hours, and the element of seasonality, it includes working for others for wages and working for one's own family. The majority of children involved in paid work labour hard and full time. Even for those not involved in paid work all around the year, the period for which they are employed involves hard work for long hours. Work for 'own family' is more flexible and varies in its 'toughness'.

The present legislation on child labour does not cover 85 per cent of earning children. It is important to expand the scope of legislation to include all children employed for wages. The availability of paid work for children makes it an important option available to parents in times of crises. However, mere legislation will not be able to stop the practice. In any case, it is not possible for any legislation to include unpaid activities for one's own family, whether engaging in household chores and sibling care or working in one's own field, collecting forest produce and other similar activities. Therefore, intensive social mobilization to create a norm for educating children is absolutely necessary. This kind of mobilization is important even for withdrawing children from paid work, especially those engaged as part of family-based labour. The nature of parental occupations is such in these cases that it necessitates the child's participation in work (e.g. boatmen, fishermen, seasonal work in brick kilns, sugarcane harvesting, etc.). It may require special measures such as residential educational facilities for children.

AREAS WITH SEVERE FOOD INSECURITY

In the poorest areas with chronic food crises and serious livelihood constraints, any initiative focusing on education alone is not likely to succeed in isolation. Several NGO experiments have emphasized the need for a more comprehensive approach—including the major concerns/ deprivations faced by a community/area—rather than targeting education development in isolation. In an area that faces chronic food deficits, efforts to ensure food security through diverse interventions (e.g. watershed management, women's self-help groups, grain banks, nutrition programmes for the severely malnourished, food for work, etc.) would be important. In certain tribal areas facing exploitation by traders and neglect by government agencies, an integrated approach could include leadership training for tribal youth including information on development schemes, legal issues, etc. Migration of whole families has emerged as a major constraint in the completion of schooling by children in several areas. Diversified livelihood options and greater availability of work around the year could also boost children's education.

In the present form, government funding and programme development have been largely sectoral or sub-sectoral, not taking cognizance of the requirements of these areas. What is important in this respect is a recognition of the existence of food insecurity, livelihood constraints, and unstable life situations as major issues in many parts, and a review of policies that impact upon these directly or indirectly. Here, too, a long-term vision is critical for a definite and sustainable shift in conditions.

QUALITY OF GOVERNANCE AND SOCIAL SECURITY

It is important to realize that the issue of basic social security in terms of opportunities to earn enough for subsistence and provisions for basic minimum needs such as food, safe drinking water, and health care facilities are crucial for creating stability, which is in turn important for building commitment towards the education of children. People cannot be empowered without providing them the basics of life. Therefore, the functioning and delivery of the primary health care system, food grain programmes, housing and loan schemes, etc., become crucial for a stable and secure life situation. However, these schemes and structures also suffer from similar design and implementation problems that also plague the education schemes and structures. The benefits rarely reach those who deserve the most and therefore fail to bring about any significant change in their life situations. Corruption is also rampant at all levels, eroding the faith of people in these institutions. Hence, the quality of governance in delivery of services in social sectors is a major issue and needs to be addressed. It is a big challenge considering it requires radical changes in the functioning of government machinery as well as institutions like panchayats. This requires changes in attitudes of elected representatives and government personnel at all levels, which is a long and painstaking process.

COLLABORATION OF DIFFERENT AGENCIES

In view of the need for intensive work with communities and diversified strategies to reach the goal of UEE, it is important to recognize that partnership between government and NGOs or other such citizen-based groups is crucial. In fact, the partnerships may go beyond the government and NGOs and may involve more institutions and organizations. UEE is a national concern and it is the common responsibility of all to work towards it. It is the government, however, which should be responsible for encouraging and facilitating such partnerships and collaborations. These collaborations can be of different types and at different levels, and also for different purposes. The DPEP and similar programmes did make an effort in this direction by bringing together universities, NGOs, and other institutions with varied roles in programme designing, implementation, and evaluation. However, this needs to be taken forward and made more meaningful and vibrant in the future.

Finally, what emerges is that the goal of universalizing elementary education cannot be achieved unless the 'real' issues are recognized and confronted directly. The majority of children not attending school regularly are girls and children belonging to marginalized groups, mainly from poor households. The problems related to basic livelihood security are real for them, impacting on their life situations significantly. Adverse socio-political positioning adds to their marginalization, making them more vulnerable. A clear sense of hopelessness about any change in their socio-political and economic positions is visible among poor families in areas where levels of school participation are really low. Poor governance in general, and the lack of school accountability in particular, both reflect and add to their powerlessness. It is not easy to build commitment to sustained schooling of children in such situations without a clear political commitment and concerted action at all levels. The issues of equity have so far been largely over-simplified in policy and delivery modes. Simple, tokenistic, easy-to-implement measures take precedence over those which require radical shifts in approach and functioning of the schooling system. The universalization of elementary education, however, cannot be achieved without a fundamental change in the approach and functioning of the schooling system, on the one hand, and socio-political empowerment of the poor and the deprived, on the other.

Notes

1. See Tilak (1999) for a discussion on costs of schooling.
2. In response to a Public Interest Litigation on the Right to Food, the Supreme Court has recently (in 2001) given a directive to governments to provide a cooked midday meal in all primary schools in the country.
3. See Bashir (2000) for a discussion on government expenditure on elementary education in the 1990s.
4. See *Education in India and Selected Educational Statistics*, published by the Ministry of Human Resource Development for different years.
5. See Nambissan and Sedwal (2002) for a discussion on Dalit habitations remaining uncovered by schools.
6. See Sharma and Gopalakrishan (1998) and the PROBE report (1999) for discussions on NFE.
7. From 2002, the scheme has been merged with the Sarva Shiksha Abhiyan.
8. See Vyasulu (2000), Jha (2000), Srivastava (2000), Rahul (2000) and Educational Consultants India Limited (1999) for feedback on EGS in MP.
9. See Educational Consultants India Limited (1999a) for different approaches and focuses of Alternative Schooling Programmes initiated under DPEP.
10. See Ramachandran (2002) for a discussion on the issue of gender equity in classrooms and the recent experiences from the field.
11. See Jha and Bhardwaj (2000) for a discussion on women teachers in rural India.
12. See GOI (1990), *Ramamurti Committee Report*, p. 307.
13. See GOI (1992); POA, 1992, p. 111.
14. See Jha, Saxena and Baxi (2001) for a discussion on management of information in elementary education.
15. See the Gram Swaraj Adhiniyam, passed by the MP government in 2001.
16. One important effort in this context is the increased focus on including children with disabilities in schooling. This issue was highlighted in the POA, 1992, and concerted efforts were made to facilitate this, especially under the DPEP.

APPENDICES

Appendix 1

Table A1: The Study Villages: Infrastructure Development Indicators—An Index

State	District	Village	Distance from road (in kms.)	Distance from town (in kms.)	Public transport	Upper primary school	*Anganwadi*	Elect	Dist. PHC/ Hospital	Drinking water	Grade
Jharkhand	Palamu	Ukamand	0	8	Average	No	Yes	No	8	Average	B
Jharkhand	Palamu	Lanka	3	3	None	No	Yes	No	3	Average	B
Jharkhand	Palamu	Ayodhya Kolhua	0	10	Average	No	No	No	9	Bad	C
Jharkhand	Palamu	Khudakhurd	0	13	Bad	No	No	No	13	V. Bad	D
Bihar	Arari	Kismat Khabaspur	1.5	23	None	No	No	No	2	V. Bad	D
Bihar	Arari	Mudballa	0	9	Bad	No	No	No	9	V. Bad	C
Bihar	Arari	Rahatmina	8	13	None	No	No	No	10	Average	D
Bihar	Arari	Doriya	0	10	None	No	No	No	10	Bad	D
Gujarat	Dang	Mahal	0	27	Average	No	Yes	Yes	12	Average	B
Gujarat	Dang	Wakarya	1	27	Average	No	No	Yes	4	Average	B
Andhra Pradesh	West Godavari	Gavaravaram	0	2	Good	Yes	Yes	Yes	2	Good	A
Andhra Pradesh	West Godavari	Bayyannagudem	0	8	Good	Yes	Yes	Yes	2	Good	A
Karnataka	Chamrajnagar	Chandukatte Mole	2	6	Average	No	No	Yes	6	Average	B
Karnataka	Chamrajnagar	Honnahalli	0	14	Good	Yes	No	Yes	5	Good	A
Karnataka	Chamrajnagar	Doddathupur	0.5	6	Average	Yes	Yes	Yes	6	Good	A
Karnataka	Chamrajnagar	Maddur Colony	1	22	Bad	No	No	Yes	2	Good	B
Maharashtra	Pune	Karandi Khedebare	5	8	None	No	Yes	Yes	4	Good	B
Maharashtra	Pune	Malegao	0	1	Good	No	Yes	Yes	1	Good	A
Madhya Pradesh	Sidhi	Naudhiya	4	5	None	Yes	No	Yes	5	Bad	C
Madhya Pradesh	Sidhi	Barambaba	0	20	None	Yes	No	Yes	0	V. Bad	C
Madhya Pradesh	Sidhi	Kursa	4	8	None	Yes	Yes	No	8	Average	C
Madhya Pradesh	Sidhi	Jogini	0	6	Good	No	No	Yes	6	Average	C

(contd.)

Appendix 1 (contd.)

Uttar Pradesh	Shravasti	Mashakala	13	10	None	No	No	No	12	Average	D
Uttar Pradesh	Shravasti	Sultanpur	1.5	12	None	No	No	No	4	Average	C
Uttar Pradesh	Shravasti	Balanagar Kodri	1	12		No	No	No	8	Average	C
Uttar Pradesh	Shravasti	Kathkuiyakalan	1	12	None	No	No	No	7	Average	C
Assam	Dhubri	Bhamandanga Pt. II	3	5	Average	No	No	No	15	Average	C
Assam	Dhubri	Ramraikuti Pt. II	6	6	Average	No	No	4	6	Average	C
Assam	Dhubri	Bamunigaon Pt. I	5	10	Bad	No	No	No	5	Average	C
Assam	Dhubri	Tiapara	1	5	None	No	No	No	3	Average	C
Orissa	Koraput	Mulasar	3	13	None	No	Yes	No	3	Bad	C
Orissa	Koraput	Mohul Bhatta	8	7	None	No	Yes	No	3	Bad	C
Orissa	Koraput	Bharwa Munda	3	20	Bad	No	Yes	Yes	10	Average	C
Orissa	Naupara	Kermeli	6	10	None	Yes	Yes	Yes	5	Average	B
Orissa	Koraput	Padheiguda	2	8	Bad	No	No	No	5	Average	C
Orissa	Naupara	Ratapalli	1	6	Average	No	yes	Yes	2	Average	A
Orissa	Naupara	Cherichuan	9	21	None	No	No	No	–	Average	D

Total Score:
45 and above : A [6]
31-44 : B [8]
21-30 : C [15]
10-20 : D [6]

1. Distance from road
0 : 9
Up to 1 km. : 7
1-3 km. : 5
4-5 km. : 3
More than 5 km. : 1

2. Distance from town
Up to 3 km. : 9
4-8 km. : 7
9-14 km. : 4
15 and above : 1

3. Public transport
Good : 9
Average : 7
Bad : 4
Very Bad : 1

4. Upper Primary school within village
Yes : 6
No : 0

5. *Anganwadi* within village
Yes : 3
No : 0

6. Electricity
Yes : 4
No : 0

7. Distance PHC / hospital
Up to 2 km. : 9
3-5 km. : 7
6-10 km. : 4
More than 10 : 1

8. Drinking water facilities
Good : 9
Average : 6
Bad : 3
Very Bad : 0

Appendix 2

Table A.2: Schools and the Schooling Participation Status in the Study Villages

District	Village	Efficiency Grade	Student-Classroom Ratio [Grade]	People Perception [Grade]	% Enrolled (in total pop)	% Regularly going (in total pop)
Dhubri	Jhakuapura	[D]	[C]	C	80.9	33.89
	Ramrai Kuti	[C]	[D]	C	87.8	27.22
	Bamunigaon	[C]	[D]	B	73.8	36.90
	Tiapara	[C]	[A]	C	72.5	90.62
Araria	Mudballa	[C]	[A]	C	20.0	5.46
	Khabaspur	[D]	[B]	D	40.8	14.56
	Rahatmina	[D]	[D]	B	58.6	53.09
	Doriya	[D]	[D]	C	78.3	26.07
Palamu	Khurkhurd	[D]	[C]	C	46.7	18.16
	Ayodhya Kolhua	[B]	[D]	B	64.9	45.95
	Lanka	[C]	[A]	C	86.0	56.16
	Ukamand	[A]	[C]	A	51.1	40.31
Nuapara	Kermeli	[C]	[C]	C	87.8	80.51
	Ratapalli	[B]	[B]	A	91.5	78.41
	Cheri Chuan	[A]	[B]	B	60.0	57.93
	Bharua Munda	[C]	[A]	B	13.2	88.04
Koraput	Mohul Bhatta	[D]	[B]	B	61.1	38.86
	Mulasar	[C]	[B]	C	49.0	13.72
	Padheiguda	[B]	[D]	C	60.6	43.75
Sidhi	Nauirya-1	[B]	[D]	A	79.0	32.23
	Nauirya-2	[B]	[D]	D		
	Barambaba [Til]	[D]	[C]	B	72.9	36.45
	Barambaba-1	[B]	[A]	C		
	Kursa (EGS)-1	[D]	[B]	D	79.7	48.30
	Kursa-2	[D]	[D]	D		
	Jogini-2	[C]	[D]	D	63.5	31.75
	Jogini-1	[D]	[B]			
Shravasti	Balanagar Kodri	[B]	[D]	D	68.2	37.64
	Sultana	[D]	[D]	C	36.7	24.48
	Kathkuiyan Kalan	[D]	[D]	B	37.0	15.24
	Mashakalan	[D]	[D]	C	53.2	66.5
Dangs	Mahal	[C]	[A]	A	71.2	53.40
	Wakaria	[B]	[A]	A	75.9	68.46
Chamraj-nagar	Chandukatte-1	[A]	[D]	C	80.0	61.04
	Chandukatte-2	[C]	[D]	B		
	Moddur Colony	[C]	[A]	C	64.7	64.70
	Doddathapur	[A]	[B]	A	88.1	85.54
	Honahalli	[A]	[C]	C	85.3	61.40

(contd.)

Appendix 2 (contd.)

District	Village	Efficiency Grade	Student-Classroom Ratio [Grade]	People Perception [Grade]	% Enrolled (in total pop)	% Regularly going (in total pop)
West Godavari	Garvavaram-1	[C]	[D]	A	66.7	46.02
	Garvavaram-2	[A]	[D]			
	Bayyanagudem-1	[B]	[D]	A	72.3	70.20
	Bayyanagudem-2	[C]	[B]			
Pune	Karandi	[A]	[B]	A	74.4	74.40
	Malegaon (1)	[A]	[A]	A	61.1	61.10

NOTES: * Based on combined score of PTR, Attendance-Enrolment Ratio, Class V as a proportion of Class I Enrolment, and the difference between Boys' and Girls' enrolment. The brackets for score are given below.

Scores given for each indicator are as below:

1. Column 3 in Table A.2:

PTR			Attendance/Enrolment			Enrolment in Class V / 1		
0-20	:	14	5-20	:	2	0-20	:	2
20-40	:	12	20-30	:	4	20-30	:	4
40-60	:	10	30-40	:	6	30-40	:	6
60-80	:	8	40-50	:	8	40-50	:	8
80-100	:	6	50-60	:	10	50-60	:	10
100-150	:	4	60-70	:	12	60-80	:	12

Boys' minus Girls' Enrolment			Total score given in Column 3 in Table A.2		
0	:	14	45 above	:	A
1-10	:	12	40-44	:	B
10-20	:	10	31-39	:	C
20-30	:	8	Upto 30	:	D
30-40	:	6			
40-60	:	4			

2. Column 4 in Table A.2:
   Student-Classroom Ratio

Upto 30	:	14 [A]
30-50	:	10 [B]
50-70	:	6 [C]
70-100	:	2 [D]
Above 100	:	0 [D]

3. Column 5 in Table A.2 is based on grading of people's perceptions as revealed during Focus Group Discussions.

Appendix 3

Table A 3: NGO Initiatives in Working with Difficult Groups – A Few Examples

S.No.	Programme	Approach and Strategies	Learning
1.	Pratham, Mumbai	Work towards the creation of a social mission for universal primary education 1. *Balwadis* for 3-6 year-old children 2. Bridge courses for mainstreaming out-of-school children 3. Support to municipal schools through para teachers. Attempt to influence the municipal education system 4. 'Out reach' programme	• Networking of NGOs, professionals, corporate houses, and the government is useful. • For UPE, it is important to encourage early childhood education. • The process of change within the government school system is slow and painstaking.
2.	MV Foundation, Andhra Pradesh	There must be total abolition of child labour. All children must be in formal, full-time day schools. A consensus should be created about the norm that every child should be in school. 1. Creation of a demand for education 2. Bridge residential camps, short-and long-term non-residential bridge courses 3. Support to formal schools in newly enrolled bridge courses for children through para teachers	• The key to universalizing education in child labour pockets or low-demand areas is large-scale, sustained 'societal mobilization'. Poor parents can make sacrifices to send children to school if a consensual norm emerges for education • Schools need to be strengthened to ensure the continuation of such children in school. Teachers, educational bureaucracy, and policy makers need to be first sensitized and convinced on UEE issues. • Demonstration of success on a small scale in the initial stages is crucial to replication. • A dedicated group of volunteers committed to the cause is an essential starting point in this process. • For very difficult groups of children like bonded labourers or wage-earning children, residential camps are necessary in the initial stages. Some children require residential facilities to continue their education.

(contd.)

Appendix 3 (contd.)

S.No.	Programme	Approach and Strategies	Learning
			• It is more difficult to ensure enrolment and retention of girls, who are involved in all kinds of household work, including sibling care.
3.	CINI–ASHA Kolkata	(a) Providing services and facilities for street children, mobilizing the community, empowering children, sensitizing the police, etc. 1. Drop-in centres 2. Half-way homes 3. Night shelters 4. Sick bays, outreach clinics 5. Special intervention for children of sex workers (b) Sensitizing children, parents, community, youth clubs, employees, schools on child labour issues and advocacy, formal compulsory education. 1. Bridge courses in preparatory centres 2. Hard-core child labourers withdrawn from their environment and placed in residential camps 3. Supporting pre-school education of 3-6 year-old children 4. Coaching centres for children enrolled in formal schools after completing bridge courses	• Crucial role of contact and report/ support-building activities for street children. • Need for diverse and flexible strategies. • Need for providing basic needs for street children for shelter, recreation and emotional support, healthcare, etc., in addition to education. • Intensive work with parents, community, influential leaders and employers is a prerequisite for UPE intervention • Preparatory courses are needed for out of school children. There have to be residential for more difficult groups. • Continued support to these children in formal schools is essential. Sensitization and involvement of formal municipal schools and teachers is crucial.
4.	CRREDA Mirzapur, Uttar Pradesh	- Mass mobilization around issues of child labour - Establishment of community schools for children withdrawn from work - Social mobilization of different stakeholders including children, parents, loom holders, media, panchayats, teachers, government officials, etc. - Community-based and supported schools - Some work on self-help credit groups of women.	• Where deep-seated vested interests are involved, the mobilization effort has to be intensive and all-encompassing • Work with the community has to include other aspects such as economic upliftment as well.

5.	Concerned for Working Children (CWC) Karnataka	On child labour issues, CWC holds that the child-work situations are varied and there is a need to work with children to explore reasons/factors underlying the problem and find solutions by providing political space to such children and their families. The 'Bhima Sangha' is a programme for providing this platform to working children. The 'Toofan Panchayat' programme has attempted to evolve child- centred developmental processes for rural areas, including strengthening of panchayats, schools, etc., and also enabling the creation of child labour-free and child-friendly panchayats. Children are involved in a variety of institutions of village improvement. CWC has also worked on the empowerment of the functioning of the formal primary and middle schools.	• The best way to empower children is to work with them directly. • The child labour issue is complex. Legislation necessary, cannot in itself bring about any results. • It is useful to work on a wide range of issues of village development rather than focus only on education. • Empowerment of stakeholders in the education process, e.g. children, parents, panchayats, leads to greater pressure on the system to perform. • This kind of work with children and the community has to be very intensive and painstaking .
6.	Prachiti, Jhana Prabodhini Maharashtra	Children who migrate for 6 months with families to sugarcane-growing areas: 100 days intensive (12 hours each day) school for children who migrate with parents to sugar factory areas. Schools run in/near the sugar factories. Flexible strategies for children depending on their level/ability.	• Detailed planning and preparatory work in and around the area of migration. • Flexible approach to maximize learning in a course of 16-weeks' duration, with emphasis on language and mathematics.
7	Udaan, Sarvodaya Ashram, Hardoi and CARE-India, UP	Providing education to girls in the 10-14 years age group equivalent to Classes V of formal schools in residential schools through a one-year rigorous course. Focus on equipping them with critical thinking abilities, an independent personality, decision-making ability, and developing a spirit of enquiry. Continuous community contact and opinion building on basic women's empowerment, as well as other social issues.	• Intensive work with the community generates confidence and builds a commitment to education. Getting girls away from home environments and staying together facilitates intensive work. • Focus on rigour and empowerment in curriculum transaction leads to perceptible changes. However, many aspects are suited for residential teaching of these curricula and can be successful only when this is possible. • Success of some girls leads to change in outlook and generates further interest in a norm of schooling.

Appendix 3 (contd.)

S.No.	Programme	Approach and Strategies	Learning
			• Residential programmes require high investments: financial and human resources. • Intensive follow-up required to enable girls to continue with their education.
8.	Movement for Alternatives and Youth Awareness (MAYA), Bangalore	Working, school-going and loitering children Crèches and play schools for 2-6 year-old children Non-formal education programmes leading to main-streaming. Supplementary education programme to support school-going children. Pre-vocational programme for 12-14 year-old children.	• Need for diverse strategies. • Dedicated community workers. • Follow-up of children enrolled in schools.

Appendix 4

Equity and Decentralization in Education: An Uphill Task—The Assam Experience

Dhir Jhingran

For almost two years, during 2002 and 2003, I worked as Mission Director, Elementary Education, Assam, responsible for the implementation of the District Primary Education Programme, the Sarva Shiksha Abhiyan (SSA) and a major reform agenda for the mainstream elementary education system of the state. The understanding of and sensitization about the problems and issues in working for the universalizing of elementary education among the marginalized groups that I had developed during the conduct of this study guided me to make *equity* the overarching yardstick of all our interventions. It was clear to us that the disadvantaged areas and groups needed more resources, greater attention, and flexible, contextual strategies. These were areas where there were the highest proportion of children not attending school needed special attention. The schools in these areas were poorly provided for and did not function regularly. The challenge was to compensate for decades of neglect of such areas and groups and to bring about a total shift from the completely uniform and strait jacketed planning and implementation for the state as a whole.

Some of the initiatives that translated our commitment to equity into action were:

(a) Selected villages and panchayats were officially notified as '*disadvantaged*', based on the criteria of remoteness, high proportion of 'out of school' children, and presence of groups suffering serious social disadvantage or neglect (e.g. the tea garden community). *These areas became eligible for compensatory packages* that could be locally designed or put together from a menu of flexible strategies, including intensive mobilization activities, community-based village motivators, preferential allocation of funds for school improvement activities such as school libraries and mothers' groups, and grants to NGOs for working in these areas.

(b) *For specific marginalized groups* like the tea garden community, minority (Muslim) populations residing in temporary riverine settlements, and some tribal groups, *special strategies were designed for social mobilization and school improvement* in consultation with community-based organizations.

(c) A large number of decisions under the SSA, including placement of additional teachers, selection of schools for construction grants, selection of villages for conduct of bridge courses or schools for remedial coaching classes, were made based on the data collected from every village and school and clear norms and criteria, which were widely publicized. *This transparent, norm-based selection ensured that deprived areas and social groups were benefited the most through greater attention and resources.*

(d) To send out a message that the *most under-privileged children were a priority for us,* we initiated programmes reaching out to children working in shops and hotels, domestic servants, quarry workers, and street children.

The norms for expenditure, the allocations against each scheme, and the final accounts at each level were made public through leaflets, newspaper advertisements, and meetings. This transparent and norm-based work also helped to create a climate of trust for the programme amongst the people. School managing committees, village education committees, and panchayats were empowered to take decisions and spend funds for school improvement. Apart from the decentralization of powers to panchayats and schools, there was significant administrative and financial delegation within the education system to the district and block levels.

A major thrust of our initial work was to ensure 'basic learning conditions'—an adequate number of teachers, adequate space per child, textbooks, and TLM in every school. The effort was to ensure that every school reaches predefined minimum standards on these requirements and continues to remain above these standards. A series of initiatives was also taken to ensure that schools in remote and disadvantaged areas functioned for the prescribed hours and days. These included empowerment of school committees and panchayats to modify school timings and calendars locally, holding of *shiksha adalats*, more intensive supervision of schools in such areas, involvement of the district administration and other development departments in visiting schools on a regular basis. We considered the regular and reliable functioning of schools with regular availability of teachers as the most important precondition for ensuring learning.

The Assam elementary education mission implemented a massive programme of bridge courses for older children who had never been to school or had dropped out before completing the primary stage. While more than 4,00,000 children completed these bridge courses and were 'mainstreamed' into regular schools, we felt that much more intensive effort was required for mobilizing parents and sensitizing the schools to ensure that such children attend regularly, and are able to adjust to the school environment. This realization was a result of the understanding developed during the fieldwork for the study of the complex interplay of family and school factors that shapes the commitment of poor and deprived parents to regular schooling of children. Our experience in Assam validated this finding when we observed that some of the more disadvantaged children were not regular in the bridge courses and were likely to drop out after joining school. However, in several states, bridge courses are now being implemented in a mechanistic manner without the realization that comprehensive processes need to be undertaken for the mobilization of parents and for 'preparing' the schools to ensure regular participation of vulnerable children. Also, the present thrust on 'universal enrolment' by 2003 is being implemented mainly by ensuring that every child's name is entered into the school admission registers, which glosses over the real challenge of ensuring the regular participation of vulnerable children.

In Assam a major exercise for the sensitization of teachers, academic personnel, and education administrators was undertaken on the 'right to education' and its implications for work in education offices and schools. At the school level, the accountability of the school for ensuring learning by all children was stressed through the Learning Assurance Programme and the Reading Guarantee Campaign. These programmes stressed additional in-class academic support to the poorly performing children on a regular basis and special strategies for children who had serious learning problems because their mother tongue was very different from the medium of instruction employed at school. We realized the crucial role of equity in the quality improvement effort if the goal is to ensure that *all* children learn adequately.

The entire UEE effort in Assam was implemented through the mainstream education department, which was a real challenge. For years, the education system had worked on the basis of centralization of powers at the state level and a complete lack of transparency in its functioning. The political system, especially the legislators, had a vice-like grip on the district and sub-district education offices and enjoyed formal and informal powers of decision making on teachers' selection and transfers, award of grants for construction, and the management of schools. While the panchayats and school committees were very enthusiastic about the decentralized and the criteria-evidence-based approach initiated by the mission, the legislators were extremely unhappy since such processes reduced or eliminated the discretion and nepotism in the selection of schools, villages, and teachers. The education system had been working on the basis of arbitrary, or at best uniform, resource allocations across districts and blocks. It was, therefore, a very difficult task to convince the political executive and the education bureaucracy to agree to a system of preferential allocation of resources to disadvantaged areas, groups, and schools.

The education system, as most other parts of the government in Assam (as in several other states) is fairly corrupt, and it was a major challenge to introduce transparency in the utilization of funds. The education system was also slow to respond to the rights-based approach and the thrust on accountability. It was also clear that the education structures lacked the managerial capacity to implement the wide range of activities involved in the SSA and spend the huge funds allocated each year to each district. Our effort at introducing accountability in the education system remained a limited and imperfect attempt since institutional reforms could not be carried to their logical conclusion. Reforms like transparent and merit-based selection and transfer of teachers threatened power relationships and could not be implemented owing to the lack of political commitment. Decentralization and empowerment of people was a clearly stated goal of the government of Assam and was strongly espoused by the chief minister himself. Still, in the face of opposition from legislators, this agenda had to be virtually given up by the government.

It became clear that making the right to basic education a reality requires a long-term vision backed up a sustained effort, political commitment to decentralization and empowerment of people, and a basic change in the functioning of the education system. This kind of effort is not to be seen in government programmes for UEE in most states. It is high time that the education discourse in the states, within and outside the government, focuses on the processes of marginalization and exclusion that prevent the most disadvantaged children from participating and successfully completing elementary-level schooling. Merely counting 'admitted children' to show increased enrolments, managing to spend larger sums on elementary education, or implementing state-wide teacher training programmes would mean that some of the real challenges of universalization, as outlined in this study, would remain unaddressed.

Bibliography

Acharya, Sarthi (2001), 'Access to Primary Education: Rural Maharashtra and Madhya Pradesh', in A. Vaidyanathan and P.R. Gopinathan Nair (eds.), *Elementary Education in Rural India: A Grass-roots View,* Sage Publications.

Agarwal, Bina (1989), 'Rural Women, Poverty and Natural Resources: Sustenance, Sustainability and Struggle for Change', *Economic and Political Weekly,* 28 October 1989.

—— (1990), 'Social Security and the Family: Coping with Seasonality and Calamity in Rural India', in Ehtisham Ahmad, Jean Dreze, John Hills and Amartya Sen (eds.), *Social Security in Developing Countries,* Oxford University Press.

Aggarwal, Yash (2001), *Progress towards Universal Access and Retention (Analytical Report),* NIEPA.

Agrawal, Rashmi (1999), *Street Children: A Socio-psychological Study,* Shipra Publications.

Ahmad, Aijazuddin (ed.) (1994), *Muslims in India: Their Educational, Demographic and Socio-Economic Status with Inter-Community Comparisons Based on Field Survey Conducted in 1991 [Different Volumes],* Hamdard Education Society, Inter-India Publications.

Ahmad, Imtiaz (1978), 'Endogamy and Status Mobility among the Siddiqui Sheikhs of Allahabad, Uttar Pradesh', in Imtiaz Ahmad (ed.), *Caste and Social Stratification among Muslims in India,* Manohar.

—— (1983) (ed.), *Modernization and Social Change among Muslims in India,* Manohar.

—— (2001), *Muslim Empowerment* (Mimeo).

—— (2002), 'Secularism, Hindus and Muslims', *Hindu, 24 May 2002.*

Ali, Hasan (1978), 'Elements of Caste among the Muslims in a District in Southern Bihar', in Imtiaz Ahmad (ed.), *Caste and Social Stratification among Muslims in India,* Manohar.

Ambasht, N.K. and K.B. Rath (1995), 'A Study of the Effect of Household, Community and School Factors on the Enrolment, Retention and Achievement of ST Children at the Primary Level', in A.K. Sharma (ed.), *School Effectiveness and Learning Achievement at the Primary Stage: International Perspectives,* NCERT.

Ananda, G. (1994), *Ashram Schools in Andhra Pradesh,* Commonwealth Publishers.

Areeparampil, Mathew (1993), 'The Impact of Uranium Mining and Processing on the Indigenous Peoples of Singhbhum Distt. in Chotanagpur', in Walter Fernandes (ed.), *The Indigenous Questions: Search for an Identity,* Indian Social Institute.

Bashir, Sajitha (2000), *Government Expenditure on Elementary Education in the Nineties,* European Commission.

Basu, Aparna (1999), 'Women's Education in India: Achievements and Challenges', in Bharati Ray and Aparna Basu (eds), *From Independence Towards Freedom:*

Indian Women since 1947, Oxford University Press.
Betéille, André (ed.) (1992), *Society and Politics in India: Essays in a Comparative Perspective,* Oxford University Press.
Betéille, André (2000), 'Changing Socio-Economic and Political Profile of Scheduled Castes in Uttar Pradesh' *Journal of Indian School of Political Economy,* vol. XII, nos. 3 and 4, July-Dec. 2000.
Bellow, Rosemary T. and Elizabeth M. King (1993), 'Educating Women: Lessons from Experience', in Elizabeth M. King and M. Anne Hill (eds.), *Women's Education in Developing Countries,* Johns Hopkins University Press.
Bhatt, Zarina (1978), 'Status and Power in a Muslim Dominated Village of Uttar Pradesh', in Imtiaz Ahmad (ed.), *Caste and Social Stratification among Muslims in India,* Manohar Publications.
Bremen, Jan (1985), *Of Peasants, Migrants and Paupers: Rural Labour Circulation and Capitalist Production in West India*, Oxford University Press.
Burra, Neera (1995), *Born to Work: Child Labour in India,* Oxford University Press.
Chambers, Robert (1992), 'Poverty in India: Concept, Research and Reality', in Barbara Harris; S. Guhan; R.H. Casen (eds.), *Poverty in India: Research and Policy,* Oxford University Press.
Chanana, Karuna (1988), 'Social Change or Social Reform: The Education of Women in Pre-Independence India', in Karuna Chanana (ed.), *Socialisation, Education and Women: Explorations in Gender Identity,* Orient Longman Ltd.
—— (1988a), 'Introduction in Socialisation Education and Women: Explorations', in Karuna Chanana (ed.), *Gender Identity,* Orient Longman Ltd.
Chelliah, Raja J. and R. Sudarshan (1999), *Income, Poverty and Beyond (Human Development in India),* Social Science Press.
Child In Need Institute (1998), *Urban Community-Based Rehabilitation Project in India [A Draft Report for Discussion at a National Workshop],* Child In Need Institute.
Chitnis, Suma (1978), 'Education for the Scheduled Castes and Scheduled Tribes in Maharashtra', in *The Social Context of Education: Essays in Honour of Prof. J.P. Naik,* Allied Publishers Pvt. Ltd.
Desai, I.P. (1978), 'Education of the Scheduled Castes and Scheduled Tribes in Gujarat', in *The Social Context of Education: Essays in Honour of Prof. J.P. Naik,* Allied Publishers Pvt. Ltd.
Devendra, Kiran (1992), 'Education of the Tribals', *Journal of Indian Education,* vol. XVIII, no. 4, 1992.
Dreze, Jean and Amartya Sen (1990), 'Public Action for Social Security: Foundations and Strategy', in Ehtisham Ahmad, Jean Dreze, John Hills and Amartya Sen (eds.), *Social Security in Developing Countries,* Oxford University Press.
—— (1995), *India Economic Development and Social Opportunity,* Oxford University Press.
Dreze, Jean and Harris Gazdar (1996), 'Uttar Pradesh: The Burden of Inertia', in Jean Dreze and Amartya Sen (eds.), *Indian Development: Selected Regional Perspectives,* Oxford University Press.
Dreze, Jean and Amartya Sen (2002), *India Development and Participation,* Oxford University Press.
Dubey, Amaresh and Shubhashis Gangopadhyay (1998), *Counting the Poor,* Department of Statistics, Government of India.

Dutta, S.C. (1983), *Education for All: An Alternative Strategy, Indian Journal of Adult Education,* vol. 44, no. 12, 1983.

Educational Consultants India Ltd. (1999), *Strategic Breakthrough: Micro Initiatives for Girls' Education: Experiments in DPEP,* Educational Consultants India Ltd.

—— (1999), *Reaching out Further: Para-teachers in primary education,* Educational Consultants India Ltd.

Fernandes, Walter and Arundhuti Roychaudhury (1993), 'Search for a Tribal Identity: The Dominant and the Subaltern', in Walter Fernandes (ed.), *The Indigenous Question: Search for an Identity,* Indian Social Institute.

Fernandes, Walter (1993), 'Natural Resources, Self-Determination and the Indigenous Identity: An Introduction', in Walter Fernandes (ed.), *The Indigenous Question: Search for an Identity,* Indian Social Institute.

Fernandes, Walter (ed.) (1996), *The Emerging Dalit Identity: The Re-assertion of the Subalterns,* Indian Social Institute.

Filmer, Deon and Lant Pritchett (1999), 'Educational Enrolment and Attainment in India: Household Wealth, Gender, Village and State Effects', *Journal of Educational Planning and Administration,* vol. 13.

Gangopadhyay, Shubhashis and Wilima Wadhwa (2000), *Economic Reforms for the Poor,* Konark Publishers Pvt. Ltd.

Gathia, Joseph (1999), *Child Prostitution in India,* Concept Publishing Company.

Government of India (year not mentioned), *Sarva Shiksha Abhiyan: Broad framework for implementation,* Ministry of Human Resource Development.

—— (1983), *Report of High Powered Panel on Muslims, SC, ST and weaker sections constituted by the Ministry of Home Affairs headed by Dr. Gopal Singh (sample studies in 45 districts in 12 states),* Ministry of Home Affairs, Government of India.

—— (1986), *National Policy on Education,* Ministry of Human Resource Development.

—— (1988), *Report of the Commissioner for Scheduled Castes and Scheduled Tribes: Twenty-Eighth Report* (*1986-87*), Govt. of India, Office of the Commissioner for SCs and STs.

—— (1990), *Towards an Enlightened and Humane Society (Ramamurti Committee Report),* Government of India.

—— (1990a), *Report of the Commissioner for Scheduled Castes and Scheduled Tribes: Twenty-Ninth Report,* Govt. of India, Office of the Commissioner for SCs and STs.

—— (1990b), *Forty-Third Round Survey (1987-88),* National Sample Survey Organisation.

—— (1992), *Programme of Action, 1992,* Ministry of Human Resource Development.

—— (1998), *Report of the Committee on Prostitution, Child Prostitutes and Children of Prostitutes and Plan of Action to Combat Trafficking and Commercial Sexual Exploitation of Women and Children,* Ministry of Human Resource Development.

—— (1998a), *Report of the Group of Experts on the Financial Resource Requirements for Operationalising the Proposed Constitutional Amendment Bill Making the Right to Free and Compulsory Education upto 14 Years of Age a Fundamental Right' (mimeo) (Tapas Majumdar Committee Report),* Department of Education, Ministry of Human Resource Development.

—— (1998b), *Attending an Educational Institution in India: Its Level, Nature and Cost,* National Sample Survey Organisation, GOI.
—— (different years), *Selected Educational Statistics,* Ministry of Human Resource Development.
——(Different years), *Education in India,* Ministry of Human Resource Development
Govinda, Rangachar (1995), *Status of Primary Education of the Urban Poor in India: An Analytical Review,* UNESCO.
Hamdard Education Society (1983), *All-India Survey (1982-83) of Muslim-Managed Educational Institutions,* Hamdard Education Society.
Harris, Barbara (1992), 'Poverty in Rural India: Micro-level Evidence', in Harris Barbara, S. Guhan, R.H. Casen (eds.), *Poverty in India: Research and Policy,* Oxford University Press.
Harris, Barbara, S. Guhan, R.H. Casen (eds.) (1992), *Poverty in India: Research and Policy,* Oxford University Press.
Hasan, Zoya (2000), 'More Equal but Still Not Equal?: State and Inter-Group Equality in Contemporary India', in Partha S. Ghosh, Imtiaz Ahmad and Helmut Redfield (eds.), *Pluralism and Equality: Values in Indian Society and Politics,* Sage Publications.
Hossain, Mahabub (1995), 'The Social Composition of Poverty: Socio-economic Characteristics of the Poor', in Hossain Zillur Rahman and Mahabub Hossain (eds.), *Rethinking Rural Poverty: Bangladesh as a Case Study,* Sage Publications.
International Institute for Population Sciences (2000), *National Family Health Survey – 2,* International Institute for Population Sciences.
Jain, S.P. (1978), 'Caste Stratification among Muslims in a Township in Western U.P.', in Imtiaz Ahmad (ed.), *Caste and Social Stratification among Muslims in India,* Manohar.
Jain, Meenakshi (1996), 'Backward Castes and Social Change in UP and Bihar', in M.N. Srinivas (ed.), *Caste: Its Twentieth-Century Avatar,* Penguin Books.
Jangira, N.K. (1991), *Indian Society and Education of the Disadvantaged,* NCERT.
Jayachandran, V. and Damodar Sahu (1998), 'School Attendance and its Correlates in India', in Yash Aggarwal and Kusum K. Premi (eds.), *Reforming School Education: Issues in Policy Planning and Implementation,* Vikas Publishing House.
Jha, Hetukar, 'Promises and Lapses: Understanding the Experience of Scheduled Castes in Bihar in Historical Perspective', *Journal of Indian School of Political Economy,* vol. XII, nos. 3 and 4, July-Dec. 2000.
Jha, Jyotsna (2000), 'Education Guarantee Scheme and Alternative Schooling: Community-based initiative in primary education in Madhya Pradesh', in *From Your School to Our School,* Rajiv Gandhi Shiksha Mission, Government of Madhya Pradesh.
Jha, Jyotsna and Meenakshi Bhardwaj (2000a), *Increase in Number of Women Teachers in Rural India,* UNESCO.
Jha, Jyotsna, K.B.C. Saxena and C.V. Baxi (2001), *Management Processes in Elementary Education: A Study of Existing Practices in Selected States in India,* European Commission.
Julka, Anita (2000), *Taskforce on Children with Special Needs,* Department of Education of Groups with Special Needs.
Karlekar, Malavika (2000), 'Girls' Access to Schooling: An Assessment', in Rekha

Wazir (ed.), *The Gender Gap in Basic Education: NGOs as Change Agents,* Sage Publications.

Kaur, Kuldip (1990), *Madrasa Education in India: A Study of its Past and Present,* Centre for Research in Industrial and Rural Development.

Khan, Shahrukh R. (1993), 'South Asia', in Elizabeth M. King and M. Anne Hill (eds.), *Women's Education in Developing Countries,* Johns Hopkins University Press.

King, Elizabeth M. and M. Anne Hill (1993), 'Women's Education in Developing Countries: An Overview', in Elizabeth M. King and M. Anne Hill (eds.), *Women's Education in Developing Countries,* Johns Hopkins University Press.

Krishnaji, N. (2001), 'Poverty, Gender and Schooling: A Study of Two Districts in Andhra Pradesh', in A. Vaidyanathan and P.R. Gopinathan Nair (eds.), *Elementary Education in Rural India: A Grass-roots View,* Sage Publications.

Majumdar, Tapas (1983), *Investment in Education and Social Choice,* Cambridge University Press.

Michael, S.M. (ed.) (1999), *Dalits in Modern India: Vision and Value*, Vistaar Publications.

Minz, Nirmal (1993), 'Identity of Tribals in India', in Walter Fernandes (ed.), *The Indigenous Question: Search for an Identity,* Indian Social Institute.

Mohsini, S.R. (1991), 'The Status and Education of the Girl Child', in Leelamma Devasia and V.V. Devasia (eds.), *Girl Child in India*, Ashish Publishing House.

Mukherjee, K.K. and Deepa Das (1996), *Prostitution in Metropolitan Cities of India,* Central Social Welfare Board.

Nambissan, Geetha B. (2000), 'Identity, Exclusion and the Education of Tribal Communities', in Rekha Wazir (ed.), *The Gender Gap in Basic Education: NGOs as Change Agents,* Sage Publications.

Nambissan, Geetha B. and Mona Sedwal (2002), 'Education for All: The Situation of Dalit Children in India', in R. Govinda (ed.), *India Education Report: A profile of basic education,* Oxford University Press.

National Council of Applied Economic Research (1999), *India Human Development Report [A Profile of Indian States in the 1990s],* Oxford University Press.

National Institute of Urban Affairs (1993), *Urban Child: Issues and Strategies,* National Institute of Urban Affairs.

Nayar, Usha (2001), *Education for All: Education of Girls in India: An Assessment,* NIEPA.

Osmani, S.R. (1990), 'Social Security in South Asia', in Ehtisham Ahmad, Jean Dreze, John Hills and Amartya Sen (eds.), *Social Security in Developing Countries,* Oxford University Press.

Pai, Sudha (2000), 'The Politics of Untouchability and Social Change: A Study of the Scheduled Castes of Maharashtra', *Journal of Indian School of Political Economy,* vol. XII, nos. 3 and 4, July-Dec. 2000.

Pande, Anuradha (2001), 'Education of Rural Children in UP Himalayas', in A. Vaidyanathan and P.R. Gopinathan Nair (eds.), *Elementary Education in Rural India: A Grass-roots View,* Sage Publications.

Parthasarathi, Vibha (1988), 'Socialisation, Women and Education: An Experiment', in Karuna Chanana (ed.), *Socialisation, Education and Women: Explorations in Gender Identity,* Orient Longman Ltd.

Punalekar, S.P. (1991), 'Gender, Class and Culture: Situation of Girl Children in

India', in Leelamma Devasia and V.V. Devasia (eds.), *Girl Child in India*, Ashish Publishing House.

Quibria, M.G. (ed.) (1994), *Rural Poverty in Developing Asia [vol. 1]: Bangladesh, India and Sri Lanka*, Asian Development Bank.

Rahman, Hossain Zillur and Mahabub Hossain (eds.) (1995), *Rethinking Rural Poverty: Bangladesh as a Case Study*, Sage Publications.

Rahman, Hossain Zillur (1995), 'Dimensions of Poverty: Crisis and Insecurity: The Other Face of Poverty', in Hossain Zillur Rahman and Mahabub Hossain (eds.), *Rethinking Rural Poverty: Bangladesh as a Case Study*, Sage Publications.

Rahul (2000), 'On Education Guarantee Scheme in Madhya Pradesh', in *From Your School to Our School*, Rajiv Gandhi Shiksha Mission, Government of Madhya Pradesh.

Ramchandaran, Vimala (2002), *Gender and Social Equity in Primary Education*, European Commission.

Rao, M.S.A (ed.) (1986), *Studies in Migration: Internal, and International Migration in India*, Manohar Publications.

Ray, Bharati and Aparna Basu (eds.) (1999), 'Introduction', in *From Independence Towards Freedom: Indian Women since 1947*, Oxford University Press.

Reddy, V. Eswara (1995), 'Primary Education in the Web of Poverty Culture', in A.K. Sharma (ed.), *School Effectiveness and Learning Achievement at the Primary Stage: International Perspectives*, NCERT.

Ruhela, Satya Pal (1997), *Children of Indian Nomads: Studies in Enculturation and Socialisation*, Regency Publications.

Sachchidananda (1999), 'Education of Scheduled Castes and Scheduled Tribes', in Marmar Mukhopadhyay and Madhu Parhar (ed.), *Indian Education: Development since Independence*, Vikas Publishing House Pvt. Ltd.

Sainath, P. (1996), *Everybody Loves a Good Drought*, Penguin Books.

Salim, A. Abdul (1998), 'Education of Muslims in Kerala since Independence', in *Education and Muslims in India Since Independence*, Institute of Objective Studies.

Saraswati, Baidyanath (1996), *Swaraj in Education: Experience and Experiment in Primary Education* [The Cultural Dimension of Education, 3 vols.], UNESCO, IGNCA.

Saxena, N.C. (1983), 'Public Employment and Educational Backwardness among Muslims in India', *Man and Development*, December 1983.

Sen, Amartya (1996), 'Radical Needs and Moderate Reforms', in Jean Dreze and Amartya Sen (eds.), *Indian Development: Selected Regional Perspectives*, Oxford University Press.

Sen, Binayak (1995), 'The poor and the poorest', in Hossain Zillur Rahman and Mahabub Hossain (ed.), *Rethinking Rural Poverty: Bangladesh as a Case Study*, Sage Publications.

Sengupta, Chandan, 'Cities, Poverty and Vulnerability: Observations on a study of nine cities in India', *paper presented in a seminar on Social Dimensions of Urban Poverty*, Mimeo.

Seshadri, C. and Rajamani (1995), 'Home Language, School Language and Learning Achievement: A Study of Scheduled Caste Children', in A.K. Sharma (ed.), *School Effectiveness and Learning Achievement at the Primary Stage: International Perspectives*, NCERT.

Shah, A.M. (1996), 'The Judicial and Sociological View of Other Backward Classes', in M.N. Srinivas (ed.), *Caste Is Twentieth-Century Avatar* , Penguin Books India.

Shah, Vimal P. and Tara Pate (1985), *School Contexts of Tribal Education,* Concept Publishing Company.

Sharma, A.N., S. Sarkar, A.K. Karan, V. Gayathri and Pushpendra (monograph), *Dynamics of Poverty Employment and Human Development in Bihar,* Institute for Human Development.

Sharma, A. and R. Gopalakrishnan (2000), 'Bringing the People Back In: From Lok Sampark Abhiyan to Education Guarantee Scheme in Madhya Pradesh', in *From Your School to Our School,* Rajiv Gandhi Shiksha Mission, Government of Madhya Pradesh.

Sharma, B.K. (ed.) (2001), *Socio-Economic Profile of Child Labour in a Developing Economy,* Himalaya Publishing House.

Shukla, Neerja (1995), 'Effectiveness of Various Interventions for Improving Tribal Education', in A.K. Sharma (ed.), *School Effectiveness and Learning Achievement at the Primary Stage: International Perspectives,* NCERT.

Siddiqui, Mohammad A. (1998), 'Development and Trends in Madrasa Education', in Qadri Khan and Siddiqui (eds.), *Education and Muslims in India Since Independence,* Institute of Objective Studies.

Singh, Bhupinder and Neeti Mahanti (eds.) (1995), 'Issues in Tribal Education', *in Tribal Education in India.*

Singh, Jagpal (1998), 'In Search of Quality Education: Alternative Schooling in Meerut District of Western Uttar Pradesh', in Yash Aggarwal and Kusum K. Premi (eds.), *Reforming School Education: Issues in Policy Planning and Implementation,* Vikas Publishing House Pvt. Ltd.

Singh, K.S. (1994), *The Scheduled Tribes* [People of India: National Series, vol. III], Oxford University Press.

—— (1995), *The Scheduled Castes* [People of India: National Series, vol. II], Oxford University Press.

Singh, Shyamanand (1991), *Tribal Education in India,* Uppal Publishing House.

Sinha, Shantha (2000), 'Child Labour and Education in the Gender Gap', in Rekha Wazir (ed.), *Basic Education: NGOs as Change Agents,* Sage Publications.

Srinivas, M.N. (ed.) (1996), *Caste: Its Twentieth-Century Avatar,* Penguin Books India.

Srivastava, Ranjana (2000), 'Evaluation of community-based primary schooling initiative in Madhya Pradesh: Education Guarantee Scheme and Alternative School', in *From Your School to Our School,* Education Guarantee Scheme, Rajiv Gandhi Shiksha Mission, Government of Madhya Pradesh.

Sujatha, K. (1999), 'Education of Weaker Sections in India', in Marmar Mukhopadhyay and Madhu Parhar (eds.), *Indian Education: Development Since Independence,* Vikas Publishing House Pvt. Ltd.

—— (2000), *Education of Indian Scheduled Tribes: A study of Community Schools in the District of Vishakhapatnam, Andhra Pradesh,* UNESCO.

The Probe Team (1999), *Probe Report,* Oxford University Press.

Thomas, Joseph A. (2001), 'Dynamics of Educational Development: A Case Study of Selected "Backward" Villages in Kerala', in A. Vaidyanathan and P.R. Gopinathan Nair (eds.), *Elementary Education in Rural India: A Grass-roots View,* Sage Publications.

Tilak, J.B.G. (1993), 'East Asia', in Elizabeth M. King and M. Anne Hill (eds.), *Women's Education in Developing Countries,* Johns Hopkins University Press.

—— (1996), 'How Free is "Free" primary education in India', *Economic and Political Weekly*, 3 February 1996.

Vaidyanathan, A. and P.R. Gopinathan Nair (ed.) (2001), *Elementary Education in Rural India: A Grass-roots View,* Sage Publications.

Velaskar, Padma (1998), 'Ideology, Education and the Political Struggle for Liberation: Change and Challenge among the Dalits of Maharashtra', in Sureshchandra Shukla and Rekha Kaul (ed.), *Education Development and Underdevelopment,* Sage Publications.

Vyasulu, Vinod (2000), 'In the wonderland of primary education', in *From Your School to Our School,* Rajiv Gandhi Shiksha Mission, Government of Madhya Pradesh.

Wazir, Rekha (2000), 'Profiling the Problem', in Rekha Wazir (ed.), *The Gender Gap in Basic Education: NGOs as Change Agents,* Sage Publications.

Webster, John C.B. (1999), 'Who is a Dalit?', in S.M. Michael (ed.), *Dalits in Modern India: Vision and Value,* Vistaar Publications.

World Bank (1990), *Poverty [World Development Report 1990],* Oxford University Press.

—— (1998), *Reducing Poverty in India: Options for more effective public services,* World Bank.

Index